INSIDERS' GUIDE® TO THE MONTEREY PENINSULA

Help Us Keep This Guide Up to Date

Every effort has been made by the authors and editors to make this guide as accurate and useful as possible. However, many things can change after a guide is published—establishments close, phone numbers change, hiking trails are rerouted, facilities come under new management, etc.

We would love to hear from you concerning your experiences with this guide and how you feel it could be improved and be kept up to date. While we may not be able to respond to all comments and suggestions, we'll take them to heart, and we'll also make certain to share them with the authors. Please send your comments and suggestions to the following address:

The Globe Pequot Press
Reader Response/Editorial Department
P.O. Box 480
Guilford, CT 06437

Or you may e-mail us at:

editorial@globe-pequot.com

Thanks for your input, and happy travels!

Insiders' Guide® to the Monterey Peninsula

THIRD EDITION

Tom Owens and Melanie Bellon Chatfield

INSIDERS' GUIDE®

Guilford, Connecticut
An imprint of The Globe Pequot Press

The prices and rates in this guidebook were confirmed at press time. We recommend, however, that you call establishments before traveling to obtain current information.

Previous editions of this book were published by Falcon Publishing, Inc. in 1998 and 2000.

Front cover photo by Charles Benes/Index Stock
Maps by Geografx ©The Globe Pequot Press

ISSN 1540-1758
ISBN 0-7627-2255-X

Manufactured in the United States of America
Third Edition/First Printing

Contents

Directory of Maps

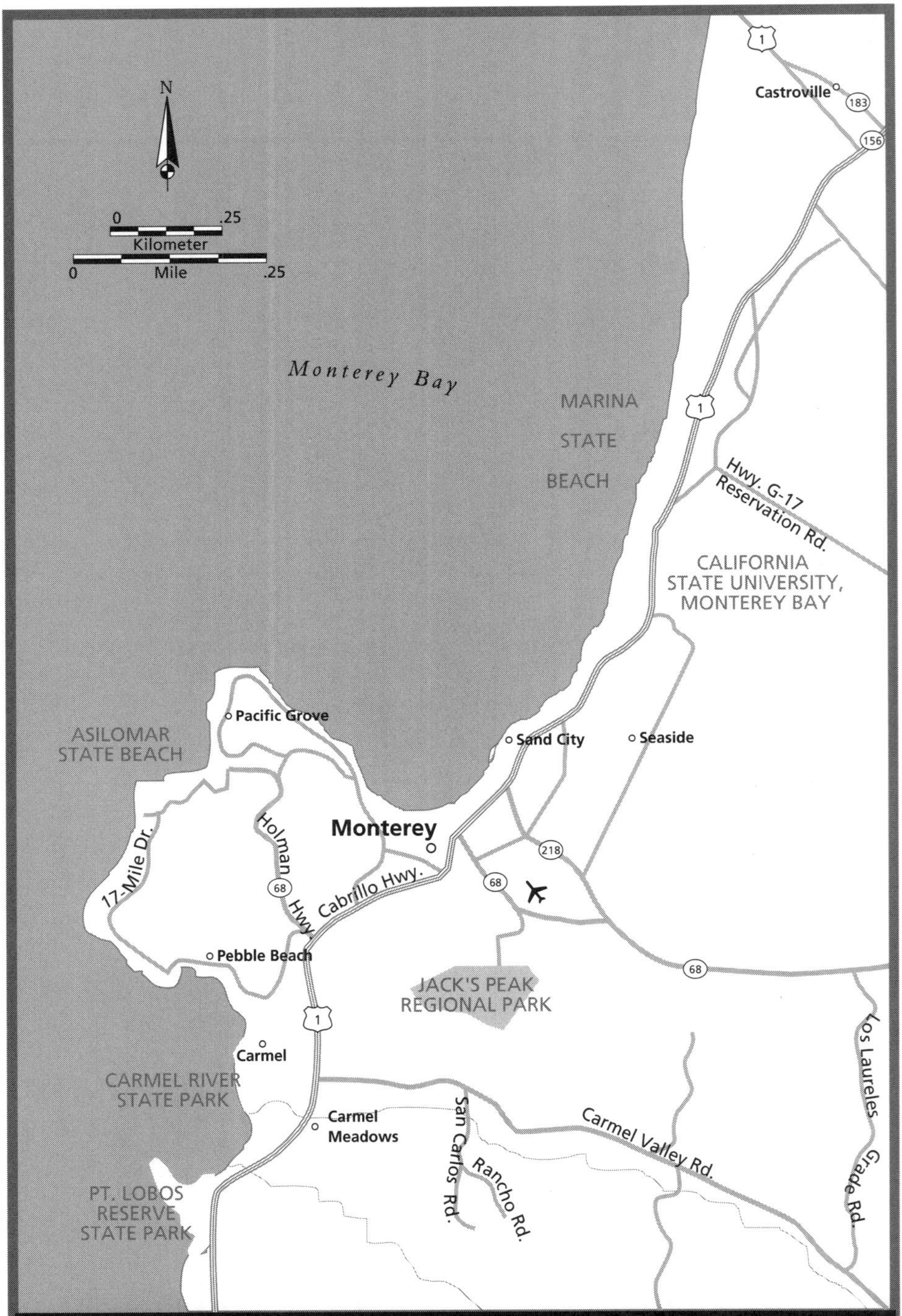

MONTEREY PENINSULA

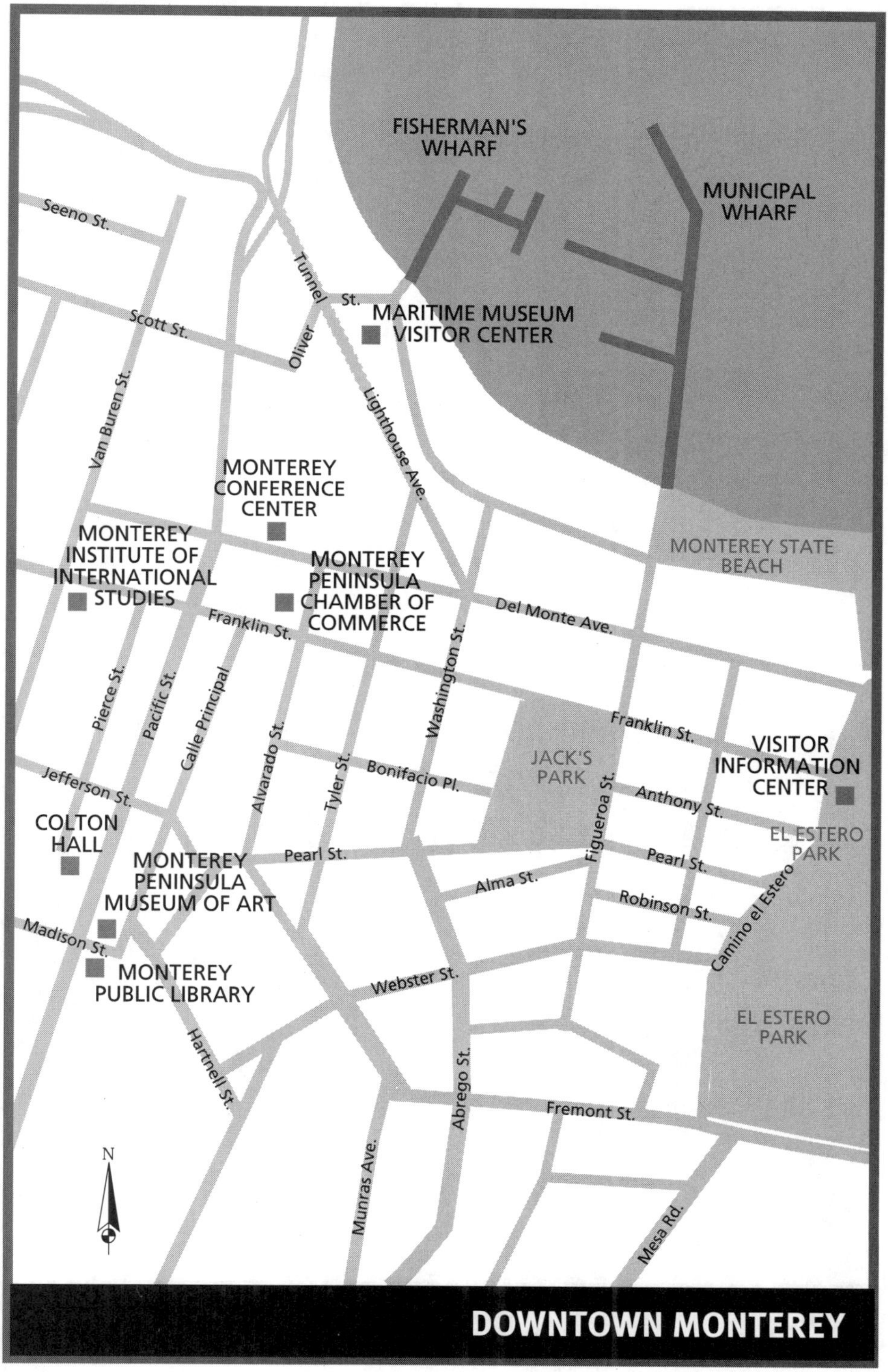
FISHERMAN'S WHARF
MUNICIPAL WHARF
Seeno St.
Tunnel St.
Scott St.
Oliver
MARITIME MUSEUM VISITOR CENTER
Van Buren St.
Lighthouse Ave.
MONTEREY CONFERENCE CENTER
MONTEREY INSTITUTE OF INTERNATIONAL STUDIES
MONTEREY PENINSULA CHAMBER OF COMMERCE
MONTEREY STATE BEACH
Del Monte Ave.
Franklin St.
Washington St.
Pierce St.
Pacific St.
Calle Principal
Alvarado St.
Tyler St.
Bonifacio Pl.
JACK'S PARK
Franklin St.
VISITOR INFORMATION CENTER
Figueroa St.
Anthony St.
EL ESTERO PARK
Jefferson St.
COLTON HALL
Pearl St.
MONTEREY PENINSULA MUSEUM OF ART
Alma St.
Pearl St.
Robinson St.
Camino el Estero
Madison St.
MONTEREY PUBLIC LIBRARY
Webster St.
EL ESTERO PARK
Hartnell St.
Abrego St.
Fremont St.
N
Munras Ave.
Mesa Rd.
DOWNTOWN MONTEREY

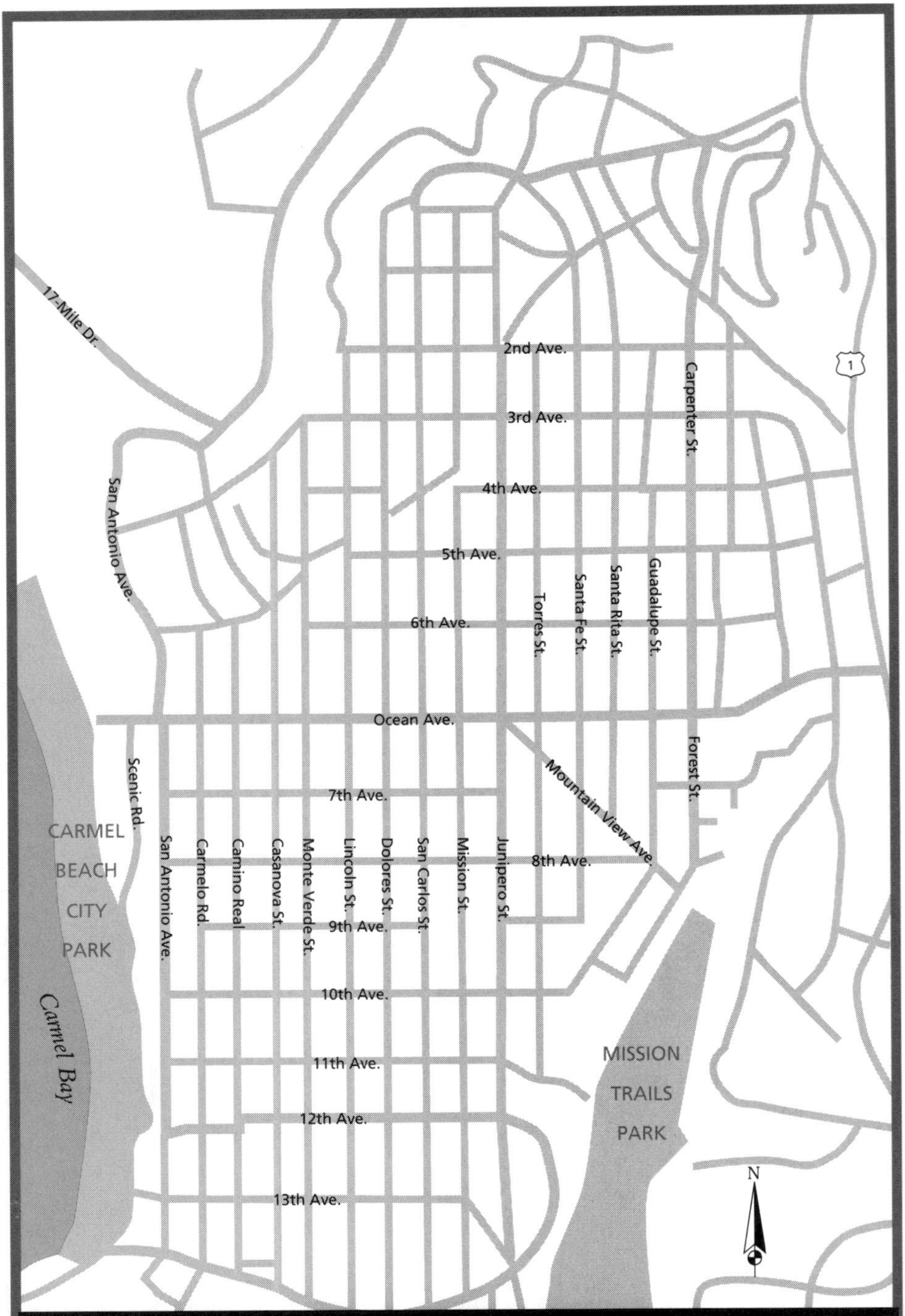

DOWNTOWN CARMEL

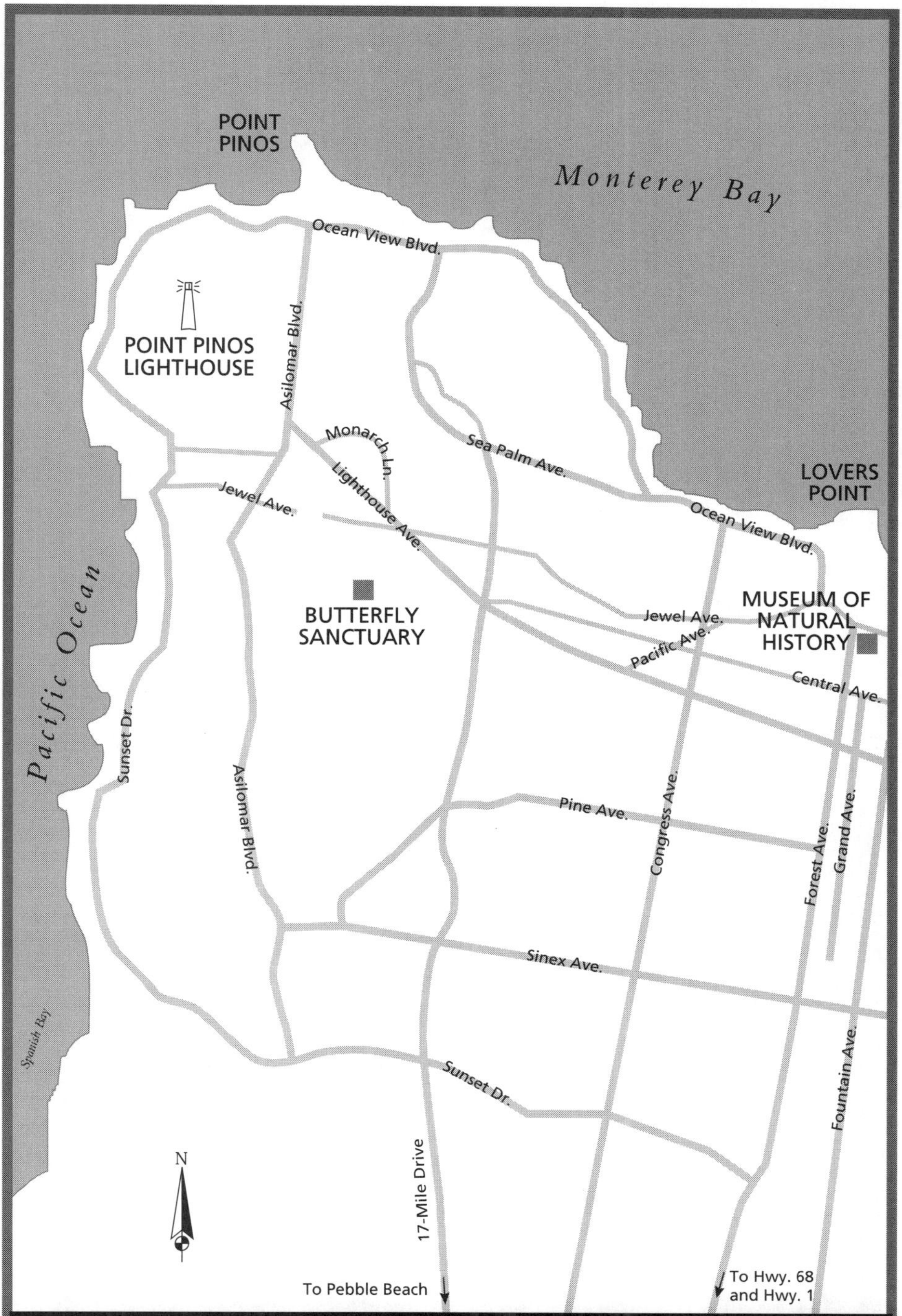

PACIFIC GROVE

Preface

Welcome to the Monterey Peninsula!

The natural splendor and scenic wonders of our area are magical and inspirational. If you are looking for a place to relax, unwind, and slow down for just a little while, you've chosen the ideal location. Sit on the beach and watch the sparkling waves, or listen to the sacred silence in one of our many forested parks. Feel the tranquillity of your surroundings. The magnetic environment of this particular stretch of California coast has attracted and encouraged world-class writers, artists, photographers, and performers, due in part to the continual inspiration provided by the incredible beauty of the Monterey Peninsula.

But the spectacular scenery is only one of the Monterey Peninsula's many attractions. The Monterey Bay Aquarium is internationally famous for its stunning exhibits and informative tours. Our wine region rivals Napa County in wine production; many of these local wineries have tasting rooms and tours open to the public. Our art galleries offer an unbelievable variety of art styles and many specialize in the works of regional artists. Recently, the opening of several fabulous spas has added one more entry to our never-ending list of things to see and do while visiting the area. Many of our festivals and special events draw a returning crowd each year: auto races at Laguna Seca, major golf events at Pebble Beach, the Monterey Jazz Festival, the Carmel Bach Festival, the list goes on and on. . . .

Each town in our fascinating Peninsula has a distinctive character and unique appeal. Though close in proximity, the types of activities, style of architecture, and layout of the land vary from one town to the next. Monterey, as California's first state capital is steeped in history and filled with historic buildings including California's First Theater and the oldest building in California, the Royal Presidio Chapel. Pebble Beach, though not a city but a planned community, is in the midst of the Del Monte Forest and is known the world over for its luxury resorts, estates, and famed golf courses. Carmel is famous for its wide sandy beaches, numerous art galleries, high-end shopping, and quaint cottages. Pacific Grove is a seaside Victorian village with a beautiful ocean drive, many shops and restaurants, and its famed Monarch butterfly sanctuary.

In addition to the usual information you would expect to find in a tourist guide (accommodations, restaurants, shopping, attractions), you will also find chapters highlighting relocation information, such as education, worship, media, healthcare, and retirement. Visitors to the Peninsula will find the guide especially useful and even longtime residents who read the Insiders' Guide will discover something new about the Monterey Peninsula.

It is with an unending respect and appreciation for our beloved home that we encourage you to use this publication to fully enjoy the sights and delights of the Monterey Peninsula. We have done our best to give you an accurate representation of the wonder and majesty of our magnificent area. Enjoy!

Acknowledgments

Where to start is easy. Dear Emily, thank you for covering for my mental and physical absence while I whiled away the hours on the road and at the dining room table on my laptop. Your strength, support, and understanding made this all possible. I love you. And thanks to my pride and joys, Kate and Anna, for forgiving Dad who wasn't always there on school nights and weekends because he had homework of his own. I love you two, too, and am so proud of both of you.

And to my cohorts, Melanie, Julia, and Judy, it has been an adventure, hasn't it? Exploring our hometown as if we didn't live here. I appreciate your talent, your effort, and your support.

For my daytripping buddies, thank you. Thanks to my family again for that great long and winding road south through Big Sur. Thanks to Leslie and Em for Salinas Valley and all that wine. To Martha, my dear friend, for a smile-filled day of monks, more wine, and muddy roads of Carmel Valley. For Dan and Gena for wonderful hospitality (and needed shoulder massages) in San Francisco.

Thanks to my editor Lynne Arany for her direction, understanding, forgiveness, patience, great talent, and support. For all you others at Insiders' Guide and The Globe Pequot Press, thank you for this opportunity and your efforts. I know what it takes.

Many thanks to all of you other friends and good sports out there who helped me through this project with your words, guidance, answers, kindness, encouragement, and support in getting this done.

And to my wonderful mother, who understood that her son had a commitment to keep and maybe didn't phone or drive down to L.A. as often as he should. I love you, Mom. And you, too, sisters one and two. Ciao, Cyn and Deb.

Finally, I dedicate this effort to my father, who passed away just before I started the first edition of this book. He taught me the quiet dedication and perseverance needed to complete the job. Thanks Pops.

—Tom Owens

As in any dynamic environment, many changes, updates, closures, openings, and new twists occurred that required a great deal of checking, double-checking, and rewriting. My husband of a few months and partner for many years, Michael, not only put up with my long hours staring into the manuscript and at my computer screen, he worked with me to gather the reams of data that go into a new edition. He makes it all fun and I love him.

My brother Skip (real name is Clair, but he's 6′4″ and we're all scared to call him that) fuels my drive with his confidence in and pride of me. I've never met another human being (although Michael's a close second) who has set such an example of courage, passion for life, and love of family. Thanks to him and his wife, Kathy, I can enjoy children, niece Megan and nephew Dalton, without having to go through the pain of childbirth or the expense of providing for college educations. I love you!

Loving thanks to my father for giving me the support, encouragement, and freedom to grow as a person and as a professional writer. And to my dearest friends, the PowerBabes—Susan, Carolyn, Jan, Kathy, Jane, and Jackie—I think you know how important you are to me.

A special thank you to my coauthor, Tom Owens, who gave me this opportunity. He has a great sense of humor and a true talent for creative writing, and he's a joy to know. Thanks also to The Globe Pequot Press and my editor, Joshua. Last but not least, major kudos to photographers extraordinaire, Barbara and Fernando of Batista Moon Studio in Monterey and Kelli Uldall, also of Monterey, who made even me look good in a photo.

—Melanie Bellon Chatfield

How to Use This Book

From the beginning of this project, we wanted to write a friendly book. We wanted to write a useful book that would paint a true picture of our home (through only slightly rose-colored glasses) so you could better plan your stay. We wanted to write a book that you'd keep by your side during your travels on the Monterey Peninsula and that would help you make the most of your time here. And we wanted to write a book that, if you lived here or dreamed of living here, gave you insight into everyday life on the Monterey Peninsula.

Eight months later (only slightly less time-consuming than bearing a child), we thought we had written a pretty darn good first edition of that book we envisioned. And with the subsequent editions, we corrected our mistakes, updated what had changed, and polished our prose. We have dug deep to uncover what we feel is the best our neck of the woods has to offer. We organized the chapters by subject matter so you can easily access the information you need. We used bold headings and individual listings to make it easy for you to skim through the chapters and pinpoint exactly what you're looking for. We included in-depth descriptions to allow you to get the inside scoop when you need it. Plus, we have tried to make this book fun and interesting reading, in the event you want to sit down for a while, at home or on one of our many gorgeous beaches, and get a good taste of this place.

We hope by the end of your stay on the Monterey Peninsula that this book is torn, dog-eared, marked up, smelling of the sea, and stained with wine, coffee, or some of the many other good things our home has to offer. Then we will know we did our job, and you put this book to good use. We also hope you discover your own favorite places, and tell us about them. We trust you'll let us know if you found our descriptions incorrect or off base. The information we gathered here is based on our combined decades living on the Peninsula and the best research we human beings could gather, arrange, and compile within our allotted time. Please take the time to let us know your thoughts and comments by writing to: Insiders' Guides, The Globe Pequot Press, P.O. Box 480, Guilford, CT, 06437-0480, or visit our Web site at www.insiders.com and make your comments there.

How This Book Is Organized

The Insiders' Guide® to the Monterey Peninsula provides extensive coverage to the cities of Monterey, Pacific Grove, Carmel, and Pebble Beach. Geographically, these communities make up all of the Monterey Peninsula proper and spill a mile or so farther inland and up and down the California coast at the southern end of Monterey Bay. We have also included a daytrip section, which will provide overviews of outlying areas, including Big Sur, Carmel Valley, and Salinas Valley. In fact, we take you all up and down the California central coast from San Francisco to San Luis Obispo.

The subject matters covered are outlined in the table of contents. We suggest you fold or tab the corner of that page for repeated reference. A detailed index in the rear of the book is especially helpful for finding particular places and specific things by name. Within most of our chapters you will find an introductory description followed by individual entries categorized by subject and listed alphabetically. Whenever the number of entries warrants (as with accommodations and attractions), we also divide categories by locale in the following sequence: Monterey, Pacific Grove, Carmel, and Pebble Beach.

Close-ups provide additional information about people, places, and things of note, while Insiders' Tips highlight helpful advice and interesting notes designed to make your visit more enjoyable.

When writing this book, we found that the lines of distinction were not always clear for some of our entries. For instance, many of the finest restaurants in the area are also some of its hottest spots for nightlife. Thus, you'll see numerous places listed more than once, with cross-references throughout the book to help you find just the information you are looking for.

The area code for the Monterey Peninsula is 831. Our daytrip chapter does venture outside the county, and neighboring area codes are given where appropriate.

Finally, we look forward to revisiting this book for subsequent editions, hearing your comments, and gaining from your perspective on the Monterey Peninsula. We hope you enjoy this book, and we know you'll enjoy your time in our own backyard. Do us a favor, will you? Look at our smiling faces on the About the Authors page. Then if you happen to see either of us walking through the streets of Pacific Grove, sitting along the beach in Carmel, or strolling along Fisherman's Wharf in Monterey, say hello. We'd love to welcome you personally to the Monterey Peninsula.

Area Overview

Weather and Climate
Commerce and Industry
Crime
The Neighbors
The Peninsula Towns

The Monterey Peninsula, one of the most picturesque spots in North America, if not the world, is a can't-miss destination for anyone traveling in and around the state of California. Yet miss it is exactly what explorer Juan Rodriguez Cabrillo did in 1542, sailing his galleon right past the Peninsula and Monterey Bay as he headed up the coast of this newfound continent. It wasn't until nearly 60 years later that Captain Sebastian Vizcaino came ashore on this rocky headland at "El Puerto de Monterey," which he named in honor of the Viceroy of New Spain, Count de Monte Rey.

The Monterey Peninsula sits 125 miles south of San Francisco, 345 miles north of Los Angeles, and 17 miles west of Salinas, the largest city in the agricultural region of Monterey County known as the Salad Bowl of the World. To the north of the Peninsula is the spectacular Monterey Bay, a National Marine Sanctuary with abundant sea life and an undersea canyon deeper than the Grand Canyon. With its rich harvest of seafood, the Bay has long been the source of livelihood for Peninsula residents, but it now attracts as many fishers of tourism dollars as it does fishers of fish. To the west is the Pacific Ocean, creating spectacular meetings of land and sea as waves crash along the rugged shoreline in Pacific Grove, Carmel, and Pebble Beach.

Today the Monterey Peninsula proper, a compact landmass of fewer than 25 square miles, is made up of three incorporated cities—Monterey, Carmel, and Pacific Grove—and an unincorporated area of Monterey County known as Pebble Beach. Immediately east of the Peninsula are the bedroom communities of Seaside and Del Rey Oaks and the small industrial/retail town of Sand City. To the southeast is sunny Carmel Valley, with its oak-covered hills and Western-style flair. Farther south is the spectacular Big Sur Coast, a 90-mile stretch of unrivaled scenic beauty. To the northeast, up the coast, lie Marina, Castroville (Artichoke Capital of the World), Watsonville, and, at the northern tip of Monterey Bay, Santa Cruz with its famous Beach Boardwalk.

Approximately 125,000 residents populate the Monterey Peninsula and the immediate surrounding communities. They are host to more than two million annual visitors who arrive year-round to enjoy the natural beauty, world-class accommodations, and historic attractions.

Weather and Climate

Geographically, the Peninsula features a mix of rocky coastlines, gentle sand dunes, and native forests of Monterey pine and cypress. After more than a century of development, the forests have been cut back significantly within the city limits of Pacific Grove and Monterey, but substantial wooded areas remain in Pebble Beach and the northern end of Carmel. This seaside forest environment is the direct result of a mild, ocean-influenced climate that envelops the Peninsula.

Many "California-Dreaming" tourists arrive on the Peninsula during the summer with suitcases full of shorts and tank tops only to scurry to a local clothier for long pants and a sweater. While the Peninsula's temperature occasionally reaches into the 80s and infrequently hits 90, the average summer temperature is only a daytime high of 68 and a nighttime low of 51. The average winter temperature is a slightly cooler high of 61 and low of 44.

Why the mild summers in a Golden State known for its warm sun, sand, and surf? During the summer, as the inland California

Nature's beauty and power is evident across the Monterey Peninsula. PHOTO: ROSS ANDRÉSON

Central Valley swelters above 100 degrees, air rises, pulling the cool marine air above the cold waters of the Pacific over the Peninsula. This effect can engulf the Monterey Peninsula in fog, sending temperatures plunging. If you don't like bundling up in blankets and sweaters during those foggy days of July or August, a 10-minute drive inland to Carmel Valley or toward Salinas usually finds warm, if not hot, sunshiny weather. Insiders suggest dressing in layers that may need to be peeled off and put back on repeatedly throughout your stay.

The warmest and most pleasant months of the year are September and October, the only months when average highs exceed 70 degrees. May and June are also nice, typically dry, and in the mid-60s. The rainy season runs from November to April, with January and February the wettest months. Average seasonal rainfall is 18 inches, but rarely is there an "average" year. The Peninsula tends to go through cycles of heavy rain and drought, often influenced by the ocean current phenomena El Niño and La Niña.

This unpredictable rainfall plays havoc with the area's freshwater supply. Not connected to the elaborate California aqueduct system that irrigates the arid southern part of the state, the Peninsula depends on local groundwater and on area rainfall gathered behind small dams up the Carmel River. If you arrive during one of the periodic droughts, be prepared to experience water rationing at the hotels, inns, and restaurants. Locals have learned to live with the on-again, off-again water restrictions (repeatedly voting down measures to build new, larger dams), and they appreciate the cooperation of visitors in their water-preservation efforts.

Commerce and Industry

Tourism is by far the leading industry in the area. Fishing remains prevalent, but much of the commercial activity has moved north up the Bay to Moss Landing. Squid, or calamari, not sardines, is now the silver harvest of the Bay. The agriculture industry is huge in Monterey County but not on the Peninsula. The limited land is just too valuable to be used for growing crops. A once-large military presence was scaled down dramatically with the closure of the Fort Ord Army Base in the mid-1990s. Still, the armed forces retain a significant presence with the United States Naval Postgraduate School, the United States Army Defense Language Institute (the largest foreign-language school in the country), and a United States Coast Guard Station.

Educational facilities also play a key part of the Peninsula makeup, with California State University Monterey Bay (located on the former site of Fort Ord), Monterey Peninsula College, the Monterey Institute of International Studies, and other small colleges and private prep schools.

A recent trend finds small high-tech and service companies discovering the attractions of the Monterey Peninsula and relocating from Silicon Valley and San Jose, just 70 miles to the north. With advancements in technology such as the Internet, firms are realizing they no longer have to be physically located next to their clients or suppliers and can run their businesses in any locale they want to live in.

For those who can afford it, the Monterey Peninsula isn't a bad choice as a place to set up shop. The cost of living on the Peninsula is high, much like the San Francisco Bay Area to the north. Homes on the Peninsula proper begin at around $300,000, and that's for a small one-bedroom, one-bath fixer-upper. A standard three- or four-bedroom home is likely to be in the $500,000 to $800,000 range, and from there, the sky's the limit. You can read more about homes and home prices in our Real Estate chapter.

But along with those high costs of living come some perks that are standard equipment on the Monterey Peninsula. Locals enjoy daily walks on spectacular beaches; strolls through native forests along narrow trails that only Insiders know about; fantastic restaurants of all sizes, shapes, and ethnicities; cultural richness in the fine and performing arts; a mild climate free of the extremes of snowstorms or humid heat waves; decent to top-rated schools; and a low to moderate crime rate.

Crime

While we're on the subject of crime, burglary represents the biggest threat of misdeed to visitors on the Monterey Peninsula. As in any tourist area, a certain criminal element preys on the fact that motel rooms and parked cars full of valuables are left vacated for hours while visitors are out having a wonderful time. Valuables left clearly visible from the outside are likely targets. Simple precautions, such as keeping locks locked and valuables stored out of sight, go a long way toward preventing you from becoming a victim. It may seem like paradise, but keep alert when carrying valuables.

The Neighbors

As you get out and about and mix with the natives, you'll find that most Peninsula neighborhoods are involved communities,

Insiders' Tip

Alvarado Street in Monterey is home to the Old Monterey Marketplace, which offers fresh produce, local artwork, good food, and live music every Tuesday afternoon.

Downtown Monterey is adjacent to Fisherman's Wharf and the Monterey Harbor and Marina.
PHOTO: STEVE PROEHE/MONTEREY PENINSULA VCB

each with great pride in its particular city or area. Each community also has a distinct personality, and Montereyans, Carmelites, and Pagrovians can be very different animals, as can the residents of Pebble Beach. We'll get more into that a bit later in this chapter. Ethnically, the Peninsula is a diverse community. Spaniards, Mexicans, Italians, Chinese, Japanese, Portuguese, Filipinos, and Caucasian and African-American descendants from the dust bowl era (a la the Joad family in Steinbeck's *The Grapes of Wrath*) make up a patchwork of cultures that have arrived at various periods of Monterey's history and left their marks on the Peninsula. Each has brought along the riches of its culture, as evidenced by the many popular ethnic festivals and other celebrations that take place throughout the year.

Visitors will likely find the Peninsula a diverse, accommodating community. Most local citizens realize how fortunate they are to live here, and they are happy to share their corner of the world with visitors who equally enjoy and—importantly—respect the spectacular beauty of the place.

Now let's take a little closer look at the four unique communities that make up the Monterey Peninsula.

The Peninsula Towns

Monterey

Rich in history that dates back prior to the pilgrims' landing at Plymouth Rock, Monterey is a multifaceted city that seeks to preserve its long, rich heritage while at the same time thriving in the 21st century. Culturally diverse Monterey is a true ethnic melting pot that reflects the city's storied past. You'll find, for instance, two and three generations of Italian fishing families still playing a central role in community leadership and still gathering to play some serious bocce ball down at the Custom House Plaza every weekend. Mixed with that rich heritage is a new generation of Montereyans, many of whom have relocated from Los Angeles and other hectic urban areas and fallen in love with the city's laid-back, almost Mediterranean lifestyle. Many baby boomers have found Monterey and the rest of the Peninsula a near-perfect spot for raising families, so children seem ever-present. The local foreign-language schools, which have led to Monterey's designation as a "language capital of the world," add a dash of international flavor to the city.

The heart of Monterey remains Alvarado Street, the longtime business district of the city. Today a potpourri of shops, restaurants, and local businesses, Alvarado Street reflects a blend of Monterey's old-town stability and vibrant new life. This area provides an ample supply of coffeehouses, juice bars, movie theaters, sports bars, and nightclubs and is a popular gathering spot for students, the military, and other young adults. For locals, it's where it's happening within the overall scope of the rather docile Monterey Peninsula. Visitors likely find it low-key by urban standards, but it's about the only game in town.

The downtown area surrounding Alvarado Street is home to most of Monterey's splendid adobes and other historic highlights, including Fisherman's Wharf, Custom House Plaza, and Colton Hall. It's truly a town to discover on foot (see the Monterey Path of History in our Attractions chapter), so leave the car in one of the many parking lots and take a walk.

The largest of the Peninsula's cities with a population of approximately 30,000, Monterey spreads out in all directions from the downtown area and covers almost 9 square miles. Due north is Fisherman's Wharf and Monterey State Beach, great for a relaxing day on the Bay. To the east toward Seaside are the greenbelts of El Estero Park, Monterey Peninsula College, the Naval Postgraduate School, and Old Del Monte Golf Course. Northwest toward Pacific Grove is the Presidio of Monterey, and beyond that is the residential area of town known as New Monterey, with small businesses along Lighthouse Avenue, and historic Cannery Row. Southwest toward Pebble Beach lie the Skyline Forest and Jack's Peak areas of pastoral hillside homes,

Monterey Harbor is home to an active group of local sailors. PHOTO: JANA MORBA

and the Community Hospital of Monterey Peninsula. To the southeast, out along the Highway 68 corridor east toward Salinas, lie the Monterey Peninsula Airport and the Ryan Ranch Business Park, a modern light-industry center.

Pacific Grove

Pacific Grove goes by two monikers: "Butterfly Town USA" and "The Last Hometown." The former name is earned as a result of P.G.'s famous stands of pines, cypress, and eucalyptus trees to which the Monarch butterfly returns like clockwork every fall and winter for the Peninsula's mild climate. The latter name, which some consider a bit presumptuous, reflects the pride of the city's 16,000 inhabitants and their determination to keep Pacific Grove a safe refuge for a family lifestyle reminiscent of days gone by.

The stately Victorian homes and turn-of-the-century architecture create a proper setting for this bit of Americana. But it is the steadfast citizenry who make sure "progress" is kept in check and treasured values are retained. Nothing is more evident of this mindset than a not-too-distant hoopla over the proposed introduction of a new Taco Bell fast-food restaurant into Pacific Grove. City ordinances were passed a decade or so back prohibiting any new fast-food establishments within city limits. The prospective new franchisee, however, took the ordinance head on, arguing that his proposed business was actually a sandwich shop, which the ordinance didn't cover. City Hall became a hotbed of debate as forces pro and con debated whether or not a taco was a sandwich and whether the new franchise was really a threat to all that Pagrovians hold dearest. In the end, the fast-food franchisee tucked his tail between his legs and abandoned his plans. And all was right again in Pacific Grove.

Kidding aside, preservationists deserve a lot of credit for keeping the character of Pacific Grove as special as it is. A trip through the downtown district on Lighthouse Avenue quickly takes you back to a time when Main Street USA was a way of life. The huge Holman Building, a former family department store that now houses an antiques mall, stands proudly near the town entrance, its magnificent stained-glass butterfly window celebrating our special winter guests.

Insiders' Tip

Leave your butterfly nets at home. In Pacific Grove it's against the law to harass Monarch butterflies.

Victorian storefronts line both sides of the street and are occasionally interrupted by more modern architecture, but they're still prevalent enough to retain the town's overall character. Stately Queen Anne–style homes pepper the town, with many now serving as restaurants or bed and breakfast inns rather than private residences.

Downtown Pacific Grove has experienced quite a revival in the last few years. It wasn't too long ago that the Holman's Building stood vacant, a victim of America's preference for mega-shopping malls over stand-alone department stores. The local five-and-dime and other longtime merchants also closed down as Peninsula residents chose to do their buying in the new discount shopping centers surrounding the larger cities of Monterey and Salinas.

Today, Pacific Grove is reinventing itself as a home and garden design mecca. Antiques shops, interior design studios, plant boutiques, and stores of similar ilk are attracting attention from all over Monterey County and beyond. Suddenly there's more to do in Pacific Grove than simply enjoy the serenity and scenery.

Despite the revival, P.G. is still the quiet side of town, even by Peninsula standards. Visitors looking to simply relax and get away from it all will have a hard time finding anything to beat this tranquil locale. Check in at a quaint bed and breakfast inn or family-run motel and kick your shoes off. Stroll along the beach and boardwalk on the spectacular Asilomar coastline. Take in a meditative afternoon at the Monarch Butterfly Sanctuary. Or

Pacific Grove begins near the Monterey Bay Aquarium on Cannery Row and extends to the northernmost reach of the Peninsula at Point Pinos. PHOTO: STEVE PROEHE/MONTEREY PENINSULA VCB

picnic at Lovers Point or one of the many secluded coves along Ocean View Boulevard. Ask a local for a restaurant recommendation and you'll likely obtain a host of choices for breakfast, lunch, or dinner. And don't miss the beach sunsets with the Point Pinos Lighthouse pulsating gently in the background.

Carmel

To some it's Carmel-by-the-Sea. To most Insiders, however, it's simply Carmel. But whatever you call it, this lovely seaside village and artists colony is just about as storybook as it gets. Picture Hansel and Gretel on Rodeo Drive. That's Ocean Avenue, the main shopping and dining thoroughfare through downtown Carmel. Then for two to three blocks east and west of Ocean Avenue and down most of its north-south length are streets and streets of quaint shops, hideaway restaurants, charming inns, and almost secret courtyards that contain their own hidden treasures.

Despite a population of only 4,100 and an area of only 1 square mile, Carmel is truly a tale of two cities. First there's the bustling Carmel commercial shopping district of art galleries, clothiers, specialty shops, and exceptional restaurants most visitors become familiar with. Its quaint village character has been preserved by strict building codes and regulations that prohibit neon signs, parking meters, souvenir shops, and high-rise structures. Then there's the picturesque residential Carmel of neither sidewalks nor streetlights, where the inhabitants largely conduct their daily lives away from downtown.

You'll immediately notice that Ocean Avenue and its environs are not designed to meet the day-to-day needs of locals. How many sweaters can you wear, paintings can you hang, or figurines can you dust? Ocean Avenue is for the visitor, who can find the perfect outfit or the special piece of artwork to capture the memory of a magical moment. Yes, there are a few markets and stores that can provide some

Insiders' Tip

Bring your flats to Carmel: An ordinance still on the books outlaws high heels in order to protect the city from liability lawsuits for trips and falls on the town's uneven streets.

of the necessities of life. But if you need staples like milk, bread, and toilet paper, it's often less of a hassle to head on over to the more resident-friendly mouth of Carmel Valley or even into Monterey or Pacific Grove.

Still, there's a strong local culture in downtown Carmel, made up of resident artists, writers, shopkeepers, gallery and restaurant owners, and other longtime Carmelites. Part of that local culture is spawned at the Carmel Post Office, where citizens gather to collect their daily mail and exchange the latest news and gossip. There's no mail delivery in most of Carmel proper, which is good for the mailcarrier because there aren't any street addresses either.

If a local is giving directions to his or her home, it usually goes something like this: "It's the stone house on the beach side of Ocean View between Bay View and Stewart." Or, the house may enjoy its own personal name, such as "Knot Very Lodge" or "The Holly House." The same thing goes for most Carmel shops, galleries, and restaurants. "Ocean between Mission and Junipero" or "Sixth between Lincoln and Dolores" is about as specific as addresses get. But with a street map in hand, even first-time visitors find Carmel easily navigable on foot. And the key words here are "on foot." Parking has always been and likely always will be a problem in Carmel, particularly during the peak summer tourist season. So, should you find

Carmel Beach is a favorite spot for couples to unwind after a busy day of shopping, golf, or sightseeing.
PHOTO: TOM OWENS

Pine trees, ocean views, and golf are among the trademarks of Pebble Beach. PHOTO: TOM OWENS

that rarest of all species, an available parking space on Ocean Avenue, grab it and milk it for all it's worth.

Carmel is truly a shopper's and art lover's paradise. Its rich cultural history, embodied in the Sunset Cultural Center since its founding in 1964, adds an air of elegance to this remarkable town. The white sandy beach at the end of Ocean Avenue can be absolutely spectacular on a perfect day, and the picturesque residential cottages off the beaten path elicit thoughts of a quaint English village. World-class hotels, inns, and restaurants are the topper for an enchanting stay.

Pebble Beach

It's known worldwide as an exclusive address. Its seashore villas are home to the rich and famous. (Robin Leach could shoot a season's worth of episodes along 17-Mile Drive alone.) Visitors must pass through guarded gates to gain admittance. If you're dropping in just for a quick look-see, it will cost you a $7.50 entry fee. If you're staying for a round of golf at The Links, Spyglass Hill, Poppy Hill, or Spanish Bay, the price of admission just got considerably higher—if you can get a tee time. Stay a few days at The Lodge or The Inn at Spanish Bay, and you may have to bring more than your American Express.

Pebble Beach is the geographic heart of the Monterey Peninsula. The widely held image of wealth and exclusivity conjured at the mention of the name is accurate, at least along the coastal route of 17-Mile Drive and surrounding the famous Lodge. But not every home is a mansion and not every one of the approximately 5,000 residents is a movie star, oil baron, or silver-spoon-fed millionaire. In fact, some abodes in the Del Monte Forest might even be called rustic or modest by Peninsula standards. And some residents are hardworking stiffs just trying to make ends meet.

Beyond being a famous resort destination, Pebble Beach is also a company town. Not being an incorporated city, there's no

Monterey Peninsula Vital Statistics

Mayors:
Monterey: Dan Albert
Carmel: Sue McCloud
Pacific Grove: Sandy Koffman

California governor: Gray Davis

Area (square miles): 24.5 miles

Nickname/motto:
Monterey: California's first capital
Pacific Grove: Butterfly Town USA
Carmel: A city in a forest

Average temperatures: July (high/low) 68/51
January (high/low) 60/43

Average rainfall/days of sunshine: 19.29 inches/298 days

Cities founded: Monterey, 1850; Pacific Grove, 1889; Carmel, 1916

Major university: California State University Monterey Bay

Important dates in history:

1542: La Bahía de los Pinos (Bay of Pines) was first discovered by Juan Rodriguez Cabrillo.

1602: Sebastian Viscaino officially named the port Monterey, in honor of the Viceroy of New Spain.

1770: Gaspar de Portolá and Franciscan Father Junipero Serra came to Monterey to establish a mission.

1776: Spain named Monterey as the capital of Baja (lower) and Alta (upper) California. Captain Juan Bautista de Anza arrived from Sonora with the first settlers for Spanish California.

1818: Argentinean revolutionary privateer Hippolyte Bouchard arrived and burned the compound at the Royal Presidio Chapel in an effort to destroy Spain's attempt to colonize California.

1822: Mexico seceded from Spain bringing Monterey and all of California under the rule of Mexico.

1842: The United States established a consulate in Monterey and Thomas Larkin was appointed first consul to Mexico.

1846: Commodore John Drake Sloat's flagship arrived in Monterey Bay and the American flag was raised.

1848: Treaty of Guadalupe Hidalgo was signed, making California part of the United States. In Monterey, Chaplain Walter Colton, U.S. Navy, was appointed as Monterey's first American alcalde, a position defined as mayor and judge. He established *The Californian*, California's first newspaper. Colton Hall was built to serve as a public school and town meeting hall.

1849: Colton Hall was chosen as the site for the convention where delegates drafted and signed California's first state constitution.
1850: California becomes 31st state to enter the Union.
1875: Pacific Grove was settled as a Methodist retreat.
1897: Del Monte golf course opened, first course west of the Mississippi.
1906: San Francisco earthquake occurred; artists began to move to Carmel.

Major area employers:
County of Monterey; The United States Government (U.S. Navy, U.S. Army); Community Hospital of the Monterey Peninsula; Pebble Beach Company

Famous sons and daughters:
John Steinbeck, author; Edward Weston, photographer; Ansel Adams, photographer; Robinson Jeffers, poet; Clint Eastwood, actor; Leon Panetta, politician; Alan Funt, television personality; Hank Ketcham, cartoonist; Mary Austin, author; Doris Day, actress; Emily Fish, Point Pinos Lighthouse lightkeeper.

State/city holidays:
New Year's Day; Martin Luther King Day; Presidents' Day; Easter; Memorial Day; Independence Day; Labor Day; Thanksgiving Day; Christmas Day

Chamber of commerce:
Monterey Peninsula Chamber of Commerce
380 Alvarado Street
Monterey, CA 93940
(831) 648–5360
Fax (831) 649–3502
www.mpcc.com

Major airports/interstates:
Monterey Peninsula Airport (Monterey), San Jose International Airport (San Jose); Highway 1, Highway 68, U.S. Highway 101

Public transportation: Monterey-Salinas Transit (bus); Amtrak (train)

Military bases:
Naval Postgraduate School; Defense Language Institute (Presidio of Monterey)

Driving laws:
Seatbelts must be worn by all passengers; right turns permitted on red; speed limit is as posted; maximum speed is 65 on Interstates.

Alcohol laws:
Legal drinking age is 21 years; blood/alcohol level of 0.8 or higher is a DWI; it is unlawful to drive with an open container of alcohol in the car.

Daily newspaper: *The Monterey County Herald*

Sales tax: 7.25 percent city/state taxes on all retail sales mayor, no city council, and no police department. Instead there's the Monterey County Sheriff and The Pebble Beach Company, which owns much of the property and serves largely as lord and master over the forest.

As ruler over this prime primeval real estate, The Pebble Beach Company (now owned by an investment group that includes Clint Eastwood, Arnold Palmer, and other celebrities) often finds itself in a somewhat awkward position. It constantly finds itself trying to balance its role as a responsible corporate citizen (its community work and monetary contributions to good causes are legendary) and profitable corporate entity. On the one hand, The Pebble Beach Company is expected by residents and neighbors to preserve and protect what remains of the undeveloped forest, providing whatever maintenance and tending is deemed necessary to keep pest and pestilence away. On the other hand, the company is called to task by preservationists whenever it tries to recoup its shareholders' considerable investment by further developing its valuable land holdings. It's an age-old battle that continues behind the scenic scenes on what seems like a daily basis.

Insiders' Tip

The 200- to 300-year-old Lone Cypress, one of California's most famous landmarks, is a copyrighted symbol of The Pebble Beach Company.

Such rumblings remain largely inaudible to the casual visitor, and that's the way it should be. Your senses should be overwhelmed with the sights of awe-inspiring natural beauty, the smells of pine forests and salty ocean air, the sounds of squawking sea gulls and barking seals, the feel of ribbed seashells and smooth ocean pebbles, and the taste of delectable meals served in delightful surroundings. If you're fortunate enough to stay at The Lodge or The Inn at Spanish Bay, take full advantage of the amenities that await you. Even if you're just driving through, an hour or two perusing the shops or sampling the food and drink is an unforgettable taste of the good life.

Getting Here, Getting Around

To travel to the scenic Monterey Peninsula you have several choices—by air, by roads, and by sea. Once here, the choices continue; rental cars are readily available at the airport if you choose to drive, but taxicabs and public transportation are also an option. Many locals and visitors alike prefer to explore Monterey, Carmel, and Pacific Grove on foot; don't forget to pack your walking shoes! Biking, in-line skating, or walking along the bike path is a great way to get around and provides up-close views of beautiful Monterey Bay.

The daily rise and fall in temperature in the coastal areas call for a mixture of layered clothing. Early mornings and late afternoons tend to be cooler and windier than the midday; which in September and October can be quite mild and pleasant. A warm sweater or light jacket is recommended, especially if you will be spending a lot of time enjoying the area's spectacular beaches or tide-pooling along the rocky coast.

By Air

Commercial Flights

Monterey Peninsula Airport
200 Fred Kane Drive, Suite 200, Monterey
(831) 648–7000, www.montereyairport.com

The Monterey Airport is small, friendly, and centrally located, providing easy access to all cities within the county. The airport offers about 50 conveniently scheduled daily arrivals and departures with connecting flights to anywhere in the world. The following airlines currently serve the airport: America West Express, American Airlines/American Eagle, and United/United Express. Ask your travel agent about fares from your home city to Monterey. Sometimes the fare is only a few dollars more than flying into San Francisco or San Jose airports.

There is one restaurant at the airport, the Golden Tee. A snack bar and coffee cart can provide something quick if you're in a rush. Five major car rental companies operate out of the airport: Avis, Budget, National, Enterprise, and Hertz. (For more on rental cars, see our "Ground Transportation" section in this chapter.) Ground transportation service, including taxis and Monterey-Salinas Transit (city bus), is offered in front of the airport.

Other Options

You can fly into San Francisco International Airport or San Jose International Airport via most major airlines. From there you can rent a car and drive to Monterey or take the Monterey-Salinas Airbus (see our "By Bus" section in this chapter). The San Francisco airport is approximately 100 miles from Monterey, and San

Insiders' Tip

Monterey's aviation history began in 1910, when James Radley, a British flyer, staged exhibition flights in his Bleriot plane for several hundred people on the northwest side of what is now the Monterey Airfield.

Jose is about 70 miles away. Follow the signs from either airport to U.S. 101 South to the Salinas and the Monterey Peninsula exits.

If you own your own plane, you can fly into the Monterey Airport by utilizing Million Air, (831) 373-4151; Del Monte Aviation-East, (831) 373-3201; and Monterey Jet Center, (831) 373-0100. These companies are at the airport and offer tie-down service, hangars, fuel, and repairs for various types of planes.

Charter Flights

Three charter companies serve the Monterey Peninsula area. Rates for their service depend on the type of aircraft, the destination, and wait time for the pilot. You can expect to pay a rate starting at $200 an hour up to $4,500 per hour or more depending on the type of aircraft.

Million Air Monterey
100 Sky Park Drive, Monterey
(831) 373-4151, www.millionairmonterey.com

Million Air Monterey, a division of Del Monte Aviation, offers premier charter flights in the private plane of your choice to your desired destination. Services for pilots include aircraft fuel, cleaning and maintenance of aircraft, hanger space and tie-down rental, comfortable terminal and pilots' lounge, and air shares and aviation sales.

The Monterey Airplane Company
514 Airport Way, Monterey
(888) 843-7031, www.flymac.com

The Monterey Airplane Company provides aircraft charter and air ambulance services. When flying commercial is not an option, their fleet of two Astra 1125 jets and a Rockwell Turbo Commander turboprop provide on-demand service to domestic and international destinations. MAC also has an aircraft management service. Customers can add their aircraft to the Monterey Airplane Company fleet, providing cost reduction in flight crews and maintenance. Your plane can also be leased to other customers when you are not using it.

Monterey Jet Center
Airport Road, Monterey
(831) 373-0100

The Jet Center offers charter service to the location of your choice as well as air shares and aircraft sales. It also provides aviation fuel services, cleaning and maintenance of aircraft, hangar and tie-down rental, and pilots' lounge.

By Sea

Monterey Bay, a broad 20-mile-wide, open roadstead, is between Point Pinos and Point Santa Cruz. The shores vary. Some are low with sandy beaches backed by dunes or low, sandy bluffs; others are rocky with heavy surf. Salinas Valley, the lowland extending eastward from about the middle of the Bay, is prominent from seaward as it forms the break between the Santa Lucia Range southward and the high land of the Santa Cruz Mountains northward.

The Bay is free of dangers and has a 10-fathom curve lying at an average distance of 0.7 mile offshore. The tidal currents in the Bay are weak. The submarine Monterey Canyon heads, near the middle of the Bay at a depth of more than 50 fathoms, lie about 0.5 mile from the beach near Moss Landing. Shelter from southwesterly winds is afforded at Monterey Harbor off the southern shore.

When arriving by boat, you will find Monterey Harbor, a compact resort harbor with some commercial activity and fishing, 3 miles east of Point Pinos.

Insiders' Tip

The first U.S. ship to enter California waters sailed into Monterey Bay in 1796. The ship's name was Otter, and it was under the command of Yankee skipper Ebenezer Dorr.

Prominent landmarks include the granite Presidio Monument on the brow of a barren hill and a radio tower 0.6 mile north of the monument. A large red-roofed building is conspicuous on a bluff above the shore 4 miles northeastward from the breakwater. Two radio towers just inshore from the sand dunes at Marina, 6 miles northeastward from the breakwater, are conspicuous in the southern part of Monterey Bay. An aero light at Monterey Peninsula Airport is 2.2 miles southeastward of Monterey Harbor breakwater light.

A breakwater extends from the foot of Spence Street in an easterly direction for about 1,700 feet. This affords excellent protection in northwesterly weather. The outer end is marked by a light and in the daytime usually by the loud barking of sea lions. A Coast Guard Station is near the inner end.

The outer harbor and entrance offer depths of more than 20 feet, and the small-boat basin is 8 to 10 feet deep. There are many sport-fishing landings here, and the small-craft basin provides good shelter for about 350 vessels.

Transients should report to the harbor office at the head of Municipal Wharf #2 for berth assignments. The harbormaster can be contacted on channel 5 or 16. Quarantine, customs, and immigration services are handled by representatives from San Francisco, (831) 373-1155.

The easterly municipal wharf is 1,600 feet long and 86 feet wide at the outer end. Depths alongside the outer east and west sides are 24 feet. Freight and supplies are trucked directly to the wharf, and a 10-ton hoist is available. There is a fog signal on the northern end of the wharf.

Monterey Bay Boatworks/Breakwater Cove Marina
32 Cannery Row, Monterey
(831) 373–7857, www.montereybayboat works.com

Restoration, repairs, and fabrication are provided for both motor and sail vessels to 70 tons. A special keel lift is available for wood vessels. Spray painting and welding are also available.

Monterey Marina
Del Monte Avenue, Monterey
(831) 646–3950, www.monterey.org/harbor

The Monterey Marina is between Fisherman's Wharf and Wharf #2. Gasoline, diesel oil, water, and ice are available at Breakwater Cove. Several machine shops operate in Monterey, and marine supplies are readily available.

By Land

Three major highways lead to the Monterey Peninsula: U.S. 101/156 West/Highway 1 from the north and from the south; and Highway 68, also known as the Monterey-Salinas Highway, from the east.

Highway 1 is the most direct route to the Monterey Peninsula. It was appointed one of six All-American Roads by the Federal Highway Administration. If you are coming from the Bay Area or farther north, take the Highway 1 South /Pacifica exit and wind your way down a breathtaking stretch of the Pacific Coast until you reach the Monterey/Highway 156 West exit. Once in Monterey, Highway 1 cuts across the Peninsula, north to south, providing easy access to Carmel, Carmel Valley, and farther south to Big Sur. From Southern California, take Highway 1 North at Santa Barbara and enjoy an equally inspiring drive north until you see the signs for Monterey. Highway 1 is by far the most scenic route, not necessarily the fastest. If time is an issue, take U.S. 101.

U.S. 101 can take you to the Monterey area from the north or south as well. If you are coming from the north, take U.S. 101 South until you reach Salinas and the Monterey Peninsula exit. This exit connects you to Highway 68, or the Monterey-Salinas Highway, which traverses west to Monterey Peninsula cities. The directions are the same for Southern California, except of course, you will be traveling on U.S. 101 North until you arrive at Salinas.

Highway 68 originates in Salinas, and after a short diversion onto Highway 1, travels across the Peninsula ultimately providing access to Pebble Beach and

Surreys are popular along the recreation trail on Cannery Row. PHOTO: HEMP: CANNERY ROW CO./MONTEREY PENINSULA VCB

Pacific Grove, the westernmost point on the Peninsula.

Ground Transportation

Rental Cars

Five major car rental companies serve the area, most with offices at the Monterey Peninsula Airport. Rental rates vary based on the length of rental and time of year. The airport is a short drive from Peninsula hotels and attractions. Advance reservations are strongly recommended.

Avis Rent A Car
Monterey Peninsula Airport, Monterey
(831) 647–7140, (800) 831–2847
www.avis.com

Budget Rent A Car
Monterey Peninsula Airport, Monterey
(831) 373–1899, (800) 527–0700
www.budget.com

Enterprise Rent-A-Car
1178 Del Monte Avenue, Monterey
(831) 649–6300, (800) RENTACAR
www.enterprise.com

Hertz Rent A Car
Monterey Peninsula Airport, Monterey
(831) 373–3318, (800) 654–3131
www.hertz.com

National Rent A Car
Monterey Peninsula Airport, Monterey
(831) 373–4181, (800) 227–7368
www.nationalcar.com

Monterey Rent-A-Roadster
229 Cannery Row, Monterey
(831) 647–1929

Travel around the Peninsula in style by renting a reproduction of a 1929 Mercedes, Model A, or Phaeton roadster. These specialty cars are fun and easy to drive, making any occasion a memorable one. Hourly rates start at around $30. Monday through Friday you get three hours for the price of two. Reservations are required.

Taxi and Limousine Service

If you don't drive your own vehicle or haven't rented a car, there are several other options including taxis, limousines, shuttles, and motor coaches. Cab fees vary depending on the destination, but the starting fee is $1.50 followed by a mileage rate of $1.75. Limousine and shuttle services vary a great deal depending on the number of people, the amount of luggage, the destination, and driver waiting time. These vehicles also have a three-hour minimum. Limousine rentals range from $45 to $85 per hour, and minivans cost about $50 to $60 per hour. Motor coaches require a four-hour minimum, and the price range is from $60 to $80 per hour. For specific price information, call the company directly. The following companies currently serve the Monterey Peninsula area:

A-1 Chartered Limousine Service,
(831) 899–2707

Adventure Tours, (831) 375–2409

Airport Yellow Cab Company, (831) 646–1234

Carmel Taxi, (831) 624–3885

Monterey Limousine Service, (831) 646–9635

Your Maitre d' Limousines, (831) 624–1717

Bus Service

Greyhound
1042 Del Monte Avenue, Monterey
(831) 373–4735
19 W. Gabilan Street, Salinas
(800) 231–2222, www.greyhound.com

Bus service to anywhere in the continental United States is available from the Monterey terminal. Eight buses leave daily, four northbound and four southbound. Services at the station include rest rooms, snacks, and a delivery service for packages.

Monterey-Salinas Transit
1 Ryan Ranch Road, Monterey
(831) 899–2555, www.mst.org

Monterey-Salinas Transit (MST) covers the entire Peninsula area from Watsonville to the north, Big Sur to the south, Salinas to the east, and Pacific Grove to the west. Buses run from 6:00 A.M. to 11:00 P.M. Monday through Saturday and from 8:00 A.M. to 6:00 P.M. on Sunday. Fees vary depending on distance. Exact change is required on all MST buses. Special-rate passes are available. Wheelchair lift buses are available, and the use of the bike racks is free on all MST routes.

Monterey/Salinas Airbus
Monterey
(831) 883–2871, (800) 291–2877
www.montereyairbus.com

The bus arrives and departs at the Monterey Transit Plaza in Monterey at the corner of Pearl and Alvarado streets. There are 10 departure/arrival times, the first at around 4:00 A.M. From Monterey the route continues to the Amtrak station before departure to San Jose airport (approximately two hours) or the San Francisco airport (approximately three hours). A prepaid round-trip fare is around $50. Holiday schedules vary, and reservations are recommended.

Waterfront Area Visitors Express
(The WAVE)
1 Ryan Ranch Road, Monterey
(831) 899–2555, www.mst.org

The WAVE is a real plus for summer visitors to the area because it offers a special fare of only $1.00 per day for routes running along the waterfront from the Point Pinos Lighthouse in Pacific Grove, through Cannery Row and Old Monterey to the Del Monte Shopping Center. The WAVE stops at most major hotels along the way. Seniors, children, and the disabled ride for 50 cents. The WAVE operates from Memorial Day weekend through Labor Day weekend. Hours of operation are from 9:00 A.M. to 6:30 P.M. daily.

Trains

Amtrak
11 Station Place, Salinas
(800) 872–7254, www.amtrak.com

Amtrak provides service from Monterey to 39 points on the West Coast on its Coast Starlight route. Amtrak Thruway Bus Service is the easy, convenient way to reach cities where Amtrak trains do not stop. Amtrak offers coordinating connecting schedules, guaranteed connections through ticketing and thoroughfares, and direct service to and from the Amtrak rail station. From Monterey the service includes nine trains and buses. The Monterey Marriott, Monterey Hyatt, the Monterey Bay Aquarium, Monterey Travelodge, and the Monterey Transit Plaza serve as departure points from Monterey.

Parking

Parking in Pacific Grove is usually not a problem. Street parking is not metered, and most spaces have a 90-minute limit. Pacific Grove has two large public parking lots, one in front of Fandango restaurant (between 16th and 17th Streets) and the other behind Lighthouse Cinema (between Fountain Avenue and 15th Street).

Parking spaces in Carmel generally have a 90-minute limit, although there are quite a few spaces with shorter time allotments so be sure to check the signs and the curb for the exact parking time limit for each available space. There is no metered street parking, and the only lot is the garage behind Carmel Plaza (between Ocean and 7th Avenues). A tight blend of residential and commercial real estate, Carmel can present a challenge in terms of finding a free parking space. Be persistent; the quaint architecture, great shopping, diverse selection of art galleries, and excellent food are worth it.

There are 31 parking facilities in Monterey, ranging from 10-space parking lots to a 1,000-space, state-of-the-art, award-winning parking garage. These facilities total 3,504 off-street parking spaces. Lots are located throughout the city and are affordable, safe, and clean.

In addition to off-street parking, there are 3,312 metered on-street spaces in the downtown, Cannery Row, and Lighthouse Avenue areas. The following page highlights a small selection of the parking options available.

Public Garages

Cannery Row
Foam Street, Monterey

This 1,000-space garage is between Hoffman and Prescott Streets. It provides the best parking for Cannery Row, the Aquarium, and the recreation trail.

East Custom House
Washington Street, Monterey

This parking garage, between Franklin Street and Del Monte Avenue, has 590 spaces. There is a ticket dispenser that accepts cash or credit cards. It is close to Fisherman's Wharf and the marina and is the best spot to park in downtown Monterey.

West Custom House
Tyler Street, Monterey

This 229-space garage is between Franklin Street and Del Monte Avenue. It is close to Fisherman's Wharf, the marina, and downtown Monterey.

Calle Principal Garage
Calle Principal, Monterey

Between Franklin and Jefferson Streets, this 124-space garage provides nearby parking for Colton Hall Museum, Monterey Peninsula Museum of Art, downtown Monterey, and City Hall.

Parking Lots

Waterfront Lot #1
Del Monte Avenue, Monterey

The 324-space lot, between Washington Street and Fisherman's Wharf is close to the Wharf, the marina, and the recreational trail.

Waterfront Lot #2
Del Monte Avenue, Monterey

This lot, between Washington Street and Fisherman's Wharf, contains 235 spaces and provides ample parking for Fisherman's Wharf, the marina, and the recreational trail. Trailer parking is available in this lot.

Lot #21
Foam Street, Monterey

Insiders' Tip

When parked in a non-metered, timed zone in Monterey, vehicles need to be moved a minimum of 120 feet before the time expires. Parking officers used to use chalk to mark tires and many people would simply roll the car a few inches to hide the mark. Now the city is experimenting with a system that combines GPS technology and license plate scanning devices. If the time expires, a ticket will arrive in your mailbox a few days later.

Lot 21 is between Cannery Row and Reeside Avenue and provides 79 spaces for parking for Cannery Row, the recreational trail, and San Carlos Beach Park. Trailer and RV parking is allowed here.

Coast Guard Lot
Cannery Row, Monterey

This 47-space lot is by the Coast Guard Pier at the south end of Cannery Row, providing the best parking for Cannery Row and the recreational trail. Trailer and RV parking is allowed, and shower facilities are available.

Lot CR-5
Cannery Row, Monterey

On Cannery Row between Hoffman and McClellan Avenues, this lot has 76 parking spaces. It is close to the Aquarium and Cannery Row. Trailer and RV parking is allowed.

Cannery Row Lot 7
David Avenue, Monterey

This 103-space lot, between Foam and Wave Streets, is close to the Aquarium and Cannery Row.

Alternative Transportation

Bicycle and Moped Rentals

Adventures by the Sea
299 Cannery Row, Monterey
201 Alvarado Mall, Monterey
Lovers Point Park, Pacific Grove
(831) 372–1807,
www.adventuresbythesea.com

Kayak tours and rentals, bicycle and surrey rentals, fully catered themed group events on the beach for up to 1,000 people or indoors for up to 350 with entertainment... is there anything these guys *don't* do? The oldest business of its kind on the Monterey Peninsula has something for everybody from the casual day-tripper wanting to see the sights from the recreation trail to the hard-core kayak trekker wanting to get up close and personal with the marine life of the Monterey Bay Marine Sanctuary. Kayaks are rented for a full day and include all gear and a safety and paddling orientation. That nemesis of the bicycling user of the recreation trail, the two- or four-person surrey, can be rented by the hour. Serenely pedaling past dozing sea lions and feeding sea otters is a lovely way to spend an afternoon in paradise.

Insiders' Tip

Biking along the Monterey Recreation Trail is a great way to get around and provides close-up views of beautiful Monterey Bay.

Bay Bikes
99 Pacific Street/Fisherman's Wharf, Monterey
(831) 655–8687

This well-known business has 21-speed bikes, wide-tire bicycles, and four-wheel surreys. It carries men's, women's, and children's frames in addition to child trailers, baby seats, and trunk racks. Bikes can be delivered to your hotel 24 hours a day by calling (831) 659-BIKE. Their brochure has a map to guide you to some of the best cycling around. Call for hourly, daily, and weekly rates.

Monterey Moped Adventures
1250 Del Monte Avenue, Monterey
(831) 373–2696

Exploring the Monterey Peninsula on a moped can be an exciting alternative. Monterey Moped Adventures has single- and double-seated mopeds, motorcycles, and bicycles available for rent. Helmets and area maps are available at no extra charge. They even rent baby strollers and carriages to go with bicycles so the little ones can tag along.

Moped drivers must be at least 18 years old (unless accompanied by a parent) and possess a driver's permit or driver's license. Call for hours and pricing information.

Bike Trails

A recreation trail runs along the coastline from Pacific Grove to Marina. Most of the other Peninsula cities offer a bike lane for two-wheeled travelers. Caution should be taken since the trail is popular with cyclists as well as those traveling on foot, on in-line skates, or by surrey.

Sharing Rides

Rideshare
(831) 422–POOL, www.ambag.org/sharing

Call or visit the Web site for information on carpools, vanpools, and other alternative commute options. The carpool lot is at the corner of Laureles Grade and Highway 68. The lot has 20 parking spaces for autos, but no bike lockers.

Special Needs

RIDES
(831) 373–1393, www.mst.org

RIDES is a transit service for seniors or special-needs riders. It offers curb-to-curb service anywhere in the county for $1.00 each way. Hours of operation are from 7:00 A.M. to 7:00 P.M. daily. It is best to reserve your ride 24 hours in advance to ensure service.

On Foot

The Monterey Peninsula is an area where walking is not only possible, but also very pleasant. The cities of Monterey, Pacific Grove, and Carmel are especially suited to exploration on foot. Each city provides ample sidewalks with crosswalks at major intersections.

In addition, the recreation trail provides a path for walking from Lovers Point in Pacific Grove to Canyon Del Rey Road in Seaside. The trail is shared also by skaters and bicyclists in Monterey, so caution is recommended.

If you are interested in a guided or self-guided walking tour, the Monterey Path of History Tour, (831) 649-7118 and Carmel Walks, (831) 642-2700 are two organizations designed to provide you with specific area information to discover while walking your way through town.

History

Monterey
Pacific Grove
Carmel
Pebble Beach

The history of the Monterey Peninsula area is rich and sustaining; many historic events happened right here in the "Cradle of California History." The tales of each of the early cities are as unique and diverse as the individuals who settled Monterey, Carmel, Pacific Grove, and Pebble Beach. The Peninsula's history is a collection of adventures that starts with the first Native Americans and continues to the present-day residents. This area has been called home by the practical and the posh, from cannery workers and fishermen to celebrities and government leaders. Today, the Peninsula includes other lively and growing communities—Seaside, Sand City, Del Rey Oaks, and Marina—however, we've chosen to highlight the earlier settlements in these pages.

Monterey

Monterey's earliest Spanish settlers can be traced back to June 3, 1770, with the arrival of Gaspar de Portolá and Father Junipero Serra. Wishing to secure the area north of Mexico before other nations could lay claim, Spain's King Charles III established 21 missions in California. Father Serra, leader of the California missions, oversaw the founding of the first nine, including those in Monterey, Carmel, and the Presidio of Monterey.

Monterey was named capital of Alta (upper) and Baja (lower) California in 1777. Felipe de Neve, the new Spanish governor, developed a code of laws that regulated both civil and military affairs. He is also credited for the improvement of the Presidio by converting it to an adobe structure.

Mexico granted the pueblo lands to Monterey in 1830 and set territorial boundaries. Fourteen *ranchos* existed in Monterey County in 1834. The ranchos, with Spanish names like Aguajito, Laguna Seca, El Pescadero, and Cañada la Segunda, were huge tracts of land. The Punta de Pinos *ranchero* encompassed the entire Monterey Peninsula. During this time, the human population of 2,000 was greatly outnumbered by nearly 140,000 head of cattle. After Mexico's independence from Spain in 1822, the nonmilitary citizens living near the Presidio headquarters were organized into the "Pueblo de Monterey" or village of Monterey.

Monterey continued to serve as the capital of Alta California under the Mexican government until 1846, when relations with Mexico began to break down. The United States had two allies in California during this time, Mr. Larkin, a consul and confidential agent of the United States who resided in Monterey, and Captain John C. Frémont, an officer in the U.S. Army.

Larkin was instructed to bring about, if possible, a nonviolent penetration of American citizens into California. He also was to support Californians in asserting and maintaining their independence from Mexico.

Frémont, the son-in-law of U.S. Senator Thomas Hart Benton, had set out to defeat Mexican power in California of his own accord. His idea was to establish a military presence in California, though he apparently was under no authorization from President Polk or the United States War Department. He arrived in Monterey with a ragtag band of 24 Americans, among them Kit Carson. He eventually left Monterey and gained control of Sonoma, where he established the Bear Flag Republic.

U.S. Commodore John Drake Sloat arrived in Monterey Harbor on July 2, 1846 carrying with him instructions from the U.S. government to capture all California ports and hold them in the event of a

Insiders' Tip

Pacific Grove's religious beginnings made the city the last "dry town" in California. The sale of alcohol was legalized in the city in 1969.

war between the United States and Mexico. He sent for Larkin and learned of the Bear Flag Republic and Captain Frémont's participation in it. On July 7, he sent four of his officers ashore with a demand to the Mexican commandant to surrender the port of Monterey with all its troops, arms, and other public property. The commandant replied that he had neither troops nor arms to surrender. Upon receipt of this message, Sloat disembarked and declared American freedoms for the Californians and that "henceforth California will be a portion of the United States."

Troubled, weary, and in poor health, Sloat turned over his command to Commodore Robert F. Stockton, who had arrived in Monterey a few days earlier. Stockton was more of a militant, uncompromising executive who sought to immediately conquer all of California. Frémont, who heard the news and came to Monterey to confer with Sloat, related to Stockton easily and planned an attack to the south to drive the Mexican authorities from the region. Frémont and his battalion were taken into the naval service and he was made major in command. The whole contingent sailed to San Diego to seal off California from further invasion by Mexico.

From the beginning Monterey seemed destined to become known as a place of "firsts." In California, Monterey was the site of the first newspaper, theater, library, post office, and real estate transaction.

The discovery of gold in the Sierras, in 1848, nearly made a ghost town out of Monterey and several other California cities. Despite the exodus of those seeking a fast fortune, Monterey was finally declared a city on June 10, 1889.

David Jacks, owner of the 3,323-acre Rancho Aguajito, was one of the most influential people in Monterey County. Jacks, born in the town of Crieff in Perthshire, Scotland, came to the United States in 1841. He worked for a few years in New York and in April 1849 he came to California, traveling immediately to the Sierra gold mines. Not liking what he saw there, he went to San Francisco in 1850 and worked in a grocery and dry goods store. He moved to Monterey a year later and became a herdsman for government horses and sheep on Rancho San Francisquito. Later, Jacks was employed by a fellow Scotsman, James McKinley, in his grocery and dry goods store.

Mr. Jacks became the Monterey County Treasurer in 1852. He began acquiring land through direct purchase, buying up tax-delinquent tracts, exchanges, and foreclosures. His land holdings in Monterey County totaled more than 70,000 acres. His purchase of 30,000 acres of Monterey city land made David Jacks the most hated and feared man in the county. Jacks acquired the property by foreclosing on city lands for a debt Monterey owed his attorney. The city was forced to auction its land in order to satisfy the debt. Jacks and his attorney were apparently the only two bidders at the auction.

From that point on Jacks became almost a marked man. He always traveled with a bodyguard, especially if he left the Monterey area. He was so despised, local legend has it, that someone placed a curse on him to prevent his family name from surviving another generation. In spite of his bad reputation, Jacks was a God-fearing man who taught Sunday school. He generously donated property and funds to the Methodist church for the establishment of a summer camp in Pacific Grove.

For nearly a century Monterey was a sleepy little ranch community. Its citizens lived in adobes, spoke Spanish, and maintained Latin customs. The arrival of the Southern Pacific Railroad to the Peninsula, in 1880, signaled a rapid change.

Point Pinos Lighthouse, built in 1885, is the oldest lighthouse in continuous operation in California.
PHOTO: JANA MORBA

Tourism, recreation, fishing, and agriculture became new industries drawing thousands to Monterey County.

Monterey didn't have a Gold Rush, but made up for it with the Silver Rush, a dramatic increase in the harvest of sardines from the Bay. Sardines had always been caught in the Bay, but after 1900 the sardine catch became an industry.

The birth of the industry actually began in 1909 when Frank Booth set up a tiny plant near the present-day Fisherman's Wharf to can salmon. Impressed by the large schools of silver-sided sardines, he began canning them in small tins. At that time the fish were caught in gill nets strung in the path of a school of sardines. The nets caught only a small percentage of the fish and many of those slipped away as the fish were passed from sailboats to the cannery in wire baskets. The fish were then cut by hand and cooked in wire baskets that were pushed through troughs of boiling oil. After the cooking process they were hand-packed in tins and hand-soldered. This method allowed for the production of only 400 cans per day.

When Booth's plant burned down, he established another at the foot of Alvarado Street. Proximity to the Bay was important because the fish had to be transported to the cannery from the ship. Booth hired Knute Hovden, a young Norwegian who had graduated from National Fisheries College in his country. He also hired Pietro Ferrante, a Sicilian immigrant whose family was involved in the fishing industry. Coupled with the introduction of the *lampara* net by Pietro Ferrante and dozens of machines that helped streamline the canning process invented by Knute Hovden, Monterey was geared up for the making of a legend.

By 1918 the canneries were producing little one-pound oval cans from the 50,000 tons of sardines caught in the Bay. The invention of purse seiners in the 1920s replaced the lampara nets. These vessels bore huge nets, with the depth of a 10-story building, encircling an area the size of a football field. In the years that followed, more than 70 seiners, with seasonal catches soaring to 215,000 tons, fished Monterey Bay. For 30 years Cannery Row

Insiders' Tip

The oldest public building still standing in California is Monterey's Custom House.

was the "Sardine Capital of the World." In its heyday, it had 30 canneries employing 2,500 full-time workers and thousands of part-timers.

For years Ed Ricketts, a marine biologist and longtime Cannery Row resident, urged officials to adopt a conservation program. (Ricketts was immortalized by John Steinbeck as Doc, in *Cannery Row*.) His warnings continued to fall on deaf ears, and the sardine catch of 1948 was the worst ever. It rebounded in 1950 to 132,000 tons, but by the next season it was all over. The sardine canning industry, sustained only a half-century, was gone for good. Life on the Row ground to a halt, and the canning machinery was sold off to foreign buyers.

A remnant of this bygone era started the revival of Cannery Row; the Hovden Cannery, built in 1916, became the nucleus for the new Monterey Bay Aquarium. The opening of the aquarium in 1984 laid the cornerstone for new vitality on Cannery Row. Today the Monterey Bay Aquarium is recognized as one of the world's premier aquariums.

The legend of Cannery Row continued as other businesses were quickly established. Today visitors stroll through several blocks of gift and specialty shops and art galleries. New restaurants, many with unobstructed ocean views, continue to breathe new life into this historic district.

The arrival of the railroad was the genius of Charles Crocker, one of four rail barons who owned Southern Pacific Railroad. Crocker envisioned Monterey as a resort and lost no time in erecting a magnificent Victorian castle at the site of the Naval Postgraduate School. Crocker spent $1 million building the Hotel Del Monte in a mere 100 days.

When the doors opened in 1880, the hotel was an immediate success. It was built in a park-like setting, and no expense was spared to provide guests every possible amenity. Each room had a telephone, and the bath was equipped with hot and cold running water, both rarities in the late 1800s.

Tragedy struck on March 31, 1887, when the "Queen of American Watering Places," as the hotel had become known, was completely destroyed by fire. Although no lives were lost in the flames, the hotel was reduced to ashes.

The following year the Hotel Del Monte was rebuilt in a Gothic-Victorian architectural style and was even more sumptuous. It covered 16 acres and could lodge 700 guests. The spacious dining room, with four fireplaces, seated up to 750 people. The hotel grounds boasted a 15-acre lake, lawn tennis courts, archery ranges, exotic gardens, and miles of walking paths. An immaculate stable and carriage house held the surreys used to transport guests to the Del Monte Forest for picnics on the pebbled beach. A beachfront bathing pavilion, the largest in the world at the time, was also built. It contained 210 dressing rooms and four swim tanks, each tank measuring 70 by 170 feet. Three of the pools were heated to different temperatures. This allowed swimmers to prepare for a dip in the chilly bay by moving from pool to pool.

A second fire in 1924 again destroyed the hotel, and it was rebuilt in a Mediterranean style with a fireproof red-tile roof. The third Hotel Del Monte, the one that exists today, was even larger and more elaborate than the other two. Unfortunately it never quite regained its previous status as a luxury hotel because the Great Depression curbed travel and extravagance for even the elite.

Much of Monterey's culture and history are revisited through the many festivals and events that take place throughout the year (see our chapter on Annual Events), and many historic buildings in Old Monterey have been preserved. The promotion of economic growth while maintaining the historic quality of Monterey is of great concern to city officials, business owners, and residents. For example, Monterey's Alvarado Street has successfully blended a variety of hotels, shops, service-oriented businesses, and eating establishments with charming adobe buildings of historical significance.

Pacific Grove

The first development in Pacific Grove was the installment of a lighthouse that began operating at Point Pinos in 1855. The lighthouse served as a guide to mariners entering Monterey Bay. The lighthouse keeper, Captain Allen Luce, received authorization in 1874 to cut a trail through the forest from Point Pinos to Monterey. This trail became what is now known as Lighthouse Avenue.

Pacific Grove is located where the Pacific Ocean meets the waters of the Monterey Bay. This area was formerly Rancho Punta de Pinos, one of the great *ranchos* of the Spanish/Mexican era in California history. Methodist Church officials founded Pacific Grove in 1875 as a religious and cultural retreat. The retreat consisted of 100 acres of dense pine forest.

Reverend Ross, a Methodist minister, convinced the Bishop of the Methodist Church to purchase headlands northwest of Monterey, owned by David Jacks, for a summer camp. At a meeting in San Francisco on June 1, 1875, a new organization, the Pacific Grove Retreat Association, met and formed the first Board of Trustees. With the donation of the land and the financial assistance of David Jacks, the association laid out the first lots for tenting in 1875.

The first camp meeting officially opened August 8, 1875, and became the forerunner of the summer religious meetings and Chautauquas that followed. The Chautauqua, a religious camp meeting consisting of sermons, educational lectures, family get-togethers, and the singing of Psalms, originated on the East Coast. The first West Coast meeting of the Chautauqua Scientific and Literary Society was held in Pacific Grove in 1879. A large tent was set up for group meetings on present-day Forest Avenue.

Every year the summer retreat groups grew larger. Eventually tents were set up on 30-by-60-foot lots, each selling for $50. A large meeting place, Chautauqua Hall, was completed in 1881. The building seated about 1,500 people.

The last Pacific Grove Chautauqua was held on August 7, 1926. Changes in lifestyle brought an end to nearly five decades of the religious camp meetings that led in the development of Pacific Grove.

In 1881, David Jacks sold 7,000 acres of ranch land on the Peninsula to the Southern Pacific Railroad, the sister company of the Pacific Improvement Company. He also sold several thousand acres of the Pescadero and Point Pinos *ranchos* to the Pacific Improvement Company in 1881 and 1883. The sale of the property eventually led to the religious retreat becoming more of a secular location as more and more people, some uninterested in religion, came to Pacific Grove. All parties agreed that the Pacific Grove Retreat Association would maintain control over the grounds. In 1919, Samuel F. B. Morse and other investors purchased the holdings of the Pacific Improvement Company; the new company, called Del Monte Properties, was formed with Morse serving as its president.

In the early 1850s a community of Chinese immigrants began settling in the area where Hopkins Marine Station stands today. It wasn't long until the population of Chinatown grew to about 500. They built wooden cottages perched above the water on stilts and rocks; some cottages included balconies. The Chinese were industrious, hardworking people who prospered by cultivating the area's natural resources. Some grew vegetables in little gardens, while others set up shell stands along 17-Mile Drive.

The truly ambitious relied on the ocean for their livelihood. By day they fished for rockfish, cod, halibut, red and bluefish, yellowtail, mackerel, and sardines. Nighttime would find them bobbing along the Bay amongst a fleet of about 30 junkets and sampans. A fire of pitch logs laid out on wire racks attached to the stern of their boats attracted squid to the water's surface. By early morning the nightly catch was spread out to dry on the ground; the potent odor of the drying

The protected waters of Lovers Point provide a unique backdrop for concerts and festivals. PHOTO: JANA MORBA

squid was not fully appreciated by the residents of Pacific Grove. In addition, the Italian fishermen from Monterey grew increasingly threatened by the Chinese presence in the Bay.

On the night of May 16, 1906, Pacific Grove's Chinatown was completely destroyed by fire. Flames roared through the village, quickly burning the wooden cottages. Those who fled the disaster watched in horror as the deadly blaze destroyed their homes and all of their earthly possessions. The fire was especially tragic for the San Francisco Chinese, who had recently come to the Peninsula in hopes of building a new life after losing everything six weeks earlier in the great earthquake.

The settlement burned to the ground as firefighters worked desperately to get water in and quench the flames. It was later discovered that the fire hose connected to the two-inch water main had been cut when the fire first started. Although authorities suspected the fire was not accidental, no further investigation took place. Once in motion, the rumor mill produced stories that implicated the Pacific Improvement Company. The rumors stemmed from the fact that Pacific Grove was continually growing and the demand for housing was becoming greater. The waterfront property where Chinatown stood was now prime real estate, and the company had previously considered evicting the Chinese.

To further fan the flames, after the fire the Pacific Improvement Company fenced in the former village and prohibited the Chinese from entering. This thwarted the efforts of the Chinese who wanted to rebuild their homes. A small Chinese village was established at McAbee Beach near the present-day Steinbeck Plaza. It should be noted that the Chinese played a great part in establishing Monterey as a fishing port, ranking second only to San Francisco.

On July 16, 1889, Pacific Grove was incorporated as a city. Mr. O. S. Trimmer was appointed as the first president of the Board of Trustees. Pacific Grove became a chartered city on April 22, 1927. This resulted in the calling of a general election for a mayor and city council.

The quality of life in Pacific Grove attracted people who were not necessarily interested in religion. The leaders of the retreat drew a dim view of these outsiders.

In the early 1900s, blue laws were put into effect in order to maintain the lifestyle of the Methodists.

Not only was the use of liquor against the law, but the sale of alcoholic beverages was strictly prohibited within the city limits. (Pacific Grove remained a "dry" town until 1969 when the city council adopted an ordinance repealing prohibition. Voters enthusiastically approved the repeal of the ordinance, which legalized the sale of alcoholic beverages.) Curfew laws went into effect stating that residents were required to keep their window shades up until 10:00 P.M. At that time, the shades were to be pulled down and all lights turned off.

Around 1915 it was determined that it was in the best interest of the city to own its own waterfront. Provisions were made to curtail development on the waterfront without the approval of Pacific Grove's residents.

The city of Pacific Grove purchased Lovers Point from the Pacific Improvement Company in 1902 to develop a park. Lovers Point and its beaches have been a focal point since the early days of Pacific Grove. The protected waters and white sand on the main beach were a very popular place. Gatherings such as prayer meetings, band concerts, and festivals were held there.

Lovers Point was the original site of Hopkins Marine Station. In those days it was called the Hopkins Seaside Laboratory. In 1891, Timothy Hopkins, the adopted son of Mark Hopkins (one of the "Big Four" rail barons of the Southern Pacific Railroad), established this important laboratory.

After visiting Dr. Anthony Dohrn's Zoological Station in Naples, Italy, Timothy approached several professors at Stanford University about opening a laboratory in Pacific Grove. With the help of the Pacific Improvement Company, a large two-story building was constructed. By the early 1900s the lab needed a larger facility and moved to Cabrillo Point where the Chinese village had once been.

After the move, the lab became known as the Hopkins Marine Station of Stanford University. Over the years it has become a well-known and esteemed research facility, gaining the respect of scientists throughout the world.

No history of Pacific Grove would be complete without mentioning Asilomar, the "Refuge by the Sea." This beautiful facility came into existence in 1913 with a gathering of girls from the Young Women's Christian Association (YWCA). Architect Julia Morgan, who developed Hearst Castle, designed the early plans for the grounds and original structures. The original 30-acre site was a gift of the Pacific Improvement Company.

From 1936 to 1941 Asilomar was leased and operated as a public resort. During WWII the National Youth Authority used it as a training facility. The YWCA resumed its normal operations there in 1946. In 1956 the YWCA offered to sell the property, now 60 acres, to the state of California providing it be used for a state park. The state purchased the property and added to it another 34 acres, renaming it Asilomar State Beach and Conference Grounds.

The name Pacific Grove was appropriate for the area, because in the early days there was nothing but a grove of trees here. The city became known by various other names including the Christian Seaside Retreat, Methodist Episcopal Encampment Grounds, Pacific Grove Retreat, Piney Paradise, the Grove, and the Retreat. It was also know as Chautauqua-by-the-Sea, the City of Churches, and the City of Homes. Today, Pacific Grove is called " P.G." by Peninsula residents and other Insiders. The town is promoted outside the area as Butterfly Town USA and America's Last Hometown.

Today, Pacific Grove still maintains its small-town atmosphere. Residents are active in the community and take a strong interest in local politics. The people who live and work in P.G. are proud of their business district, which has seen a revival in the past several years. The opening of the historic Holman building as an antiques mall and the arrival of several new businesses have filled long-vacant large retail sites, giving locals and visitors an added incentive to shop Pacific Grove.

Carmel

Present-day Carmel received its name in 1602 from two Carmelite friars traveling with Don Sebastian Vizcaino. Upon entering Monterey Bay they noticed a valley beyond the hills to the south of Monterey and named it Carmello.

Father Junipero Serra founded the Mission and Presidio of San Carlos Borromeo de Monterey in 1770. The following year it was determined that the land was more fertile to the south, so the mission was moved, and San Carlos Borroméo de Carmelo was established to provide for the agricultural needs of the new community.

The restoration of the mission was undertaken in 1883, with the financial support of Mrs. Leland Stanford. A new, steep-pitched, shingle roof was added, and the mission grounds were restored.

The area surrounding the mission was desolate, but with its restoration, it was hoped the area could be developed. The aesthetic quality of the land wasn't enough to attract real estate buyers in 1886. What mattered to most buyers was if the land was good for raising crops and cattle or if it contained timber or mineral resources. Carmel had little to offer because the dunes, scrub oaks, twisted pines, and high chaparral rendered it useless in the development of these industries.

The idea of promoting the mission as a tourist attraction was developed in 1888 by Santiago J. Duckworth, a Monterey real estate dealer, and his brother, Belisario E. Duckworth. Their idea was to develop the area into a Catholic summer resort, somewhat like that of Pacific Grove's Methodist retreat. They purchased 234 acres of the Las Manzanitas ranchero, where Carmel now stands. With no reliable water source except a Pacific Improvement Company water line across the bottom end of the property, the land was considered worthless.

A map of Carmel City was filed in May 1888 after a survey by W.C. Little, the city engineer of Monterey. By July of that same year, 200 lots were sold. The price of these lots, located east of Junipero, was an astounding $20 for inside lots and $25 for corner lots.

The Duckworths planned to sell $50 lots where the current business district is located, turning the money over to Catholic Societies of California for use in building convention halls and establishing a school or college. The brothers firmly believed that Southern Pacific Railroad would reach the mission in the near future, but this never happened. An insufficient water supply further complicated development plans. Most of the water was still hauled in barrels from the Pacific Improvement Company's pipeline. A windmill pump managed by Carmel Waterworks proved inadequate for the needs of a growing population.

About 10 families were established in Carmel at this time. Even though the Duckworths gave up their plan in 1894, most of these families stayed on. There were also three cabins (one of which was around prior to any development by the Duckworths) that housed a tiny Mexican community.

Two developers, Frank Powers and James Devendorf, with the formation of the Carmel Development Company, established Carmel-by-the-Sea in 1902. Frank Powers was a real estate developer with subdivisions near San Jose, Stockton, Morgan Hill, and Gilroy. Powers exchanged his Stockton properties for Carmel. Before long M.J. Murphy came to the little city. Murphy built his first house at age 17 and went on to build much of Carmel.

Carmel owes a debt to Powers and Devendorf, who were largely responsible for planting the trees that created the wooded village valued by residents today. In the early 1900s Carmel was practically barren, but beginning in 1904, Devendorf began planting thousands of trees each winter. Up to that time Ocean Avenue was a wide dusty strip in summer and muddy bog each winter. Planting the trees and installing a boardwalk helped to rectify the situation.

Since the beginning, the area has attracted creative people such as artists, writers, musicians, and educators. The beauty of Carmel attracted them, inspired them, and captivated them: Many decided to set up permanent residence here. Carmel became appealing to several Bohemian writers and artists in the 1920s; among these early residents were George Sterling, Mary Austin, Upton Sinclair, William Rose Benét, Sinclair Lewis, and Robinson Jeffers. These six artists laid the foundation for the arts community in Carmel, which still is an active and vibrant part of the charm of Carmel. Approximately 90 art galleries catering to a wide range of tastes and styles form the majority of the town's businesses.

Carmel is also referred to as Carmel-by-the-Sea. Picturesque houses have whimsical or romantic names such as "Frivolity" or "Song of the Sea." Photogenic gates, doorways, and secret gardens are reminiscent of a tiny English village. The architecture of the houses is fascinating—from tiny, thatched-roof cottages to palatial estates.

In many ways Carmel has stuck to its early, small-town traditions by prohibiting the use of neon lighting, high-rises, and parking meters. From its very beginnings Carmel was free of racial prejudice, and, in fact, there was quite a cosmopolitan air about the place. This impression still carries today. Each year thousands of visitors from all socioeconomic levels meander through the streets and wander down Ocean Avenue to Carmel's gorgeous beach.

It might have been the absence of trees in early Carmel that has fueled an obsession with them today. The city of Carmel has gone above and beyond the call of duty in preserving trees. Winding, narrow streets are built around the trees. Architectural plans for houses and businesses incorporate trees, a tradition started by James Devendorf. The center strip of trees in the middle of Ocean Avenue, planted by Devendorf, still stands in beautiful tribute to his vision.

Carmel is home to scores of art galleries, specialty shops, and exceptional restaurants, all compactly located within a square mile radius of "downtown." Walk around this picturesque section of the Peninsula and appreciate the natural beauty, the slower pace, and quaint character of Carmel-by-the-Sea.

Insiders' Tip

Many of the San Francisco writers, artists, and musicians left homeless by the terrible earthquake of 1906 re-established themselves in Carmel.

Pebble Beach

In 1840, Pebble Beach was part of a rancho owned by Maria del Carmen Garcia Barreto Madariaga. Maria, a widow, inherited the ranch after her husband's death. Being more of a city girl, she felt lonely and isolated on the ranch. In 1846 she sold the entire estate, over 4,000 acres, for $500 and purchased an adobe in Monterey. The ranch passed through a series of owners and 16 years later fell into the hands of David Jacks, who purchased the property at a sheriff's sale for 12 cents an acre.

In 1868 Jacks leased the area now known as Stillwater Cove to the China Man Hop Company. By 1888 this Chinese village had more than 30 residents. When 17-Mile Drive opened in the early 1900s, Chinese entrepreneurs set up shell stands along the drive, selling polished abalone shells to the tourists. Due to the stiffening of immigration laws, changes in the fishing industry, and the development of the surrounding land, the last Chinese villager left Pebble Beach in 1912.

Pebble Beach, the resort and community in Del Monte Forest, began in 1907 when Charles Crocker purchased the land from David Jacks for $5.00 an acre. Crocker was a member of the "Big Four," a group including Leland Stanford, Collin Huntington, and Mark Hopkins. The Big Four were rail barons of the Central Pacific Railroad and also owned the Pacific Improvement Company. Crocker, who thought Pebble Beach would make a good summer resort, also owned the luxurious Hotel Del Monte in Monterey.

CLOSE-UP

The Duke Builds The Links

When Yale graduate Samuel F. B. Morse, a transplanted Easterner, first saw the Del Monte Golf Course, he was amazed at its unimaginative design.

The 29-year-old Morse got to work. As the new manager of the Del Monte unit of the Pacific Improvement Company, he had already revamped and renovated the Del Monte Hotel. Now he turned his full focus to the golf course. He created distinct enhancements in the existing course and immediately began developing plans for his vision: brand new golf links in a section of the property that was being used as a picnic site.

Before hiring a designer, Sam Morse, "The Duke of Pebble Beach," interviewed international golfers for their input on how to build a golf course, created several initial plans, and then hired John F. "Jack" Neville to shape his concepts into reality. Jack Neville was an accomplished golfer with two California State Amateur winnings to his credit when he agreed to design his first golf course; his full-time occupation was in real estate sales for Del Monte Properties Company. Douglas Grant, another amateur golfer, was hired specifically to assist Jack with the bunker design and engineering; his credentials in this area included substantial time in Scotland where he had devoted his attention to golf greens and bunkers. What was to become a world-renowned golf experience began in the capable hands of two amateurs.

According to Neville, "it was all there in plain sight." His initial proposal to Morse was accepted and remains effectively unchanged; it was a design that follows the rugged Pacific Ocean coastline as closely as possible. A brilliant use of land and careful attention to the condition of the greens were important components of the overwhelming success of the Pebble Beach Golf Links.

A group of friends, a little golf, and a "clambake" essentially sum up the beginnings of what is now the AT&T Pebble Beach National Pro-Am—an annual event that now raises millions of dollars for local charities. Known as "The Crosby" to locals and insiders, the 54-hole Bing Crosby National Pro-Am debuted on the Peninsula in 1947. And it's become an event around which local people plan their schedules in order to share in the rich traditions. Each year, the Peninsula is transformed into a paradise for those who enjoy golf from the fairways and greens, the bleachers, or their living rooms.

Local resident Clint Eastwood is now one of the owners of this magnificent property and its famed golf courses.

Development in Pebble Beach began in 1908 when Crocker built a log cabin where The Lodge now stands. As little as it was, the presence of the cabin led to the opening of the first Pebble Beach post office on October 4, 1909. Charles Fahl served as the first postmaster. Crocker's cabin provided a comfort stop for people traveling through the Del Monte Forest. The cabin was destroyed by fire in 1917, but two years later it was replaced with the elaborate Del Monte Lodge, under the direction of Samuel F.B. Morse.

Samuel Finley Brown Morse, the nephew of the inventor of the telegraph, came to the Peninsula in 1915. Morse, who eventually became known as "The Duke of Pebble Beach," was hired to manage the Pacific Improvement Company.

During his first year with the company, Morse laid out the Pebble Beach Golf Course using all but 4 percent of the property's shoreline for the course. Construction on the course began in 1916 when Morse hired Douglas Grant and John F. Neville. Grant was a student of architecture, and both gentlemen were amateur golf champions.

The course, named Pebble Beach Links, was dedicated on February 2, 1919. It was only a matter of time before the Links became the world's most celebrated golf course. In 1919 Samuel F. B. Morse, with other investors, bought the holdings of the Pacific Improvement Company for a reported $1.3 million.

Having completed the Links and the Del Monte Lodge, today known as The Lodge at Pebble Beach, Morse turned his attention to the completion of 17-Mile Drive. He also laid out more than 100 miles of bridle paths, and some of these riding trails are still in use today. It was Morse's dream to see Pebble Beach become one of the world's most fashionable resorts.

Though fashionable, the Del Monte Lodge was a boring place throughout the 1920s, except when an orchestra played dance tunes on Saturday nights. More than anything, the Lodge was meant to serve as a watering hole for the small, exclusive circle of Pebble Beach residents and for golfers who played the Links.

What the Lodge lacked in excitement, the residents of the Forest made up for by entertaining the "beautiful people" at private parties in their lavish Pebble Beach mansions. The parties were quite spirited in spite of the subdued mood in the rest of the country brought on by Prohibition. Some say illegal aqua vitae was frequently brought in, throughout the 1920s, by boats that landed in the Point Lobos area.

The devastating effect of the stock market crash finally touched the elite of Pebble Beach in 1933. Nearly 85 percent of all hotels in the United States went into receivership, including San Francisco's Mark Hopkins, The Fairmont, and the Clift Hotel. Although this wasn't the fate of The Pebble Beach Lodge or the Del Monte Hotel, during the Great Depression Samuel F. B. Morse reported losses of more than $300,000. In the early 1930s, Pebble Beach real estate sales fell from more than a million dollars to nothing.

Throughout its history, Pebble Beach has been the home of many events including the Bing Crosby Golf Tournament (now the AT&T National Pro-Am), which opened in 1947. Every year, in February, the AT&T Tournament brings together celebrities with professional and amateur golfers for a week of golf that raises millions of dollars for local charities. Another world-renowned event, the Concours d'Elegance, a premier competition of classic and vintage cars, began in 1950 and was the brainchild of Gwenn Graham. Today, it remains one of the classiest and best-attended events on the Peninsula.

Samuel F. B. Morse died in 1969 but not before he saw the realization of his dream: Pebble Beach did indeed become one of the most highly acclaimed resorts in the world. The beautiful scenery that first attracted the wealthy to Pebble Beach continues to draw visitors from around the globe. The area is also a magnet for movie directors who use Pebble Beach as a backdrop for films set in the French or Italian Riviera, Isle of Capri, or parts of Britain. Recently, several famous residents, including the former mayor of Carmel, Clint Eastwood, purchased the Pebble Beach Company, returning it once again to local ownership.

The renowned 17-Mile Drive, which, incidentally, is now only 12 miles, remains a toll road. Meandering along the drive today, motorists or cyclists pass several championship golf courses. The Links at Spanish Bay; Poppy Hills, home of the Northern California Golf Association; Spyglass Hill, ranked one of the top 40 courses in the United States; the world-famous Pebble Beach Links; and the nine-hole Peter Hay course, are all open to the public. In 2001, the Pebble Beach Company hosted the 100th anniversary of the U.S. Open. Sam Morse's dream continues to expand and grow long after its initial inception.

Hotels and Motels

It's hard for locals to imagine that there could be enough visitors to fill all the available rooms on the Monterey Peninsula. Yet on many of the special-event weekends, finding a room on the Peninsula can be as difficult as finding a midmorning tee time at Pebble Beach on a Saturday. Drive into town during the Monterey Jazz Festival, the Concours d'Elegance, or a big weekend racing event at Laguna Seca, and you may have trouble finding a room for the night. That's nearly always the case if you have your heart set on a room with a view along the Pacific Grove coastline, near Cannery Row, or in central Carmel or Pebble Beach. (This is especially true for bed and breakfast inns, which we cover in our next chapter.)

Despite an abundance of accommodations of all types and price ranges, the key phrases to remember are "special-event weekend" and "advance reservations." If you've read our Annual Events chapter, you'll know that festivals and other special events occur throughout the year on the Monterey Peninsula. If you're planning to attend a major event, it isn't out of line to be thinking about reserving your room up to a year in advance. For any nonevent weekends during the summer or holidays, it's still a good idea to make your reservations two to six months in advance if you want to make sure you'll get into your choice of locations. Even during the off-season, a month's advance planning is recommended at the most popular hotels and motels. That's not to say you can't pull into town without reservations and find a great room, especially on a weeknight. Cancellations and other strokes of good fortune do happen. Just don't expect to have a wide choice of prime locations.

Also be aware that many of the hotels and motels on the Peninsula have two- or three-night minimum stays during all peak-season, special-event, and holiday weekends. Peak season is generally June through September. Some of the most popular establishments impose the two-night weekend minimum year-round. But again, exceptions to these restrictions are made if the hotel or motel has unexpected vacancies.

Amenities offered at the hotels and motels vary widely. However, you'll find that a great majority of the establishments offer both smoking and nonsmoking rooms, cable television (many with premium movie and sports channels and/or VCRs with videotape rentals), and in-room telephones. Most accept major credit cards such as Visa, MasterCard, Discover, and American Express. Unless the listings in this chapter note otherwise, you can safely assume that these conveniences are provided. Sorry, pets are probably not allowed unless we note otherwise. Where they are okay, be sure to call in advance to confirm any room fees, deposits, and restrictions. Virtually all hotels and motels, except for a few historic inns, are wheelchair accessible, but inquire about your specific needs.

Price Code

Prices for accommodations on the Monterey Peninsula cover a wide range, from less than $60 per night to more than $1,000. In fact, the very same room may cost you twice as much or more during the peak season (June through September) or a special-event weekend than it does on a weekday during the quiet off-season. These codes represent the average price of a double-occupancy room during the peak season, taxes not included. This average may represent a wide range of room prices, with added amenities and ocean views hiking up the price of a standard room. Be sure to confirm the current rates and available methods of payment when making your reservation.

Insiders' Tip

Take advantage of the Web site listings for Monterey Peninsula hotels and motels. Some allow you to make your reservations on-line; others provide pictures or virtual tours of the accommodations.

$	less than $90
$$	$90 to $130
$$$	$131 to $190
$$$$	$191 and more

Where to Stay

So where should you stay during your time on the Monterey Peninsula—Monterey, Pacific Grove, Carmel, or Pebble Beach? That will depend on your preferences and your pocketbook. Below, we describe the types of accommodations found in each of the four locales and then list some specific establishments representing your range of choices.

Monterey

For hotels and motels, Monterey is by far your best bet for finding a full range of accommodations representing all price ranges. From budget motels to luxury hotels, Monterey has it all. And you'll find that particular sections of town are home to particular types of accommodations. Generally speaking, the farther away from the water and major attractions you get, the less expensive your night's stay will be.

If you're simply looking for a clean, inexpensive room and don't particularly give a darn about a great ocean view or being within walking distance to the major attractions, try the stretch of motels along Fremont Boulevard east of Highway 1. Here you'll find a choice of rooms for about $70 to $80 a night, which is just about as inexpensive as it gets in these parts during peak seasons. This stretch of Fremont Boulevard is near the Monterey Fairgrounds, home of the Monterey Jazz Festival and Monterey Blues Festival. Rates seem to mysteriously skyrocket at most of these establishments during these two weekends in June and September (see our Annual Events chapter).

Another great spot for motels is Munras Avenue, just off of Highway 1 near the Del Monte Shopping Center. The south side of the street is a virtual motel row; many of the establishments are of 1960s vintage with heated pools. Expect to pay anywhere from $80 to $120 here, depending on season and amenities. Note that weekend rates at some of these motels can be substantially higher than weekday rates, so weekenders are often able to find a nicer, quieter spot in, say, Pacific Grove, for about the same price.

If you prefer larger hotels complete with restaurants, lounges, pools, and exercise rooms, downtown Monterey should be your cup of tea. Centrally located and within walking distance of Fisherman's Wharf and Cannery Row, the downtown hotels are typically $100 and up a night. That also includes the smaller hotels and inns that populate the historic downtown Monterey area. The Cannery Row area has its share of upscale hotels and motels as well. Again, you're likely to find rooms in the $100-plus range, but the views and easy access to the Monterey Bay Aquarium and the Monterey Peninsula Recreation Trail make this area a great choice for a special family vacation.

Following is a selection of hotels and motels in the city of Monterey, representing all of the areas mentioned above and even a few more. The list is far from exhaustive but offers a good range of choices.

Bay Park Hotel $$
1425 Munras Avenue, Monterey
(831) 649–1020, (800) 338–3564,
www.bayparkhotel.com

Nestled among the pines at the top of Munras Avenue between Highway 1 and the Del Monte Shopping Center, the Bay

Park Hotel offers 80 clean and comfortable rooms in a central location providing easy freeway access. Many of the rooms in this full-service hotel have bay or wooded hillside views to enjoy from your patio or balcony. A full-size outdoor pool, a whirlpool spa with a brick patio, and a rustic gazebo add to an enjoyable stay. The Bay Park Hotel is home to the Crazy Horse Restaurant, which features an exceptional salad bar and hearty fare, as well as the Safari Club lounge for evening cocktails. Locally owned and operated by Kurt Lang, the Bay Park Hotel is known for its friendly, long-term staff, many of whom have welcomed visitors here for more than 10 years. Pets okay.

The Beach Resort $$$
2600 Sand Dunes Drive, Monterey
(831) 394–3321, (800) 528–1234,
www.montereybeachresort.com

The Beach Resort by Best Western has perhaps the best ocean view of any hotel in the area. Right on a long stretch of sandy beach east of the Peninsula proper, the hotel looks across Monterey Bay toward the Monterey Harbor, Cannery Row, and the Pacific Grove coastline. Both day and night views are breathtaking, and sunsets can be downright awesome. The hotel has 196 rooms, an outdoor pool, a whirlpool spa, and a fitness room. A comfortable lounge with a fireplace and baby grand piano is a great spot to enjoy the complimentary afternoon hors d'oeuvres, and the Cafe Beach restaurant on the fourth floor offers a spectacular vantage point from which to enjoy your breakfast, lunch, or dinner. The Sandals Lounge has live entertainment Thursday through Saturday evenings. Pets okay.

Cannery Row Quality Inn $$$
200 Foam Street, Monterey
(831) 649–8580, (800) 228–5151,
www.qualityinn.com

Just a block above Cannery Row, this inn offers 33 nonsmoking rooms, each with a fireplace. You can chose from king- or queen-size beds in the ample rooms. Eight specialty rooms offer great bay views from private balconies. In-room coffeemakers and pastries are provided. An inviting hot tub is just the thing after a day of walking Cannery Row.

Carmel Hill Lodge $$
1374 Munras Avenue, Monterey
(831) 373–3252, (888) 551–4455

Situated across Munras Avenue from the Del Monte Shopping Center, the Carmel Hill Lodge offers comfortable and affordable rooms and friendly service. The 38 units are nothing fancy, but the good-sized outdoor pool will be a hit with the kids.

Casa Munras Garden Hotel $$$
700 Munras Avenue, Monterey
(831) 375–2411, (800) 222–2558,
www.casamunras-hotel.com

Casa Munras Garden Hotel is a historic 3-acre adobe property near downtown Monterey. The hotel is built around the original hacienda of Don Esteban Munras, the last Spanish diplomat to California.

Its 166 rooms are situated in an idyllic garden setting reminiscent of old Monterey. The rooms are pleasantly furnished with comforters, armoires, shuttered windows, and other warm touches. Selected rooms have fireplaces and balconies, and spacious specialty suites are available. A large heated outdoor pool is a great spot to while away the day. The Casa Cafe & Bar serves a varied menu for breakfast, lunch, and dinner. The happy hour with live entertainment draws a local crowd. Casa Munras is a good choice for first-time visitors looking for a taste of old Monterey.

Clarion Hotel Monterey $$
1046 Munras Avenue, Monterey
(831) 373–1337, (800) 821–0805

Groovy is the word to describe this 1960s-style, 52-unit motel recently purchased and remodeled by Clarion Hotels. Executive suites have king-size beds, full kitchens, and fireplaces. The honeymoon suite has an in-room spa and private patio. All guests can enjoy the only indoor heated pool on Munras Avenue. Continental breakfast and in-room coffee is available to all guests. A little kitsch, the Clarion Hotel Monterey will bring back memories of those '60s vacations in the family station wagon.

The Colton Inn $$$
707 Pacific Street, Monterey
(831) 649–6500, (800) 848–7007,
www.coltoninn.com

If a motel on a quiet corner along a meandering creek sounds appealing, try The Colton Inn. Situated on Pacific Street a few blocks north of the downtown area, this inn offers 50 amply sized rooms, many with special amenities such as wood-burning fireplaces, whirlpool tubs, kitchenettes, microwave ovens, and refrigerators. A honeymoon suite is fully equipped with these and other extras, including a great sound system. A private dry sauna and a sundeck with a barbecue grill are available to guests. A continental breakfast of fresh-made muffins, Danish rolls, and coffee is included in the room price.

Cypress Gardens Resort Inn $$
1150 Munras Avenue, Monterey
(831) 373–2761, (877) 922–1150,
www.innsbythesea.com

On the site of a former Monterey nursery, the Cypress Gardens Inn is an Insiders' favorite, with 46 good-sized rooms in a lush garden setting. Many of the private balconies overlook the garden and the 55-foot heated outdoor pool (Monterey's largest) and hot tub. Each room has its own refrigerator, and a continental breakfast is available in the lobby. Pets are allowed in some rooms. A special two-story townhouse features a full kitchen, large fireplace, dining room, and queen bedroom up a spiral staircase.

Cypress Tree Inn $
2227 N. Fremont Street, Monterey
(831) 372–7586, (800) 446–8303,
www.cypresstreeinn.com

One of the true bargains in Monterey, Cypress Tree Inn offers 55 clean rooms and amenities such as hot tubs, fireplaces, sauna, barbecue patio, coin-operated laundry, and even an on-site bake shop. Divers will appreciate the dip tanks and hanging area for their gear. There are even RV hookups. Yes, you are east of Highway 1, away from the beaches and major attractions, but for the price you'll be hard-pressed to find a better stay in the area. The Cypress Tree Inn is also a favorite of jazz and blues festival fans, so book your room for those events far in advance.

Del Monte Pines $$
1298 Munras Avenue, Monterey
(831) 375–2323, (800) 633–6454

Directly across Munras Avenue from the Del Monte Shopping Center is the Del Monte Pines Motel. This cozy two-story complex of 19 rooms has a heated outdoor pool, and some of the rooms include fireplaces and hot tubs. Movie rentals are available. A continental breakfast is served each morning in the lobby, and all rooms have coffeemakers.

DoubleTree Hotel $$$$
2 Portola Plaza, Monterey
(831) 649–4511, (800) 222–8733,
www.doubletreemonterey.com

The large, 380-room DoubleTree Hotel lies in the heart of Monterey. Just steps from Custom House Plaza and Fisherman's Wharf on one side and facing downtown's Alvarado Street on the other, it's centrally located, allowing guests to enjoy most of Monterey's attractions on foot. The hotel itself features a heated outdoor pool, hot tub, day spa, and complete fitness room. The California Grill restaurant serves breakfast, lunch, and dinner and is noted for its fine salad bar and excellent steak dinners. Some upper-story rooms have great bay vistas, and the large rooftop two- and three-bedroom suites enjoy spectacular views. For nightlife, the DoubleTree has a lobby bar and is also home to Peter B's microbrewery, which serves up many fine local brews as well as delectable light fare. The Monterey Conference Center is adjacent to the hotel.

El Adobe Inn $$
936 Munras Avenue, Monterey
(831) 372–5409, (800) 433–4732,
www.el-adobe-inn.com

El Adobe Inn provides clean and comfortable rooms at a reasonable price. The 26 units are nicely decorated, and the service is friendly. A secluded hot tub provides a great place to relax. In-room coffeemakers and refrigerators are available. A complimentary continental breakfast is served in the lobby. Pets are welcome in the smoking rooms only.

Embassy Suites $$$
1441 Canyon Del Rey, Seaside
(831) 393–1115, (800) EMBASSY,
www.embassy-suites.com

Located in the neighboring community of Seaside, the Embassy Suites deserves your consideration when visiting the Monterey Peninsula. Each of the 225 suites has a separate bedroom and living area, including a queen-size sleeper sofa. A wet bar with sink, refrigerator, microwave, and coffeemaker makes quick snacks a snap. The indoor heated swimming pool (kept at a constant 85 degrees), whirlpool, and fitness center provide for relaxation and recreation. All guests receive a complimentary full breakfast each morning and a complete choice of beverages during a two-hour manager's reception each evening. The Pacific Cafe specializes in steak and seafood, and the Cypress Lounge is a great place to relax at the piano bar and enjoy the 1,000-gallon saltwater aquarium. Friday at happy hour, the Cypress Lounge at Embassy Suites typically presents the best free live jazz and blues in the area.

Hilton Monterey $$$$
1000 Aguajito Road, Monterey
(831) 373–6141, (800) 774–1500,
www.monterey.hilton.com

Formerly the Holiday Inn Resort, this 204-room hotel recently went through a thorough renovation. Amenities include an outdoor pool, an indoor whirlpool spa, his and hers saunas, a fitness room, two tennis courts, a putting green, table tennis, and shuffleboard. The Pacific Grille restaurant serves coastal California cuisine, and all guests can enjoy a private patio and in-room coffeemakers. A few of the larger suites have kitchen facilities.

Hotel Pacific $$$$
300 Pacific Street, Monterey
(831) 373–5700, (800) 232–4141,
www.hotelpacific.com

Planning a weekend getaway, California style? Hotel Pacific pays homage to Old Monterey with 105 magnificent adobe-style suites that take you back to an earlier time in the Golden State. Rooms include Spanish-tile floors, fireplaces, impressive wooden furniture, feather beds, vaulted ceilings, wet bars with minifridges, and 500 square feet of space so you can stretch out. The lobby and salon feature intriguing artifacts, such as the buffalo-hide chairs. In the two gardens you'll find whirlpool spas, decorative fountains, and bright and colorful plantings. In historic downtown Monterey, Hotel Pacific treats guests to continental breakfast and afternoon tea. Truly an experience to remember, the Hotel Pacific is built for the romantic at heart.

Hyatt Regency Monterey $$$$
1 Old Golf Course Road, Monterey
(831) 372–1234, (800) 824–2196,
www.hyatt.com

The largest hotel complex in Monterey, the 575-room Hyatt Regency Monterey offers amenities such as two heated outdoor pools, two whirlpool spas, six tennis courts, a fitness club, massage services, a game room, and a hair salon. Plus, it's on the Pebble Beach Company's Del Monte Golf Course, the oldest 18-hole course west of the Mississippi. Hotel guests enjoy discounted greens fees. Camp Hyatt for Kids provides arts, crafts, and other activities for kids ages three to 15. The Restaurant and Cafe offer a wide choice of entrees for breakfast, lunch, and dinner, while Knuckles Historical Sports Bar features drinks, light fare, and plenty of sports on television in a fun-filled setting. Regency Club members receive complimentary breakfasts and other extras.

Merritt House $$$
386 Pacific Street, Monterey
(831) 646–9686, (800) 541–5599,
www.merritthouseinn.com

Want a real taste of Monterey history? Here's your chance to stay in an authentic Monterey adobe (circa 1830), the former home of County Judge Josiah Merritt. The home is divided into three suites, each decorated in 19th-century style. Twenty-two additional units surround

On Pacific Street in downtown Monterey, Merritt House, a historic adobe c. 1830, offers three suites decorated in 19th-century style. PHOTO: MONTEREY PENINSULA VCB

the adobe. All suites have fireplaces, and some have private balconies overlooking the historic home and its grand old fig tree and courtyard rose garden. A complimentary continental breakfast is included in the room package. Merritt House is centrally located near historic downtown Monterey and is along the Monterey Path of History.

Monterey Bay Inn $$$$
242 Cannery Row, Monterey
(831) 373–6242, (800) 424–6242,
www.montereybayinn.com

Right on the water at historic Cannery Row, the Monterey Bay Inn offers spectacular views and special amenities for active vacationers. Large sliding glass doors and private balconies take full advantage of this prime bayfront location. Binoculars are provided! A soak in the rooftop whirlpool spa at sunset is a moment to remember. All 47 units feature king-size beds and honor bars, and guests can lounge in plush terry cloth robes. Some rooms have cozy fireplaces. Enjoy a continental breakfast brought right to your room, or feel free to enjoy your pastries, fruit, and coffee on the second-floor outdoor garden patio. Divers will appreciate the handy scuba facilities, including lockers and rinse-off showers, and the inn has an exercise room. The Monterey Bay Inn is a nonsmoking facility.

The Monterey Fireside Lodge $$
1131 10th Street, Monterey
(831) 373–4172, (800) 722–2624 (Calif. only),
www.montereyfireside.com

This comfortable hotel features gas fireplaces in each of its 21 rooms. It also has an outdoor whirlpool spa. Family units have kitchenettes and refrigerators, and all guests enjoy complimentary continental breakfasts. Near Lake El Estero off Camino Aguajito, this hotel is just off Highway 1. Pets okay.

The Monterey Hotel $$$
406 Alvarado Street, Monterey
(831) 375–3184, (800) 727–0960

The pride of Alvarado Street, The Monterey Hotel is a historic Victorian inn that was renovated from top to bottom in 1996. The 1904 building is simply charming, including its two-story atrium, second-floor lobby with carved crown molding and gallery railing, and the original Hammond elevator with gilt-edged molding and bevel leaded glass. The 45 rooms are all exquisitely furnished with reproduction hand-carved furnishings, ceiling fans, and plantation shutters. Master suites have harbor views, fireplaces, and oversized tubs in the marbled-floor bathrooms. Guests are treated to a continental breakfast, afternoon tea, and milk and cookies at bedtime. Lovers of historic hotels shouldn't miss this 100-percent nonsmoking facility.

Monterey Marriott Hotel $$$
350 Calle Principal, Monterey
(831) 649–4234, (800) 228–9290,
www.marriotthotels.com/mryca

Dominating the downtown Monterey skyline, the 363-room Monterey Marriott is a modern luxury hotel with all the amenities. Overlooking the Monterey Harbor, it's close to Fisherman's Wharf and adjacent to the Conference Center, making the Marriott popular among both the vacation and business set. A heated outdoor pool, whirlpool spa, and 24-hour health club provide ample opportunity for relaxation and recreation. The Three Flags Cafe prepares buffet breakfasts, while Characters Sports Bar and Grill dishes up all-American food as well as plenty of sports programming and memorabilia for the avid fan.

Monterey Plaza Hotel & Spa $$$$
400 Cannery Row, Monterey
(831) 646–1700, (800) 368–2468,
www.montereyplazahotel.com

If you're looking for luxury on Cannery Row, the Monterey Plaza Hotel has it. Built right on the edge of Monterey Bay, the hotel affords spectacular views from the bayside rooms. Lobbies are replete with Italian marble and rich Brazilian teakwood. Luxury penthouse suites have bayfront balconies and are exquisitely appointed with Biedermeier-style armoires and writing desks. Plush terrycloth robes invite visitors to lounge to their hearts' content. A European-style health spa and fitness room provides a place to work off those extra ounces you may have put on at the Duck Club Restaurant or Schooners Bistro on the Bay. The Monterey Plaza Hotel is a good choice for an anniversary or other special occasion.

Padre Oaks Motel $
1278 Munras Avenue, Monterey
(831) 373–3741, (888) 900–6257

Here's one of the best bets for motel fans who like quaint, well-maintained, and modestly priced properties. This small 20-room motel has been recently redecorated and landscaped and provides a heated outdoor pool. A continental breakfast and in-room coffee are included. Some rooms have private decks.

Sand Dollar Inn $$
755 Abrego Street, Monterey
(831) 372–7551, (800) 982–1986,
www.sanddollarinn.com

A good value, the Sand Dollar Inn is a modern 63-unit motel complex on the outskirts of the historic district of downtown Monterey. Amenities include a large heated pool and outdoor spa, guest laundry facilities, continental breakfast, and in-room coffeemakers and minifridges. Deluxe rooms have fireplaces, wet bars, and private balconies or patios. Two-bedroom family suites are also available. For a heartier breakfast or late-night snack, Denny's restaurant is right next door.

Spindrift Inn $$$$
652 Cannery Row, Monterey
(831) 646–8900, (800) 841–1879,
www.spindriftinn.com

A favorite among honeymooners, Spindrift Inn combines life in the heart of Cannery Row with unsurpassed luxury accommodations. The 42 rooms in this classic small hotel include antique decor, hardwood floors with Oriental rugs, half-canopied goose-feather beds with down comforters and pillows, marble baths, wood-burning fireplaces, honor bars, and

The Monterey Plaza Hotel & Spa overhangs the shoreline on Cannery Row. PHOTO: ROSS ANDRÉSON window seats or balconies. Imagine: all of these creature comforts available in a hotel that's right on the beach of Cannery Row, with breathtaking bay views in many rooms. Complimentary continental breakfast is brought to your room on a silver tray. Afternoon tea includes pastries, wine, and cheese. Enjoy the rooftop garden and private beach. The Spindrift Inn is a truly memorable place for those who want a real taste of the romantic side of Monterey.

Travelodge, Monterey Downtown $$
675 Munras Avenue, Monterey
(831) 373–1876, (800) 578–7878,
www.montereytravelodge.com

You'll find no surprises here. You get everything you've come to expect in a Travelodge motel, including a clean room, a comfortable bed, and an outdoor pool. The special feature here is location—51 rooms right downtown in historic Monterey, within walking distance of most major attractions.

Victorian Inn $$$
487 Foam Street, Monterey
(831) 373–8000, (800) 232–4141,
www.victorianinn.com

A short block from Cannery Row, the Best Western Victorian Inn offers 68 well-appointed rooms. Each room has a marble fireplace, honor bar, and either a private patio, balcony, or window seat. Deluxe suites feature bay views, feather beds, jetted tubs, CD players, and microwave ovens. All guests can enjoy the garden courtyard hot tub. Continental breakfast and afternoon wine and cheese are served in the parlor of the 1907 Victorian home that serves as the lobby and office. Pets okay.

Way Station Monterey $
1200 Olmstead Road, Monterey
(831) 372–2945, (800) 858–0822,
www.waystationmonterey.com

The affordable Way Station Monterey is near the Monterey Airport off Highway 68. That makes it convenient for air travelers as well as those attending events out at Laguna Seca Raceway (though event-weekend rates are somewhat higher). About five minutes from downtown Monterey, the Way Station has 46 units including luxury suites with fireplaces, wet bars, and refrigerators. Most rooms have private decks overlooking a parklike setting. Continental breakfasts are provided.

Pacific Grove

Is your trip to the Monterey Peninsula one of those I-just-want-to-get-away-from-it-all-and-relax kinds of vacations? Then consider Pacific Grove for your accommodations. The rates for a simple room are equivalent to those of the motels on the major thoroughfares of Fremont and Munras in Monterey, but the locale is much more peaceful. Spend a bit more and you'll have your choice of family and beachfront motels, forest cottages, historic hotels, and stately Victorian mansions (see our Bed and Breakfast Inns chapter). A few of the accommodations are in and around downtown Pacific Grove, but the great majority are farther north out the Peninsula toward Point Pinos. Most of the motels down Lighthouse Avenue are traditional family-style establishments. Those out Asilomar Boulevard are more cottage-like and situated beneath tall Monterey pines. All are in easy walking distance of the spectacular Pacific Grove coastline, and all are (fellow visitors permitting) quiet, quiet, quiet. Be prepared for cool, maybe foggy weather out here on the point—just the ideal climate for a brisk, bundled-up walk along the sand dunes and rugged coast.

Andril Fireplace Cottages $$
569 Asilomar Boulevard, Pacific Grove
(831) 375–0994, www.andrilcottages.com

For a week in a woodland cottage by the seaside, think Andril Fireplace Cottages. You'll find 16 separate cottages set under tall pines in a quiet corner of P.G. Each unit has a full kitchen and wood-burning fireplaces. A luxury suite has skylights and a private deck. Barbecues and Ping-Pong add to the fun. From June through September, Andril's has a standard five-night minimum stay. (But Insiders know that, depending on how reservations book

Insiders' Tip

Services such as Monterey Peninsula Reservations, (888) 655-3424, can assist you in finding just the right accommodations for your needs.

up, you might be able to squeeze your way in for just a couple of nights.) Daily rentals are available in the off-season. Enjoy amenities such as VCRs with free tape rentals. Pets okay.

Asilomar State Beach and Conference Grounds $
800 Asilomar Boulevard, Pacific Grove
(831) 372–8016, www.visitasilomar.com

The Asilomar Conference Grounds, on 105 beautiful acres of pine forests and rolling sand dunes on the northern end of the Monterey Peninsula, is part of the California State Park system. The original buildings were designed by noted California architect Julia Morgan and opened in 1913, providing a spectacular yet rustic setting ever since for the many conferences that are held here year-round. For vacationers, the Asilomar Conference Center provides very affordable accommodations on a space-available basis. The staff recommends calling no more than 30 days in advance of your planned date of arrival to check on room availability. Guests are treated to a complimentary full breakfast and can also have lunch and dinner in Crocker Dining Hall for an additional charge. (Listen for the meal bell, which is rung on the meal hour.) Several of the rooms have fireplaces, some have private decks, and a few have kitchenettes. Cottages sleep up to seven. The 314 rooms don't have televisions or phones, but there are plenty of pay phones throughout the grounds. You can take advantage of recreational facilities, such as a heated outdoor pool, Ping-Pong, pool tables, and volleyball courts as well as partake in evening barbecues and bonfires. A winding boardwalk provides a direct path to the beach through rolling dunes. Asilomar Conference Center is a nonsmoking facility.

Beachcomber Inn $$
1996 Sunset Drive, Pacific Grove
(831) 373–4769, (800) 634–4769

Location, location, location: the Beachcomber Inn has it. There is nothing special about the accommodations themselves, but look out back from one of the private patios, and you're sitting right on the edge of Spanish Bay and Asilomar Beach. The 25-room motel is a nonsmoking establishment with an outdoor heated pool and sundeck protected from the wind by a glass enclosure. Complimentary bicycles are available for exploring the Asilomar area. Speaking of location, right next door is the highly acclaimed Fishwife restaurant, a locals' favorite for breakfast, lunch, or dinner. If your idea of an ideal weekend is surfing the wild Pacific or combing the Pacific Grove beaches, the Beachcomber Inn isn't a bad choice for a clean and comfortable bed.

Bide-A-Wee Motel and Cottages $$
221 Asilomar Boulevard, Pacific Grove
(831) 372–2330

If you're looking for a quiet and quaint motel setting, consider the Bide-A-Wee. Located near Point Pinos and a quick stroll from the beach, this recently remodeled 11-unit and nine-cottage charmer is no-frills but provides a great hideaway. You'll enjoy a continental breakfast and in-room coffeemakers. Most of the cottages have kitchens and living rooms; one has a fireplace. Pets okay. And how could you not like the name?

Borg's Ocean Front Hotel $$
635 Ocean View Boulevard, Pacific Grove
(831) 375–2406

Owned by the Borg family for more than 50 years, this motel right on the waterfront has some of the best oceanview rooms on the Peninsula, many with great balconies for taking in Lovers Point and the Bay beyond. Borg's has 60 rooms and four feature kitchenettes. No in-room coffeemakers are available, but you can get hot beverages in the lobby. There's nothing fancy about the accommodations, but the clean and comfortable rooms with a view are a great place from which to enjoy the beauty of the Bay.

Butterfly Grove Inn $$$
1073 Lighthouse Avenue, Pacific Grove
(831) 373–4921, (800) 337–9244,
www.bflyinn.qpg.com

For a true feel of Pacific Grove, consider a stay at the Butterfly Grove Inn during the Butterfly Parade weekend in October (see our Annual Events chapter). The 28 one- and two-bedroom units (including family units in a large Victorian home) are right next door to the Monarch Grove Sanctuary (see our Attractions chapter). That makes it a good spot for both summer and winter visits. You'll find a heated outdoor pool, hydrojet spa, shuffleboard, croquet, volleyball, continental breakfast, and an in-room refrigerator and coffeemaker. A few units have kitchenettes with microwaves, and a couple have fireplaces. Upstairs rooms offer peeks at the ocean. Divers will appreciate the outdoor wash lines.

Lighthouse Lodge & Suites $$$
1150 and 1249 Lighthouse Avenue, Pacific Grove
(831) 655–2111, (800) 858–1249, www.lhls.com

On both sides of the northern end of Lighthouse Avenue, the Lighthouse Lodge and Suites are actually two separate facilities. The Lodge is a Best Western motel with 68 units. Guests can enjoy a heated outdoor pool, whirlpool spa, and sauna. A deluxe continental breakfast is served, and summer poolside barbecues are held for guests when weather permits. Some rooms have fireplaces, and pets are welcome. The 31-unit Lighthouse Suites across the street provide Cape Cod–style luxury accommodations that include king-size beds, down pillows, fireplaces, whirlpool tubs, terry robes, honor bars, and kitchenettes. For the ultimate in a group vacation, the Executive Residence sleeps six adults and has three bathrooms, three marble fireplaces, a gourmet kitchen, laundry facilities, a fully fenced backyard, and a rooftop deck. All guests at the Lodge enjoy a full chef-prepared breakfast and an evening hospitality reception of wine and hors d'oeuvres.

Olympia Motor Lodge $
1140 Lighthouse Avenue, Pacific Grove
(831) 373–2777

On Lighthouse Avenue, backed up to the Pacific Grove Municipal Golf Course, the Olympia Lodge is a good value motel in the peace and quiet of P.G. You'll find a charming Asian motif, heated outdoor pool, and complimentary continental breakfast. Eight of the 38 units have sitting areas and kitchenettes with fridges and two-burner stoves. Twenty rooms have balconies with peeks at the ocean through the trees. Pets are allowed in the off-season only.

Pacific Gardens Inn $$$
701 Asilomar Boulevard, Pacific Grove
(831) 646–9414, (800) 262–1566,
www.pacificgardensinn.com

Situated across from the Asilomar Conference Center, the Pacific Gardens Inn offers 28 rooms under a canopy of pines. Guests can enjoy two outdoor hot tubs, a buffet continental breakfast, wood-burning fireplaces, and complete kitchens with refrigerators and popcorn makers (nice touch!). A two-bedroom cottage with living room and deck is available. Wine and cheese are served in the evening.

Rosedale Inn $$$
775 Asilomar Boulevard, Pacific Grove
(831) 655–1000, (800) 822–5606,
www.rosedaleinn.com

A great place to unwind, the Rosedale Inn features in-room Jacuzzi tubs, wet bars, fireplaces, fridges, sinks, coffeemakers, microwaves, and cathedral ceilings with fans in the 19 units. Complimentary continental breakfasts are served each morning. Sofa beds and private patios on some suites add to the pleasure. If you're looking for nothing more rigorous than a walk on the beach, this is a nice choice for some serious R and R. An added feature is the Rosedale Inn's own handthrown pottery gallery, with a unique selection of gifts for the folks you left back home.

Insiders' Tip

Planning to visit the Peninsula during the off-season? Always ask about special vacation packages. They can save you big bucks!

The Sunset Inn $$
133 Asilomar Boulevard, Pacific Grove
(831) 375–3936, (800) 525–3373,
www.montereyinns.com

Built in 1939, The Sunset Inn has a long history of providing a quaint and quiet place to stay near Point Pinos. A half-million dollar renovation brought this charming 20-unit motel back to its former glory. Each room has a cozy fireplace, some wood-burning, some gas. The remodeled interiors with high ceilings provide a classic atmosphere. Some rooms have in-room two-person spas, and all have refrigerators. If you've enjoyed your stay here in the past, you won't believe the love and attention given to this Pacific Grove landmark.

The Feather Bed Inn $$$
1095 Lighthouse Avenue, Pacific Grove
(831) 373–4382, (800) 525–3373,
www.montereyinns.com

A longtime favorite of Pacific Grove visitors, The Feather Bed Inn (formerly Terrace Oaks Inn) recently enjoyed a refreshing face-lift. Window treatments, Italian-tile floors, paint, and artwork have livened up the place, but it still provides an affordable and homey stay. The 12 nonsmoking units present a variety of accommodation choices, including suites with formal bedrooms and rooms with kitchenettes, fireplaces, Jacuzzi tubs, and outdoor verandahs or patios. Continental breakfast is provided in the lobby, and it's a short walk to the beach or the Monarch Grove Sanctuary (see our Attractions chapter).

The Wilkie's Inn $
1038 Lighthouse Avenue, Pacific Grove
(831) 372–5960, (866) 372–5960,
www.wilkiesinn.com

Another moderately priced family motel in Pacific Grove, The Wilkie's has 24 units, with peeks of the ocean from some upstairs rooms. There's a complimentary continental breakfast and in-room coffee. Two units have full kitchens. Be sure to visit The Butterfly Shop, which sells just about anything you can think off that's about or in the shape of a Monarch butterfly. Proceeds support the Friends of the Monarch, a local environmental group. The motel is a short stroll from the Monarch Grove Sanctuary.

Carmel

How do you spell romance? Around these parts, it's C-A-R-M-E-L. And that's especially true when you're talking about accommodations. While families of four or five are likely to find Monterey to their liking, parties of two owe it to themselves to give Carmel an extra-close look. Known for its quaint inns, charming cottages, and splendid hotels, Carmel boasts some of the most unique and memorable accommodations you'll find anywhere. Prices won't be cheap, yet some are surprisingly reasonable during the off-season. Here's a sample representation of what you'll find in the village of Carmel.

Candle Light Inn $$$
San Carlos Street and 5th Avenue, Carmel
(831) 624–6451, (800) 433–4732,
www.innsbythesea.com

This 20-unit Tudor-style inn provides a nice heated outdoor pool, picnic-basket breakfast with a newspaper, and in-room coffee. Some rooms provide wood-burning fireplaces, whirlpool spas, and kitchenettes. All rooms have refrigerators and loveseat-size sofa hideaway beds. Friendly, attentive service is a hallmark of the Candle Light Inn.

Carmel Country Inn $$$
Dolores Street and 3rd Avenue, Carmel
(831) 625–3263, (800) 215–6343,
www.carmelcountryinn.com

This small 12-room, nonsmoking inn is a real country-style charmer with many modern amenities. All but one of the one- and two- bedroom suites have a fireplace, and some provide private decks. Kitchenettes with refrigerators and tables are also available. A generous continental breakfast is served, and off-street parking is provided. Pets okay.

Carmel Mission Inn $$
3665 Rio Road, Carmel
(831) 624–1841, (800) 348–9090,
www.carmelmissioninn.com

This 165-room Best Western hotel near the mouth of Carmel Valley has some of the least expensive rooms in town as well as some large specialty suites. An outdoor heated pool and two spas are relaxing spots to enjoy the sunshine, while the Villa Carmel Restaurant and Beethoven's Bar & Grill provide fun places to recall your day's adventure. In-room coffeemakers and private decks are among the amenities. Although outside of downtown Carmel, the Carmel Mission Inn is conveniently located near the Barnyard and Crossroads shopping centers. Pets okay.

Carmel Oaks Inn $$$$
Mission Street and 5th Avenue, Carmel
(831) 624–5547, (800) 266–5547,
www.carmeloaksinn.com

This California-country-style inn prides itself in providing the little extras that make a visit to Carmel something special. Start the day with an in-room picnic-basket breakfast you can enjoy on your private deck. Later, sample the homemade candies that are a Carmel Oaks specialty. Wine in the evening tops your splendid day. This is an all nonsmoking, 17-room establishment that provides in-room refrigerators. One room has a kitchenette. There's plenty of off-street parking to make your stay in Carmel hassle-free.

Carriage House Inn $$$$
Junipero Street and 8th Avenue, Carmel
(831) 625–2585, (800) 433–4732,
www.innsbythesea.com

The Carriage House Inn is well known as a favorite honeymoon spot in Carmel. Secluded and quiet, it's a great spot to cuddle under a down comforter in front of a wood fire and enjoy a late-morning, made-to-order continental breakfast that's delivered right to your door. Among the 13 rooms, special suites include whirlpool spas and baths. Walk a couple of short blocks down Junipero, and you're at the trendy Carmel Plaza shopping center. In the evening, enjoy wine and hors d'oeuvres in the library. Three is definitely a crowd at the Carriage House Inn.

Casa de Carmel Inn $$$
Monte Verde Street and Ocean Avenue, Carmel
(831) 624–2429, www.vagabondshouseinn.com

This cute two-story inn has only seven guest rooms, making for an intimate setting. It's a quiet and comfortable place without a lot of extras, but fresh-cut flowers are always on hand to brighten up your day. Rather than providing a continental breakfast, Casa de Carmel gives each guest a coupon for breakfast at the nearby Merlot Bistro on Ocean Avenue at Lincoln Street. This is a nonsmoking inn.

Coachman's Inn $$$
San Carlos Street and 7th Avenue, Carmel
(831) 624–6421, (800) 336–6421,
www.coachmansinn.com

With a European decor of Old World timber and stucco, the Coachman's Inn provides a quiet stay in downtown Carmel. The 30 rooms include queen, king, and family units, some with kitchens, whirlpool tubs, and wet bars, and a few with fireplaces. Complimentary continental breakfast is provided each morning, and coffee, tea, and hot chocolate are available to guests throughout the day. Evening sherry is also on the house. All rooms have in-room coffeemakers. Off-street parking is provided.

Cypress Inn $$$$
Lincoln Street and 7th Avenue, Carmel
(831) 624–3871, (800) 443–7443,
www.cypress-inn.com

A Carmel landmark since 1929, this fabulous Moorish Mediterranean-style hotel with a Spanish-tile roof offers the best in elegant comfort. Walk in the ornate entrance to find a spacious living room

The Moorish Mediterranean architecture and friendly service has made Cypress Inn a Carmel favorite since 1929. PHOTO: TOM OWENS

lobby with a large fireplace. Down the hall is a cozy cocktail lounge with a full bar—a popular spot with Insiders. The 33 rooms themselves are one of a kind. Some have fireplaces, whirlpool tubs, private verandahs, intimate sitting rooms, and stylish wet bars. Guests can enjoy afternoon tea and complimentary hors d'oeuvres in the lounge. Co-owner and animal lover Doris Day probably has something to do with the fact that this small luxury hotel accepts up to two pets per room. Continental breakfast is served in a sunny breakfast room and secluded courtyard garden.

Dolphin Inn $$$
San Carlos Street and 4th Avenue, Carmel
(831) 624–5356, (800) 433–4732,
www.innsbythesea.com

Accommodations at the Dolphin Inn are friendly and comfortable with pleasant touches such as fresh flowers, a picnic-basket continental breakfast brought to your door, in-room coffee and refrigerators, and a nice heated outdoor pool. Many rooms have fireplaces; specialty rooms include the two-bedroom, two-bath family suite and the deluxe suite with living room, whirlpool tub, and fireplace.

Highlands Inn $$$$
120 Highland Drive, Carmel
(831) 620–1234, (800) 682–4811,
www.highlands-inn.com

South of Carmel, about 15 minutes down Highway 1, lies the Highlands Inn, now a Park Hyatt Hotel. At the gateway to Big Sur, this spectacular 142-room inn is world famous for its California coastline views, its superb restaurants, and its hosting of the Masters of Food and Wine festival each spring. The inn features one- and two-bedroom suites as well as 37 guest rooms with unsurpassed coastal views. A heated outdoor pool, three outdoor spas, and two great restaurants provide more reasons to not set foot off the property. Most suites have wood-burning fireplaces; some have view decks, double spa baths, and fully equipped kitchens. Expect to find terry bathrobes and binoculars in your room. Special amenities such as massages and complimentary bicycles are also provided. The elegant Pacific's Edge restaurant offers a 180-degree panoramic view, great food, and a 28,000 bottle wine cellar that was one of fewer than 100 to win *Wine Spectator* magazine's Grand Award (see our Restaurants chapter). The more casual California Market offers a variety of fares for breakfast, lunch, or dinner, enjoyable from inside the restaurant or outside on the breathtaking cliffside deck. The Sunset & Lobos Lounge provides a spectacular afternoon and evening view over Point Lobos State Reserve while you sip your favorite beverage and listen to a live jazz trio. Pets okay.

Hofsas House $$
San Carlos and 4th Avenue, Carmel
(831) 624–2745, (800) 221–2548,
www.hofsashouse.com

You might think you're spending a summer in the Bavarian Alps, perched on a hillside overlooking a green forest. But that's the Pacific Ocean beyond and you're at Hofsas House, the big pink Carmel landmark near Carmel Woods. Each of the 39 rooms is unique, including the popular Bridal and Private Lanai rooms. Some have wood-burning fireplaces, sundecks, and/or kitchenettes; most have ocean views. Continental breakfast is served in the lounge, and all rooms have coffeemakers. Guests can enjoy the heated outdoor pool and dry saunas.

Horizon Inn and Ocean View Lodge $$$
Junipero Street and 3rd Avenue, Carmel
(831) 624–5327, (800) 350–7723,
www.horizoninncarmel.com

These two properties, across Junipero Street from each other, provide a choice of accommodations. The Horizon Inn has 21 smartly redecorated rooms, most with gas fireplaces and some with kitchenettes and in-room whirlpool baths. The more expensive Ocean View Lodge offers six minisuites with separate living rooms, wood-burning fireplaces, and some private balconies with nice ocean views. Rooms at Ocean View Lodge have either a full-size Jacuzzi tub or a fully equipped kitchen. Each establishment offers access to a heated outdoor pool, a picnic-basket continental breakfast delivered to your room, and in-room coffeemakers.

Lamp Lighter Inn $$$
Ocean Avenue and Camino Real Street, Carmel
(831) 624–7372

Hansel and Gretel could live here. With the official title of "The most photographed inn in Carmel," The Lamp Lighter Inn consists of five turn-of-the-century baby-blue cottages set in a fairy tale garden, complete with elves. All cottages are nonsmoking and have private baths, Dutch doors, and quilts on the beds. A kitchen and fireplace are available in the renovated Hansel & Gretel Cottage. The Lamp Lighter has performed the commendable task of developing an inn that can please both honeymooners and families with small children. While lovers snuggle in the cozy Treetop House, kids will be fascinated by the special kid's bedroom in the Bluebird Cottage. Pets okay. In-room coffee is provided.

La Playa Hotel $$$
8th Avenue and Camino Real, Carmel
(831) 624–6476, (800) 582–8900,
www.laplayacarmel. com

Originally a private Carmel mansion built for a member of San Francisco's famous Ghirardelli chocolate family, La Playa Hotel is a true classic. Noted Norwegian-born painter Christopher Jorgensen, who was inspired by the stone and heavy beam of the nearby Carmel Mission, designed the original home in 1902. Much of the mansion has been expertly preserved as part of the current 80-room La Playa (a charter member of the Historic Hotels of America). In 1983, the Cope family of San Francisco (owners of the city's prestigious Huntington Hotel) purchased and fully refurbished La Playa and its large award-winning garden with wrought-iron gazebo to create a magical atmosphere. You'll find a few rooms with fireplaces, others with great ocean views. A heated outdoor pool provides recreation and relaxation, and the popular Terrace Grill restaurant serves up excellent California cuisine for breakfast, lunch, dinner, and Sunday brunch, either indoors or alfresco on the heated open-air terrace. La Playa also offers five storybook cottages with full kitchens, wood-burning fireplaces, private patios, and extras such as wet bars and stereo systems.

Mission Ranch Lodging $$
26270 Dolores Street, Carmel
(831) 624–6436, (800) 538–8221

A truly unique experience at a very reasonable price, the Mission Ranch is unlike any other lodge in Carmel. Built on ranchlands behind the Carmel Mission, it consists of 11 buildings ranging from the rustic to the sublime, with 31 guest rooms available. The grounds include an

The Lamp Lighter Inn's storybook charm has made it "the most photographed inn in Carmel," and a favorite among honeymooners and families alike. PHOTO: TOM OWENS

1850s farmhouse and enchanting fields of grazing sheep, with Carmel Bay and Point Lobos as the backdrop. Complimentary continental breakfast and in-room coffee are provided in this fully nonsmoking facility. Most rooms have fireplaces, and the higher-end ones feature whirlpool tubs and breathtaking views from your private deck. The Mission Ranch restaurant, an Insiders' favorite, serves up delectable California cuisine. Six championship tennis courts and a workout room are available. Did we forget to mention that Clint Eastwood is the proprietor? If you're really lucky, you might even find Clint tickling the ivories one evening in the Mission Ranch piano bar within the restaurant. Make your reservations well in advance for this very popular spot.

Normandy Inn $$$$
Ocean Avenue and Monte Verde Street, Carmel
(831) 624–3825, (800) 343–3825 (Calif. only), www.normandyinncarmel.com

Looking for an Old European-type inn in the center of downtown Carmel? The Normandy Inn is a charming 45-room hotel and three family cottages, each with three bedrooms and two baths. All feature French-country decor and cozy feather beds; some have fireplaces. On Ocean Avenue only blocks from the beach, this nonsmoking establishment has beautifully landscaped gardens. Guests can enjoy a heated outdoor pool, continental breakfast, in-room coffee, and afternoon sherry.

Pine Inn $$$
Ocean Avenue and Monte Verde Street, Carmel
(831) 624–3851, (800) 652–2632, www.pine-inn.com

Built in 1889, the Pine Inn was the first Carmel inn. Originally a few blocks away, it was moved to its current location in 1903. Enter the plush red and dark wood interior, and you're immediately hit with the inn's warm, sophisticated elegance. The decor reflects that of a world traveler, with European and Far East influences coming together most effectively. With 49 rooms, the Pine Inn has everything from simplicity to opulence, with amenities such as whirlpool tubs, fireplaces, and private entrances. For dinner, enjoy Il Fornaio, a cozy Italian restaurant on premises.

Quail Lodge Resort & Golf Club $$$$
8205 Valley Greens Drive, Carmel
(831) 624–2888, (888) 828–8787, www.quail-lodge-resort.com

The ultimate in rustic, upscale elegance, Quail Lodge is situated on 850 acres within sunny Carmel Valley. Beautifully

The pastoral splendor of Mission Ranch in Carmel makes it a great choice for a romantic weekend.
PHOTO: TOM OWENS

landscaped grounds, tranquil lakes, rolling hills, and an 18-hole championship golf course provide the setting for the 100 luxurious guest rooms. You'll enjoy four tennis courts, two outdoor heated pools, a soothing redwood hot tub, miles of jogging and hiking trails, and a complete workout facility. There's refined dining with European and Mediterranean cuisine at the award-winning Covey Restaurant (see our Restaurants chapter) and enjoyable breakfast and lunch at the casual Country Club dining room. All guest rooms are stylishly furnished and feature private decks or patios, fresh fruit baskets, and in-room coffee as well as plush terrycloth bathrobes. Most have minifridges, and some have fireplaces. Twelve cottages are available with up to five rooms each, and the Executive Villa offers the ultimate in privacy and luxury. Guests enjoy a favorable rate when playing at the Golf Club at Quail Lodge. One pet per room is allowed, and pet-sitting services are available. Quail Lodge is truly a five-star experience.

The Sandpiper Inn $$$
2408 Bay View Avenue, Carmel
(831) 624–6433, (800) 633–6433,
www.sandpiper-inn.com

Fewer than 100 yards from the white sands of Carmel Beach, the Sandpiper Inn is an excellent choice for those who want to get away from it all and enjoy the sights and sounds of the open sea. This romantic 1929 California-style country inn has 17 rooms, several with ocean views and some with fireplaces. But you'll find neither television nor in-room phones. (Sounds pretty good, doesn't it?) A fine continental breakfast is served, and you can enjoy a good book all snug in the library nook or in front of the Carmel stone fireplace in the lounge. Award-winning gardens provide the perfect surroundings for a most restful stay.

Insiders' Tip

Many hotels and motels sell Monterey Bay Aquarium tickets right in the lobby. This guest service can save you from having to wait in long ticket lines at the aquarium.

Sundial Lodge $$$
Monte Verde Street and 7th Avenue, Carmel
(831) 624–8578, www.sundiallodge.com

Here's a great European-style inn right in the heart of downtown Carmel. The 19 nonsmoking rooms surround a beautiful brick courtyard full of brightly colored plants. The rooms are tastefully furnished in wicker, English Victorian, or French Country, and the private baths have plenty of brass and marble. All rooms include a refrigerator, and some have kitchenettes. Guests enjoy a deluxe continental breakfast, afternoon sherry or port, and evening tea and cookies.

Svengaard's Inn $$$
San Carlos Street and 4th Avenue, Carmel
(831) 624–1511, (800) 433–4732,
www.innsbythesea.com

Country decor and a beautiful garden setting are the hallmarks of the 35-room Svengaard's Inn. You can enjoy the heated courtyard pool and in-room continental breakfast and coffeemakers. Many rooms have fireplaces, kitchenettes, and Jacuzzi tubs.

Tally Ho Inn $$$
Monte Verde Street and Ocean Avenue, Carmel
(831) 624–2232, (800) 652–2632,
www.tallyho-inn.com

Across Monte Verde Street from the Pine Inn is the Tally Ho Inn, run by the same owners. Here in the former residence of cartoonist Jimmy Hatlo (creator of Little Iodine), you'll find 12 lovely rooms and patios with an English-countryside atmosphere. Most rooms have fireplaces and private decks, some have in-room whirlpool spas and ocean views. An expanded continental breakfast is served, and room service is available from Il Fornaio, the Italian restaurant across the street at Pine Inn.

Tickle Pink Inn $$$$
155 Highland Drive, Carmel
(831) 624–1244, (800) 635–4774,
www.ticklepink.com

South of Carmel approximately 10 minutes down Highway 1 is the legendary Tickle Pink Inn. Long a favorite spot for honeymooners and the romantic at heart, the inn is on the hills of Carmel Highlands and has some of the most breathtaking views of the California central coast you'll ever find. The 35 rooms include 12 suites, all of which have fireplaces and private decks. A few units have full kitchens. The secluded Senator's Cottage features two bedrooms, a kitchenette, and private patio. A continental breakfast and in-room coffee are provided in all rooms, and an outdoor hot tub is sure to please any pair of lovebirds. An evening wine and cheese reception in the Terrace Lounge or on the outdoor Cliffside Deck provides the opportunity to get acquainted with your fellow guests.

The Village Inn $$$
Ocean Avenue and Junipero Street, Carmel
(831) 624–3864, (800) 346–3864 (Calif. only),
www.carmelvillageinn.com

The Village Inn offers 34 rooms right on Ocean Avenue at the entrance to downtown Carmel. Lovely landscaped gardens and the post-adobe construction create a warm atmosphere. Complimentary continental breakfast and in-room coffee are provided. Five suites feature fireplaces, living rooms, and full kitchens. There is plenty of off-street parking. If you enjoy being at the head of the action, The Village Inn is for you.

Wayside Inn $$$
Mission Street and 7th Avenue, Carmel
(831) 624–5336, (800) 433–4732,
www.innsbythesea.com

One of the better spots for families in Carmel, the 22-unit Wayside Inn offers suites with full kitchens and extra bedrooms or queen-sized sofa hideaway beds. Pets are welcome at no extra charge, although it's preferred that you not leave them alone in the room. On a quiet corner of Carmel, the Wayside Inn is a cozy place with lots of wood-burning fireplaces and a few private balconies and patios. There's no pool on the grounds, but guests can use an outdoor pool at one of the other sister properties in Carmel owned by Inns By The Sea. A complimentary picnic-basket breakfast is provided.

Pebble Beach

For many an avid golfer, a stay at one of the Pebble Beach resorts is a lifelong dream. And since you may only live once, we suggest that you golfers live out your dream. Sure, it's expensive. But how can you put a price on walking up to the 18th green at Pebble Beach Golf Links? Even when you're not out on the course, the ambiance of these world-class resorts is a memorable experience. Here's a quick snapshot of what you can expect at The Inn at Spanish Bay and The Lodge at Pebble Beach, the sister resorts of Pebble Beach Company.

The Inn at Spanish Bay $$$$
2700 17-Mile Drive, Pebble Beach
(831) 647–7500, (800) 654–9300,
www.pebblebeach.com

Overlooking the 18-hole Links at Spanish Bay and the Pacific Ocean beyond, The Inn at Spanish Bay is a splendid Old Monterey and Spanish California-style resort. Of its 269 guest rooms, 145 enjoy ocean views, while the rest overlook the Del Monte Forest. Each room has two queen- or one king-size bed, a living room, fireplace, dressing area, private deck or patio, and a large bathroom with Italian marble and brass decor. Sixteen special suites provide additional luxurious amenities.

Guests receive special rates for the inn's linksland golf course and any of the other Pebble Beach Company golf courses.

Guests at the opulent Inn at Spanish Bay in Pebble Beach can enjoy outdoor dining or refreshments along with spectacular views of the golf links and the Pacific Ocean beyond. PHOTO: TOM OWENS

You can also take advantage of the Spanish Bay Club with heated outdoor pool, spas, steam rooms, and a complete fitness center. The Tennis Pavilion has eight outdoor tennis courts, one stadium court designed for tournaments, a pro shop, lockers, and expert instruction. There are also excellent walking and jogging trails along the boardwalk and sandy beaches. Plus, don't forget to indulge at the Spa at Pebble Beach, a complete health resort near The Lodge and available to guests at Spanish Bay.

For full meals or quick snacks, Spanish Bay provides some excellent choices. Roy's at Pebble Beach presents great breakfasts, lunches, and "Euro-Asian" dinners from the menu of world-famous chef Roy Yamaguchi (see our Restaurants chapter). Peppoli at Pebble Beach provides an intimate and elegant atmosphere for Northern Italian cuisine, while Traps, an 80-seat lounge, is perfect for catching your favorite sporting event on TV or for an evening cigar and scotch. The Lobby Lounge serves refreshments and cocktails around a wood-burning fireplace, with live entertainment Thursday through Saturday. Retail shopping includes Breezes for fashion and the Ansel Adams Gallery for fine art.

The Inn at Spanish Bay has been honored with many awards, including the title of "Number One Mainland Resort," bestowed by *Condé Nast Traveler* Readers Choice Awards and "Best North American Hotel," from *Travel & Leisure* magazine. The Inn at Spanish Bay is a stay to remember, with golf, fine dining, opulent accommodations, and a lone kilted Scotsman who serenades the sunset each evening with his bagpipe.

The Lodge at Pebble Beach $$$$
17-Mile Drive, Pebble Beach
(831) 624–3811, (800) 654–9300,
www.pebblebeach.com

For golfers, it just doesn't get any better. Overlooking the Links at Pebble Beach with Carmel Bay and Point Lobos as your backdrop, The Lodge at Pebble Beach is a world-class experience. The 155 luxury rooms, five spa rooms, and one spa suite have a relaxed elegance that sets the tone for your stay in Pebble Beach. All but seven of the rooms (which average more

Carmel Bay and Point Lobos are your backdrop at The Lodge at Pebble Beach. PHOTO: JANA MORBA

than 560 square feet) have fireplaces, and many enjoy balconies overlooking the seaside fairways.

Built in 1919, The Lodge provides a full range of activities to fill your day. In addition to receiving special rates to play Pebble Beach Golf Links, one of the most famous golf courses in the world, guests are provided privileges to Poppy Hill Golf Course, the Links at Spanish Bay, and the Del Monte Golf Course in Monterey. Then there's the great Beach and Tennis Club that offers 12 tennis courts and a heated pool right on the edge of Carmel Bay. The Spa at Pebble Beach offers such luxuries as therapeutic baths, body wraps, massages, and facials as well as healthy cuisine. The Pebble Beach Equestrian Center is only a few blocks away for an incredible trail ride through the forest and to the beach. For shopping enthusiasts, the Lodge offers a breezeway of 15 specialty shops with an emphasis on golf, fashion, accessories, and gifts to appease the jealous folks who had to stay back home.

For dining, the Lodge offers a great variety of choices. The Cypress Room serves a nice breakfast, lunch, and dinner with panoramic views of the 18th green and Carmel Bay. On the lower level, Club XIX is a perfect spot to enjoy a sandwich for lunch on the outdoor patio or have contemporary French cuisine for an intimate evening. The Tap Room has just the right friendly pub atmosphere for embellishing your latest round of golf and enjoying the memorabilia from "The Crosby." Finally, across from The Lodge is The Gallery, providing breakfast and lunch overlooking the first tee. Winner of numerous awards, including being named the "Best Resort in Northern California" by *San Francisco Focus* magazine, The Lodge at Pebble Beach will put a wide smile on your golfer's face. All rooms are nonsmoking, and small pets are accepted.

Bed and Breakfast Inns

The Monterey Peninsula is world-famous for its bed and breakfast inns, particularly those in Pacific Grove and Carmel. From stately Victorian mansions to quaint cottages, you'll find a host of comfortable accommodations for a very special stay.

Before we highlight the individual inns, let's go over a few of the basics. It's no secret that most of the bed and breakfast inns are designed for romance, and you'll find many honeymooners, anniversary celebrators, and other romantic couples among your fellow guests. While some inns do accept children, it's a good idea to remind the kids that they need to be on their best behavior. Many of the inns are classic homes, some National Historic Landmarks, filled with delicate and breakable antiques. If your clan is subject to bed-jumping, tag-playing, noisemaking, and other hyperactive types of family vacation fun, consider a sturdier hotel or motel instead.

Breakfasts at these inns will vary from full sit-down meals to in-room deluxe continentals. City safety and health regulations limit the types of kitchens and therefore the types of meals that the small inns may provide in particular parts of the Peninsula. Therefore, you won't be able to find cooked meats, for example, at all of the establishments. But most bed and breakfast inns offer egg dishes, waffles or pancakes, baked goods, hot and cold cereals, and a variety of fresh juices, coffees, and teas.

Since most of the bed and breakfast inns have a small number of guest rooms available, last-minute cancellations can be especially hard on the innkeepers' pocketbooks. Therefore, be sure to ask about reservation and cancellation policies, which can be strict. Most inns accept major credit cards. If you pay by personal check, you may be required to submit a deposit weeks in advance of your stay. Smoking is typically prohibited and few inns accept pets, but ask about it when making reservations. Wheelchair access may be limited at some of these historic inns, so check in advance if it is important to you.

Most of the innkeepers we talked to recommend making your reservations at least two to three months in advance during the peak season (June through September) and for holiday weekends. Some special-event weekends may require bookings up to a year in advance. During the off-season, rooms can often be found up to the week of your stay, sometimes at great special rates. But if you have your heart set on a special room at a popular inn, avoid disappointment by reserving your accommodations as early as possible. With these caveats, let's take a look at some of the most popular of the Monterey Peninsula's bed and breakfast inns.

Insiders' Tip

When inquiring about your stay at a bed and breakfast inn, be sure to ask specifically about the menus and dining arrangements, especially if you have special dietary needs or desires.

Price Code

Prices for accommodations in a bed and breakfast on the Monterey Peninsula cover a wide range, from less than $90 per night to more than $1,000. In fact, the very same room may cost you twice as much during the peak season (June through September) or a special-event weekend than it does during the quiet off-season. These codes represent the average price of a double-occupancy room during peak season. This average may represent a wide range of room prices, with added amenities and ocean views hiking up the price of a standard room. Be sure to confirm the current rates and available methods of payment when making your reservations.

$	less than $90
$$	$90 to $130
$$$	$131 to $190
$$$$	$191 and more

Monterey

Del Monte Beach Inn $
1110 Del Monte Avenue, Monterey
(831) 649–4410

For a very reasonably priced small bed and breakfast hotel in the European tradition, try the Del Monte Beach Inn. This quaint 1929 beach hotel right across the street from the Bay was once home to whaling captains, cannery workers, and other merchants of the sea. Today, it is an 18-guest room bed and breakfast inn (nonsmoking) that offers no-frills but comfortable accommodations. An extended continental breakfast featuring hot baked goods and fresh fruit is offered buffet style on crisp linens in the downstairs dining room. The single television is in the library, and the phone is down the hall. Each room has a sink and vanity, but only two have full private baths. One of those rooms is a suite that sleeps five and includes a kitchenette. (This is the only room that accepts children.) Pets okay. Divers will appreciate the rinse tank out back.

The Jabberwock $$$
598 Laine Street, Monterey
(831) 372–4777, (888) 428–7253,
www.jabberwockinn.com

Situated in New Monterey on the hill above Cannery Row, The Jabberwock is a 1911 Craftsman-style home offering seven cozy guest rooms with goose-down pillows and comforters and a decidedly *Alice In Wonderland* theme. For 30 years, this splendid home served as a Victory Mission Sisters' convent and later as a church retreat. Since 1982, it has provided a serene haven for visitors who enjoy the spacious common areas and outdoor garden. Three of the rooms of this whimsical inn (The Brillig, The Mome Rath, and The Borogove) have fireplaces, one (The Toves) has a secret garden, and five have ocean views. The Mome Rath also has a great big Jacuzzi tub for fabulous soaks for two. Five rooms also have private baths, while two attic rooms (The Mimsy and The Wabe) share a bathroom. Complete breakfasts include fanciful specialties like Snackleberry Flumpsious (crème brûlée) and a surprise egg dish called Humpty Dumpty. Afternoon nibblers and evening homemade cookies and milk add to the bemusement. Sherry and hors d'oeuvres add a touch of elegance. Children older than 12 are welcome at this nonsmoking inn.

Old Monterey Inn $$$$
500 Martin Street, Monterey
(831) 375–8284, (800) 350–2344,
www.oldmontereyinn.com

Though not as well known as some of its more famous bed and breakfast brethren in Pacific Grove and Carmel, the Old Monterey Inn is on par with the best on the Peninsula. In fact, it was recently named one of the top 12 inns by *Country Inns* magazine. Up a quiet residential neighborhood above Pacific Street, this 10-guest room, ivy-covered English Tudor-style country home is on one and a half wooded and garden acres. It was built in 1929 for the first mayor of Monterey, Carmel Martin. An inn for more than 20 years, this property features private baths and sitting areas in all guest rooms, wood-burning fireplaces in most, and whirlpool tubs in three. A favorite among repeat guests is the Library Room with a private sundeck, and honeymooners fall in love with the Garden Cottage and the Chawton, a comfy and romantic room with a whirlpool tub for two, fireplace, and secluded garden entrance. A few in-room phones and televisions are available upon request. The innkeepers serve a full gourmet breakfast. Enjoy it in the dining room by the massive ironwork fireplace, out in the sunny English garden—or even in bed! The sunset wine hour is a great time to enjoy the wooded gardens, which afford many quiet sitting areas and hammocks for some serious R and R. In-room massage and day membership at the Monterey Sports Center are among the amenities offered. A true romantic getaway, the nonsmoking Old Monterey Inn allows children older than 12. However, the inn limits reservations to two guests per room.

Pacific Grove

The Centrella Inn $$$
612 Central Avenue, Pacific Grove
(831) 372–3372, (800) 233–3372,
www.centrellainn.com

An 1889 National Historic Landmark, the Centrella Inn takes you back in time to turn-of-the-century Pacific Grove. The classic Victorian design and small but comfortable, high-ceilinged guest rooms are a real treat to behold. Located between downtown P.G. and the beach, the main hotel has 26 rooms. All rooms have in-room phones and private baths, many with claw-foot tubs, and a few rooms have ocean views, including the airy attic suites. A favorite among honeymooners is the Garden Room, with a Jacuzzi tub, pot-belly stove, canopy bed, wet bar, and private entrance. Outside within a peaceful garden are five cozy cottages, each with a fireplace, wet bar, and private bath. All guests enjoy an extended sit-down continental breakfast (ask about the inn's famous waffles) and a light repast at the evening social hour. Children younger than 12 are allowed in the cottages only.

Gatehouse Inn $$$
225 Central Avenue, Pacific Grove
(831) 649–8436, (800) 753–1881,
www.sueandlewinns.com

A picturesque Victorian home circa 1884, the Gatehouse Inn is one of the better-kept secrets among Pacific Grove's Victorians. While not right on the waterfront, it does enjoy some nice bay views from the upstairs rooms. Homey and cozy, this nine-guest room inn features private baths (most with claw-foot tubs), in-room phones (no TVs),

The Centrella Inn in Pacific Grove is an 1889 Historic Landmark with 26 rooms and five cozy cottages out back. PHOTO: MARTIN BROWN/MONTEREY PENINSULA VCB

and full gourmet breakfasts. Some rooms have fireplaces or wood stoves, others have private decks and porches. A favorite is the Langford Room (named after original owner Benjamin Langford, a California senator), with a sitting area, wood stove, ocean view, queen-size bed, and claw-foot tub. An early-evening tea with wine and home-baked goodies allows you to visit with fellow guests by the fireplace in the parlor. And you can raid the cookie jar all day long! Children must be older than 10 to stay here.

Gosby House Inn $$$
643 Lighthouse Avenue, Pacific Grove
(831) 375–1287, (800) 527–8828,
www.foursisters.com

Welcoming guests to downtown Pacific Grove for more than 100 years, Gosby House Inn is one of the most recognized landmarks in Butterfly Town USA. The stately Queen Anne Victorian mansion provides 22 antique-filled guest rooms plus two romantic carriage-house rooms with spa tubs, fireplaces, and private balconies. All but two of the mansion's guest rooms have private baths, and many have sitting areas, each of which has a fireplace, private patio entrance, and/or window seat from which to view the ocean or hometown scenery. Lavish breakfasts are a hallmark of the nonsmoking Gosby House, and afternoon teas with wine and sherry are a great way to meet fellow guests and share your day's activities. For a small charge, you can even have champagne and truffles delivered to your room.

Grand View Inn $$$$
557 Ocean View Boulevard, Pacific Grove
(831) 372–4341, www.pginns.com

Elegant is the only word to describe this lovely 1910 Edwardian-style mansion, situated on the waterfront with a spectacular view of Lovers Point in Pacific Grove. The 22-guest room, nonsmoking Grand View Inn, originally home to noted marine biologist and P.G.'s first woman mayor Julia Platt, has been extensively renovated by its current owners and is now a showcase of the post-Victorian era. The dining room features oak columns, a marble fireplace, and exquisite antique furniture and has ocean views that will make your full breakfasts and afternoon teas simply unforgettable. Guest rooms feature marble-tiled private baths (plush bathrobes too), patterned hardwood floors, and striking antique furnishings. There are no televisions or in-room phones, but who needs them? Well-behaved children older than 12 are welcome.

Insiders' Tip

Some of the smaller bed and breakfast inns have strict payment policies. Make sure you ask about acceptable forms of payment and cancellation policies to avoid any unpleasant surprises.

Green Gables Inn $$$
104 5th Street, Pacific Grove
(831) 375–2095, (800) 722–1774,
www.foursisters.com

Perhaps the best-known Pacific Grove bed and breakfast (and a favorite of this Insider), the Green Gables Inn was named the number one bed and breakfast inn in North America by the Official Hotel Guide's 1997 travel agent survey. This 11-guest room inn and carriage house is right on the corner of Ocean View Boulevard and 5th Street and affords warm and comfortable accommodations with spectacular waterfront views. See our Close-up on the Green Gables Inn in this chapter.

The Inn at 213 Seventeen Mile Drive $$$
213 17-Mile Drive, Pacific Grove
(831) 642–9514, (800) 526–5666,
www.innat17.com

This is the newest and the youngest of the Pacific Grove bed and breakfast inns, welcoming its first guests in 1998. All we can say is take advantage of this reasonably

CLOSE-UP

And the Winner Is: Green Gables Inn

Okay, so if we Insiders could pick just one place to stay on the Monterey Peninsula for a warm, cozy, romantic night it would be—a difficult choice. But if push came to shove, our numero uno bed and breakfast inn would be the Green Gables Inn, at 104 5th Street, Pacific Grove.

First of all, we're partial to Pacific Grove with its quiet charm and hometown casualness. Second, a Queen Anne mansion sitting right on the edge of the Bay is pretty hard to beat. The Seven Gables Inn and the Grand View Inn, just down Ocean View Boulevard, probably have even more spectacular views, but their high-brow opulence and antiques don't bring the down-to-earth comfort level we'd be looking for to get that ultimate rest and relaxation.

And we Insiders are not alone in picking Green Gables Inn as the crème de la crème. In fact, Green Gables Inn was voted North America's number one bed and breakfast inn by none other than the Official Hotel Guide's (OHG) travel-agent survey. (The annual OHG Readers' Choice Awards survey is based on responses from 20,000 subscribers who rated properties across 51 categories. OHG is said to be the world's largest supplier of information and services for the travel industry.)

A visit to the Green Gables Inn confirms that these travel agents know what they're talking about. The 1888 National Historic Landmark is a multigabled Queen Anne right on the waterfront at the corner of 5th Street and Ocean View Boulevard. The 11-room mansion and carriage house are painted white with dark green trim. The windows, fixtures, and woodwork are all original features. Walk up the front steps into the warm and cozy living room of the main house, and you immediately

Green Gables Inn is a Pacific Grove landmark and our #1 bed and breakfast inn. PHOTO: MONTEREY PENINSULA VCB

feel at home. The six guest rooms in the main house feature English antiques, comfortable beds, and snuggly teddy bears to welcome you.

Each guest room has its own special touches. The Chapel Room features a rich mahogany interior, while the Gable Room has a sturdy ladder that takes you up to the cozy attic room in the main gable itself. Canopy bed aficionados will appreciate the aptly named Lacey Room. Rooms in the main house share baths (some consider this one of the few drawbacks), except for the two-room suite. Out back, the carriage house has five more rooms, each with a fireplace, queen bed, bath, and extra foldout sofa bed. Each guest room is tastefully decorated with romantic wallpaper and fabric. All guests enjoy a full breakfast each morning in the oceanview dining room. Wine and hors d'oeuvres are served in the afternoon next to the parlor fireplace. Call (831) 375–2095 or (800) 722–1774 for reservations.

So if Green Gables Inn tops the charts in Pacific Grove, what about Monterey and Carmel? Again, there are many splendid choices and our top picks would vary depending on our mood. But for unbeatable B&Bs, try:

Old Monterey Inn, Monterey, (831) 375–8284. This English Tudor-style inn is off the beaten path and secluded within lush wooded and garden acres. For a real Monterey getaway in plush surroundings, stay here (see listing).

Green Lantern Inn, Carmel, (831) 624–4392. We pick the Green Lantern because it epitomizes what Carmel is all about. Quaint, charming, storybook cottages in a splendid garden setting, easy walking distance to the beach, and close to Ocean Avenue shopping (see listing).

priced jewel before the rest of the world finds out! The main Craftsman-style house, built in 1925, features seven tasteful rooms, each with its own motif. Some have Asian influence in recognition of the area's rich Chinese heritage; others honor the Monarch butterfly or the area's nautical legacy. Each is named for a local seabird. Then there are seven more rooms on the spacious grounds, including the Pelican cottage and the entirely redwood Guillemot loft. An outdoor spa and fountain add to the tranquility. A large buffet breakfast and evening hors d'oeuvres and wine provide a great opportunity to mingle with your hosts and fellow guests. Innkeepers Tony and Glynis Greening are avid runners and kayakers and relish in sharing their favorite spots for each.

The Martine Inn $$$$
255 Ocean View Boulevard, Pacific Grove
(831) 373-3388, (800) 852–5588,
www.martine.com

Perched on a small bluff overlooking the rocky coastline of Monterey Bay, The Martine Inn was built in 1899 and was originally the opulent home of Laura and James Parke of Parke-Davis Pharmaceuticals. Today, after many renovations, it is a striking 23-guest room inn with special touches that please the most discerning visitor, as evidenced by its place on a number of travel magazine top-12 lists. Think elegant. Breakfast is served on Victorian china with old Sheffield silver and crystal goblets. Lunches and dinners are based on the 1880s "White House" cookbooks and are lengthy multicourse affairs that may even include Victorian spoon warmers. The furnishings are museum quality. Bedroom ensembles include the Malarin Estates mahogany suite exhibited in the 1893 Chicago Words Fair; an 1860 Chippendale Revival four-poster bed with canopy and side curtains; and Edith Head's bedroom suite complete with her early commissioned portrait. All rooms have private baths, some with claw-foot tubs as well as in-room phones. Many guest rooms have wood-burning fireplaces, and smoking is allowed in these rooms only. You can enjoy a comfortable library, enclosed courtyard (where antique MG automobiles are on display), a garden conservatory with a hot tub spa, and a game room with a 1917 nickelodeon and an 1890 white oak pool table. At twilight the inn serves wine and hors d'oeuvres around the knabe reproducing Baby Grand Piano, where you can take in the spectacular bay view. Wine, champagne, and picnic-basket lunches can all be provided. The Martine Inn prides itself in hosting spectacular weddings, and an on-staff consultant will help organize and coordinate the entire event.

The Old St. Angela Inn $$$
321 Central Avenue, Pacific Grove
(831) 372–3246, (800) 748–6306,
www.sueandlewinns.com

Formerly a rectory and later a convent, The Old St. Angela Inn is now a comfy Craftsman-style bed and breakfast inn. The circa-1910 inn may lack the opulence of some of Pacific Grove's more stately Victorian Queen Annes and Edwardians, but it offers a comfortable stay at a reasonable price. There are nine guestrooms, including the upstairs Whale Watch, with an ocean view from the private balcony, fireplace, and Jacuzzi tub. Each room has a private bath, and most have either a fireplace or cast-iron stove. Breakfast is served in a bright redwood and glass solarium or in the oceanview dining room. Home-baked cookies and other treats are a specialty and can be enjoyed before the cut stone fireplace in the living room. Those scrumptious cookies are especially good with evening wine, tea, or coffee. A garden gazebo and spa add to the enjoyment. Some rooms accommodate children and all are nonsmoking.

> **Insiders' Tip**
>
> Sure, bed and breakfast inns are great for a romantic getaway for two. But take advantage of sit-down breakfasts and evening sherry and tea to meet other guests and make new friends.

Pacific Grove Inn $$$
581 Pine Avenue, Pacific Grove
(831) 375–2825, (800) 732–2825

This 1905 Victorian mansion at the corner of Pine and Forest Avenues is a marvel in its detail. Carved oak walls, a round turret room with a 30-foot pointed ceiling, and antique Oriental carpeting are just a few of the highlights. In its main house and guesthouse, the nonsmoking Pacific Grove Inn has a total of 16 guest rooms, each with a private bath featuring a full-sized tub and heated towel racks. All rooms have brass beds, fireplaces, televisions, and phones; a few rooms feature extras like a whirlpool tub, an enclosed sundeck, or an open-air porch. The four-room, oceanview suite is perfect for families. Children of all ages are welcome. The large buffet breakfast includes waffles, eggs, baked goods, juices, six choices of coffee, and 14 kinds of tea.

Seven Gables Inn $$$$
555 Ocean View Boulevard, Pacific Grove
(831) 372–4341, www.pginns.com

Like its sister Grand View Inn next door, the Seven Gables Inn offers a breathtaking view of Lovers Point and Monterey Bay that in itself is worth the price of a night's stay. But the classic inn, with its many gables, sun porches, beveled glass windows, and gilded and inlaid antique furniture, gives the ocean view a run for its money in both beauty and elegance. The showy 1886 Victorian main house topped by the Breakers room, along with its guesthouse and cottages, offers 14 guest rooms, each with a full private bath and queen-size bed. Virtually all of the rooms have a spectacular view of the Bay, and one of the carriage-house rooms adds a cozy fireplace. The host Flatley family's

Seven Gables Inn is a showy 1886 Victorian located across the street from Lovers Point in Pacific Grove.
PHOTO: ELLIOTT SCHERLING/MONTEREY PENINSULA VCB

eclectic collection of fine antiques adds both opulence and warmth. A full breakfast and elegant afternoon high tea are served in the grand Victorian dining room. The Seven Gables is a nonsmoking inn, and children younger than 12 are not allowed because of the low windows, sharp corners, and delicate furnishings. For sheer beauty indoors and out, it's tough to top the Seven Gables Inn.

Carmel

Carmel Wayfarer Inn $$
4th Avenue and Mission Street, Carmel
(831) 624–2711, (800) 533–2711

Established in 1929, the nonsmoking Carmel Wayfarer Inn has 18 comfortable rooms, all with private baths, coffeemakers, and refrigerators. Most rooms in this small hotel-like facility have fireplaces; some have ocean views. Rooms are situated around a quaint courtyard garden that has a cozy outdoor fireplace with plenty of fireside seating. An extended continental breakfast is served buffet style in a common dining area, with a menu of fresh fruits, baked goods, and other treats.

Cobblestone Inn $$$
Junipero Street and 7th Avenue, Carmel
(831) 625–5222, (800) 833–8836,
www.foursisters.com

This English-style country inn combines warm charm with modern amenities. Stone from the Carmel River covers the first level of this two-story inn and is also used in the fireplaces that grace every one of the 24 rooms. The slate courtyard in the center of the horseshoe-shaped building is a great place to enjoy a full gourmet breakfast during warm weather. When the fog rolls in, you can move into the enclosed dining room or have breakfast in bed. All rooms have refrigerators stocked with cold beverages, and wine and hors d'oeuvres are served each afternoon. A special honeymoon suite features a four-poster bed with a European cutwork canopy. Use the complimentary bicycles to explore the back

Insiders' Tip

Historic inns might have limited wheelchair access, narrow winding staircases, no in-room televisions or phones, and shared bathrooms. Check for details if these limitations are important to you or someone you're traveling with.

streets of Carmel. The large stone fireplace in the comfortable parlor is a great place to unwind at the end of the day.

The Green Lantern Inn $$$
7th Avenue and Casanova Street, Carmel
(831) 624–4392, (888) 414–4392,
www.greenlanterninn.com

Of all the inns in Carmel, perhaps none epitomize English country charm as much as The Green Lantern Inn, established in 1926. The historic main house and five cottages, nestled in a quaint garden of roses, azaleas, and other flowers amid pine and oak trees, offer 18 guest rooms, each with an individual charisma. The Cedar room is a spacious room with queen bed and a private Carmel stone patio. The Holly has a hipped vestibule with a narrow stairway leading up to the "lighthouse" bedroom. The high-ceiling Cypress is a fireplace suite with a spacious loft and two queen beds. The Maple is large with two queen beds and a secluded redwood deck. You get the idea. Guests enjoy a buffet breakfast in the cozy fireside room or out in the courtyard. All rooms are nonsmoking and have private baths, some with full-sized tubs. It's a short walk to the beach and downtown, if you can pull yourself away. Afternoon wine and cheese are served in the fireside room.

Happy Landing Inn $$
Monte Verde Street and 6th Avenue, Carmel
(831) 624–7917

This storybook 1929 Comstock house has seven guest cottages, each with a cathedral ceiling, private bath, and stained-glass window. The two-room suite with fireplace is a favorite among repeat visitors. You'll find televisions but no phones in the rooms—a guest phone is available off the living room. Rooms look out over a lovely courtyard garden with a vine-covered gazebo, frog pond, and many, many flowers. The Happy Landing Inn serves a gourmet continental breakfast with a unique custom: In the morning, you pull up your window shade as a signal you're ready, and the staff brings the breakfast to your room. Feel free to enjoy your morning meal out in the garden gazebo. Evenings include tea and cookies served in the main house and in-room sherry. The Happy Landing Inn is a nonsmoking establishment that provides quiet comfort in residential Carmel and is just blocks from downtown and the beach.

Holiday House $$$
Camino Real and 7th Avenue, Carmel
(831) 624–6267

Built in 1905 as a summer home for a Stanford University professor, the shingle-covered, Craftsman-style Holiday House has six guest rooms, two with ocean views. Dormer windows and quilted bedspreads add to a cozy atmosphere that makes you feel like you're part of the family. The emphasis here is on rustic simplicity. Although most rooms have private baths, only one has a television. And if you need to call home or the office, you'll have to use your cell phone or the coin phone in the lobby. A full breakfast is served buffet style in the dining room. Afterward, enjoy a relaxing moment in front of the living room's big wood-burning fireplace or cuddle up with a good book in the well-stocked library. A walk down the Carmel stone paths through the peaceful garden is a pleasantry before your afternoon sherry. The Holiday House, known as Carmel's oldest guesthouse, is a nonsmoking inn.

Monte Verde Inn $$$
Monte Verde Street and Ocean Avenue, Carmel
(831) 624–6046, (800) 328–7707

Built as an inn in 1900, the Monte Verde Inn has been welcoming guests to Carmel for nearly 100 years. The Mediterranean-style villa offers 10 nonsmoking guest rooms, two with fireplaces and a few with private balconies or decks. One large suite has two queen-size beds, a sitting room, and full kitchen. Another has an ocean view, a sitting room, and a balcony. A secluded brick patio provides a great place to enjoy the fresh ocean air. Guests receive an extended continental breakfast in the sunny dining room. All rooms have private baths, and there is ample off-street parking. The Monte Verde Inn is only a half-block from downtown and 3 blocks from the beach.

San Antonio House $$$
San Antonio Avenue and Ocean Avenue, Carmel
(831) 624–4334

The four-guest room San Antonio House was built in 1927 and is one of the smallest bed and breakfasts in Carmel. All rooms have in-room televisions and phones, private baths, cozy fireplaces, breakfast patios, and their own entrances to heighten privacy. There is a quaint outdoor garden so you can enjoy the mild Carmel days. A gourmet continental breakfast of fruit, granola, yogurt, and pastries is delivered to your room. Accommodations are comfortable, with a cozy put-up-your-feet, don't-worry-about-the-furniture ambiance. Plus, you can't get a room much closer to Carmel Beach than at the San Antonio House.

Sea View Inn $$
Camino Real and 11th Avenue, Carmel
(831) 624–8778

This turn-of-the-century, three-story Victorian offers eight nonsmoking guest rooms in quiet residential Carmel, about as far away from downtown as you can get. Antique accents and comfortable surroundings make this a great spot to sit back and relax in real peace and quiet. There are no in-room phones or televisions to distract you. Six rooms have private baths; two attic rooms share a bath. The large front porch and lush back garden make great spots for reading, writing, or just enjoying the moment. A full breakfast is served in the spacious dining room on weekend mornings, and generous continental breakfasts are offered on weekdays. Enjoy wine and cheese in the evenings before a crackling fire. Children 11 and older are welcome.

The Stonehouse Inn $$$
8th Avenue and Monte Verde Street, Carmel
(831) 624–4569, (877) 748–6618,
www.carmelstonehouse.com

The Stonehouse Inn is a 1906 Carmel home that gets its name from the rugged stone exterior that was hand-shaped by local Native Americans. Among the guests of original owner, Josephine "Nanna" Foster (who had a penchant for inviting San Francisco writers and artists to her home for long conversations), were Jack London and Sinclair Lewis. Subsequent owners included cartoonist Gene Byrnes (of *Reg'lar Fellers* fame) and A. T. Hyde, of the Mentholatum fortune. Today, you enter The Stonehouse through a long glass-enclosed porch and walk into a large living room with an impressive stone fireplace—ask the innkeeper to show you the hidden vault! Each of the seven guest rooms has its own unique charm, but the big favorite is the upstairs suite with an ocean view and the George Sterling hand-carved canopy bed. Two of the light and airy rooms have private baths, the other four share. Amenities include cozy quilts, plenty of pillows, and a full sit-down breakfast in the sunny dining room. Breakfast includes omelets, bacon, fruit, juices, baked goods, and coffee or tea. Ever tried southern-style banana rice pancakes? Enjoy wine in the evening before the living room fireplace. A large backyard patio is a great relaxation spot on warm afternoons. Smoking is not permitted, and children must be 12 or older.

The Sunset House $$$
Camino Real and Ocean Avenue, Carmel
(831) 624–4884, www.sunset-carmel.com

If you're looking for a Carmel inn with all the special touches, The Sunset House may be just your cup of tea. With only four

The award-winning cobblestone courtyard and gardens provide a tranquil oasis for guests at Carmel's Vagabond's House Inn. PHOTO: TOM OWENS

spacious guest rooms, all with private baths and some with great ocean views, this nonsmoking inn caters to your every need. Great breakfasts, delivered to your room by the innkeepers, feature hand-squeezed juices, freshly baked goods, specially made granola, and a special house-blend gourmet coffee. Floor-to-ceiling brick fireplaces in each room come complete with hand-split wood, expertly mixed to provide just the right heat, scent, and color of fire. Wet bars, kitchenettes, Jacuzzi tubs, hide-a-beds, sitting areas, and outdoor decks and patios are other available extras. Phone lines are wired to handle your laptop computer. Built in 1960, The Sunset House may not be a picturesque historic inn, but it has a charming fountain garden and all the modern conveniences. Plus, it's just a short walk from the beach or downtown Carmel.

Vagabond's House Inn $$$
Dolores Street and 4th Avenue, Carmel
(831) 624–7738, (800) 262–1262,
www.vagabondshouseinn.com

The Vagabond's House Inn was originally built in the 1940s as housing for officers at Fort Ord to the north of Monterey. Today, these English Tudor shingle-roofed cottages have been transformed into comfy rooms and suites situated in a horseshoe around a secluded cobblestone courtyard with waterfall pool, beautiful award-winning gardens, and a stately oak tree. There are 11 guest rooms and two suites in this nonsmoking inn, the favorites being rooms 1 and 11, which have great courtyard views. Each room is decorated in a unique theme or style, such as nautical or floral, with many antiques and a notable Ralph Lauren influence throughout the inn. Most rooms have fireplaces, coffee bars, and refrigerators, and all have private baths. An elaborate continental breakfast is delivered on a tray to your room each morning. Complimentary sherry, coffee, and tea cap your evening. Children 12 and older are welcome. Pets okay.

Vacation Rentals

Visitors looking for a vacation rental on the Monterey Peninsula may be in for a bit of a surprise. Yes, there is an ample supply of single-family homes, apartments, and condominiums available to rent as vacation getaways. They range from small studios, cottages, and beach bungalows to expansive estates.

However, you might have to plan on an extended stay to be able to enjoy many of these homes. Ordinances in the cities of Monterey, Carmel, and Pacific Grove require a minimum of a 30-night stay in many vacation rentals. Why? Unlike most resort communities, the Monterey Peninsula does not have vicinities devoted to short-term vacation properties. Most of the vacation rentals here are second homes that owners live in part time and rent out the rest of the year through a property-management firm. These houses are primarily in residential neighborhoods, surrounded by the homes of full-time residents. Understandably, some of these residents object to having their quiet neighborhoods turned into a weekly merry-go-round of active new visitors. They took their complaints to the city governments, who established ordinances calling for 30-night minimum stays to establish some semblance of neighborhood stability.

That being said, there are still opportunities to find a vacation rental on the Peninsula for a weeklong stay. A seven-day minimum, not the 30-night ordinance, applies to the unincorporated areas of the Peninsula. That includes all of Pebble Beach and many neighborhoods commonly considered Carmel and Monterey but actually outside the boundaries of the incorporated cities. Some vacation rentals within Monterey, Carmel, and Pacific Grove commercial zones are also exempt from the 30-day minimum.

How to Find Rentals

Vacation rentals can be found through a variety of sources. You can check the classified ads in the local newspapers for private owners who are renting their second homes. Some of the larger Monterey Peninsula real estate companies handle property rentals as well (see our Real Estate chapter). The primary source is a handful of property-management firms that specialize in vacation rentals. These are listed at the end of this chapter.

The Cost

How much can you expect to pay for a vacation rental? That will depend on the size and location of the property, the duration of your stay, and the time of year you're coming into town. At the low end of the price spectrum, small studios and one- or two-bedroom houses and condominiums start around $800 per week or $1,700 per month in the off-season. At the high end, large estates can run $5,000 or more per week and into the tens of thousands per month during the peak months. While it's difficult to pinpoint a typical rental price, you can expect to pay $1,500 to $2,500 per week or $3,500 to $5,000 per month during the peak summer season for a comfortable home in a nice location with ample room for a family of four to stretch out. Weekly rentals in unincorporated locales will also include a 10.5 percent occupancy tax.

What You Get

If you deal with a specialist property-management firm, you'll likely get a fully

Vacation rentals on the Monterey Peninsula are primarily located in residential neighborhoods.
PHOTO: TOM OWENS

furnished, clean home complete with bed and bath linens, dishes, cooking equipment, a telephone, a television, and a VCR as standard equipment. Many of these homes also have fireplaces (complete with a supply of wood), washers and dryers, a microwave oven, a deck or patio, and a barbecue grill. Some include stereo systems, pools, hot tubs, spas, fax machines, and even computers. In many cases, all you need is clothing and groceries. (Property-management firms may also provide faxes, copy machines, express mail, and other administrative services through their offices.)

Of course, for a price, extra amenities are always available. Maid service, grocery shopping, and catering as well as massages and baby-sitting can be arranged through the property-management firm or an independent contractor. Cribs, high chairs, rollaway beds, cars, bicycles, and other equipment can also be rented. Some firms will even arrange tee times at local golf courses. Just ask, and you can probably get it. Many vacation homes are nonsmoking properties, and pets are typically excluded. But exceptions can often be made in exchange for an added cleaning fee and/or security deposit.

Making Arrangements

Property-management firms recommend reserving vacation homes eight months to a year in advance for the peak seasons. That includes the summer months of June through August, the winter months of January through March and the major holiday weekends. During the off-season, generally spring and fall, try to make your reservations three to six months in advance. Security deposits (typically $300 and more) are usually required to hold a property. Full payment is often due 30 days in advance of your stay. Still, don't be afraid of calling for a vacation property a week before your planned trip—or even dropping in on a property-management firm when you arrive in town. You never know what might be available due to an unusually slow week or a last-minute cancellation.

Property-Management Firms

Although a number of real estate agencies, private individuals, and property-management firms handle vacation homes on the Monterey Peninsula, the majority of the business is handled by four firms, each with a solid local reputation. Check out a variety of sources, but be sure to include these firms in your search for that perfect Monterey Peninsula vacation home.

Insiders' Tip

Be a good neighbor. Your Monterey Peninsula vacation rental is likely in a residential area, so respect the requests of others and try to blend in with the neighborhood ambiance.

Monterey Bay Property Management
816 Wave Street, Monterey
(831) 655–7840, www.montereyrentals.com

In business for 15 years, Monterey Bay Vacation Properties handles more than 100 fully furnished vacation rentals, ranging from small studio apartments and condominiums to luxury estates; from the quaint to the exotic. Properties are located throughout Monterey, Carmel, Pacific Grove, Pebble Beach, and Carmel Valley as well as the South Coast and other surrounding unincorporated areas. Weekly and monthly rentals are available from this agency that prides itself on its customer service. The firm also specializes in second-home purchases for out-of-area buyers.

Pine Cone Property Management
26613 Carmel Center Place, Carmel
(831) 626–2800, www.pineconerentals.com

From golf course country club homes to beachfront bungalows, Pine Cone Property Management offers a wide range of properties in Monterey, Carmel, Pacific Grove, Pebble Beach, and surrounding unincorporated areas. Most rental properties are nonsmoking, and pets are allowed only by prearranged permission with a deposit required. Pine Cone Property Management prefers not to give out a full list of available properties. Instead, you provide a description of your dream vacation home, and they present a selection of homes that make a good match. Cashiers checks are required on walk-in rentals.

San Carlos Agency
26358 Carmel Rancho Lane, Carmel
(831) 624–3846, www.sancarlosagency.com

With nearly 50 years in the business, San Carlos Agency is the oldest and largest vacation-property specialist on the Monterey Peninsula. Representing up to 150 vacation rental properties in Pebble Beach, Carmel, Pacific Grove, and surrounding unincorporated areas, the firm is a member of the Vacation Rental Managers Association, a national group. Visitors to the Peninsula can drop in to view photos of the properties. Rent a property, and you typically have first choice to rebook the home during the same period the following year. As a full-service real estate company, San Carlos Agency can also handle all types of residential and vacation-property sales and then provide continuing property-management services.

Vintage Property Management
San Carlos Street and 7th Avenue, Carmel
(831) 624–2930

Owner-operated Vintage Property Management prides itself in being a full-service vacation-rental agency. It offers single-family vacation homes in Carmel, Pebble Beach, Pacific Grove, Carmel Valley, and surrounding unincorporated areas. Vintage does not handle condominiums or apartments, and all properties are nonsmoking and no-pet homes.

Restaurants

The culinary selections on the Monterey Peninsula are as bountiful and satisfying as the glorious ocean that graces our coast and the fertile fields of the inland areas. Many of the innovative chefs in this area make use of the abundant fresh seafood, herbs, and vegetables available. Our proximity to the Salinas Valley for lettuces and vegetables, Castroville for artichokes, Gilroy for garlic, and the Pacific Ocean for crab, calamari, fish, and rock shrimp leads to the superb quality and freshness of area cuisine.

While many establishments pay homage to the Italian origins of many Peninsula residents, there is also an eclectic offering of international cuisine and cooking styles. From American comfort food to Thai and Indian fare, and representing just about every point on the globe, you'll find a place to indulge your culinary cravings.

Although we have by no means even scratched the surface of the Peninsula's dining and snacking options, our hope is to give you a small sampling of the range of possibilities. For your convenience we have organized the chapter by categories based on the type of food offered. Within each category, the selections are presented alphabetically.

Here are a few other guidelines to keep in mind. Reservations are not generally required. However, in most cases they are suggested, especially on weekends and during any of the area's many festivals and events. To avoid disappointment, it is best to call ahead. Smokers be warned that all restaurants and bars in California are, by law, nonsmoking establishments.

Although some national chain restaurants are located here, you won't find them among our listings. We prefer to focus on unique eating environments in the descriptions that follow. With few exceptions, we have not mentioned restaurants within hotels or shopping centers. If there is something you are looking for that we didn't have space to cover, you'll find a complete listing of restaurants in the local Yellow Pages. Newsstands, visitor centers, and the concierges of many hotels also have several publications to assist you in your dining discoveries. If you're looking for places the kids will enjoy, see our Kidstuff chapter. Buon appetito!

Price Code

The following dollar-sign codes are designed to give you an idea of the approximate price range for each restaurant. The codes represent the price of dinner entrees for two, without cocktails or wine. We have not included tax and gratuity in our price code. Cash, travelers checks, and most major cards are the norm for payment -unless otherwise noted, you can expect major credit cards to be accepted at all restaurants listed. If you are concerned about which credit cards are accepted, just call ahead to check the restaurant's current policy.

$	Less than $25
$$	$25 to $40
$$$	$41 to $55
$$$$	$56 and more

American

Em Le's $
Dolores Street between 5th and 6th Avenues, Carmel
(831) 625–6780

There's no place like home, unless it's Em Le's. Savor home-style foods such as homemade meat loaf or chicken-fried country steak served with real mashed potatoes and gravy. Nothing will wet your whistle better than a glass of ice-cold lemonade. You can order beer, wine, or champagne if you prefer. How does a visit to an old-fashioned soda fountain sound? Em Le's offers big banana splits, with a choice of hot fudge, strawberry, pineapple, or caramel toppings. Be sure to try a malt or ice cream float. If you're in the mood for breakfast, you can order it anytime of day—try the three-egg omelets. Em Le's is open for breakfast and lunch every day.

Forge in the Forest $$
Junipero Street at 5th Avenue, Carmel
(831) 624–2233, www.forgeintheforest.com

Welcome to the Forge, a unique collection of buildings, patios, and gardens that includes a blacksmith shop, an old-fashioned general store, a wine cellar, and a Gold Rush–era bar. Find a seat in the most appealing area to you and peruse the creative American menu. Lunch favorites are the baked onion soup, Caesar salad (with or without chicken), and the seared ahi tuna salad. A genuine deli selection of sandwiches, with authentic New York pastrami heading the list, is another lunch option. Six different kinds of steak, juicy baby back ribs, roasted duck, and several seafood and pasta entrees are some of the tantalizing dinner choices. Visit this Carmel landmark restaurant for lunch or dinner.

The Old Monterey Café $
489 Alvarado Street, Monterey
(831) 646–1021, www.cafemonterey.com

Each meal at this warm, friendly cafe is cooked-to-order, wholesome food made with fresh ingredients. Now for the best part—breakfast is served all day. The four-egg, extra fluffy, rolled-up omelets are reminiscent of a true back-to-the-farm breakfast. The big Belgian waffles and buckwheat pancakes are also generously portioned home-style treats. Burgers, a variety of salads, homemade soups, and vegetarian entrees are a few of the lunch menu selections. The Old Monterey Cafe serves breakfast and lunch only.

Tarpy's Roadhouse $$
Highway 68 at Canyon Del Rey, Monterey
(831) 647–1444, www.downtowndining.com

The historic vine-covered stone ranch house with indoor and outdoor seating sets the stage for a true roadhouse dining experience. The courtyard, with an arched entrance enclosed by the stone walls of the ranch house, offers delightful garden dining, weather permitting. Inside, the stone house has seven separate dining rooms, including perfect spots for a cozy meal in front of the fire. One intermittent drawback is the roadhouse's location under the flight path to the airport. Momentary pauses in conversation are a remedy, and the food and service are certainly worth it. Tarpy's is famous for its wood-burning grill that brings out the special flavors of vegetables, steak, wild game, and fresh seafood. Innovative salads, vegetarian selections, daily specials, and delectable dessert creations are additional specialties of the house. The award-winning wine list and full bar compliment the food. Tarpy's is open for lunch or dinner.

The Tinnery $
Lovers Point Park, 631 Ocean View Boulevard, Pacific Grove
(831) 646–1040, www.thetinnery.com

This popular oceanfront spot is prized for affordable, casual dining. Cooks put the spin on ordinary scrambled eggs with a feast of sides that include Italian sausage, filet mignon, and calamari. Quiche Lorraine, cheese blintzes, and eggs Alaska (similar to eggs Benedict but using crabmeat) also receive top billing. At lunchtime, choose from an extensive selection of various salads, sandwiches, chicken and beef dishes, and pizza. Seafood and other American fare, including roast prime rib, are highlighted at dinner. The oceanview

Insiders' Tip

The Monterey Peninsula is a relatively small area, but it boasts a staggering array of dining choices. Just about every ethnic and national fare is represented here. One could literally choose a different restaurant every night for a month and never repeat cuisines.

lounge features live entertainment Tuesday through Saturday. The Tinnery is open every day for breakfast, lunch, and dinner.

Toasties Café $
702 Lighthouse Avenue, Pacific Grove
(831) 373–7543

This cozy cafe serves breakfast fare that includes homemade hash, eggs Benedict, French toast, and pancakes. For lunch try the specialty sandwiches, yummy fresh salads, or the fajitas, if you're in the mood for something a little different. A partial listing of the dinner menu includes pork chops, chicken, and a steak and scampi combo. Desserts are all-American here too: You'll find both apple pie and chocolate cake. Home-style atmosphere and meals, reasonable prices, and friendly staff make this a great spot for breakfast, lunch, or dinner.

Asian

Chopsticks Café $
209 Forest Avenue, Pacific Grove
(831) 375–7997

The cuisine at Chopsticks Café is traditional Japanese with Southeast Asian influences and a California flair. The menu reflects a blend of favorites—tempura, sushi, sashimi, teriyaki—and contemporary, innovative creations utilizing seafood or unusual Asian pasta. You'll also find several vegetarian items. Chopsticks Café combines high-quality, imaginative food with truly affordable prices. Beer and wine are available. It's open for lunch and dinner.

The Orient Restaurant $
1760 Fremont Boulevard, Seaside
(831) 394–2223

Tucked into an otherwise nondescript strip mall, this unpretentious restaurant serves pho, a beef noodle soup considered to be the national dish of Vietnam. A steaming bowl of rice noodles, onion, paper-thin slices of beef, and star anise-scented beef broth arrives at your table along with a plate of bean sprouts, basil or cilantro, chili peppers, a hot chili sauce, and lemon for customizing this little bowl of heaven. Other Vietnamese specialties and a wide variety of exotic Asian dishes round out the menu.

Sapporo Japanese Steakhouse & Sushi
$$
Fisherman's Wharf #2, Monterey
(831) 333–1616

This teppan grill-style restaurant makes the claim, "Where every meal is a performance," and they don't disappoint. Customers are seated around a large hibachi grill, set in a room with sweeping views of the Monterey Harbor. After choosing from a dizzying array of combinations of meat and seafood, a chef approaches the grill and the show begins. All flying knives and flailing food, the experience brings new meaning to the term "dinner theater." Particularly entertaining is the onion volcano, made by stacking sliced onions in a conical shape and lighting brandy sprayed inside. Each meal comes with soup and salad, a shrimp appetizer, rice, and vegetables. An adjacent sushi bar serves all the standard sushi fare. A full bar, beer, and wine are also available.

Thai Bistro II $$
159 Central Avenue, Pacific Grove
(831) 372–8700

From the outside, Thai Bistro looks like grandma's house, all old-fashioned Americana. Upon entering, however, you'll find yourself in a pleasantly decorated Asian atmosphere where the walls are lined with pillowed benches and adorned with an eclectic mixture of Asian and local art. But make no mistake; the food is Thai through and through. They serve up good-sized portions of traditional favorites such as chicken and beef *sa-tay* with peanut sauce for dipping, *phad thai*, and *tom kah kai*—a spicy coconut milk-based soup with lemongrass, fresh mushrooms, and chicken. A variety of noodles, rice dishes, curries, salads, and soups make Thai Bistro a great choice for lovers of Southeast Asian cuisine.

Californian

Pacific's Edge $$$
Highlands Inn–A Park Hyatt Hotel, Highway 1, 4 miles south of Carmel
(831) 622–5445, www.highlands-inn.com

Quite possibly one of the most inspiring spots on the California coast, Pacific's Edge affords breathtaking ocean views accented by a jagged seacoast and wind-blown cypress trees. The accolades from national and international food critics for the regional cuisine at Pacific's Edge continue. New menu items include yellow fin tuna sashimi and seabean salad with rice chips, and coriander-crusted ahi tuna with orange citrus sauce. The *Wine Spectator* Grand Award wine list is a perfect complement to the exquisite food. A special four-course prix fixe dinner menu is available nightly; the menu changes every two weeks. Indulge in sensational food and wine. Pacific's Edge is open for lunch, dinner, or Sunday Brunch.

Rio Grill $$
Highway 1 at Rio Road, Carmel
(831) 625–5436, www.downtowndining.com

For well over a decade, people have considered the Rio Grill an extraordinary place to have fun and enjoy fine dining. There is a Southwest influence in the preparation of the California foods served here. Entrees like smoked chicken served with mild smoked chili butter and filet mignon with wild mushroom and guajillo chile salsa prove the point. If you want to have something sweet afterward, you'll love the ice cream sandwich with almonds, strawberries, and chocolate packed between two cookie wafers. The creative, colorfully presented food, impeccable service, and festive atmosphere make the Rio Grill a locals' favorite. The colorful artwork and sculptures throughout the restaurant enhance the artistic food presentations. There is even a cup full of crayons and butcher paper over each tablecloth to encourage your own artistic inclinations. The full bar offers cocktails, premium liquors, and a selection of wines by the glass. Rio Grill is open for lunch and dinner and on Sunday for brunch.

Tillie Gorts Café $
111 Central Avenue, Pacific Grove
(831) 373–0335

Long known as the premier vegetarian restaurant on the Peninsula, the menu at Tillie Gorts also features beef and turkey burgers, chicken entrees, sandwiches, soups, and salads. The cafe also features pasta, including a rich spinach and cheese lasagna, spinach ravioli, or fettuccine served with fresh vegetables and your choice of Alfredo or marinara sauce. Sample one of the homemade desserts after dinner. Tillie's serves beer and wine. It is open for breakfast, lunch, and dinner.

English Pubs and Tea Rooms

London Bridge Pub $
Fisherman's Wharf #2, Monterey
(831) 655–2879

This traditional English pub serves up fish and chips made with true Atlantic cod. Other dishes include cottage pie, bangers and mash, seafood salads, and a ploughman's lunch. Stop in anytime for cream tea, coffee, or specialty drinks. In the English manner, join friends for afternoon tea accompanied by scones, cream, and jam. The pub features live entertainment in the evenings, but most people show up for the beer. There's an impressive selection of more than 60 international beers, all served with good cheer at Monterey's only waterfront pub. You'll have a jolly good time at lunch or dinner.

Tuck Box English Tea Room $ no credit cards
Dolores Street between Ocean and 7th Avenues, Carmel
(831) 624–6365, www.tuckbox.com

The Tuck Box looks like a storybook English cottage. Built in 1927, the cozy building is the perfect setting for a breakfast of waffles, pancakes, French toast, or eggs served just the way you like them. The delicious scones, a Carmel tradition for over 50 years, are the perfect light breakfast or snack. They're served with the Tuck Box's own house-made preserves. Lunch fare is light; choose from a variety of sandwiches, salads, or soups. Afternoon tea at the Tuck Box is a perfect respite from sightseeing or shopping. The Tuck Box is open for breakfast and lunch almost every day from 8:00 A.M.

European/Mediterranean

Anton & Michel $$$
Mission Street between Ocean and 7th Avenues, Carmel
(831) 624–2406, www.carmelsbest.com

A fine dining spot for both lunch and dinner, Anton & Michel has been a favorite of locals, restaurant critics, and visitors for more than a decade. The setting is sublime, an elegant and romantic interior with original oil paintings, soft colors, and dramatic windows. Outside on the patio are gracious gardens and two soothing fountains. The well-crafted menu showcases a highly acclaimed rack of lamb in addition to grilled lamb medallions with mint pesto sauce. The catch of the day and other seafood creations are magnificent. Even the most discriminating wine lover will appreciate the award-winning wine list with a good showing of California wines from Napa Valley and Monterey County. The regions of Burgundy and Bordeaux have a prominent place on the wine list as

Quaint architecture distinguishes many Carmel eateries. The Tuck Box is a prime example. PHOTO: ELLIOTT SCHERLING/MONTEREY COUNTY CONVENTION & VISITORS BUREAU

well. Exquisite flaming desserts include bananas Foster and crepes Suzette. The wonderfully dark cocktail lounge is a good meeting place for pre-dinner libations. Lunch and dinner are served.

Fandango $$
223 17th Street, Pacific Grove
(831) 372-3456,
www.fandangorestaurant.com

European country cuisine is presented in an inviting Mediterranean setting at Fandango. Fresh-cut flowers adorn the tables, and a crackling fire warms the place. If weather permits, dine on the cheerful outside patio with colorful, flower-filled window boxes. The earthy scent of fruitwood and mesquite will tempt you to order one of the seafood specialties prepared on the wood-burning grill. Or set your sights on fresh pasta, paella, or couscous. Glacé with raspberry sauce is one of their most tempting desserts. Fandango has a full bar with an exceptional list of wines from Spain, France, Germany, Italy, Algeria, Morocco, and California vineyards. It serves lunch and dinner, and the Sunday brunch is splendid.

Montrio $$
414 Calle Principal, Monterey
(831) 648-8880, www.downtowndining.com

Montrio is in a richly restored 1910 historic firehouse in downtown Monterey. The menu is influenced by the foods of France, Italy, and America. The dining room is simultaneously sophisticated and casual with the feel of an upscale European bistro. The Dungeness crab cakes accompanied by a spicy remoulade are a house specialty. The grilled portobello mushroom with a ragout of vegetables is another excellent choice. Choose from grilled favorites such as rosemary garlic chicken or Black Angus rib-eye cooked to perfection on the wood-burning rotisserie. Numerous side dishes, both unusual and delicious, are presented using beans, grains, and locally grown vegetables.

Desserts at Montrio look and taste like works of art. The excellent wine list includes a few French and Italian selections. A fully stocked bar is available. If you can't make it for lunch or dinner during the week, a spectacular brunch is served on Sunday.

Insiders' Tip

The Tuck Box in Carmel has been using the same recipe to make its popular scones for more than 50 years.

Stokes Restaurant & Bar $$
500 Hartnell Street, Monterey
(831) 373-1110, www.stokesadobe.com

Stokes Restaurant & Bar, located in an adobe structure built in 1833, has an ambiance that speaks well of the friendly people and casual atmosphere that define Monterey. You'll feel comfortable socializing with friends while lingering over a splendid meal. Country Mediterranean cuisine in both small and large plate portions create the menu. Some sample selections of the innovative culinary presentations are grilled lavender-infused pork chop with leek-lemon bread pudding and plum chutney. Relax and enjoy a charming setting and wonderful food. Choose from a specially selected variety of wines from California, France, and Italy. Stokes Restaurant serves lunch and dinner.

Taste Cafe & Bistro $$ no credit cards
1199 Forest Avenue, Pacific Grove
(831) 655-0324, www.tastecafebistro.com

A comfortable mix of high and low tables affords a full view of the open-style kitchen at Taste. Sit back and observe the new chef/owners, Bill Karaki and Jay Dibs, create visually appealing, quality entrees. The original menu of European-influenced, old-world favorites has remained intact during the transition from one group of owners to the next. You are presented with a range of choices such as herb-roasted chicken, grilled rabbit, fresh-made sausage, or salmon filet baked in parchment. For lighter fare, the pasta dishes are exquisite, especially when paired with soup or a crisp salad. Enjoy a sweet ending by choosing either the decadent brioche bread pudding or hazelnut chocolate torte. Taste, open for lunch and dinner, is closed on Monday.

The Village Corner $$
Dolores Street and 6th Avenue, Carmel
(831) 624-3588, www.carmelsbest.com

The quaint family atmosphere, reminiscent of a Mediterranean bistro, and a solid reputation for good food has made the Village Corner a favorite for many years. Dine alfresco by the fireplace on the pleasant outdoor patio. Order chicken, lamb, or your pick of the fresh pasta dishes. Beer and a variety of Monterey County wines are available with your meal. One of the many after-dinner temptations is the incredible chocolate espresso bread pudding. The Village Corner serves lunch and dinner and is also one of the most popular breakfast spots in Carmel.

French

Club XIX $$$$
The Lodge at Pebble Beach, 17-Mile Drive, Pebble Beach
(831) 625-8519, www.pebblebeach.com

French elegance, eclipsed by unparalleled views of Carmel Bay and the legendary 18th green of the Pebble Beach Golf Links, has earned Club XIX a distinguished international reputation. Elegant appetizers include sautéed Monterey Bay abalone and artichoke hearts with truffle vinaigrette. Stunning entrees such as Rabbit Three Ways with chanterelle mushrooms and caramelized shallots and Crisp Skin Black Sea Bass with arugula, carrots, and cumin showcase the chef's mastery of technique. Impeccable, attentive, and gracious service enhances the experience.

Club XIX serves lunch and dinner.

French Poodle $$$$
5th Avenue and Junipero Street, Carmel
(831) 624-8643

The American Academy of Restaurant Sciences has recognized this elegant dinner house as one of the Top 10 French restaurants in the United States. It serves classic, light French cuisine. House specialties include crab legs, duck, abalone, lamb, and fresh fish. One of the most requested appetizers is Les Escargot de Bourgogne, six imported French snails prepared with homemade lemon garlic and shallot butter. Popular entrees include grilled sliced breast of duck in Port wine sauce; Provimi veal T-bone with fresh cream and morel mushrooms; and fresh Morro Bay abalone (when available). French Poodle's famous French Floating Island, a creamy dessert fit for royalty, is unsurpassed. Wine offerings include Port, Sauternes, and Madeira selections. The French Poodle serves dinner only and is closed on Sunday.

Fresh Cream $$$$
99 Pacific Street, Monterey
(831) 375-9798, www.freshcream.com

Since its opening in 1978, Fresh Cream continues to be recognized as one of the Top 100 restaurants in the nation. The stylish interior, dazzling bay view, and impeccable epicurean reputation make this a distinctive favorite. The culinary presentations combine classic French with California flair in a well-balanced mix of meat, poultry, seafood, and vegetarian entrees. The melt-in-your-mouth fillet of ahi tuna, prepared blackened, is served with a delicious pineapple rum butter sauce. A selection of well-chosen California and French wines complement the choice foods featured on the menu. The friendly and knowledgeable servers can help you with your decisions. After dinner, try the Grand Marnier soufflé; it's a masterpiece. Fresh Cream serves dinner only.

La Boheme $$$
Dolores Street between Ocean and 7th Avenues, Carmel
(831) 624-7500, www.laboheme.com

This inviting Carmel restaurant features casual French country decor, a three-course prix fixe menu (the entree selection changes nightly), and attentive service. Each meal begins with a crisp salad, made from organically grown lettuce and vegetables from the Salinas Valley and served family style. The first course is followed by a special soup prepared with the chef's own stock. Entrees range from filet mignon with a Roquefort-wine sauce to Scampi Conquistador, served with a compote made of fresh corn, roasted bell peppers, chili pepper, cilantro, and black beans. A vegetarian plate is available nightly. A choice of tempting desserts, such as chocolate mousse or a light lemon tart, round out an exceptional meal. California and French wine selections feature Bordeaux half-bottles and vintages. La Boheme serves dinner only.

Robert's Bistro $$$
217 Crossroads Boulevard, Carmel
(831) 624–9626

The bistro has a country French ambiance highlighted with graceful archways, exposed wood beam ceilings, a cozy fireplace, and walls like weathered stone. Robert's serves classic bistro cuisine, adding special touches such as Cassoulet a la Robert, a casserole of white beans, grilled duck confit, rabbit sausage, and garlic prawns. Signature dishes include roasted duckling with wild cherry sauce and grilled Holland Dover sole with a lemon-caper sauce that is presented whole on a platter and deboned at your table. The fish, flown in fresh from England, is exquisite. You won't be able to pass up house specialty Pithivier, an almond creme-filled, circular puff pastry drizzled with raspberry sauce. Robert's Bistro is open daily for dinner.

Italian

Allegro Pizzeria $
3770 The Barnyard, Carmel
(831) 626–5454,
www.allegrogourmetpizzeria.com

Flavorful fare has made Allegro a local favorite for lunch and dinner. A children's menu offers rotelli served with a variety of sauces. Allegro also offers special heart-healthy recipes such as garlic chicken, pasta with marinara, and pasta primavera. The light eater will be pleased with the selection of salads, which include Mediterranean Chicken Salad and Salade Nicoise. Several varieties of calzone and pizza are popular choices. The spinach pesto pizza or Del Mare, prepared with rock shrimp, sea scallops, garlic, chives, and mozzarella are standouts. Beer and wine are served.

Cibo Ristorante Italiano $$$
301 Alvarado Street, Monterey
(831) 649–8151, www.cibo.com

Drop into Cibo (pronounced chee-bo) and you've dropped into one of the area's only restaurant/bars that also serves up nightly live jazz (except Monday). Having undergone an extensive remodel in late 2001, the casually elegant setting showcases photography, paintings, sculpture, and handblown glass by local and Bay Area artists. Owned and operated by Rose and Mario Catalano, mother and son, Cibo specializes in modern adaptations of old family recipes that reflect their Sicilian heritage. Carpaccio, Bresaola, gnocchi, risotto and pasta, beef, veal, chicken, and seafood, all prepared under the supervision of Chef Rose, provide ample choices. This establishment offers an extensive list of Italian and California wines as well as cordials and creative cocktails. Live music is featured every night (except Monday) in a central area where it can be enjoyed by patrons of the bar and restaurant. Sunday, Tuesday, Wednesday, and Thursday the live jazz begins at 8:30 P.M. and runs through 12:30 A.M., with quieter sets during dinner hours. Friday and Saturday, the music is decidedly livelier with jazz, R&B, soul, and funk from 10:00 P.M. to 1:30 A.M. Cibo serves dinner only from 5:00 to 10:00 P.M. The bar is open 5:00 P.M. to 2:00 A.M.

Pasta Mia Trattoria $$
481 Lighthouse Avenue, Pacific Grove
(831) 375–7709

Try to reserve the table in what was once the restaurant's foyer. Surrounded on three sides with windows and looking out over Pacific Grove's Lighthouse Avenue, it's perfect for two. The food, in a word, is outstanding. The menu features a good selection of antipasti including Melazane

CLOSE-UP

With a passion for food, family, and friends, Rose Catalano has left her mark on the Monterey dining landscape.

Monterey is home to a number of Sicilian families who came here after World War II in pursuit of a better life. At 17, Rose traveled with her mother and three sisters from Mondello (near Palermo) to Monterey where her father had settled into the fishing trade.

Having cooked beside her mother since she was a very young child, Rose decided to look for work in a local restaurant. "My mother, Rosalia, always set up a small pot for me so I could make what she was making," recalls Rose. "I learned by doing and by following my mother. She loved making people happy through her wonderful food. I came to enjoy that too."

Not long after arriving in Monterey, she went to work at Neptune's Table, an Italian family-owned restaurant. (Coincidentally, it was located on the lot that holds Cibo Ristorante Italiano, a restaurant that Rose opened in 1989.) After 14 years, Rose left to work at the Monterey Hyatt. Watching and learning during the next 22 years, she held on to the dream of opening her own restaurant. "I stole everything with my eyes," says Rose. "I put everything away in my head. I knew that I could make people happy with my food and by giving them something different."

Rose and her two sons, with the support of husband Johnnie, established Cibo Ristorante Italiano. Rose joined the Chef's Association in 1990 to increase her knowledge and skills and is the restaurant's chef to this day. She uses family recipes handed down through the generations and infuses them with her own style, a trademark of the restaurant. A family affair, son Mario Catalano is the restaurant's general manager and introduced and manages Cibo's nightly live jazz program.

The extensive menu is innovative with flavorful entrees like Pollo Nina, named after Johnnie's mother, and Filetto Alla Siena and Vitello Ariana, named after Rose's grandchildren—Mario's daughters. Her signature lasagna is in high demand with locals and the Gnocchi Gran Festa is a personal favorite. Each of the many antipasti, pastas, pizzas, and entrees is presented artfully by a professional and attentive staff. They also offer a wine list with an extensive selection of fine California and Italian vintages.

Rose's dream was to create something unique where her love of cooking—and people—could be put to work. She and son Mario have grown Cibo into the type of establishment where other restaurateurs, especially those of Italian heritage, enjoy dining. In fact, although Cibo is open for

Rose Catalano with son Mario. Together they bring the taste of Sicily to the Monterey Peninsula.

PHOTO: © BATISTA MOON STUDIO (WWW.BATISTAMOON.COM)

dinner only, Rose is often requested to prepare special luncheons for these discriminating entrepreneurs.

Rose Catalano views every day as a challenge and an opportunity to be a little better at what she does. In November 2001, Cibo underwent an extensive remodel. The decor features fine art—paintings, photography, handblown glass, and sculpture by local and Bay Area artists. "My joy is having my friends, family, and customers come by to eat my food and enjoy the beautiful art and atmosphere." She visits Sicily at least once each year to eat at the restaurants of her friends and "steal" more ideas with her eyes, recipes that she brings back to the delight of her loyal patrons.

alla Mia, a savory blend of eggplant with tomato sauce, basil, and asiago cheese. Entrees, served with your choice of soup or salad, include Ravioli Grande (ricotta cheese and chives with tomato meat sauce) and Linguini alla Puttanesca (a southern sauce of black olives, capers, tomatoes, anchovies, and spicy red peppers). Don't overlook Nero & Bianco—black and white linguini with scallops, caviar, cream, and chives! House specialties include dishes such as Scampi al Modo Mio, prawns in a champagne cream sauce served over a bed of homemade fettuccine. The homemade desserts are excellent, especially the tiramisu and the chocolate torte. Beer and wine are served. Pasta Mia serves dinner only.

Tutto Mondo Trattoria $$
Dolores Street between Ocean and 7th Avenues, Carmel
(831) 624–8977, www.mondo.com

Tutto Mondo, a true Italian old-world trattoria, offers the romance of Italy to visitors of Carmel and some of Carmel's famous citizens (it is a favorite of Clint Eastwood, among others). Lovers of Italian food will treasure the cozy atmosphere that is both welcoming and relaxed. Select regional specialties from both North and South Italy, such as homemade ravioli, lasagna, and other pasta dishes combined with various sauces. Light eaters can choose from a selection of insalate, bruschetta, antipasti, and minestre. Those needing something more substantial can feast on homemade pizza or veal and seafood specialties. Italian wines, especially well-known Chiantis, are favored on the wine list, along with a good selection of French and California choices. Lunch and dinner are served at this award-winning Italian restaurant.

Seafood

Bubba Gump Shrimp Co. $$
720 Cannery Row, Monterey
(831) 373–1884, www.bubbagump.com

This theme restaurant, with its re-created scenes and props from the popular movie, is one the whole family will enjoy for lunch or dinner. Its menu boasts "down-home cooking with down-home warmth." Enjoy shrimp kabobs, shrimp scampi, shrimp cocktail, shrimp gumbo, butterfly shrimp, and peel and eat shrimp—but that's not all. There is fresh Pacific Northwest salmon, crab legs, bone-in rib-eye steaks, roasted pork chops, and the bucket o' lobster tails. The Alabama Hula Pie made with macadamia nuts, chocolate ice cream, whipped cream, and caramel is a fabulous finish. There is also a kids' menu with foods the little ones will love. Adults will appreciate the gorgeous view of the Monterey Bay and Bubba Gump's full bar.

Cafe Fina $$
47 Fisherman's Wharf #1, Monterey
(831) 372–5200, www.cafefina.com

A popular dining spot on the wharf, Cafe Fina is owned by the Mercurios, a third-generation Italian family. Dig your fork into appetizers like deep-fried artichoke hearts or oysters Rockefeller. Don't pass up one of the 8-inch authentic Italian pizzettes baked in a Milanese wood-burning brick oven. Cafe Fina makes its own pasta and covers it with fresh herb sauces. Daily specials include tempting concoctions made with snapper, calamari steak, salmon, swordfish, and other fresh seafood. All fish entrees are served with two fresh vegetables and pasta. Veal, chicken, lamb, and steak are non-seafood entree alternatives. California, French, and Italian wines comprise the wine list. Enjoy an after-dinner drink of Amaro or Grappa from the full bar. Cafe Fina serves lunch and dinner.

The Fish Hopper $$
700 Cannery Row, Monterey
(831) 372–8543, www.fishhopper.com

The Fish Hopper's view of the Monterey Bay is one of the best, and you can enjoy it from the oyster bar, dining room, or outside deck. For starters select the Crab Cakes Monterey or the award-winning clam chowder. Signature dishes include Fish Hopper Combo (a deep-fried mix of prawns, cod, and calamari) and The Hopper Mixed Grill (prime top sirloin, baby back ribs, and jumbo prawns). Both dishes are served with garlic mashed potatoes. Seafood prepared a number of ways is also featured, along with pasta, beef, ribs, and chicken. The Fish Hopper has a full bar with a drinks menu featuring its famous Bucket of Fire, a blend of island spirits and tropical juices topped with a flaming sugar cube. Lunch and dinner are served.

The Fishwife $$
1996 Sunset Drive, Pacific Grove
(831) 375–7107
789 Trinity Avenue, Seaside
(831) 394–2027, www.fishwife.com

The Fishwife is known for flavorful, fresh food at affordable prices. Located near Asilomar, the restaurant is an ideal place to have dinner after taking a sunset walk along the beach. California cuisine with a touch of Caribbean influence is reflected in offerings like Prawns Belize and Snapper Lafayette. Feast on fresh chowder, grilled oysters, sautéed calamari, one of several seafood pastas, or a Sea Garden Salad. The famous Key lime pie is the perfect conclusion to a pleasurable meal. Well-chosen, moderately priced, premium California wines are poured by the glass or bottle. Sunday brunch features seafood Benedict and other egg dishes. The mimosas made with fresh-squeezed orange juice are the brunch beverage of choice! The Fishwife is open daily for lunch and dinner.

Monterey's Fisherman's Wharf abounds with restaurants and cafes offering fresh crab and other seafood from area waters. PHOTO: RANDY TUNNELL, © 2002 FISHERMAN'S WHARF ASSOCIATION

Monterey's Fish House $$
2114 Del Monte, Monterey
(831) 373–4647

The homelike, jovial atmosphere at Monterey's Fish House will win you over, as will the California-style cuisine served in generous portions. Begin with the fresh barbecued oysters or sautéed mussels served at the horseshoe bar. You can also opt for the house-made soups and salads. The menu features fresh Sicilian pasta, most prepared with seafood; fish, including snapper, sole, salmon, and swordfish; and meats such as rib-eye steak, pork chops, and chicken cooked on an oak barbecue pit. Death by Chocolate cake for dessert needs no further description. The Fish House has a good wine list featuring California wines and champagne, all available by the glass. It serves lunch and dinner.

Rappa's Seafood Restaurant $$
End of Fisherman's Wharf #1, Monterey
(831) 372–7562, www.rappas.com

Rappa's, a Monterey landmark, offers sensational views of the Monterey Bay. Its motto of "if it's not fresh, we don't serve it" assures you of the freshest fish possible. Choose (as available) Monterey Bay salmon, sea bass, or Alaskan halibut prepared flame broiled or blackened. House specialties include Rappa's famous cioppino, a flavorful blend of herbs, spices, and tomato with golden crab legs, shrimp, clams, mussels, halibut, calamari, salmon, and bay scallops. Combination platters of fish and shellfish are other popular choices. Pasta selections are also good, especially the crab ravioli prepared with baby shrimp in a light tomato sauce. Enjoy a piece of amaretto devil's food fudge cake with espresso as the finishing touch to a memorable meal. Diners can meet for a predinner drink at Rappa's cocktail lounge. Bayside lunch and dinner are served.

Sardine Factory $$$$
701 Wave Street, Monterey
(831) 373–3775, www.sardinefactory.com

The Sardine Factory, which fostered the resurgence of Cannery Row, has satisfied locals, visitors, and celebrities with its fine food and wine, exquisite desserts, and impeccable service for more than 30 years. A winner of *Wine Spectator*'s Grand Award and Distinguished Restaurants of North America Award, the restaurant houses an impressive collection of 30,000 bottles of wine with 1,200 labels. Four distinctive dining rooms highlight the Sardine Factory dining experience. Take the canopy-covered steps to the Cannery Row Room and elevated Grill Room and bar, all adorned with rich wood, soft leather, and walls reflecting the area's history with photographs, paintings, and documents. The Wine Cellar Banquet Room contains a 25-foot-long table and 16th-century antiques. The intimate Captain's Room glows from the light of the fireplace and candlelit tables. In the glass-domed Conservatory a center statue, fully surrounded by lush greenery, sits beneath a crystal chandelier. The menu features appetizers such as "The World Famous" abalone bisque, which was served at the Taste of America for President Reagan's Inaugural. For intermezzo order fresh fruit sorbet elegantly served in a graceful carved-ice swan. House specialties include fresh swordfish with Catalina sun-dried tomato tapenade and seared ahi tuna crusted with black sesame seeds. Sardine Factory desserts are also splendid. We recommend you try the delectable crème brûlée.

Stillwater Bar & Grill $$$
17-Mile Drive, Pebble Beach
(831) 625–8524, www.pebblebeach.com

Join the fun in this casual, two-level dinner spot overlooking the legendary 18th green of the Pebble Beach Golf Links. Be sure to select something from the raw bar, offering freshly shucked oysters, clams, mussels, and other seafood delicacies. Although this is primarily a seafood grill, the fresh fish menu options include tempting appetizers such as House Smoked Salmon Carpaccio and Osetra Caviar with Lemon Crème Fraîche. Feeling extravagant? How about a Seven-Year-Old Monterey Bay Red Abalone with potato-parsnip risotto and black truffle vinaigrette?

Your knowledgeable waitperson can readily suggest pairings from the award-winning wine list. Stillwater Bar & Grill serves breakfast, lunch, and dinner.

Insiders' Tip

The Sardine Factory restaurant, which opened in 1968, signaled the beginning of a rebirth for Cannery Row.

Superb views and excellent food are the hallmark of restaurants along Cannery Row and on Fisherman's Wharf. PHOTO: ELLIOTT SCHERLING/MONTEREY COUNTY CONVENTION & VISITORS BUREAU

Take-Out

Bagel Bakery $
452 Alvarado Street, Monterey
(831) 372–5242
1132 Forest Avenue, Pacific Grove
(831) 649–6272
2160 California Avenue, Sand City
(831) 392–1581
539 Carmel Rancho, Carmel
(831) 625–5180

The Bagel Bakery has been providing quality food at reasonable prices since 1976. It offers omelet-on-a-bagel breakfast sandwiches, wraparounds (peaches and cream cheese wrapped in a bagel crust) for breakfast or lunch, and special combination bagel sandwiches. Basic bagels come in a variety of flavors including plain, poppy seed, blueberry, sesame seed, onion, garlic, salt, pumpernickel, whole wheat, and superseed. Top your bagel with plain or flavored cream cheese such as herb, walnut-olive, date-nut, strawberry, garden veggie, and lox spread. Bagel Bakery also sells muffins, cookies, and juices. The Sand City location has drive-through service.

Goodies $
518 Lighthouse Avenue, Pacific Grove
(831) 655–3663

Goodies has uncommonly good deli-type foods including 18 sandwiches and 10 types of salads. Made fresh daily, salad selections might include breast of chicken, Caesar with pasta, red-skin potato, curried rice pilaf, or tuna-stuffed tomato on greens. Goodies also has hot foods such as quiche, pastries, tortas, knishes, veggie burritos, and soup.

Santa Lucia Market $
484-A Washington Street, Monterey
(831) 333–1111

A European-style deli and market, Santa Lucia Market carries imported German and Italian meats, a variety of European cheeses, and a host of European imported specialty food products. It also stocks organic produce and grocery foods in addition to coffee, tea, and both imported and domestic wine. Gourmet salads, desserts, and pastries are also sold. Design your own sandwiches choosing from several kinds of bread, spreads, condiments, meats, and cheeses. The market also has sushi, a variety of entrees, and pizza.

World Flavors

Epsilon $$
422 Tyler Street, Monterey
(831) 655–8108, www.mbay.net/~petros

In downtown Monterey, Epsilon has become a favorite of Greek food enthusiasts. Appealing appetizers are the traditional Greek finger foods such as dolmas or gyros. Entrees, served with a tasty Greek salad, offer choices such as perfectly grilled lamb shanks or the crispy and creamy spanakopita. Both are Insider favorites. You will be especially tempted by the baklava for dessert. Epsilon serves lunch and dinner.

India's Clay Oven $$
150 Del Monte Avenue, Second Floor, Monterey
(831) 373–2529

Escape to India's Clay Oven for lunch or dinner and sample authentic Indian cuisine. The restaurant, in downtown Monterey across from the DoubleTree complex, serves vegetarian and nonvegetarian foods. Popular starters include pakora (crispy vegetable fritters) and samosa (stuffed vegetables). A particularly savory entree is the tandoori-roasted chicken, lamb, and seafood baked in a clay oven, an Indian tradition for thousands of years. The lunch buffet features 18 different choices; it's all you can eat of exotic foods from a variety of regions in India.

Pablo's Mexican Restaurant $
1184 Forest Avenue, Pacific Grove
(831) 646–8888

This casual place serves Mexican food using no animal fats in the preparation. The result is delicious, wholesome food for lunch or dinner. Pablo's serves plentiful portions and offers daily specials along with tried-and-true combination plates. Try one of the house specialties—red snapper tacos, seafood enchiladas, or Snapper Vera Cruz. The chicken and cheese enchiladas are especially tasty, as are the tostadas. Served a la carte, the burrito is a meal in itself. For dessert, try the homemade flan—it's rich, creamy, and very delicious! Pablo's serves a variety of beer and wine.

Passionfish $$
701 Lighthouse Avenue, Pacific Grove
(831) 655–3311, www.passionfish.net

Passionfish is well known to Peninsula diners as a place for creative, innovative dishes and an ever-changing menu. This downtown Pacific Grove gem is owned and operated by Ted and Cindy Walter. A lifelong chef, Ted has an especially deft touch with seafood. But the wine list is what really sets Passionfish apart. Here is a staggering array of vintages from all over the globe, and the knowledgeable staff can help you pair just the perfect wine with your entree choice. The restaurant also maintains a very active wine club with a

Al fresco dining is very popular on the Monterey Peninsula. Many restaurants provide outdoor heaters to ward off evening chills. PHOTO: ELLIOTT SCHERLING/MONTEREY COUNTY CONVENTION & VISITORS BUREAU

newsletter and monthly wine flights paired with special menus. Passionfish is open for dinner only and is closed on Tuesday.

Worth the Drive

Cielo at Ventana Inn & Spa $$$$
Highway 1, 28 miles south of Carmel, Big Sur
(831) 667–4242, www.ventanainn.com

Absorb the famed 50-mile panorama of the Big Sur coast while dining on eclectic California cuisine at this internationally known Big Sur resort. Attention to the little details is what creates perfection. Innovative use of vegetables and herbs from the on-site organic garden is what sets Cielo apart from other restaurants. The menu highlights fresh local fish and meats; signature dishes include seared ahi tuna served with porcini mushrooms and prime New York steak served with blue cheese potato gratin. Freshly baked bread and elegant dessert creations from the on-site bakery are also on the menu. A stellar wine list of California and imported wines concentrates on vintages from the Central Coast. Cielo, which means "heaven" or "sky" in Italian, serves lunch and dinner daily; we recommend Cielo as a divine culinary adventure.

The Covey at Quail Lodge $$$$
8205 Valley Greens Drive, Carmel Valley
(831) 620–8860, www.peninsula.com

Relax and enjoy a Euro-Californian inspired dinner overlooking a glistening lake, splashing fountains, lush gardens, and splendid golfing greens. The menu changes daily, but you'll usually find a sumptuous variety of fish such as snapper, sole, salmon, and sea bass. Center-cut veal loin, roast rack of lamb, and New York steak are delectable possibilities for the meat entrees. The wine list renders a full page of half-bottles, highlighted by an award-winning selection of California and Monterey County wines. Desserts fall under the category of unforgettable dining pleasures. The Covey serves dinner only and has a recommended dress code: jackets for men and no jeans, shorts, or athletic attire.

Nepenthe $$$
Highway 1, 28 miles south of Carmel, Big Sur
(831) 667–2345, www.nepenthebigsur.com

Family-owned and operated since 1949, Nepenthe maintains a commitment to simple yet delicious food. Spacious decks overlook the Pacific Ocean, the Santa Lucia Mountains, and a 40-mile inspirational view of the Big Sur coastline. Nepenthe's famous Ambrosia burger, made with a special grind of beef, is served on a French roll with Nepenthe sauce and a choice of three salads. Vegetarians can experience the legend, too, by ordering the tofu burger, prepared in the same manner (the secret's in the sauce). Another winner is Lolly's Roast Chicken, stuffed with an aromatic sage dressing and served with cranberry sauce. The homemade desserts are abundant helpings of four-layer chocolate cake, apple pie, and triple berry pie, just to name a few. Lunch and dinner are served. Breakfast and lunch are also served at the open-air cafe, Keva, from March to early January (weather permitting).

Phil's Fish Market & Eatery $
7600 Sandholdt Road, Moss Landing
(831) 633–2152

It's unpretentious, informal, and downright funky, but that's what makes this Moss Landing restaurant charming and fun. The entrance to the restaurant is through the fish market; whole fish on ice are everywhere. You can't go wrong with any of the fresh seafood selections here! The Sicilian artichokes, stuffed with bread crumbs and whole garlic cloves and poached in white wine and garlic, are tremendous. Pasta lovers will appreciate the huge platter of linguini smothered with olive oil, garlic, olives, capers, mushrooms, white wine, and Dungeness crab. Phil's serves beer and wine. It's open for lunch and dinner daily.

Rocky Point Restaurant $$$$
Highway 1, 12 miles south of Carmel
(831) 624–2933, www.rocky-point.com

Location, location, location . . . Rocky Point has it. This landmark restaurant, serving breakfast, lunch, and dinner, is high on top of a bluff overlooking the mighty Pacific Ocean. Floor-to-ceiling glass on the coastal side of the building means that every seat in the house has a magnificent ocean view. Weather permitting, outdoor seating allows you an even closer oceanside table. Enjoy a meal while watching for spouting whales, sea lions, otters, pelicans, and shore birds. Lunch features lighter fare including soups, salads, and a selection of South of the Border dishes. After sunset you can still enjoy an illuminated view of rocks, cliffs, and ocean. The dinner menu features steaks and fish barbecued over hardwood charcoal and mesquite. Choose from swordfish, salmon, lobster tail, prawns, chicken, pork ribs, lamb chops, or one of several cuts of beef. All dinners include an old-fashioned relish tray, toasted cheddar cheese bread, Boston clam chowder or green salad, and a large baked potato with cheddar cheese butter. For steak-house style food in an unbeatable locale, stop in at Rocky Point.

Sole Mio Caffé Trattoria $$
3 Del Fino Place, Carmel Valley
(831) 659–9119

Prepare yourself for romance at this authentic Southern Italian restaurant tucked away in the village of Carmel Valley. A tiny patio enshrouded by flowering vines creates a garden setting. The addition of umbrella tables and cozy gas heaters make this a year-round option. Adding to the ambiance inside are cheery Mediterranean colors, checkered tablecloths, and Chianti bottles with drippy candles. Antique cooking utensils, straw baskets, and garlic strands accent the Italian decor. The food is no less appealing. A sun-dried tomato sauce and Italian bread are delivered to your table upon arrival. Pasta dishes include mouth-watering crab ravioli in a shrimp-lobster sauce or light gnocchi with a pleasing tomato-basil sauce. For those with a hearty appetite, entrees of seafood, veal, and chicken can be added to a meal of pasta. For dessert try the lemony Torta De La Nona. Sole Mio serves wine only, an excellent selection from Italy and California. It is open for lunch and dinner daily except Monday.

The Whole Enchilada $
Highway 1 and Moss Landing Road, Moss Landing
(831) 633-3038, www.wenchilada.com

For the owners of The Whole Enchilada, a Mexican meal is a melding of regional cuisine with geographic and historical influences. For example, the menu is influenced by old family recipes and the ample supply of fresh seafood from the Monterey Bay. High quality is the hallmark of this restaurant. Everything on the menu is made fresh daily. House specialties include Seafood Sopes, a delicious blend of jumbo prawns and crabmeat topped with refried beans and salsa. The Oaxacan Chicken Mole Tamales are wrapped in banana leaves, which seep a unique flavor into the tamales. Also try the chicken Chile Verde tamales. There is a full-service bar. The view of Moss Landing Harbor and live music and dancing on the weekends make this a great place to unwind. The Whole Enchilada is open for lunch and dinner every day.

Nightlife

Bars and Pubs
Billiards
Clubs
Coffeehouses
Comedy Clubs
Movie Houses

When we told friends we were working on the Nightlife chapter for this book, a common response was a sarcastic, "It will be a short chapter, won't it?" That'll give you a hint of how many locals perceive nightlife on the mostly quiet Monterey Peninsula.

It's true that compared to many larger urban areas, such as San Francisco and San Jose to the north, the Monterey Peninsula does not have a highly spirited night scene. Part of the reason can be traced back to the roots of Carmel and Pacific Grove, both of which have histories of imposing near-Puritanical restrictions on such lurid activities as drinking alcohol or playing raucous music. Monterey, however, has long been a center of nightly entertainment for, first, the merchants and laborers of the sea and, second, the soldiers stationed at Fort Ord. Readers of John Steinbeck's *Cannery Row* are familiar with the types of late-night entertainment that Monterey has historically offered. Today, even with both the canneries and the army base long gone, the Monterey Peninsula nightlife still provides a smattering of activities to please locals and visitors looking for a night on the town.

Since the Peninsula is a tourist destination, you'll find an ample supply of bars and pubs, a number of which are inside the major hotels and leading restaurants that populate the area. For live music and dancing, the choices are more limited. Still, there seems to be a sufficient number of late-night clubs to meet the not-so-high demands of local night owls. In fact, over the last few years, a number of clubs have opened and then suddenly closed their doors due to lack of community support. As the California State University at Monterey Bay continues to grow, locals hope the area will be able to support a couple more live music and dance venues. Notable nighttime choices for the teen crowd are especially lacking, but there are coffeehouses, movie theaters, and other entertainment choices to draw out people of all ages for an enjoyable night.

Note that the legal drinking age in California is 21, and minors are prohibited in most bars and pubs. Also, smoking is prohibited in nearly all indoor public establishments in the state, including bars (see our Close-up).

In this chapter we provide a list of some of the most popular Peninsula nightspots, arranged by type of activity and, where numbers warrant, by locale. This list is by no means exhaustive, and the details regarding what venues offer which entertainment on what nights change frequently. We recommend that while in town you check out the local newspapers (*The Monterey County Herald* and *The Pine Cone*) and entertainment weeklies (*Coast Weekly* and *The Sun*) for a list of the current nighttime activities (see our Media chapter for more about these publications). Have fun, but be safe and careful!

Bars and Pubs

Listed here is a sampling of Monterey Peninsula bars and pubs, including sports bars and microbreweries. A few of these establishments provide live or DJ music on the side, but the more dynamic music and dancing establishments are listed separately in this chapter under the heading "Clubs."

Monterey

Britannia Arms
444 Alvarado Street, Monterey
(831) 656–9543

At Britannia Arms, you'll find a comfortable tavern with plenty of hearty beers (24 drafts, including Guinness) and good English fare like cottage pie or bangers and mash, along with American choices. You'll find live music on Friday and Saturday, karaoke on Sunday and Wednesday, and a fun trivia contest on Thursday nights.

Bulldog British Pub
611 Lighthouse Avenue, Monterey
(831) 372–5565

Great Britain comes to Monterey at this small New Monterey neighborhood bar. You'll find plenty of English ales as well as a variety of British menu items such as shepherd's pie or bangers and mash. Darts are the game of choice at the Bulldog. Night owls will appreciate the fact that breakfast is served all hours. The Bulldog British Pub is open nightly until 2:00 A.M. but the kitchen closes weeknights at 11:00 P.M.

Casa Cafe & Bar
700 Munras Avenue, Monterey
(831) 375–2411

In the Casa Munras Garden Hotel, the Casa Cafe & Bar is a rather quiet but popular gathering spot for downtown locals and hotel guests to mix and mingle after work or on weekend evenings. There's a low-key atmosphere that allows for friendly conversation and a relaxing evening. You can enjoy live easy-listening music Friday and Saturday nights until 11:00 P.M.

Characters Sports Bar & Grill
350 Calle Principal, Monterey
(831) 647–4234

Located in the Monterey Marriott hotel, Characters is a lively downtown sports bar full of sports memorabilia and big screen TVs to catch a variety of professional and college events. The full bar features a wide selection of beers and ales, and the bar snacks and grill fare are rather good, with complimentary appetizers during weekday happy hours. DJ dance music is provided Friday nights. There is karaoke on Tuesday, Wednesday, Thursday, and Saturday evenings. Characters is open until 2:00 A.M.

Crown & Anchor
150 W. Franklin Street, Monterey
(831) 649–6496
www.crownandanchor.net

This downtown establishment was recently voted the most authentic English pub in Monterey. Models of old sailing ships and other nautical artifacts provide an ideal atmosphere. The 20 beers on tap include English ales and Irish stouts, as well as pilsners and microbrews. You'll also find nice single-malt scotches, smooth bourbons, and tasty Ports and wines. Plus, there's a full menu of traditional pub fare and great burgers.

El Palomar of Monterey
724 Abrego Street, Monterey
(831) 372–1032

Margaritas and Mexican beer are the chart toppers at El Palomar, a Mexican seafood restaurant that showcases a full bar with ample seating if you just want to drop in for some nachos and a cold one. The indoor setting is cantina-casual, while the open patio has a cozy fire pit, perfect for cuddling or relaxing on a pleasant evening. Acoustic Latin music adds to the cantina atmosphere on Saturday and Sunday nights. The bar at El Palomar is open until 11:00 P.M. on Friday and Saturday, but closes at 9:30 P.M. Sunday through Thursday.

El Torito
600 Cannery Row, Monterey
(831) 373–0611

This Mexican restaurant chain specializes in Margaritas of many flavors. It's a great happy-hour spot for inexpensive food and drink. A big plus is that you're right on the water on Cannery Row with great bayside views. El Torito is open until midnight on Friday and Saturday and until 11:00 P.M. Sunday through Thursday.

The Fish Hopper
700 Cannery Row, Monterey
(831) 372–8543

For a festive happy hour or early nightcap after a stroll down Cannery Row, consider The Fish Hopper. This popular restaurant has a large bar that offers many tropical specialties to enjoy indoors or on the outside patio. Take advantage of the great views during the weekday 4:00 to 7:00 P.M. happy hour, with inexpensive drinks and

> **Insiders' Tip**
>
> Try one of the many splendid Monterey County red or white wines during your stay on the Peninsula.

tasty seafood treats like shrimp cocktail and fresh oysters. The Fish Hopper bar usually closes by 9:00 P.M. on weekdays and 10:00 P.M. on weekends, depending on the level of restaurant activity.

Knuckles Historical Sports Bar
1 Old Golf Course Road, Monterey
(831) 372–1234

At the Hyatt Monterey, Knuckles is the biggest and typically the most active sports bar on the Peninsula. It has 17 TVs, some with satellite hookups, to provide a wealth of sports programming year-round. Local sports fans love the free popcorn and peanuts to enjoy with their choice of 16 beers, plus there's an extensive pub menu. The full bar has ample seating to accommodate big crowds. Two pool tables add to the fun. Knuckles is open until midnight Sunday to Thursday, and until 1:00 A.M. on Friday and Saturday.

Lallapalooza
474 Alvarado Street, Monterey
(831) 887–1014

Lallapalooza is a stylish martini bar and restaurant that caters to a young professional crowd that appreciates a well-made libation—including 14 kinds of martinis. Try the Classic, cold and dry, or the house special Lallapalooza martini with a citrus flair. The Big American Menu offers a choice of appetizers, salads, steaks, and pastas. Lallapalooza is open nightly until midnight and occasionally features live acoustic music.

Lighthouse Bar and Grill
281 Lighthouse Avenue, Monterey
(831) 373–4488

This casual neighborhood bar caters to the gay and lesbian community and welcomes everyone. A pool table provides friendly diversions, and the Sunday beer bust, with cut-rate brews, is a local favorite. Monday Night Football brings in a lot of people during the season. Lighthouse has a full bar, good grill fare, and a fun and friendly crowd. It's open daily until 2:00 A.M.

London Bridge Pub
Municipal Wharf #2, Monterey
(831) 655–2879

The London Bridge Pub offers more than 70 beers, festive games of darts and cribbage, and a traditional English pub menu—right at the entrance to Wharf #2. There's even a tea room in the back for traditional cream tea. The latest craze is "The Smarty Pants Show," a Monday night trivia game with lots of fun and prizes. Thursday is open-mike night and Friday and Saturday feature live music. The bar is usually open until midnight nightly and the kitchen serves food until 11:00 P.M. Friday and Saturday and 10:00 P.M. other nights.

Monterey Jacks Fish House and Sports Bar
711 Cannery Row, Monterey
(831) 655–4947

This upstairs sports bar and fish house in the heart of Cannery Row is frequented largely by a local crowd, so come prepared to root for the 49ers, Giants, and other San Francisco Bay area teams while dining on some good local seafood. Play Foosball or video games when the pros aren't in action. Monterey Jacks is open nightly until 11:00 P.M.

Montrio
414 Calle Principal, Monterey
(831) 648–8880

Montrio restaurant has a great little bar with intimate seating that's perfect for a quiet drink and sweet dessert after the movies or theater. There's also a wonderful wine list with a range of choices by the glass or bottle. Montrio is open until 11:00 P.M. on Friday and Saturday and 10:00 P.M. Sunday through Thursday.

Peter B.'s Brewpub
2 Portola Plaza Monterey
(831) 649–4511 Ext. 138

Nestled in the back corner of the DoubleTree Hotel is Monterey's favorite microbrewery. Try one of the eight Carmel Brewery exclusives—the pilsner is highly recommended—while you watch the brewmaster at work. Pizza and other pub fare are served daily until 1:00 A.M., and a happy hour is held weekdays from 5:00 to 6:30 P.M. Pool tables and plenty of sports on TV make for a lively evening.

Sandbar & Grill
Municipal Wharf #2, Monterey
(831) 373–2818

Visitors are often surprised to find a true piano bar right under Municipal Wharf #2 in Monterey. The Sandbar & Grill is a small, cozy restaurant with a great harbor view, full bar, and the soothing sounds of a live pianist Friday and Saturday evenings. It's open until midnight Sunday through Thursday and until 1:00 A.M. Friday and Saturday. There's also a fun happy hour from 4:00 to 6:00 P.M. Monday through Friday with inexpensive drinks and half-price appetizers.

Tarpy's Roadhouse
2999 Monterey-Salinas Highway, Monterey
(831) 647–1444

Got romance on the mind? Here's a great out-of-the-way restaurant and bar for a quiet after-dinner (or after-movie) drink for two. Tarpy's is in a historic stone house about 2.5 miles east of Highway 1 on the Monterey-Salinas Highway (Highway 68). It has a cozy atmosphere and a great wine list, full bar, and warm fireplace. The bar closes with the restaurant, which means most evenings by 11:00 P.M.

The Wharfside Restaurant
Fisherman's Wharf, Monterey
(831) 375–3956

Although a number of the Fisherman's Wharf restaurants have full bars that provide a nice spot for an evening drink, the downstairs bar at the Wharfside is perhaps the most popular. The atmosphere is upscale, and the appetizers are downright delicious. The weeknight happy hours include free pizza. Live music is provided Friday evenings.

Pacific Grove

Peppers Mexicali Cafe
170 Forest Avenue, Pacific Grove
(831) 373–6892

A very popular local Mexican restaurant and hangout, Peppers serves beer and wine only in its friendly, cantina-style bar. Enjoy the neighborhood ambiance with some nachos and one of the many microbrewed or Mexican beers or a tasty wine Margarita. Peppers serves more than 20 local wines by the glass and makes a nice fruity sangria. It's open until 9:30 P.M. Sunday, Monday, Wednesday, and Thursday and until 10:30 P.M. Friday and Saturday. Peppers is closed on Tuesday.

Tinnery at the Beach
Ocean View Boulevard and 17th Street, Pacific Grove
(831) 646–1040

One of the few full bars in previously dry Pacific Grove, the Tinnery provides a relaxing atmosphere to enjoy the evening—with a great ocean view. Live music, primarily light jazz and acoustic rock, is provided Wednesday through Saturday nights and during the Wednesday happy hour from 5:00 to 7:00 P.M. Other weeknights, happy hour runs from 4:00 to 6:00 P.M. with a complimentary buffet. The Tinnery is open until midnight Sunday through Thursday and until 1:00 A.M. Friday and Saturday.

Carmel

You aren't going to find too many towns with a quieter nightlife than Carmel. City ordinances prohibit such wild activities as loud music or the dastardly game of pool-which begins with P, which rhymes with T, which stands for trouble in By-the-Sea City. Seriously, though, within Carmel proper you'll find some great places to enjoy a quiet evening, indoors or out, with a refreshing drink, good food, and delightful company. Outside of the city proper,

The Sandbar & Grill offers a cozy piano bar and great views right under Municipal Wharf #2 in Monterey. PHOTO: JOHN MORBA

such as at The Barnyard and The Crossroads shopping centers at the mouth of Carmel Valley, things pick up a bit with some lively music.

Chevy's Fresh Mex Restaurant
The Crossroads,
Highway 1 and Rio Road, Carmel
(831) 626–0945

A popular chain Mexican restaurant in The Crossroads shopping center, Chevy's has a festive happy hour with half-price appetizers. First-timers should try a Fresh Mex Margarita with the fresh fruit of the month—from the traditional strawberry to the exotic prickly pear. Chevy's is open Sunday through Thursday until 10:00 P.M. and Friday and Saturday until 11:00 P.M.

The General Store
5th Avenue and Junipero Street, Carmel
(831) 624–2233

On a starry evening, sipping a hot coffee drink while snuggled around one of the two fireplaces on the beautifully landscaped outdoor patio at The General

Store can be an unforgettable Carmel experience. The indoor bar has its own crackling fire and serves 10 wines by the glass and four beers on draft. The bar at The General Store is open until midnight Sunday through Thursday and until 1:00 A.M. Friday and Saturday.

Highlands Inn's Sunset Lounge
Highway 1, Carmel Highlands
(831) 624-3801

Even if you're not staying at the Highlands Inn, a visit to the Sunset Lounge is worth the scenic drive south on Highway 1, especially for jazz fans. Plan on a cruise down the Big Sur coast to watch the sunset, then stop by this intimate piano lounge with quality music nightly by local artists. Piano music is presented 6:00 to 9:00 P.M. Thursday and Sunday, and a live jazz trio plays Friday and Saturday evenings from 9:00 P.M. until midnight. Specialty drinks include a tasty Absolut Mandarin Cosmopolitan and flavored martinis. The Sunset Lounge is open until midnight Sunday through Thursday and until 1:00 A.M. Friday and Saturday nights.

Jack London's Restaurant
San Carlos Street and 5th Avenue, Carmel
(831) 624-2336

Here's a lively local hangout, a bar and grill that offers casual fare and your favorite drink around a horseshoe-shaped bar. The pub features four beers on tap and a full Margarita menu. Happy hour with a complimentary buffet is offered Monday through Friday from 4:30 to 6:30 P.M. Jack London's is open nightly until 2:00 A.M., and the kitchen serves until 1:00 A.M.

Mission Ranch
26270 Dolores Street, Carmel
(831) 625-9040

The Mission Ranch, owned by Clint Eastwood, is a popular nightspot among local singles in the 30-plus crowd. The dining room features a festive piano bar with live music every night. There's mellow dinner music from 6:00 to 9:00 P.M. and a lively open-mike singalong from 9:00 P.M. until midnight. Food is served until 10:00 P.M.

During the summer, arrive at sunset to stroll the splendid grounds, then sit back and enjoy a friendly fun-filled evening. On Dolores Street back behind the Carmel Mission, the Ranch can be a little hard to find in the dark, but it's definitely worth the effort.

Rio Grill
101 Crossroads Boulevard, Carmel
(831) 625-5436

Here's a popular early evening choice for a drink and appetizers among the young urban professionals and local jet-setters. It's a place to see and be seen and is often frequented by out-of-town celebrities during the Pebble Beach Pro-Am and Concours d'Elegance. Besides all that, there's an extensive wine list and tasty Margaritas, including the signature Rio Rita made with premium tequilas. The food is great too. Rio Grill is open until 10:00 P.M. Sunday through Thursday and until 11:00 P.M. on Friday and Saturday.

Sade's
Lincoln Street and Ocean Avenue, Carmel
(831) 624-0787

A local hangout since 1926, Sade's (pronounced "Sadie's") is a Carmel landmark. Named after Sade Latham, a Follies Girl, this 20-stool bar has welcomed such famous visitors as Bing Crosby, Bob Hope, Eddie Cantor, and Dean Martin. Today, you can join the locals in a friendly game of dice or darts while enjoying a great Bloody Mary or your own favorite drink. Sade's is open until 2:00 A.M. nightly.

Sherlock Holmes Pub & Restaurant
3772 The Barnyard, Carmel
(831) 625-0340

This isn't really a late-night spot since it closes at 9:00 P.M. most evenings, but it's still a worthwhile mention for fans of the master sleuth. The indoor and outdoor patios, both with fireplaces, are pleasant spots to enjoy one of the 40 beer selections, including Bass and Guinness on tap. If you're hungry, Sherlock Holmes makes good American burgers with decidedly British names, as well as the traditional bangers and mash, fish and chips, and pasties.

The piano bar at Mission Ranch in Carmel is a popular nightspot among the 30-something crowd.
PHOTO: TOM OWENS

Pebble Beach

Peppoli/Lobby Lounge
The Inn at Spanish Bay, Pebble Beach
(831) 647–7500

For an early evening of live piano music Friday and Saturday, visit Peppoli at The Inn at Spanish Bay. Seating is provided until 10:00 P.M. nightly, with a full bar, an award-winning wine list, and great Italian desserts. Meanwhile, the Lobby Lounge outside of Roy's restaurant presents Brazilian jazz Thursday through Sunday from 7:00 to 11:00 P.M. Drinks and munchies are served.

Tap Room Bar & Grill
The Lodge at Pebble Beach, 17-Mile Drive
(831) 624–3811, (831) 625–8535

The Tap Room is a favorite of hotel guests and locals who enjoy mingling in the casual, elegant atmosphere of The Lodge. The full bar features dozens of beers, including local microbrews on tap. The munchies menu ranges from oysters on the half-shell to great half-pound burgers. You'll also enjoy the fascinating collection of golf memorabilia, including many celebrity photos from The Crosby. The Tap Room is open nightly until midnight.

Terrace Lounge
The Lodge at Pebble Beach, 17-Mile Drive
(831) 624–3811, (831) 625–8535

Enjoy live jazz from 6:30 to 10:30 P.M. Tuesday, 7:00 to 11:00 P.M. Wednesday and Thursday, and 8:00 P.M. until midnight Friday and Saturday. The lounge is open nightly until 1:00 A.M.

Traps
The Inn at Spanish Bay, Pebble Beach
(831) 647–7500

Here's a cozy Spanish Bay setting for a relaxing drink in a comfortable chair before a warm fireplace. There's a full bar with a terrific wine and single-malt selection plus late-night snacks and appetizers. Traps is open nightly until 1:00 A.M.

Billiards

Monterey is definitely the place on the Peninsula for a nightly game of billiards. Although many bars, pubs, and clubs provide a table or two for your enjoyment, the only two billiard halls are your best bet for a serious game of 8-ball.

Monterey

Blue Fin Cafe and Billiards
685 Cannery Row, Monterey
(831) 375–7000, www.bluefin-billiards.com

One of the busiest nightspots in town, Blue Fin Cafe offers 18 billiards tables, snooker, a shuffleboard court, air hockey, Foosball, and darts. Plus it's open every day until 2:00 A.M. The cafe serves freshly made sandwiches and other light fare all night, and the full bar features 22 ales and lagers on tap and premium single-malt scotches, enjoyable from the bayview patio. You'll find good deals on billiards and food at the 4:00 to 7:00 P.M. Monday through Friday happy hour. Live music is presented Thursday and Friday nights starting at 9:00 P.M. Tuesday is Swing Night, with free swing dance lessons at 8:00 P.M. and half-price pool all night. Wednesday and Saturday feature DJ dance parties beginning at 9:00 P.M.

Easy Street Billiards
511 Tyler Street, Monterey
(831) 333–0825

Hustlers welcome! This serious pool hall offers 13 tournament tables and some of the best billiards play in town. For refreshments, there's draft and bottled beer. Open seven days a week and all ages are welcome. Call regarding the regularly held competitive tournaments.

Clubs

Monterey

Of all the sections in this book, the following listing of clubs will probably be the most unreliable. Believe me, it's not because we were distracted or otherwise impaired while doing our research. It's just that these places tend to come and go, disappear and reappear, on a moment's notice. And even those clubs that have staying power tend to change their weekly line-ups and types of music as frequently as we change our mind. With that caveat, here's what was happening on the Peninsula club scene at the time of this writing.

Cibo Ristorante Italiano
301 Alvarado Street, Monterey
(831) 649–8151

Cibo (pronounced "chee-bow") has become one of the poshest elbow-to-elbow spots among the hip Monterey 30-ish crowd who enjoy tasty Italian food and good live music. Six evenings a week (all but Monday), jazz, rhythm and blues, and reggae draw full crowds that often pack the bar and compact dance floor. The full-size bar is known for its oversized martinis. Cibo is open until 12:30 A.M., and 1:00 A.M. on Friday and Saturday.

Club Octane
321 Alvarado Street, Monterey
(831) 646–9244, www.cluboctane.com

Okay, club freaks. This is the closest thing you're going to find to a vibrant, hot, and nasty club scene anywhere on the Peninsula. There are three bars and two separate dance floors, each catering to a target clientele on any given night. Take Friday night, for instance. The front room features hip-hop and house music, while the back room pumps out Top 40 hits. On Saturdays, it's '80s, funk, old school, and new wave out front and Eurohouse out back. Sundays feature Latin house music out front and salsa and merengue in the back. Mondays take a different twist with burlesque dancers—men grinding up front and the ladies swinging and swaying in the rear. Tuesdays are no-cover-charge nights, with house and Top 40 music, while Thursdays pulse with '80s modern rock and new wave. Take a rest on Wednesdays. There's a cover charge of $5.00 or so most nights, and you have to be 21 or over and pass the dress code to enter.

CLOSE-UP

Smoking Ban at Bars and Clubs

As the cry of "Happy New Year" rang out on January 1, 1998, a law went into effect prohibiting smoking in all California bars and clubs that have employees. Only owner-operated establishments that have no employees and bars and casinos on Indian reservations are exempt from the ban. And none of the bars and clubs listed in this chapter now allow smoking. The California law, known as SB 137, follows a 1995 smoking ban for restaurants and most other indoor workplaces. It is aimed at protecting bartenders and other employees from secondhand smoke. Bar owners face a $100 fine for a first offense and up to $7,000 for repeated violations. So, please, no smoking inside these establishments. Some bars and clubs have designated outdoor smoking areas.

The Mucky Duck
479 Alvarado Street, Monterey
(831) 655–3031

This British pub and restaurant has slowly transformed into a lively nightspot. You can dance to DJ-spun tunes on Thursday through Saturday nights around the fire pit out on the back patio. Live music is featured on Sunday, Tuesday, Wednesday, and Friday night. The indoor pub offers 70 beers, including 21 drafts, plus boisterous games of darts. The Mucky Duck is populated with the local military and college scene and draws primarily a 20-something crowd at night.

Ocean Thunder
214 Lighthouse Avenue, Monterey
(831) 643–9169

Over in New Monterey rolls Ocean Thunder. It's a kick-back, get-down, let-it-loose kind of establishment that caters to the rock and blues crowd. You'll find live bands rockin' most Friday and Saturday nights. Wednesdays you're invited to pack along your own instruments for a jam-along of rhythm and blues, and Thursdays are reserved for some really rowdy rock and roll. Sundays during the summertime there are early evening barbecues out back on the Ocean Thunder patio, and Monday is typically reserved for sports on the big screen televisions. Don't be intimidated by the lines of Harleys you might see parked out front. This is a friendly, back-slappin' kind of place that invites head-bobbing fun.

Sly McFly's Jazz and Blues Alley
700 Cannery Row, Monterey
(831) 649–8050

Traditionally a favorite bar and restaurant among auto-racing fans with its classic-car decor, Sly McFly's recently remodeled to become one of the hottest new clubs as well. Live music is now offered seven nights a week, smack dab in the center of Cannery Row. There's a 4:00 to 7:00 P.M. happy hour Monday through Friday. Sly's is a good place to meet out-of-towners; it's open nightly until 1:30 A.M.

Viva Monterey
414 Alvarado Street, Monterey
(831) 646–1415

Viva Monterey plays live, loud music nightly from 9:00 P.M. to 1:00 A.M. with no cover charge. This small, often packed club also offers three pool tables, including two black light tables where games glow in the dark. On Friday and Saturday nights there's live hard-rock music. Sunday nights feature DJ house music, while Monday and Tuesday it's bring-your-own-CDs nights, which are proving very popular. There's more DJ disc spinning on Wednesday and Thursday at

Sly McFly's Jazz and Blues Alley offers live music every night and weekend afternoons, including performances by local favorites The Blue Tones. PHOTO: TOM OWENS

open-jam night. Viva Monterey is open every night until 2:00 A.M.

Carmel

The Jazz & Blues Company
236 Crossroads Boulevard, Carmel
(831) 624–6432,
www.thejazzandbluescompany.com

A music store by day, The Jazz & Blues Company at The Crossroads in Carmel converts into an intimate live-music club about 60 nights a year (including most Saturdays) as the venue for the W. & J. Graham's Port Jazz Series. It's a recital concert atmosphere with a maximum capacity of about 70 people, so reservations are nearly always a must. No food or drinks are served, but you can bring your own beverages. Tickets are in the $20 to $30 range for these great jazz and blues shows by nationally known talents. Shows typically begin at 7:30 P.M. with artists playing two sets. Jazz fans should definitely check out the schedule while in town.

Coffeehouses

Monterey

Morgan's Coffee and Tea
498 Washington Street, Monterey
(831) 373–5601

Morgan's schedules a scattering of local and national musical acts on weekends. Typically shows start around 7:00 to 8:00 P.M. with two sets nightly. Cover charges for name acts usually range from $8.00 to $10.00, while some local acts have no cover. The upcoming schedule is available by calling (831) 642-4949. Oh yeah, Morgan's serves fine coffees, teas, and other goodies and offers indoor and sidewalk seating. It's open until 1:00 A.M. Tuesday through Sunday and until 10:00 P.M. on Monday.

Plumes Coffee House
400 Alvarado Street, Monterey
(831) 373–4526

Plumes is a popular late-night hangout for the young downtown Monterey crowd. No entertainment is provided (except from your fellow caffeine freaks), but a good variety of local pastries and decadent desserts is available. Plumes is open until 11:00 P.M. Sunday through Thursday and midnight on Friday and Saturday.

Carmel

Caffé Cardinale Coffee Roasting Company
Ocean Avenue and Dolores Street, Carmel
(831) 626–2095

Caffé Cardinale features 30 coffees roasted right on site and a full espresso bar. You can enjoy your beverage on the outdoor courtyard, which also features live music on Friday nights during the summer season. Caffé Cardinale is open until 10:00 P.M. on Friday and Saturday but closes at 6:00 P.M. other nights.

Pacific Grove

Juice & Java
599 Lighthouse Avenue, Pacific Grove
(831) 373–8652

Here's a nice spot in downtown Pacific Grove to enjoy a nighttime coffee, espresso, mocha, tea, smoothie, shake, fresh juice, or other beverage. For a real kick, come on Friday open-mike night, with local legend Rama P. Jama as your host. You're likely to catch local singers, pickers, dancers, or poets baring their souls. Juice & Java is open until 8:00 P.M. Sunday through Thursday and 10:00 P.M. on Friday and Saturday.

Wildberries
212 17th Street, Pacific Grove
(831) 644–9836

If you're looking for a quiet and cozy spot for your nightly java, pick Wildberries. In a small P.G. Victorian, Wildberries serves up a full coffee menu and a complete selection of leaf and herbal teas. Try a Chinese herbal tonic to cure what ails you. A favorite among mellow P.G. locals of all ages, Wildberries is open until 10:00 P.M. Sunday through Thursday and until 11:00 P.M. on Friday and Saturday.

Comedy Clubs

Planet Gemini
625 Cannery Row, Monterey
(831) 373–1449, www.planetgemini.com

On the third floor overlooking Cannery Row, Planet Gemini is the longtime king of comedy clubs in Monterey. You'll see both local and nationally known comedy acts Thursday through Saturday from 9:00 to 10:30 P.M., with cover charges typically $6.00 to $8.00. Afterward, Planet Gemini turns into a dance club with live bands or DJs. Sunday is salsa dance night, Wednesday features live band music, and DJs spin dance tunes Thursday through Saturday. Enjoy the full bar and light fare. Planet Gemini is open until 1:00 A.M. Wednesday through Sunday.

Doc Ricketts' Lab
180 E. Franklin Street, Monterey
(831) 649–4241

The newest Monterey nightspot, Doc Ricketts' Lab, is still finding its identity. The name conjures images of the old Doc Ricketts' Lab, the late, great basement club on Cannery Row. Currently, the new Doc's is offering stand-up comedy on Friday and Saturday nights, followed by DJs spinning funk and rhythm and blues. There's talk of live music during the summer season but plans are still in the making. You might want to check the local papers during your visit to see just what Doc's is up to these days.

Movie Houses

Monterey

Galaxy Six Cinemas
280 Del Monte Center, Monterey
(831) 655–4617

Galaxy Six, in the Del Monte Shopping Center, is one of Monterey's modern six-

Wildberries is a favorite local hangout in Pacific Grove, offering coffees, teas, and wonderful pastries.
PHOTO: JANA MORBA

plex cinemas and shows the latest first-run films. Bargain matinees are offered daily for showings before 6:00 P.M. (**Note:** Plans are in the works for building an even larger multi-screen theater at the Del Monte Shopping Center. Check out the local papers to see if it's a reality.)

Osio Cinemas
350 Alvarado Street, Monterey
(831) 844–8171

Completed in late 1999 in downtown Monterey, Osio Cinemas is the area's newest movie house. With the demise of the fabulous Dream Theater, it's the closest thing going to an art film house in the area. The Osio features six screens showing first-run films, with bargain matinees for shows starting before 6:00 P.M. Assisted listening systems are available for the hard-of-hearing.

State Theatre
417 Alvarado Street, Monterey
(831) 372–4555

The historic State Theatre in Monterey has been renovated to its former glory as Monterey's premier movie house. The large main theater provides a great atmosphere with a classic movie house architecture and house organ. Unfortunately, the balcony has been enclosed to provide a smaller separate screen upstairs. Management also owns a less opulent theater right across Alvarado Street where a third feature is shown. Definitely go for the main screen at the State Theatre. Bargain matinees are offered daily before 6:00 P.M.

Pacific Grove

Lighthouse Cinema
525 Lighthouse Avenue, Pacific Grove
(831) 372–7300

With four screens, the Lighthouse Cinema is the only movie house in Pacific Grove. It shows first-run films, offering discount prices every Tuesday and for all matinees before 6:00 P.M.

Carmel

Crossroads Cinemas
2 The Crossroads, Carmel
(831) 624–8682

Crossroads Cinema, which shows first-run movies, is a two-screen theater in the rear of The Crossroads shopping center. A classic matinee series is featured during the summer, bringing back movie favorites. Bargain matinees are offered year-round for showings before 2:00 P.M. (except for special engagements).

Forest Theater
Mountain View Road and Santa Rita Street, Carmel
(831) 626–1681

During the summer months, the Outdoor Forest Theater in Carmel presents a series of classic movies under the stars on Thursday through Saturday nights. This is a very popular Carmel tradition, where locals pack their picnic baskets (don't forget the wine), grab some warm blankets, and enjoy a memorable outdoor cinematic experience. Movies usually begin at 8:30 P.M.

Shopping

Malls, Plazas, and Outlets
Shopping Areas
Antiques
Bookstores
Farmers Markets
Gift and Specialty Shops
Home and Garden
Thrift Shops
Specialty Food Markets

From T-shirts and local souvenirs to one-of-a-kind clothing, art, and jewelry, the shopping selections on the Monterey Peninsula encompass a wide variety of tastes and budgets. We have organized this chapter to help you find the kind of shopping that's right for you. First, we provide some information about the Peninsula's malls, plazas, and outlet centers. Next, we highlight several geographic areas on the Peninsula that have a high concentration of shopping opportunities. Following that, we provide categories of our favorite places to shop for antiques, books, fresh produce, gifts, items for the home, and specialty food items. We've also added a section on thrift shops for those who enjoy finding a great bargain. Many shoppers come to the Monterey Peninsula just for the art galleries. We've included those in our chapter called The Arts and Galleries. And for the kids, we put a special shopping section in our Kidstuff chapter.

For the most part, local merchants welcome credit cards as a form of payment, and the larger shopping malls and outlets accept personal checks with proper identification. For the thrift shops and the farmers markets, we suggest you have sufficient cash available.

Malls, Plazas, and Outlets

American Tin Cannery Premium Outlets
125 Ocean View Boulevard, Pacific Grove
(831) 372–1442, www.premiumoutlets.com

This outlet center is near the aquarium in a historic cannery building. In the middle of the old cannery, you'll find an 80-foot History Wall that heralds Cannery Row's meteoric rise to become the "Sardine Capital of the World."

The multilevel center, California's first factory outlet, has all the big names you have come to expect: Anne Klein, Bass, Big Dog, Izod, Geoffrey Beene, Reebok, Van Heusen, Woolrich, and London Fog, to name a few of the many stores here.

When you need refreshment, grab a bite at any one of several food and beverage establishments. First Awakenings Restaurant is an Insiders' favorite for breakfast, and we also recommend Archie's American Diner for one of the messiest (and most delicious) burgers in town.

The American Tin Cannery is open seven days a week. Free parking is available in a lot directly behind the outlets.

The Barnyard
26400 Carmel Rancho Lane, Carmel
(831) 624–8886, www.thebarnyard.com

The Barnyard is composed of nearly 50 shops and galleries housed in rustic barns and grouped in a quaint village-like setting. Each barn, surrounded by fragrant and colorful gardens, has its own personality and charm. Women's and men's apparel, books, music, toys, antiques, fine art, home accents, jewelry, gifts, and accessories can all be procured here.

International cuisine and specialty food shops are also plentiful. Cafes and full service restaurants offer culinary delights from a multitude of different ethnic origins: Swiss, Japanese, Chinese, Italian, and American to name a few. Afterward, enjoy a cup of tea or fresh-roasted gourmet coffee from around the world at the Carmel Valley Roasting Company.

As you walk through the multiterraced center, relax and admire the gardens. Benches are thoughtfully placed where you can rest for a moment and enjoy the scenery. Join the horticulturist-led garden tour (typically Sundays at noon in front of the Thunderbird Bookshop) or just ramble through the brick walkways on your own. Many outdoor events are planned here throughout the year, taking advantage of the beautiful setting.

To get to The Barnyard from Monterey, take Highway 1 South. One mile past Ocean Avenue, turn left on Carmel Valley Road. Take a right at Carmel Rancho Boulevard, then another right onto Carmel Rancho Lane. You'll see the barns directly ahead. The Barnyard is open seven days a week. There is free parking in several large lots.

Carmel Plaza
Corner of Ocean Avenue and Junipero Street, Carmel
(831) 624–0137, www.carmelplaza.com

Carmel Plaza, an elegant garden courtyard with hanging floral baskets and fountains houses a unique marketplace with more than 50 stores, one-of-a-kind shops, and restaurants. You'll find world-famous designer names like Saks Fifth Avenue, Ann Taylor, Louis Vuitton, and Georgiou.

There's also a wide variety of merchandise, including fashions, jewelry, shoes, gifts, leather goods, accessories, art, home decor, and gourmet foods.

Any of the restaurants, some with outdoor dining, will satisfy even the most discriminating palate. Whether it's with a light lunch or a larger meal, the food choices at Carmel Plaza will leave you satisfied and ready for more shopping!

Carmel Plaza is open seven days a week. You can park without charge for two hours, with validation, in the parking garage behind the Plaza on Mission Street.

The Crossroads Shopping Village
159 Crossroads Boulevard, Carmel
(831) 625–4106

Shopping at The Crossroads, with its flower-filled streets and brick sidewalks, evokes an image of roaming through an English village. You'll shop to your heart's delight among more than 90 shopping and dining establishments. You'll find men's and women's apparel, shoes, home accents, cards, gifts, collectibles, jewelry, galleries, specialty foods, videos, a pharmacy, a grocery store, a movie theater, and restaurants. Take care of banking, make travel arrangements, get your shoes repaired, drop off your dry cleaning, or mail a package home.

Enjoy brunch, lunch, or dinner with your favorite wine or cocktail at one of several award-winning restaurants and eateries.

The Crossroads lies at the mouth of the Carmel Valley where the Santa Lucia Mountains begin. To get there from Monterey, take Highway 1 South to one mile south of Ocean Avenue, and make a left turn at Rio Road. The shopping center is on the corner to your right. There is plenty of free parking on the premises. The Crossroads is open seven days a week.

Del Monte Shopping Center
Highway 1 at Munras, Monterey
(831) 373–2705, www.delmontecenter.com

The Del Monte Shopping Center is an open-air mall, with Macy's and Mervyn's department stores serving as the anchor stores. No matter what you're in search of,

Insiders' Tip

The Old Monterey Business Association provides a brochure of shopping, dining, and entertainment possibilities in Historic Downtown Old Monterey. For a brochure, call (831) 655-8070, visit the Web site at www.oldmonterey.org, or pick one up at any of the visitor centers.

you'll surely find it here. The center's diverse selection of shops feature cards, gifts, bath and body stores, books, electronics, music, records, video, hobby items, household necessities, jewelry, maternity clothing, shoes, sporting goods, and men's, women's, and children's apparel.

Personal services include a dry cleaner, travel agent, hair salon, eye care, and banking.

Enjoy a cup of java at Starbucks, or if you want something more substantial, the many restaurants include Marie Callender's (save room for the pie), Fresh Choice, and El Indio (Mexican food), among others. If you just have to have a burger, Elli's Great American Food will satisfy your craving. For a "healthy" alternative, Whole Foods has a great gourmet deli and take-out foods section.

The shopping center is just off Highway 1. Take the Munras/Soledad Drive exit when traveling southbound; the Munras Avenue exit from the north. Access to the center is afforded by two boulevard entrances. Nearly 3,000 free parking spaces are provided. It's open seven days a week.

Shopping Areas

Carmel

Carmel is renowned internationally for its extraordinary gallery selection and shopping opportunities offering everything from apparel, books, brass, fine original art and photography, furs, jewelry, leather, linens and lingerie, and exceptional gifts. A basic understanding of Carmel is necessary before you begin a spree in its downtown area. Addresses are identified by location (i.e., Ocean between Mission and San Carlos on the southwest side of the street) because there are no street numbers. The main shopping area is two blocks on either side of Ocean Avenue between Junipero and Lincoln Streets. Wear comfortable walking shoes and plan to spend at least a day drifting around, seeking out all the quaint and charming shops located in hidden alleyways and courtyards. Like thousands before you, you're sure to find Carmel to be a shopping paradise.

At the southeast corner of Junipero Street and Ocean Avenue is the **Carmel Plaza** (see our write-up in the "Malls, Plazas, and Outlets" section).

Monterey

Cannery Row and Fisherman's Wharf

Stop at the old Monterey Canning Company building, 700 Cannery Row, where you'll find shops selling candy, jewelry, clothing, food, souvenirs, and toys. **Sand Dollar Gifts,** in the cannery building, (831) 372–2885, is the oldest store on Cannery Row. It stocks everything from sweatshirts and T-shirts to unique oceanic products plus every imaginable souvenir and memento.

Across the way at Steinbeck Plaza Two is **Pebble Beach on Cannery Row,** 660 Cannery Row, (831) 373–1500. It is a great place to pick up quality Pebble Beach apparel, golf accessories, gifts, and souvenirs from the world-famous resorts and golf courses. **Robert Lyn Nelson Studios,** 660 Cannery Row, (831) 655–8500, displays the paintings of the world's foremost marine artist, Robert Lyn Nelson.

Across the street at Steinbeck Plaza One is the **Cannery Row General Store,** 685 Cannery Row, (831) 655–7747, a Disney outlet and a one-stop shopping place for picnic supplies, film, and fine cigars. **Boyz Toyz,** located on the second floor, 685 Cannery Row, (831) 333–1060, is a shop for boyz and girlz of all ages with items such as model cars, trains, sailboats, and remote control vehicles.

Directly across the street, in the Monterey Canning Company warehouse, are numerous clothing, jewelry, gift, and specialty shops such as **Three Ladys of Cannery Row,** 711 Cannery Row, (831) 655–5688. Browse through crafts and handmade gifts from local artists and books by renowned Peninsula authors, or choose from exotic teas, incense, and jewelry.

The cluster of shops on Fisherman's Wharf are hands-down winners for their inexpensive souvenirs and mementos of

Steinbeck Plaza at Cannery Row boasts a bust of the author who made the area famous. Today, visitors have a large variety of shopping opportunities to choose from. PHOTO: GRANT HUNTINGTON/MONTEREY COUNTY CONVENTION & VISITORS BUREAU

your visit to Monterey. The smell of fresh-caught seafood will probably arouse your appetite, so relax and enjoy a sourdough bread bowl of clam chowder at one of the Wharf's many seafood restaurants.

Downtown Monterey

The historic heart of Old Monterey contains an array of shopping possibilities. Along Alvarado and intersecting streets, you will find fine jewelry and watches, clothing, fine art, musical instruments, gifts, photo supplies, flowers, and home furnishings.

Pacific Grove

The revival of downtown Pacific Grove has attracted many new businesses over the past several years. Pacific Grove is home to a number of antiques shops and thrift stores (see the category listings that follow in this chapter). You will find noteworthy galleries among shops with greeting cards, gifts, apparel, home furnishings, and accessories.

Pebble Beach

A must-do on the Monterey Peninsula is a drive along world-famous 17-Mile Drive, and a stop at the Lodge at Pebble Beach affords an opportunity for excellent shopping as well. The high-end shops here feature original gold jewelry designs, fashions for men and women, antiques, and art galleries. This being Pebble Beach, of course there are shops specializing in golf, from the Pebble Beach Pro Shop to others selling official Pebble Beach merchandise and golf antiques. Visit them on the Web at www.pebblebeach.com.

Antiques

The Peninsula is home to a bonanza of antiques shops and one award-winning antiques mall with more than 150 dealers. We've highlighted our favorites here. Look in the Yellow Pages of the phone book for complete listings. Once you have investigated the Peninsula, head north on

Highway 1 to Moss Landing or out U.S. 101 to San Juan Bautista, where you can explore additional opportunities for finding just the right antique treasure.

Antique Clock Shop
489 Lighthouse Avenue, Pacific Grove
(831) 372–6435

This restored 1887 lemon-colored Victorian in downtown Pacific Grove features hundreds of antique clocks elegantly displayed with period furniture and antique curios. When you enter the shop, a symphony of time pieces will announce your arrival. For nearly 20 years The Antique Clock Shop has repaired all kinds of clocks, from cuckoos to grandfathers.

Cannery Row Antique Mall
471 Wave Street, Monterey
(831) 655–0264, www.cannery-row.com

In 1995, on the 50th anniversary of John Steinbeck's immortal novel *Cannery Row,* Cannery Row Antique Mall opened its doors. The mall, housed in the original 1927 Carmel Canning Company Warehouse, is the largest antiques and collectibles mall on the central coast. More than 170 dealers now operate out of the two-story, 21,000-square-foot structure. The mall was named the 1996 Antique Mall of the Year by *Professional Antique Mall Magazine.*

The Carmel Canning Company Warehouse is one of only a few authentic and unchanged structures from the Steinbeck era. After the purchase of the mall in 1994, the owners applied for and received Historic Structure status from the city of Monterey, making the mall the first building on the Row so designated. The rustic, tin-clad warehouse still houses the original endless-belt conveyer.

The mall has good lighting, restrooms, a free coffee bar, and indoor and outdoor seating. There is a small parking lot, a rarity on Cannery Row. The staff is friendly, helpful, and knowledgeable.

The Antique Mall houses everything from American folk art and Oriental furniture to baseball cards and Tiffany lamps. It is also known for the extensive assortment of home furnishings—a boon to local decorators. The mall also sells price guides and books on antiques and collectibles.

Holman Antique Plaza
542 Lighthouse Avenue, Pacific Grove
(831) 646–0674, www.holmanbuilding.com

The Holman Building, in downtown Pacific Grove, houses a collection of more than 50 antiques dealers. The historic, multistory building contains period furniture, jewelry, fine art, coins, stamps, swords, decorative art, Oriental rugs, glassware, watches, dishes, dolls, china cabinets, carpets, quilts, kitchenware, and a whole lot more. The third floor is strictly for consignment items and has a wealth of high-quality bedroom and living room furniture.

Patrick's Consignment Store
105 Central Avenue, Pacific Grove
(831) 372–3995

Patrick's carries a large inventory of home furnishings and is a collective of 35 antiques dealers. You'll find estate jewelry, rugs, china, crystal, silver, lamps, chandeliers, tables, chairs, and mirrors all in one location.

Pieces of Olde
868 Lighthouse Avenue, Monterey
(831) 372–1521

This tiny cottage, with a miniature replica playhouse, is filled with an inventive selection of collectibles and Victorian and country antiques. You will encounter memorabilia, kitchen items, and lots of other intriguing things. Pieces of Olde specializes in antique dolls, teddy bears, and children's toys.

Treasure Bay
883 Lighthouse Avenue, Monterey
(831) 656–9303

This little shop is packed with an interesting ensemble of antiques. You'll find vintage clothing, furs, advertising signs, estate jewelry, glassware, dishes, and a smattering of books and other paper goods.

Trotter's Antiques
301 Forest Avenue, Pacific Grove
(831) 373–3505

Established in 1965, the spacious showroom at Trotter's allows for numerous pieces of commanding 18th- and 19th-century furniture. Also plentiful are glassware, tableware, silver, porcelain, lamps, and Oriental art. You will also see an uncommon collection of antique dolls.

Bookstores

Bookstores—from the tiny shop dealing in hard-to-find and first editions to megachains and children's bookshops—are everywhere on the Peninsula. In terms of resale, there are scores of places to find used books. Don't overlook the thrift shops; most of them carry any number of paperbacks (see our "Thrift Shops" section). Whatever kind of publication you desire, there is a book dealer on the Peninsula ready to assist you. We have listed a few to get you started.

Bay Books and Coffee House
316 Alvarado Street, Monterey
(831) 375–1855, www.montereybaybooks.com

In a former bank building in downtown Monterey, located right across the street from the Conference Center, Bay Books stocks all sorts of books and has an especially nice children's section. Foreign language books and numerous books written about the Monterey Peninsula area are in stock too. You'll discover books about marine life, kayaking, and scuba diving. If you're looking for a Monterey Bay Marine Diver's Map, you'll find it here. There is indoor and outdoor seating at a coffee bar that serves fresh-brewed coffee and espresso drinks.

Books Inc.
Carmel Plaza, Ocean Avenue, Carmel
(831) 625–0440

Downstairs in Carmel Plaza is Books Inc., housing an amazing number of books in all the expected (and some unexpected) categories and an assortment of magazines. Distinctive greeting cards and book paraphernalia such as reading lights and bookmarks are also available. The sale section with dramatically reduced overstock books is a locals' favorite.

Bookworks
667 Lighthouse Avenue, Pacific Grove
(831) 372–2242

The consummate neighborhood bookstore, Bookworks is known as a haunt for the local literary crowd. Stop in to check out the newest additions to the ever-changing inventory of fiction and nonfiction books. Bookworks also carries a good selection of magazines and newspapers. The display windows are always fun, often showcasing the talents of local school children.

Borders Books and Music
Edgewater Center, 2080 California Street, Sand City
(831) 899–6643

Borders is the giant of area bookstores. It not only carries an amazing variety of books, but also sells cassette tapes, CDs, calendars, newspapers from around the world, and magazines. The cafe and lounge area is a great place to relax. Weekly programs include lectures by authors, art talks, and musical events.

Thunderbird Bookshop and Cafe
3600 The Barnyard, Carmel
(831) 624–1803

For more than 30 years the Thunderbird Bookshop and Cafe has been a Carmel landmark. Insiders know this is *the* place to go for hard-to-find and special-order books. It carries more than 40,000 volumes as well as magazines, greeting cards, and a few games. The atmosphere is casual, and the staff is friendly and helpful. The adjoining solarium cafe is a cozy spot with a fireplace. The cafe has an espresso bar and serves homemade soups, pot pies, sandwiches, and beer and wine. On some evenings the solarium serves as a lecture hall where musical artists and authors give public talks and performances.

Farmers Markets

Agribusiness is the largest revenue-generating industry in Monterey County. With so many crops grown in the county, we are fortunate to have a bountiful selection of flowers, fruits, and vegetables year-round.

Insiders' Tip

The Wing Chong Market, 835 Cannery Row, played an important part in John Steinbeck's novel *Cannery Row*. Today it houses a gift and souvenir store.

Many chefs at local restaurants shop the farmers markets to purchase produce at peak freshness. The two farmers markets listed here take place in Monterey each week.

Old Monterey Market Place
Alvarado Street, Monterey
(831) 655–2607, www.oldmonterey.org

Alvarado Street is transformed into a market each Tuesday, rain or shine. From 4:00 to 7:00 P.M. buyers and spectators investigate the goods at up to 134 booths. They search for their weekly supply of fresh fruits, vegetables, flowers, fresh-baked bread, seafood, nuts, honey, and eggs. Each booth represents a different farm, and there are many booths with organic foods. Come hungry and have a quick bite at one of the prepared-food vendors. It's a great way to sample the fare of local restaurants. By evening the place resembles a street festival with live entertainment, face-painting, and a bookmobile. In addition to food booths, you'll find vendors offering handmade crafts, artwork, ethnic clothing, used books, and ceramics.

Monterey Bay Certified Farmers Market
Monterey Peninsula College,
980 Fremont Street, Monterey
(831) 728–5060,
www.montereybayfarmers.org

A smaller affair than the Old Monterey Market Place, this market primarily features the season's best fruits and vegetables. Vendors also sell honey, nuts, bread, and eggs. You will also find fresh-cut flowers and potted plants. The market is held in the lower parking lot at the college, just off Fremont Boulevard.

Gift and Specialty Shops

Shopping for gifts and specialty items is effortless with such numerous choices in each Peninsula city. From the beautiful yet functional to the superfluous but irresistible, you'll have no trouble finding the perfect gift for anyone on your list. Here's a list of suggestions just for starters.

Bittner's: The Pleasure of Writing
Ocean Avenue and San Carlos Avenue, Carmel
(831) 626–8828

Is there a writer on your gift list? Bittner's sells only the finest writing instruments and accessories. This shop carries exquisite products from around the world including pens by Aurora, Delta, Fabergé, and Michel Perchin. The collection includes limited-edition pens by the same companies. Personalized writing materials, journals, inks, refills, and writing paper are part of the elegant inventory.

Carmel Creamery
459 Alvarado Street, Monterey
(831) 372–4720

Handmade chocolates in unusual shapes and flavors are the main reason to stop in at Carmel Creamery, although the ice cream made fresh daily is certainly another draw. In addition to the abundance of confectioner's treats in prepared gift boxes and baskets, unique Monterey Peninsula gifts fill the retail store shelves. This local business has been supplying sweets to residents and visitors for decades.

Couroc Partners Inc.
501 Ortiz Avenue, Sand City
(831) 899–5479

In business since 1948, Couroc has become an American tradition. It fashions handmade platters, trays, trinket boxes, and other specialty items. Each piece, inlaid with inventive and colorful designs, is an object of art. Since this is a factory outlet store, you'll pay wholesale prices—a savings of 50 percent off retail. Don't miss the bargain wall, where you can choose from an irresistible display of goods.

Friends of the Sea Otter Education Retail Center
381 Cannery Row, Monterey
(800) 279–3088, www.seaotters.org

This unique nonprofit center is dedicated to the southern sea otter, an adorable marine animal found in the Monterey Bay. Sea otter gifts, clothing, and collectibles fill the shelves in the retail section; sea otter books and videos are available in the education center adjacent to the store. You can also pick up a Free Otter Spotting Guide here. All proceeds from the center directly benefit sea otter research and preservation. For more details, see our Close-up in this chapter.

Ladyfingers Jewelry
Dolores Street near Ocean Avenue, Carmel
(831) 624–2327

Is there any better gift than jewelry? Ladyfingers, established in 1977, has become a showcase for the jewelry industry's unique design talent, over 45 contemporary jewelers are featured. Represented are such renowned artists as Michael Good, whose hypnotic designs have brought him international acclaim. Check out the outrageous rubber and diamond designs by André Ribeiro and the dynamic and colorful stacking rings by designer Goph Albitz.

Two Sisters Designs
Dolores Street near Fifth Avenue, Carmel
(831) 625–1203

As the name implies, this fun studio shop is owned by two sisters. Their original designs, as well as the designs of other local artists, manifest in a wide variety of beautiful products: jewelry and accessories, ceramics, note cards, fused glass, baskets, lamps, and garden ornaments. It's a little tricky to find (it's in Pantilles Court), yet it is well worth the adventure.

Home and Garden

The Peninsula is overflowing with places to find items for the home or garden. From homey, handcrafted items to ultra-chic accessories, the possibilities are endless when it comes to finding just the right thing to decorate your home or spruce up your garden.

Brinton's
546 Carmel Rancho Lane, Carmel
(831) 624–8541, www.brintons.com

Brinton's is one of those refreshingly different hardware/housewares stores. Their line of merchandise includes garden supplies, outdoor furniture, and an abundance of functional items for the kitchen and bath.

Grove Homescapes
472 Lighthouse Avenue, Pacific Grove
(831) 656–0864, www.grovehomescapes.com

The old Grove Laundry building has been transformed into a historic treasure. Restoration began in 1994 when new owners purchased the 1927 building. They created a design showroom with a lush garden and Victorian gazebo. Inside, a sweeping staircase draws your eye to the commanding displays of artwork and home furnishings.

Parsley Sage & Thyme
149 Crossroads Boulevard, Carmel
(831) 620–0515

In the Crossroads Shopping Center, this business is a gold mine of kitchenware and hard-to-find gourmet cookery from about 160 companies throughout the world. For your convenience, the store will ship all of its products via UPS.

The Woodenickle
529 Central Avenue, Pacific Grove
(831) 646–8050

This precious shop brims with nostalgic gifts and home accessories. Vintage furniture is parceled into cheerful, matched-color vignettes. The store is packed with tea pots, cups and saucers, linens, ribbons, potpourri, things for the garden, and other items to accent every room in the house.

Thrift Shops

Shopping the thrifts is an economical way of getting just about anything at a fraction of the original price. Thrift shops here tend

CLOSE-UP

The "Teddy Bears of the Sea" Center

One of the most memorable sights on the Peninsula is a southern sea otter swimming in the Monterey Bay. These adorable marine mammals, nicknamed the "teddy bears of the sea," are celebrated in extraordinary ways at the nonprofit Friends of the Sea Otter Education Retail Center, located at 381 Cannery Row, across from the Monterey Plaza Hotel.

As you step inside, you are greeted by a colorful profusion of sea otter products, from clothing and cards to toys and holiday items. Books, tapes, and videos—all describing different facets of sea otter life and habits—are for sale. An Insiders' favorite in this category is the children's story *Adventures of Phokey the Sea Otter* book and cassette (with real sea otter sounds); both items are best sellers.

Research materials, photos, and videos create an extensive library available in the Sea Otter Education Room, adjacent to the retail store. You can even go on-line to access more facts and figures, as there are several computer stations here. Free Otter-Spotting Guides are also available.

The brainchild of Margaret Owings and Dr. Jim Mattison, Friends of the Sea Otter (FSO) began in 1968 and remains the only advocacy organization for sea otters in the world. Hunters seeking the thick and lush fur had decimated the sea otter population, once plentiful along the entire Pacific Coast. When the FSO group was formed, less than 700 of the southern sea otters remained. As a result of several decades of

Beloved by all, the southern sea otter was once hunted to near extinction. Successful conservation efforts have produced a remarkable rebound in their population. PHOTO: MARTIN BROWN/MONTEREY COUNTY CONVENTION & VISITORS BUREAU

education and advocacy efforts by Friends of the Sea Otter, currently there are about 2,000 otters in our California coastal waters.

However, the sea otter is still on the Endangered Species List. Its safety is covered under the Marine Mammal Protection Act and the Endangered Species Act. Also, California law protects the species. After a slight decline beginning in 1995, the population is now considered stable. Biologists had expected the otters to continue to recolonize south into the Santa Barbara Channel, but this hasn't occurred. Pollution, loss of habitat, and encounters with fishing gear are suspected causes. FSO is dedicated to continuing to research the changes occurring in the sea otter population and working to protect the existing community.

Here is the perfect opportunity for you to make a difference. Come on in to the Friends of the Sea Otter Education Retail Center and support an exceptionally worthy nonprofit organization by purchasing sea otter merchandise or maybe even a gift membership for yourself or someone else. You also can shop on-line at www.seaotters.org. The center is open daily. The toll-free number is (800) 279–3088.

to have high-quality merchandise in near-new condition. We have described some of our favorite places to shop for bargains in designer clothing, housewares, furniture, books, and a host of other items.

American Cancer Society Discovery Shop
198 Country Club Gate, Pacific Grove
(831) 372–0866

Savvy employees have made this one of the higher-end thrifts around, but good bargains still abound on women's and men's clothing, jewelry, books, and sometimes small pieces of furniture.

Animal Welfare Benefit Shop
206 17th Street, Pacific Grove
(831) 372–1650

The Animal Welfare Benefit Shop is chock-full of books, magazines, clothing, dishes, knickknacks, household items, and the occasional piece of furniture. There is also a good selection of women's clothing and some bedding.

Church Mouse Thrift Shop
204 17th Street, Pacific Grove
(831) 375–0838

Though small, this shop has a variety with interesting games, books, children's toys, clothing, shoes, glassware, kitchen items, bedding, and the occasional sewing and knitting accoutrements. You'll often find a good selection of table linens and suitcases too.

Goodwill Industries
571 Lighthouse Avenue, Monterey
(831) 649–6056, www.goodwill.org

Clothing is the outstanding bargain at this well-known thrift store. In addition to clothing for the entire family, they have shoes, purses, accessories, as well as some furniture. Don't forget to rummage through the huge selection of books and housewares. There are four stores in Monterey County.

Specialty Food Markets

Artichokes, garlic, carrots, lettuce, and a host of other vegetables are grown in nearby Salinas Valley. The Monterey Peninsula area has long acted as a retail outlet for these foods and products made from them. Monterey County now has over 40,000 acres of vineyards, making it one of the largest fine wine regions in the United States. In this section we emphasize a few stores that carry a cornucopia of local wines, regional and international gourmet products, and health foods.

The Bountiful Basket
157 Crossroads Boulevard, Carmel
(831) 625–4457

Retain the flavor of the Monterey Bay Peninsula long after your return home. This specialty shop stocks the pick of the crop in locally produced gourmet foods—flavored vinegar and oil, salsa, garlic, salad dressings, marinades, sardines, coffee, and tea. Shipping and local delivery are available.

The Cheese Shop
Carmel Plaza
(831) 625–2272

Just stepping into The Cheese Shop and inhaling deeply will probably raise your cholesterol 10 points. But what a way to go! Before you are arrayed hundreds of cheeses from the four corners of the earth, all available to sample. If you can think of it, it's either here or the friendly staff can find it. This shop also houses one of the finest selections of wines on the Monterey Peninsula. Picnic baskets, wine and kitchen accessories, and—of course—crackers are also available.

Cornucopia Community Market
26135 Carmel Rancho Boulevard, Carmel
(831) 625–1454

For those seeking wholesome foods, the Cornucopia is an excellent choice. Organic produce, fresh pasta, salad, sauces, sandwiches, soups, and nourishing entrees are all to be found here. Don't leave without some freshly baked bread, gourmet cheese, and wine from local suppliers.

Culinary Center of Monterey
625 Cannery Row, Monterey
(831) 333–2133,
www.culinarycenterofmonterey.com

Located in a renovated cannery building, the Culinary Center of Monterey offers a full range of cooking classes taught by professional chefs in two "dream" kitchens. Gourmet take-out foods and an in-house bakery are here, as well as a prime selection of the world's finest cheeses. A huge array of kitchen gadgetry is also on display. Join friends on the outdoor patio and enjoy a premium beer, wine, and the appetizer bar while taking in the expansive view of Monterey Bay. A class schedule is available on-line.

International Market & Deli
580 Lighthouse Avenue, Monterey
(831) 375–9451

Stepping into the International Market is an experience similar to a trip abroad! You'll hear shoppers conversing in Russian, Italian, or French. Middle Eastern and Mediterranean foods comprise much of the inventory. Scan the take-out menu, and order up some Middle Eastern dishes prepared lightly (with less olive oil). Sample some freshly made hummus, dolmas, vegetarian soup, caviar, or basmati rice. Of course, the market has bottled wines to round out your meal.

Nielsen Brothers Market & Wine Shop
Corner of 7th Avenue and San Carlos Street, Carmel
(831) 624–9463

This market can accommodate all of your grocery needs and has a deli with fresh-roasted meats, an array of international cheeses, and a wide assortment of spirits. The wine shop, Carmel's only wine-tasting room, has one of the Central Coast's most extensive selections of California and European wines. Locals regularly depend on employees to help them select just the right wine for a special meal or celebration.

Pezzini Farms Produce
102 Crossroads Boulevard, Carmel
(831) 626–2734

Artichoke lovers congregate at Pezzini Farms to snatch up artichokes harvested earlier that day in Castroville. Other ready-to-eat items found here include a wide selection of gourmet salad dressings, salsas, and a host of specialty products such as artichoke pesto, which is absolutely wonderful. A fresh and colorful portion of the gorgeous produce comes daily from Pezzini's own farm.

A Taste Of Monterey
700 Cannery Row, Monterey
(831) 646–5466, www.atasteofmonterey.com

This visually spectacular center houses the largest selection of Monterey County appellation wines on the Peninsula. The showroom boasts a panoramic ocean view, gourmet gift shop, winery maps, and tour information. County-grown wine and produce samplings are held daily at this one-stop Monterey County winetasting room. Slide into a window seat overlooking the Monterey Bay and linger over a glass of wine while nibbling delectable tidbits of local produce and appetizers. When you're finished, browse through the interesting and educational exhibits about Monterey County.

Trader Joe's
1170 Forest Avenue, Pacific Grove
(831) 656–0180, www.traderjoes.com

If you haven't already discovered Trader Joe's, you're in for a real treat. It carries a sizable variety of gourmet items such as ready-to-heat and ready-to-eat foods and frozen entrees, pasta, pesto, oil, vinegar, baked goods, cheese, cookies, wine, champagne, and spirits—all at reasonable prices. The selection changes frequently, but you will always find a bonanza of quality foods and beverages.

Whole Foods Market
800 Del Monte Center, Monterey
(831) 333–1660, www.wholefoods.com

Choose from a veritable feast of organic produce, bulk foods, health products, ready-to-eat gourmet deli items, sandwiches, juices, healthy snacks, delicious soups, and fresh-baked bread delivered daily from local bakeries.

Attractions

Monterey
Pacific Grove
Carmel
Pebble Beach

Without question, the primary attraction of the Monterey Peninsula is . . . the Monterey Peninsula. This dramatic meeting of land and sea, complete with shorelines of majestic stands of native Monterey pine and Monterey cypress, has been attracting tourists for more than a century. Still, there are many attractions other than nature-made that are a must-see to make your appreciation of the Peninsula complete. Here is the cream of the crop, sure to please everyone from serious California history and architecture buffs to Walter Mitty-esque deep-sea divers and race car drivers who can live out their high-sea and high-speed fantasies.

Monterey

Cannery Row
200 to 900 Cannery Row, Monterey
(831) 649–6690

"Cannery row in Monterey in California is a poem, a stink, a grating noise, a quality of light, a tone, a habit, a nostalgia, a dream." Those words open John Steinbeck's famous short novel, *Cannery Row,* and still hold true now. Today the stench or grating noise might come from a diesel tourist bus rather than a sardine cannery, but you can still discover the poem, the quality of light, the nostalgia, and the dream lurking behind and between today's Cannery Row attractions. The truth be told, the Cannery Row memorialized by Steinbeck was largely a thing of the past by the time his instant hit was written in January 1945. Steinbeck wrote the masterpiece from New York City, recalling a period in Monterey 10 to 15 years earlier when, as a struggling writer, he hung out with "Mack and the boys" and his biologist buddy Edward F. "Doc" Ricketts. Fortunately for us all, there are a sufficient number of local Steinbeck devotees on the Peninsula and enough Steinbeck pilgrims from all corners of the globe to keep alive what little remains of the Cannery Row entrenched in the mind of anyone who has read the novel. (*Tortilla Flat* was the first of Steinbeck's Monterey trilogy, while *Sweet Thursday* completed Steinbeck's Cannery Row tale of Doc Ricketts and this most colorful cast of characters.)

We'll begin our trip down Cannery Row, whose original name was Ocean View Boulevard, at the northern end where it intersects with David Avenue at the Monterey-Pacific Grove border. It's where you'll find the kingpin of today's Row, the **Monterey Bay Aquarium** (see separate listing). The world-renowned aquarium sits at 886 Cannery Row on the site of the former cannery of Hovden Food Products and incorporates some of the cannery's structure and equipment into its displays.

Heading south, notice the bright yellow building at 851 Cannery Row called **Kalisa's La Ida Cafe,** (831) 644–9316. That's the very same La Ida Cafe Steinbeck recounts as one of the Row's infamous houses of ill repute. Steinbeck aficionados shouldn't miss the chance to stop in for a bite, or at least a hot cup of joe. If you get the chance, say hello to owner Kalisa Moore, the reigning "Queen of Cannery Row" who has operated this fine establishment since 1957. And here's a special Insiders' tip: If you happen to see a mannequin leg in Kalisa's upstairs window, you're in luck—that means there's belly dancing tonight!

Next door to La Ida Cafe at 835 Cannery Row is the **Wing Chong Market.** Built in 1918, this grocery and dry goods store was run by Chinese businessman Won Yee. Steinbeck combined the names

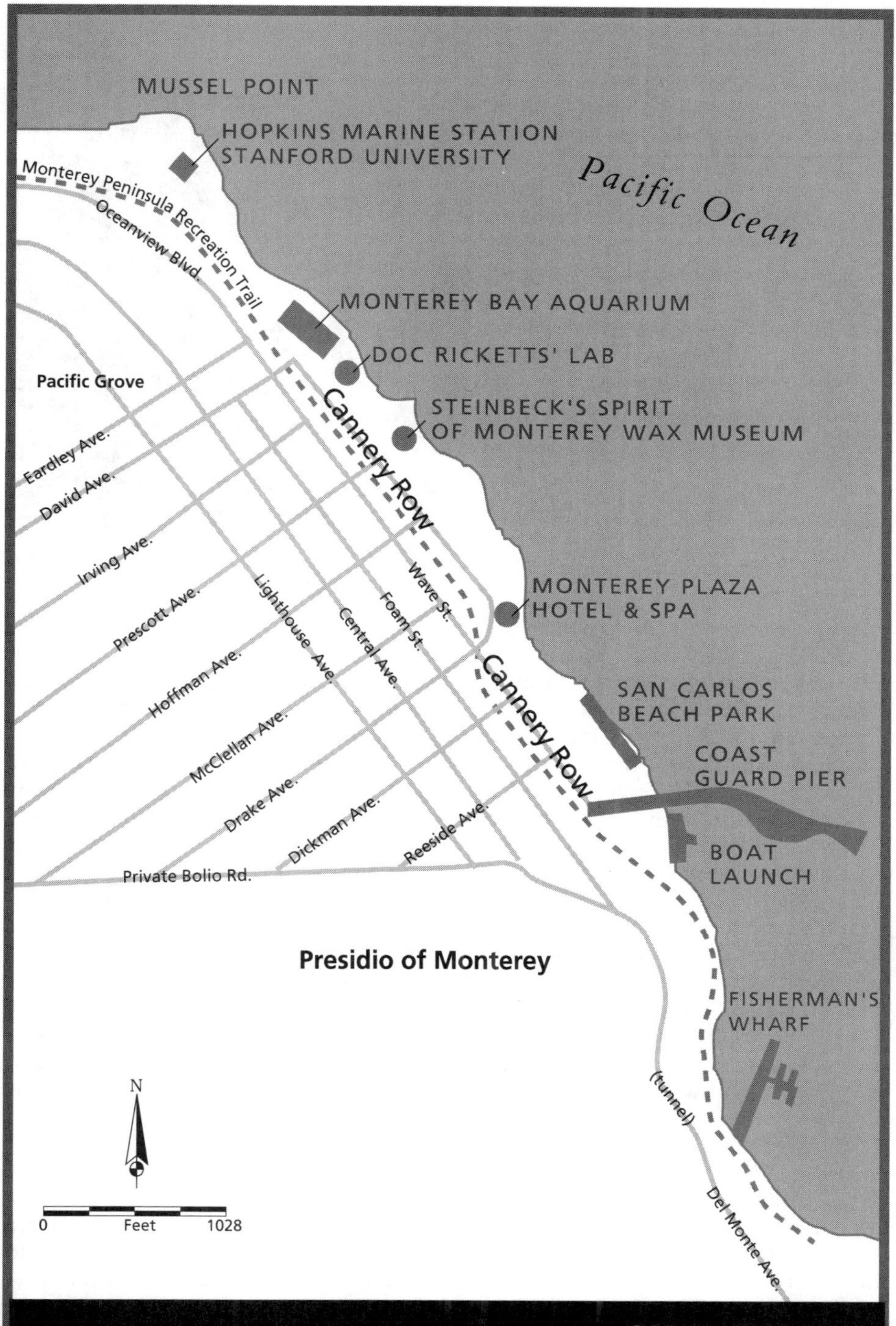
MUSSEL POINT
HOPKINS MARINE STATION
STANFORD UNIVERSITY
Pacific Ocean
Monterey Peninsula Recreation Trail
Oceanview Blvd.
MONTEREY BAY AQUARIUM
DOC RICKETTS' LAB
Pacific Grove
STEINBECK'S SPIRIT
OF MONTEREY WAX MUSEUM
Cannery Row
Eardley Ave.
David Ave.
Irving Ave.
Prescott Ave.
Lighthouse Ave.
Central Ave.
Foam St.
Wave St.
MONTEREY PLAZA
HOTEL & SPA
Cannery Row
Hoffman Ave.
McClellan Ave.
Drake Ave.
Dickman Ave.
Reeside Ave.
SAN CARLOS
BEACH PARK
COAST
GUARD PIER
BOAT
LAUNCH
Private Bolio Rd.
Presidio of Monterey
FISHERMAN'S
WHARF
(tunnel)
N
0
Feet
1028
Del Monte Ave.

CANNERY ROW

The crossovers on Cannery Row now transport tourists rather than tins of sardines from one side of the street to the other. PHOTO: TOM OWENS

of the market and the man to create "Lee Chong," the first character to appear in chapter one of *Cannery Row*. It is here that Lee Chong stood behind the cigar counter, protecting the Old Tennis Shoes and other not-so-fine whiskeys from the thirsty boys of the Row. Today, you can purchase T-shirts and souvenirs at Wing Chong Market, but, alas, nary a pint nor a quart. The building includes a small John Steinbeck museum as well, featuring newspaper clippings about the author as well as a few older editions of his books.

A stone's throw down the Row on the Bay side of the street is an unassuming wooden building with a simple staircase leading up to an even simpler door. It's **Doc Ricketts' Pacific Biological Laboratories,** or "Western Biological Laboratory" as Steinbeck named it. Here, at 800 Cannery Row, Ed Ricketts prepared the marine animals he collected in the Bay for shipment to schools, universities, and medical facilities. And it is here that Steinbeck spent countless hours in the company of his friend and the inspiration for his great work. Today, Doc's Lab is owned by a local "private men's club," whose social activities, it is rumored, would be heartily approved by Mack and the boys.

Across the street from Pacific Biological Laboratories, you'll find a small plaza and walkway called **Bruce Ariss Way,** named after one of Monterey's best-known artists and cartoonists. There, in addition to an Ariss mural of Cannery Row, stand three small one-room cabins, once homes to cannery workers. Peek inside and you'll see the typical home setting of young Spanish, Japanese, and Filipino workers. While Italians were indeed a predominant part of Monterey's fishing industry, this exhibit points out the valuable contributions of the many ethnic groups who came to stake their claim on the silver harvest of the Bay. This area of Cannery Row is also very near the original sites of the Palace Flophouse, where Mack and the boys resided, and madam Flora Wood's **Lone Star Cafe,** better known to Steinbeck readers as the "Bear Flag Restaurant."

Farther south down both sides of the Row you'll find vacant lots where abandoned cannery buildings once stood before a series of destructive fires from the

1950s to the 1980s burned them to the ground. These ghostly spaces, slotted for a new hotel, are now hidden from view by a series of colorful murals depicting historic scenes from the heyday of Cannery Row. Featured artists include local cartoonists Eldon Dedini, Jay Campbell, and Hank Ketcham, of *Dennis the Menace* fame. See if you can spot Dennis in Ketcham's mural.

Down the street at Prescott Avenue stands the epicenter of today's version of Cannery Row. On the north side of the intersection is the former Monterey Canning Company, consisting of two separate structures on opposite sides of the Row connected by an overhead walkway or "crossover." The cannery, built in 1918, is on the Bay side of the Row. It retains its landmark ornate facade, which was a marked contrast to most of the boxy commercial buildings sharing the street. Today, this building is known by its address, **700 Cannery Row,** home to a lively potpourri of more than 40 shops, galleries, eateries, and attractions. The centerpiece of 700 Cannery Row is **Steinbeck's Spirit of Monterey Wax Museum,** a veritable tourist landmark (see the separate listing in this chapter).

Wine connoisseurs will also appreciate 700 Cannery Row for a tasting room and visitor center aptly named **A Taste of Monterey** (www.tastemonterey.com). Featured here are selections from more than 35 Monterey County wineries, locally grown gourmet plates and appetizers, a large gift shop, educational displays, and even a small theater showing films on winery operations. And to top it all off, you enjoy it all from a comfortable third-story perch with a fabulous panoramic view of Monterey Bay and the scenic shoreline of Cannery Row. Wine tasting at A Taste of Monterey is reasonably priced at $5.00 for six tastes. And the charge is rebated with the purchase of any bottle of wine. A Taste of Monterey is open daily from 11:00 A.M. to 6:00 P.M. The phone number is (831) 646-5446 or (888) 646-5446. Also note that **Bargetto Winery,** (831) 373-4053, has its own tasting room on the second level of 700 Cannery Row.

On the inland side of the street, 711 Cannery Row was originally the warehouse of the Monterey Canning Company. Tins of sardines were transferred from the cannery by conveyor belt through the crossover to the warehouse for storage and eventual shipment. Today, the warehouse is home to gift stores, candy and ice cream shops, and restaurants.

Next door to the Monterey Canning Company building, Steinbeck Plaza provides an open view to the Bay at McAbee Beach. This historic site was home to Monterey's last Chinese fishing village after a 1906 fire at China Point (just north of the Monterey Bay Aquarium in Pacific Grove) forced the village to relocate here. Today **McAbee Beach** is the site of a pleasant outdoor plaza featuring beach access and a bronze bust honoring John Steinbeck. On nice days, the Bay off McAbee Beach is a favorite spot for kayakers to paddle around lush kelp forests.

The **Steinbeck Plaza** shops, situated south of the plaza on both sides of Cannery Row, are a new addition to the area. Here, you'll find some of the trendier specialty shops and galleries on the Row, including **Pebble Beach On Cannery Row,** 660 Cannery Row, (831) 373-1500; **Kinkade Family Galleries,** 685 Cannery Row, (831) 657-2365; and **Ghirardelli Chocolate,** 660 Cannery Row, (831) 373-0997.

Now hidden from Cannery Row behind the inland side of the Plaza shops is the **Edgewater Packing Company.** Facing the Monterey Peninsula Recreation Trail, this 1940s packinghouse for fishmeal and fertilizer is now home to a turn-of-the-century carousel and 21st-century video games. It's a favorite among youngsters of all ages (see our Kidstuff chapter for more about this attraction). Directly in front of the Edgewater Packing Company sit two antique railway cars. The green railcar is home to the **Cannery Row Foundation,** (831) 372-8512, a nonprofit group dedicated to preserving the heritage of the Row. Inside, you'll find pamphlets, books, and maps recalling the area's storied past. There's also an ATM if you're running a little low on cash. Docents provide guidance, directions, and occasional walking tours. The railcar is open noon to 4:00 P.M. on weekends only.

Farther south down Cannery Row are more pleasant restaurants and shops as well as the charming waterfront **Spindrift Hotel** (see our Hotels and Motels chapter). Check out the "dragon roof" architecture at 653 Cannery Row. Formerly the Marina Apartments, this 1929 building exemplifies the Chinese influence on Cannery Row.

Just past Hoffman Avenue, the Row opens up into an undeveloped area that continues to be a hotbed of local debate. Plans for future development are meeting stiff resistance from preservationists who call for a stop to the remodeling and further "touristization" of the Row.

As Cannery Row nears Drake Avenue, it veers inland. On the inland side are two green cottages, which served as the stables and servants quarters for the large Haldorn Estate, built in 1901 on the site now occupied by the stately **Monterey Plaza Hotel** (see our Hotels and Motels chapter). These cottages later served as the movie set for *Clash by Night,* a 1951 film starring Barbara Stanwyck and, in her first co-starring role (as a fish cutter), Marilyn Monroe. A few hundred feet farther, where the recreation trail crosses Drake Avenue, is the site where Doc Ricketts lost his life in an automobile collision with the Del Monte Express. (The recreation trail was built over the path of the railroad tracks that served Monterey and Pacific Grove.) A bust of Ricketts now marks the spot.

Cannery Row turns left here at Drake Avenue and continues south along the entrance to the Monterey Plaza Hotel. More shops and the **Baywood Cellars** wine-tasting room, 381 Cannery Row, (831) 645–9035, line the Row across from the hotel. Look overhead a little farther down at 299 Cannery Row, and you'll see the Aeneas Sardine Packing Company crossover. Along with the crossover of the Monterey Canning Company, it's one of only two of the original 16 crossovers to survive.

Just after the **Monterey Bay Inn** (see our Hotels and Motels chapter), Cannery Row opens up into the **San Carlos Beach Park** (see our In and Around the Water chapter). Dedicated as an access point to the Monterey Bay Marine Sanctuary, the park is a favorite among scuba divers, kayakers, and picnickers. It provides a sweeping view of Cannery Row, the Monterey Harbor breakwater, and Fisherman's Wharf. Cannery Row ends at the entrance to the breakwater and Coast Guard pier.

Additional shops and restaurants occupy the two blocks above the length of Cannery Row on Wave and Foam Streets: **The Sardine Factory,** 701 Wave Street, and **The Whaling Station Inn,** 763 Wave Street, the **Cannery Row Antique Mall,** 471 Wave Street (see our Shopping chapter), and the **John Steinbeck Bookstore & Museum** (see the separate listing this chapter).

As tourism grew, parking became a problem near popular Cannery Row. But it's a problem no more. A large multistory parking garage with more than 1,000 spaces is now situated on the full block between Foam and Wave Streets and Prescott and Hoffman Avenues. Limited on-street metered parking is available on Cannery Row itself. A quarter buys you 20 minutes, and most meters have a four-hour maximum. Also on the Row, south of Hoffman Avenue, is a parking lot with extra-large spaces for campers and RVs.

Fisherman's Wharf
99 Pacific Street, Monterey
(831) 373–0600, www.montereywharf.com

Since the time when 19th-century trading schooners arrived in Monterey Bay to unload their precious cargoes after their harrowing trip around Cape Horn, Monterey's Fisherman's Wharf has been a welcome site to Peninsula visitors. Built in 1846 as Monterey's earliest pier of stone, the wharf has gone through more metamorphoses than Monarch butterflies but it remains a monument to the fishing industry and an important economic center for the city of Monterey. Only eight years after its erection, Fisherman's Wharf became the core of a booming whaling industry. Vessels docked wharfside with their gigantic cargoes in tow as workers gathered for the arduous task of carving up these majestic behemoths. By the early 20th century, with the whale population decimated, the tiny sardine displaced the enormous mammal as the catch of the day on the wharf. Following the boom and bust of the Cannery Row sardine era, commercial fishers turned to salmon, rock cod, albacore, mackerel, and squid

An artful sign marks the entrance to Old Fisherman's Wharf and Monterey Harbor. PHOTO: JANA MORBA

for their livelihood. Today, you'll find more tourists than fishermen on the wharf, as most of the commercial fishing fleet has moved over to the neighboring Municipal Wharf, just a sea lion's bark north in Monterey, or miles up the coast to Moss Landing.

From morning till evening, Fisherman's Wharf bustles with activity. Gift shops selling everything from T-shirts to seashells, along with ice cream parlors, candy stores (sample the saltwater taffy at Carousel Fine Candies), and other attractions tempt you as you enter the wharf. But it is still the traditional fish markets, fresh seafood restaurants, and boating activities farther out on the pier that make Fisherman's Wharf so special. You'll find a wide selection of sit-down eateries of all price ranges serving full menus for lunch and dinner. Insiders' favorites include Rappa's Seafood Restaurant for a good view and good food, Abalonnetti Seafood Trattoria with calamari and pizza to die

Fisherman's Wharf offers fish markets, seafood restaurants, bay cruises, and a variety of souvenir and gift shops. PHOTO: ELLIOTT SCHERLING/MONTEREY PENINSULA VCB

for, and Old Fisherman's Grotto with its famous clam chowder served in a French bread bowl (see our Restaurants chapter for more suggestions). Many wharf restaurants advertise early-bird dinners for the budget conscious, so consider an early evening meal. Or, if you're just looking for a quick snack, try the outdoor vendors' smoked salmon, marinated octopus, fried squid (calamari), steamed mussels, and other seafood delights as you window shop and stroll in the ocean air. Fisherman's Wharf is the departure point for whale-watching expeditions, Bay cruises, glass-bottom boat harbor cruises, sailing excursions, and fishing charters (see our In and around the Water chapter for details). It is also home to The New Wharf Theatre and its American Musical Theater Festival (see our Arts and Galleries chapter).

John Steinbeck Bookstore & Museum
551 Foam Street, Monterey
(831) 646–9117

So where do you go in Monterey to find out everything you ever wanted to know about John Steinbeck? Try the John Steinbeck Bookstore and Museum, on Foam Street just two blocks above Cannery Row, between McClellan and Hoffman Avenues. This unassuming building opens into a small but thoroughly stocked book and gift store that features virtually every published work of the Pulitzer and Nobel Prize winner. You'll find new and used books, including some classic first editions; videotapes of *East of Eden, Tortilla Flat,* and other Steinbeck movies; photographs and artwork celebrating Steinbeck's Cannery Row era; and coffee, soft drinks, and snacks to enjoy as you browse through the books, gifts, and memorabilia.

The book and gift store itself is certainly worth a visit by anyone searching for the story of Cannery Row, Salinas, and the rest of Monterey County according to John. But it is the activities that go on in the back room and out the front door of the bookstore that merit special attention. Proprietor James Jay is a virtual walking Steinbeck encyclopedia and relishes sharing the legend and lore of this absorbing author. In a back room theater he holds "lecture tours" on Steinbeck, replete with stories, photographs, artifacts, and quotations that bring the words and images of John Steinbeck to life. You'll hear about the special gift that inspired nine-year-old Steinbeck to become a writer. You'll discover amazing parallels between Steinbeck and another John who became a friend and admirer in later life—John Fitzgerald Kennedy. And you'll learn why Steinbeck, now highly revered in Monterey, was not always a "favorite son."

Beyond sharing these fascinating stories, Jay also leads informative walking tours of Cannery Row, following the "Footsteps of John Steinbeck." You'll be hard-pressed to find a better guide to the past and present landmarks of this historic district of Monterey. The John Steinbeck Bookstore & Museum is open daily from 10:00 A.M. to 6:00 P.M. Lecture tours and walking tours are given by appointment only, available at 11:00 A.M. and 3:00 P.M. daily except Sunday. Driving tours can also be arranged by special request. Charges vary but average $10 per person, more or less, for a one-hour or so tour. (Jay doesn't like to be tied down to a fixed time and price. It must be the Steinbeck in him.)

Laguna Seca Recreation Area
Monterey-Salinas Highway (Highway 68), Monterey
(831) 648–5100, (800) 327–SECA, www.laguna-seca.com

Laguna Seca Recreation Area, approximately 7 miles inland from Monterey proper, is a center for a composite of activities, most of which revolve around a love of automobiles. There's the famous Laguna Seca Raceway, home of world-class motor sports competitions, including superbikes, Indy cars, and antique classics. In 2002, for example, Laguna Seca hosts the Grand Prix of Monterey featuring the Shell 300, the Honda International Superbike Classic, the 29th Annual Rolex Monterey Historic Automobile Races, and the Monterey Sports Car Championships (American LeMans Series). This is serious racing featuring the best motor sport stars from around the world.

Then there's the Laguna Seca Campground (see the County Parks section of our Parks and Recreation chapter). Motor sport enthusiasts bring their recreation vehicles, campers, trailers, tents, or just their sleeping bags and camp out in well-paved and well-maintained campsites amid scrub oak and chaparral. Some of the 100-plus sites overlook the raceway, while others have more serene views of rolling hills. The campground is also open when there are no racing activities underway. While it can't rival Big Sur camping, it does provide a reasonably priced spot to pull in your road-home away from home and put down your temporary stakes. And you're only 15 minutes inland on Highway 68 from the waters of Monterey Bay.

For those brave souls who'd rather drive Laguna Seca than simply observe it, have we got a treat for you! The Skip Barber Racing School sets up shop at Laguna Seca year-round to provide a variety of driving and racing classes (see the Close-up in our Parks and Recreation chapter).

Maritime Museum of Monterey
5 Custom House Plaza, Monterey
(831) 372–2608, www.mntmh.org/maritime.htm

What started as the private nautical collection of former Carmel mayor and seaman Allen Knight has grown into a remarkably complete history of the seafaring heritage of Monterey Bay. Salty dogs and landlubbers alike will enjoy the impressive collection of maritime artifacts spanning four centuries of men and women on the sea. Housed in the 18,000-square-foot Stanton Center, the museum is a project of the Monterey History and Art Association. Upon entry, you will embark on a high-sea adventure that takes you all the way back to the time of Spanish conquistadors. Expansive exhibit areas spread out over two stories overlooking Monterey Bay allow you to retrace the routes of Spanish sea captain Juan Rodriguez Cabrillo as he mapped out the California coast in the 16th century. Use your imagination to travel with Father Junipero Serra as he establishes Monterey's first mission settlement. Experience the drama of Commodore John Drake Sloat raising the U.S. flag over Monterey, laying

The 10,000 pound, two-story high Fresnel lens at the Maritime Museum of Monterey originally guided seafarers from atop the Point Sur Lighthouse. PHOTO: TOM OWENS

claim to the expansive California territory. View the impressive U.S. Pacific Fleet as it pulls into Monterey Bay in the early 20th century. And experience the triumphs and tragedies of the Portuguese whalers, the Chinese squid fishers, the Japanese abalone divers, and the Italian sardine fishermen as they sweat and toil to make Monterey a thriving seaport.

The Maritime Museum brims with artifacts, ship models, paintings, and photographs depicting these historic eras. Rare, finely handcrafted chronometers and sextants, original ship's logs, military weapons, and the everyday tools of the hearty seagoing sailors are all on display. The guardian over the entire museum is the original two-story-high Fresnel lens of Point Sur Lighthouse. This 10,000-pound beacon, designed in 1822 in France, was installed in 1889 to stand watch for ships navigating around treacherous Big Sur Point. For nearly 100 years, this cut-glass beauty warned mariners of the dangerous rocky shore that continues to claim ships that venture too close. Its 1,000 prisms and precision magnifying glass sent out a powerful beam that could be seen more than 20 miles offshore.

Two of the more recent additions to the Museum are an expanded World War II exhibit and new interactive video stations. The video stations allow you to select topics of interest, such as the story of the USS Macon dirigible, which crashed off the Big Sur coast, and then listen to newsreel accounts or interviews with eye witnesses.

Don't forget to sound the foghorn before completing your visit to the Maritime Museum. And kids who complete the Museum's unique treasure hunt are in for a special treat! The Ship's Store features a good selection of books, prints, postcards, toys, games, jewelry, and decorative items for your shipshape home. Ask about education programs including ship model workshops, children's activities, and a 4,000-volume library open 10:00 A.M. to 4:00 P.M. Monday through Friday. You'll find the Maritime Museum of Monterey in the historic Custom House Plaza, a short stroll from the entrance to Fisherman's Wharf. Follow signs to Fisherman's Wharf and parking. It's open from 10:00 A.M. to 5:00 P.M. Tuesday through Sunday except Thanksgiving and Christmas. Admission is $5.00 for adults, $2.50 for senior citizens and active military, $2.50 for youth (ages 13 to 17) and free for children ages 12 and younger. Memberships are available.

Monterey Bay Aquarium
886 Cannery Row, Monterey
(831) 648–4800, www.mbayaq.org

As you gaze out over Monterey Bay you can't help but wonder what goes on underneath the rolling waves, within the dense kelp forests, and among the rocky crags of the shoreline. Well wonder no more—and you don't even have to don a wet suit. The Monterey Bay Aquarium brings the Bay to Cannery Row in a breathtaking exhibit of life beneath the sea. Opened in 1984, the world-acclaimed, nonprofit, and self-supporting facility is now home to more than 300,000 creatures of the deep and not so deep, representing close to 550 species. The vast majority of residents are native to Monterey Bay. The aquarium is neatly laid out over two and three stories of more than 100 exhibits, fed by a system that pumps 2,000 gallons of raw seawater into the tanks each minute.

You'll visit the feathery inhabitants of coastal wetlands as well as the crawly creatures of deep granite reefs. A towering 28-foot-tall kelp forest sways hypnotically with the man-made tide of a 335,000-gallon tank as schools of silvery fish reflect the natural sunlight. Playful sea otters hold court before fascinated observers. Outdoor tide pools teem with life. And we haven't even gotten to the really good stuff yet!

A crown jewel of the aquarium is the Outer Bay exhibit. The only word to describe it is other-worldly (we know that's two words, but they're hyphenated). If you haven't visited the aquarium since this wing opened in 1996, a return trip is a must. The million-gallon tank is home to strange open-ocean beings normally found in waters 60 miles outside the mouth of Monterey Bay. From what is purported to be the largest window in the world (54 feet long, 15 feet tall, and 13 inches thick) you'll view giant ocean sunfish, green sea turtles, soupfin sharks, barracuda, and schools of large yellowfin tuna and bonito. Nearby tanks of jellies look for all the world like visitors from outer space rather than the outer bay.

At the "Mysteries of the Deep" exhibit you'll discover dozens of rarely seen creatures, including filetail catsharks, predatory tunicates, sea whips, spider crabs, ratfish, feather stars, eel-pouts, Pacific hagfish, and California king crabs. Monterey Bay Aquarium is the first in the world to present living displays of most of these species, who normally make their home in the mile-and-more deep submarine canyons of Monterey Bay. The 7,000-square-foot exhibit, open through October 2003, includes live exhibits, videos, and hands-on displays.

Kids of all ages enjoy the many opportunities available to get up close and personal with some slithery and slimy friends of the sea. Pet bat rays as they glide past in a wide shallow pool. Don't worry: Their stingers have been clipped. Hold sea stars and their tide pool buddies at the touch pools. Splash Zone is a family-oriented exhibit featuring black-footed penguins, moray eels, tropical sharks, and colorful corals. At *Live from Monterey,* a live video broadcast presented at most four days a week, you'll get a backseat view in a research submarine as scientists study unusual sea life in the Monterey Bay canyons. An extensive gift and bookstore provides special mementos of your visit and gifts for friends and family back home. The aquarium's Portola Cafe has a help-yourself cafeteria and a full-service restaurant and oyster bar with great ocean views.

Plan on spending at least three hours at the aquarium. Insiders suggest arriving when the aquarium opens at 10:00 A.M., visiting for a couple hours before the big afternoon crowds arrive, and getting your hand stamped for an optional return visit in the early evening. Spend the afternoon with a lunch along the beaches. Explore the real tide pools (but don't wash off your stamp!) that are only minutes down the Monterey Peninsula Recreation Trail that runs alongside the aquarium and down the shoreline in Pacific Grove. Just remember to pack out your trash, and don't disturb the protected wildlife of the Monterey Bay Marine Sanctuary.

If you've never seen an anchovy without the pizza, the Monterey Bay Aquarium is a must-see. It's open from 10:00 A.M. to 6:00 P.M. daily except Christmas. On holidays and summer months (Memorial Day to Labor Day), the aquarium opens at 9:30 A.M. Admission rates are $17.95 for adults 18 and older; $14.95 for seniors 65 or older and students (ages 13 through 17 or with a college I.D.); and $7.95 for children ages three to 12 and the disabled. Children two and younger are admitted

The Great Tide Pool at the Monterey Bay Aquarium is open to the ocean and teeming with intertidal creatures. PHOTO: RICK BROWNE/MONTEREY PENINSULA VCB

free. Memberships and group rates are available, and an extensive volunteer program allows locals to serve as guides.

Monterey Path of History
5 Custom House Plaza, Monterey
(831) 649–7118

Encompassing nearly 40 historic structures from 19th-century California, the 2.8-mile Monterey Path of History meanders throughout the entire downtown area of Old Monterey. Feel free to head out on your personal adventure with your Path of History map in hand (available at any of the visitor centers throughout town). Pick and choose from the many adobes and other storied structures along the route. Some historic buildings are now private residences that can be viewed from the exterior only. But many others open their doors to the public for interior and garden visits. If you prefer, you can take a 90-minute guided walking tour of the path, visiting selected sites. This option provides expert commentary from a local guide and includes interior and garden visits to up to four historic locations that otherwise require an admission fee equal to the cost of the whole tour.

The cost of the guided tour is $5.00 for adults, $3.00 for youths, and $2.00 for children. The guided tours begin daily at 10:00 A.M., 3:00 P.M., and 4:00 P.M. at The Monterey State Historic Park Visitor Center located in the Stanton Center, also home of the Maritime Museum of Monterey (see previous listing). The earlier starting times provide opportunities to tour the interiors of most of the historic sites. Whether you take the guided tour or walk the Path of History on your own, we suggest you begin by viewing the free 14-minute film presented every 20 minutes at the theater in the visitor center. It provides a vivid introduction to the historic sites on the path as well as insights into some of Monterey's most interesting personalities.

In this write-up we suggest a tour for adventurers who wish to see the highlights of the path on their own. These 14 buildings include the 11 structures that make up the Monterey State Historic Park as well as Colton Hall, the home of California's first constitutional convention, and the Royal Presidio Chapel, the oldest building standing in Monterey. This is a great introductory trip, but be sure to check out all of the structures listed on the Path of History map to see whether others may be of personal interest.

Note: Round markers (the new ones are yellow with the crest of Monterey; the old ones are bronze) in the sidewalks will help guide you along the Path of History route. In front of each historic site you'll find an illustrated tile, set in the sidewalk, and descriptive signs.

So slip on your good walking shoes and let's begin. Prepare for a good two to three hours, depending on how long you stay at each site. The walk itself, at a leisurely pace, takes about 90 minutes. From the Stanton Center near Fisherman's Wharf, take a quick stroll east across the Custom House Plaza to the **Pacific House and Garden.** It's the large white two-story building with dark green trim directly in front of the Stanton Center entrance. This 1847 adobe was first occupied by the U.S. Quartermaster for offices and military supplies and later became a boisterous public tavern. The walled corral behind the house is said to have been an entertainment arena for Sunday bull and bear fights, a popular spectator "sport" of the mid-19th century. Today, the Pacific House is home to two museums. The Pacific House Museum celebrates Monterey's period as capital of Spanish and Mexican California. The Monterey Museum of the American Indian is packed with Native American artifacts—and a real "growling" grizzly bear. The museums are open daily from 10:00 A.M. to 5:00 P.M.

From the front of Pacific House, follow the markers in the sidewalk north across the Plaza toward Fisherman's Wharf. Here, you'll reach the **Custom House,** the oldest public building on the Pacific Coast. Built in 1827, the Custom House presided over Mexico's only legal port of entry into the "Alta California" coast, inspecting cargoes and collecting custom duties and taxes. Later, the Custom House was the site where Commodore John Drake Sloat raised the U.S. flag on July 7, 1846, claiming more than 600,000 square miles of territory for the U.S. government. Today, you'll see a reproduction of the Custom House in action. It is filled with replicas of the types of 19th-century supplies that would likely come into port as well as the hides and tallow the Montereyans used in trade for those goods. Don't leave without your passport stamp. The Custom House is open daily from 10:00 A.M. to 5:00 P.M. and is free of charge.

From the Custom House, follow the markers east down Decatur Street. Cross Oliver Street and enter into Heritage Harbor, a retail and business center. Follow the markers about another 100 feet to a fountain. To your left, you'll discover the **First Brick House and Garden.** This is the first structure in California built by the kiln-fired brick construction method, rather than from the traditional adobe. The modest home was constructed in 1847 by the Dickinson family, original members of the Donner party who, fortunately for them, parted company with the Donners before the fateful crossing of the Sierras. Inside, you'll find displays highlighting some of the home's previous occupants. The First Brick House is open daily from 10:00 A.M. to 5:00 P.M.

Upon exiting, turn left (east) and continue just a few more steps to the **Whaling Station and Garden.** Built in 1847 as a replica of an ancestral Scottish cottage, the two-story adobe with balcony and garden was acquired in 1855 by the Old Monterey Whaling Company to house offices and employee quarters. Note the city's only remaining whalebone sidewalk in front of the building. (The Junior League of Monterey County now maintains this beautifully restored building as well as the neighboring First Brick House.)

The Path of History takes you through the garden gate at the Whaling Station. Continue through this tranquil garden (open daily from 10:00 A.M. to 5:00 P.M.) and exit in the rear, through Heritage Harbor and to Scott Street. Cross Scott Street at the corner of Pacific Street and then turn left down Scott to the chalk-rock and adobe **Casa Del Oro.** Famous Monterey businessmen David Jacks and Joseph Boston ran this 19th-century general store

Bubble windows allow Aquarium visitors to get up close and personal with sea life. PHOTO: MONTEREY BAY AQUARIUM/MONTEREY PENINSULA VCB

and gold depository. Built in 1845, Casa Del Oro is once again open for business as the Boston Store (open 11:00 A.M. to 3:00 P.M. Thursday through Sunday), a pleasant gift shop run by the nonprofit Historic Garden League. The league also runs the Picket Fence garden shop on the other side of the adjacent Casa Del Oro garden.

To continue on our path, retrace your steps back up Scott Street to Pacific Street. Cross to the southeast corner of Scott and Pacific Streets, where you'll find **California's First Theatre.** Built in 1844 by Jack Swan as a saloon and boarding house for sailors, this wooden frame and adobe structure became a venue for live theatre when the New York Volunteers, a group of local soldiers, began staging productions in 1848. The tavern and theater are still operating today, with live 19th-century melodramas and comedies held weekly since 1937 by the Troupers of the Gold Coast (see our Arts and Galleries chapter for more details on performances). The First Theatre is open for touring from 1:00 to 5:00 P.M. Thursday through Saturday.

As you exit California's First Theatre, turn right (south) and walk one block to 336 Pacific Street. Walk through the front garden gate and witness the exceptionally well-preserved **Casa Soberanes.** This thick-walled beauty is a classic example of the Monterey Colonial adobe. Built in 1842 by the commandant of the Monterey Presidio and occupied by the Soberanes family in 1860, it features interconnecting rooms filled with splendid furniture and artwork, a magnificent balcony, and beautiful well-kept gardens. Tours of the interior are available at 1:00 and 4:00 P.M.

Note: This is the first of four structures on the Path of History that have scheduled tours and charge admission, the others being the Larkin House, the Cooper Molera Adobe, and the Stevenson House. If you take the guided tour from the Stanton Center, your price of admission to each is covered. If you are on your own, one admission ticket purchased at the Stanton Center or at any of the four sites will get you into all four historic structures. As with the tour, the cost of admission is $5.00 for adults, $3.00 for youths, and $2.00 for children.

Upon exiting Casa Soberanes, continue south on Pacific Street. Pass the Merritt House, former home of Josiah Merritt, the first judge of Monterey County and continue three blocks to **Colton Hall.** (The sidewalk markers disappear on this section of Pacific Street, as the Path of History detours slightly uphill to take in a few other sites we're not visiting here.)

The first United States public building in California, Colton Hall was the site of the convention that drafted California's first constitution. Named after Walter Colton, the first Chief Magistrate of Monterey after the American occupation of California, Colton Hall was completed in 1849. Notice that it sports a definite New England style that contrasted markedly with the California adobes. It was erected, in Colton's words, "out of the slender proceeds of town lots, the labor of convicts, taxes on liquor shops, and fines on gamblers." Climb the exterior stairs to the second-story museum of this most historic California structure, and you'll enter a scene similar to that created by the 48 delegates as they debated the issues leading to California's constitution in October of 1849. Books, parchments, and fountain pens lie about the well-worn oak tables, as if the delegates had just left the room for a recess. Toward the rear of the museum are mementos of Colton Hall School, which began holding classes here in 1873. The museum is free of charge and open daily from 10:00 A.M. to noon and 1:00 to 5:00 P.M. For an entertaining side trip, follow the walkway that goes behind Colton Hall to find the **Old Monterey Jail.** This small six-cell jailhouse of granite was constructed in 1854 and served as a jail for more than 100 years—without a single reported escape. There was, however, a reported jail storming, where some 19th-century townspeople apprehended a jailed murderer and hanged him from the jail rafters! The cells are set up to re-create the quarters of incarcerated scoundrels from different eras of Monterey's colorful past—including a John Steinbeck character from *Tortilla Flat.*

Walk out to the front of Colton Hall and take the left-hand path through the tranquil garden setting of **Friendly Plaza,** a brick courtyard built in the 1930s with WPA funds. Be sure to read the unusual inscription on the monument to the city of Monterey. Then cross Pacific Street at the adjacent corner (Jefferson and Pacific Streets), and you'll be facing the rear of the **Larkin House.** Walk down Jefferson Street one block to the entrance on Calle Principal. Built by Thomas Larkin, U.S. consul to Alta California, this 1834 two-story adobe is the first example of the architectural style that has become known as "Monterey Colonial" or simply the "Monterey style." The Larkin House is now home to a fabulous collection of period furnishings and antiques from around the world. Don't miss the walled garden to experience a little piece of heaven circa 19th-century Monterey. Admission is required for the interior tours at 11:00 A.M. and 2:00 and 3:00 P.M.

As you exit Larkin House, turn right (south) down Calle Principal and walk past the quarters of William Tecumseh Sherman, the House of Four Winds, and the Monterey Museum of Art to the end of the block. Here, you'll find **Casa Gutierrez,** one of the few remaining examples of the simpler Mexican-style adobe. Built in 1841 by Joaquin Gutierrez, the nephew of Mexico's acting governor of California in the 1830s, this modest adobe was recently home to a Mexican restaurant. Today, the building is the home of the Thomas Kinkade Museum and Cultural Center (see listing in The Arts and Galleries chapter).

From Casa Gutierrez, cross Calle Principal at Madison Street and make the first left on Polk Street. Cross to the opposite side of Polk at the Gabriel de la Torre Adobe and continue north on Polk one block to Munras Avenue. You'll discover the **Cooper-Molera Adobe,** perhaps the most active spot on this Path of History and the largest complex of the Monterey State Historic Park. In fact, if you only have time to visit one of Monterey's historic adobes, this wouldn't be a bad choice. The Cooper-Molera Adobe was built in 1830 by John Rogers Cooper, a New England sea captain, as a gift for his bride. Over the years, the Cooper family added barns, servants quarters, and other structures to complete the two-and-a-half-acre complex you see today. Frances Molera, Captain

The Pacific House Museum on the Custom House Plaza now houses the Monterey Museum of the American Indian. PHOTO: TOM OWENS

Cooper's granddaughter, willed the entire grounds to the National Trust for Historic Preservation, which leases it to the State of California. The Cooper-Molera Adobe grounds are open free of charge every day from 10:00 A.M. to 5:00 P.M. from June through August, and 10:00 A.M. to 4:00 P.M. September through May. Guided tours of the interior are available at 10:00 A.M., noon, and 3:00 P.M. for the fee mentioned earlier in this entry. You're sure to enjoy the interior period garden, where chickens and other barnyard animals roam. There are also an exhibit room, barn, carriage display, and other sites of interest to see. Visit the Cooper Store, which features wooden toys, pottery, and other goods reminiscent of days gone by. Try to take advantage of the special history and art programs that are held throughout the year for both adults and children. The Cooper-Molera Courtyard is also the starting point for historic garden tours of Old Monterey on selected days (currently Saturdays and Tuesdays at 1:00 P.M.) from May through September. Adults are asked to pay a modest donation.

To proceed to our next stop, turn right (south) from the entrance of the Cooper Store and head down Munras Avenue past the Simoneau Plaza Transit Station. Cross Munras at the crosswalk, then continue across Tyler, following the brass markers. Follow a large sign pointing to a path that enters the rear garden of **Stevenson House.** (If the garden gate is closed, continue down Munras one block, take a left on Webster Avenue and another left on Houston Street to the front entrance.) Built in 1840, this historic hotel is said to have been the residence of author Robert Louis Stevenson during the fall of 1879. (There is debate whether Stevenson actually lived here or was just a frequent visitor, but who are we to quibble?) The story goes that Stevenson came to Monterey in search of his true love, Fanny Osbourne. Here, Stevenson resided in what was then known as the French Hotel as he courted his future bride. Today, you'll find period furnishings as well as perhaps the world's greatest collection of manuscripts, first-edition books, photos, and other personal belongings of the Scottish-born writer. Admission is required for the interior tours at 10:00 A.M. and 2:00 and 4:00 P.M., as mentioned earlier in this entry.

Our final destination is, fittingly, the oldest building in existence in Monterey and its last remaining structure of 18th-century Spanish origin. Exiting the front of Stevenson House, turn right (south) on Houston Street. At the first corner, turn left on Webster Street and make a right on Abrego Street, heading past Casa Pacheco. Make another left across Abrego at Church Street. Continue down Church Street a long block past San Carlos School to the **Royal Presidio Chapel.** Built in 1770 as part of California's second Franciscan mission (San Carlos de Borromeo de Monterey), the original chapel was destroyed by fire in 1789. The chapel that stands today was rebuilt in 1794 and is the oldest church in continuous service in California as well as the smallest cathedral in the United States. Note the exquisite "Virgin of Guadalupe" that adorns the facade. The Royal Presidio Chapel is open daily from 8:30 A.M. to 6:00 P.M. free of charge.

To return to our starting point, the Custom House Plaza, backtrack your route to the Stevenson House. Continue north on Houston Street to Pearl Street. Turn left (east) on Pearl and go one block to Tyler Street. Turn right (north) and go one block to Bonifacio Place. Turn left and go one block to Alvarado Street. Cross Alvarado and turn right (north) on Alvarado, following Monterey's main street through downtown until it ends at Del Monte Avenue. Cross Del Monte and continue north across Portola Plaza and along the shops outside the DoubleTree Hotel. Keep walking another few yards and you're there. After your long walk, you're probably ready for an ice cream cone, beverage, or full meal out on Fisherman's Wharf. Enjoy!

Steinbeck's Spirit of Monterey Wax Museum
700 Cannery Row, Monterey
(831) 375–3770, www.wax-museum.com

Sure, it's pure kitsch compared to computer-age standards of lifelike robotics and 3-D visual displays found at today's mega-amusement parks. But there's something pleasantly nostalgic about a genuine wax museum of sculptured figures that take you through a 20-minute Cliff Notes version of the history of Monterey. It's all here: Spanish explorers, early Native Americans, Father Serra and the missions, Robert Louis Stevenson, and John Steinbeck himself narrating stories of his *Cannery Row* characters. Some of the figurines are so lifelike, you'll swear you see them breathing. Steinbeck's Spirit of Monterey Wax Museum is open daily from 10:30 A.M. to 8:00 P.M. The price of entry is $4.95 for adults, and $2.95 for children ages seven to 12. Children six and younger get in free.

Pacific Grove

Monarch Grove Sanctuary
Ridge Road, Pacific Grove
(831) 375–2140

In 1990, the citizens of Pacific Grove enthusiastically cast their votes on a bond measure authorizing the city to spend more than $1.2 million on a rather nondescript 2.4-acre lot of spindly pine, cypress, and eucalyptus trees. As a real estate investment, the purchase certainly didn't make much sense. But for a city that proudly calls itself "Butterfly Town USA," it made all the sense in the world.

Taxpayer money was voluntarily spent to purchase this small private lot facing imminent development so it could be preserved and restored as a permanent butterfly sanctuary. Since the purchase, hundreds of volunteers organized by three citizen groups, the Monarch Habitat Restoration Committee, Friends of the Monarch, and the Pacific Grove Eco-Corps, have devoted countless hours maintaining the grounds. They've also planted hundreds of seedlings of trees and flowering plants that future generations of Monarch butterflies will call home.

The Monarch Grove Sanctuary serves as an overwintering site for Monarch butterflies from October through March. In fact, it is one of two primary sites within the city that provide the microclimate that Monarchs need to withstand the cold and wind of winter. The other site is a grove of pine trees at George Washington Park, which also has benefited from the restoration efforts of the citizen groups.

If your visit takes you to the Monterey Peninsula during the fall and winter months, take time to visit one of the Monarch habitats. Follow the clearly marked trails to the designated sites. Look up into the trees about 20 to 30 feet above the ground. On chilly, foggy, or cloudy days, you may not immediately notice the butterflies. In cold weather, they cluster with their wings closed, looking much like bunches of triangular brown leaves. Keep looking and you'll eventually spot them. When the weather warms above 55 degrees,

The Custom House, the oldest public building on the Pacific Coast, gives you a taste of 19th-century trade among early Montereyans. PHOTO: SHARON FONG/MONTEREY PENINSULA VCB

the Monarchs come to life, opening their wings and exposing the bright orange tops we're all familiar with. Should the sun warm them further, they will flutter and fly about in a showy display. Recent estimates place the winter Monarch population at more than 15,000, though the numbers can vary dramatically from year to year.

Where did they all come from? The Monarchs fly into Pacific Grove from as far north as Canada and Alaska and as far east as the Rocky Mountains. Their long journeys take up to eight months.

How the butterflies find their way back to Pacific Grove year after year is very much a mystery. Actually, the butterflies you see today are likely the great-great-great grandchildren of the Monarchs who overwintered here the previous year. Those butterflies flew east or north to lay their eggs and die. The next three to four generations fly even farther north and east, living abbreviated lifespans of just a few weeks before laying their eggs. This year's Monarch emerged from a chrysalis that hung at the farthest northern and eastern regions of the migration and made the entire return trip, flying up to 2,000 miles and reaching altitudes of 10,000 feet.

Scientists theorize that the Monarchs rely on magnetic fields, the position of the sun, or pure genetic instincts to find their way home to Pacific Grove. Regardless, they do return to be celebrated by the citizens of Pacific Grove who hold a festive Butterfly Parade on the second Saturday every October (see our Annual Events chapter).

It is important to note that the butterfly habitats are very fragile and require great care. Please stay on the trails to minimize impact on the sanctuaries. Don't disturb the clusters and watch out for butterflies on the ground. As the sign at the Monarch Grove Sanctuary says, "Leave only footprints and take away only memories."

The two butterfly habitats are open every day sunrise to sunset. The Monarch Grove Sanctuary is on Ridge Road adjacent to the Butterfly Trees Lodge. Ridge Road is off of Lighthouse Avenue, directly across from The Wilkie's Motel. George

Washington Park is at the corner of Alder Street and Pine Avenue. There is no admission charge at either site. While driving to the habitats, be alert to the "Butterfly Crossing" signs!

Pacific Grove Historic Walking Tour
Forest and Central Avenues, Pacific Grove
(831) 373–3304

While not as elaborate as the Monterey Path of History (see separate listing in our Monterey section), the Pacific Grove Historic Walking Tour is of special interest to lovers of Victorian and Queen Anne architecture. You can pick up a map of the tour at the Pacific Grove Chamber of Commerce or the Pacific Grove Museum of Natural History, both of which are at the corner of Forest and Central Avenues. The walking-tour map includes 18 points of interest, beginning with the Museum of Natural History (see separate listing). Highlights include St. Mary's By-The-Sea (a Gothic-style church with two Tiffany windows), Seven Gables, Gosby House, and Chautauqua Hall. Other than a few private residences, most of the buildings on the walking tour are open to the public during daylight hours.

Pacific Grove Museum of Natural History
Forest and Central Avenues, Pacific Grove
(831) 648–5716, www.pgmuseum.org

Recognized nationwide as one of the finest museums of its size, the Pacific Grove Museum of Natural History is a must-see for those intrigued by the fauna and flora of the Monterey Peninsula. Sandy the Whale, local artist Larry Foster's life-size sculpture of a California gray whale, greets you at the bottom of the entrance steps. Climb aboard, kids: Sandy is friendly and nearly indestructible, and she may be the most photographed gray whale in the world!

Once inside this adobe-style museum, erected in 1932, you'll see intriguing zoological specimens of many local birds, mammals, reptiles, and insects that roam throughout Peninsula beaches, forests, and streets. Unique marine creatures are on display, too, including an eerie-looking big skate. The museum's collection of more than 400 birds is especially impressive, as is the extensive multimedia exhibit honoring the local Monarch butterfly—delivered in three different languages! You'll also find artifacts from local Native Americans, such as the Costanoan, Salinan, and Esselen tribes.

An interesting exhibit of geology and mineralogy includes a working Geiger-Muller counter, an enclosed booth of fluorescent minerals, marine fossils, and impressive relief maps of Monterey County and the deep canyons of Monterey Bay, completed in 1936. A Children's Touch Gallery includes hands-on specimens and artifacts and live subtidal sea animals from the Monterey Bay. Outside, the museum grows a garden of native Monterey County plants and trees.

In springtime, be sure to catch the annual wildflower show, usually the third weekend in April. Check the museum's schedule for selected Smithsonian Institution traveling exhibitions as well. Mementos of your visit can be purchased at the well-stocked gift shop. The Pacific Grove Museum of Natural History is open Tuesday through Sunday from 10:00 A.M. to 5:00 P.M. Admission is free, though a donation is greatly appreciated. It's closed New Year's Day, Thanksgiving, Christmas Eve, and Christmas Day.

Point Pinos Lighthouse
Asilomar Boulevard at Lighthouse Avenue, Pacific Grove
(831) 648–3116, www.pgmuseum.org

The oldest continuously operating lighthouse on the West Coast of the United States, Point Pinos Lighthouse has been marking the entrance to Monterey Bay for seafarers since 1855. And what you see is what you get: The building, the lenses, and the prisms are all original equipment. The light is a third-order Fresnel manufactured in France in 1853. A whale-oil lantern was its first power source, followed by lard oil, and later kerosene. An electrical light was finally installed in 1915. Today, a 1,000-watt bulb produces a 50,000-candlepower beam that, on a clear night, can be spotted up to 15 miles offshore.

Visitors will find the procession of Point Pinos lightkeepers as interesting as

Colton Hall is the site of the drafting of California's first constitution and the first U.S. public building in the state. PHOTO: MONTEREY PENINSULA VCB

the lighthouse itself. The original lightkeeper, Charles Layton, was killed in 1856 as a member of a sheriff's posse chasing notorious Mexican outlaw Anastacio Garcia. He was succeeded by his widow, Charlotte, who served until she married her assistant in 1860. Lightkeeper Alan Luce was once host to Robert Louis Stevenson, who wrote of his pleasant visit in 1879. The most famous Point Pinos lightkeeper of all, however, was Emily Fish, known as the "Socialite Keeper." Mrs. Fish used the lighthouse to entertain many guests and kept the building well decorated and meticulously clean. Today's visitors get a glimpse of the lighthouse under Fish's 1893 to 1914 reign, as the lighthouse is decorated much as she kept it.

The Point Pinos Lighthouse shines on daily from the northernmost point of the Monterey Peninsula, sharing its scenic site with the Pacific Grove Municipal Golf Course. Parking is behind the course's 10th green, off Asilomar Avenue between Lighthouse Avenue and Ocean View Boulevard. The lighthouse is open to the public from 1:00 to 4:00 P.M. Thursday through Sunday. Admission is free, and volunteer docents are on hand to provide historical background.

Carmel

Carmel Mission Basilica
Rio Road and Lausen Drive, Carmel
(831) 624–3600, www.carmelmission.com

The Basilica of Mission San Carlos Borromeo del Rio Carmelo, or Carmel Mission, is home to some of the most significant religious artifacts in all of California. Padre (Father) Junipero Serra, founder of the California missions, is buried here and many of his personal belongings are on display. Padre Serra arrived in Monterey Bay by sea in 1770, having established the first California mission in San Diego the previous year. He chose this idyllic site in Carmel over the original Monterey site of San Carlos de Borromeo de Monterey because of its rich soil and proximity to the bountiful Carmel River. Serra took up permanent residence in the mission in 1771. At first, it was a simple wooden structure. But before long, the Spaniards enlisted the Native Americans who had converted to Catholicism to construct the more substantial adobe buildings. The mission soon became an important center of commerce, serving as a safe enclave for early Spanish settlers who sought rest, company, and supplies on their long arduous journeys up and down Alta California.

From Carmel, Padre Serra presided over the founding of nine of the eventual 21 missions in California. He passed away in 1784 at the age of 71. During his final days, Serra requested burial at Carmel Mission, beside his longtime friend Padre Juan Crespi, who had died two years prior.

Following Padre Serra's death, Padre Lasuen led Carmel Mission and, in 1793, undertook Serra's plans for building the present stone church. Built from native sandstone from the Santa Lucia Mountains in Big Sur and plastered with lime made from burnt seashells gathered along the coast, the church at Carmel Mission Basilica was completed in 1797. The turn of the 19th century marked the height of prosperity for Carmel Mission. The population of Native Americans was nearing 1,000, and the mission adobes continued to expand. But within the next 20 to 30 years, the mission began to fall into decay. By 1823 the population was less than 400. By 1836, Padre Jose Real officially moved the church to Monterey, taking most of the mission's ornaments and other effects with him. Services at Carmel Mission eventually ceased, and by 1880 the grounds were in ruin, pillaged of anything of value that had been left behind. Father Casanova's installation of a new roof on the old mission in 1884 was the first important step in its eventual restoration. The 1920s saw further restoration efforts and the erection of a memorial to Serra and the other Padres buried on the site. Then in 1931, Monsignor Philip Scher, pastor of San Carlos in Monterey, appointed Harry Downie as curator in charge of mission restoration. It was Downie who directed the painstaking rebuilding of the mission to its former grandeur.

Today, visitors can get a taste of mission life as it was in the late 18th and early 19th centuries. A mission museum displays a remarkable collection of artifacts dating back to Padre Serra's time. The spartan cell where Serra lived is recreated in detail. You'll also see his ornate "cloth of gold" vestments of Chinese silk, his personal Bible and redwood remnants of his original coffin. The museum also houses California's first library as well as a collection of tools, equipment, and appliances used by the Spaniards and Native Americans in day-to-day life at the mission. In the rear of the museum is the Junipero Serra sarcophagus, designed and created in 1924 by renowned California artist Jo Mora. At the head of the sarcophagus is a spectacular wooden cross, also a Mora design. It is a common misconception that Serra is buried beneath the sarcophagus. Actually, he is buried within the church, which is located just outside the right rear exit of the museum.

As you enter the church, notice the tower and the mission bells that date from the late 18th and early 19th centuries. The bells are still rung by hand, as they were back in 1770. Inside, the church faithfully reflects its original design, even though it was rebuilt almost totally from the ground up in the 1930s. Notice, to the left, the side chapel of Our Lady of Bethlehem with its intricately brocaded and jeweled statue. The front altar, of mid-20th-century design, contains many of the mission's original statues. Serra's grave is located under the floor on the left side of

Insiders' Tip

A little-known Carmel attraction is the colorful mural of Point Pinos and Carmel found on the side of Bruno's Market at Junipero Street and 6th Avenue. Check it out!

the altar, along with the graves of two fellow padres.

The outer grounds of the Carmel Mission are equally fascinating. Of particular interest is the cemetery to the right of the church as you face its entrance. A large cross is erected in memory of the more than 3,000 Native Americans buried in the mission grounds. To the left of the church is the main mission courtyard, a photographer's delight with the stately mission bell tower and the bright flowering bougainvillea. One final spot of interest is a small second museum near the cemetery. Here you can learn all about the exacting restoration project of Harry Downie.

To find the Carmel Mission from the Monterey Peninsula, take Highway 1 south to the mouth of Carmel Valley. Turn right at Rio Road and proceed approximately a half-mile. Off-street parking is available in front of and behind the mission. The Carmel Mission museum and gift shop are open from 9:30 A.M. to 7:15 P.M., Monday through Saturday and 10:30 A.M. to 7:15 P.M. on Sunday. A donation is requested—$2.00 for adults and $1.00 for children five to 18.

Tor House
26304 Ocean View Avenue, Carmel
(831) 624–1813 (Monday through Thursday),
(831) 624–1840 (Friday and Saturday),
www.torhouse.org

Lovers of Robinson Jeffers's poetry are in for a special treat when they visit the mystical Tor House, home to Jeffers and his wife, Una, from the time it was originally completed in 1919 until Jeffers's death in 1962. Here on Point Carmel, overlooking the Pacific Ocean, Carmel Bay, and Point Lobos, Jeffers spent his mornings penning some of his most treasured poems. Then in the afternoon, he would put aside his pen and work on his masterpiece of stone and lumber, Tor House. He spent exhausting hours carrying or rolling large granite rocks up from the shoreline to his beloved homesite set atop a large outcropping of stone, or "tor."

The original Tor House was designed and built largely by famous California architect and builder M. J. Murphy. Jeffers worked alongside Murphy and soon learned how "to make stone love stone." Later, Jeffers himself built the mystical Hawk Tower that became a special retreat for Jeffers, his wife, and their twin sons.

Today, docent-led one-hour tours take you through the main living quarters of Tor House, a quaint, unpretentious cottage of low ceilings, dark wood, and rugged stonework. See and feel where Robinson and Una lived their idyllic, somewhat spartan life during the day and often entertained world-famous poets, painters, photographers, and other luminaries of the art world in the evening. Indeed, visitors were welcome only after 4:00 P.M., as the sign Una posted on the garden gate clearly pointed out.

You'll visit the original west wing of Tor House, including the homey living room, small kitchen, and high-ceilinged dining room Jeffers later added on to entertain the growing pilgrimage of guests who came to Carmel to discover his poetic world. A memorable moment for Jeffers fans is time spent in the guest room that includes the bed by the window where Jeffers correctly prophesied he would die.

Throughout the house and lush outdoor gardens, docents point out special stones, shards of ancient pottery, and other artifacts from around the globe that were gifts from Jeffers's world-famous friends. They were brought to Jeffers specifically to be built into Tor House. You'll find pieces of history, such as the Great Wall of China, Pompeii, and the Pyramid of Cheops, in the walls, garden paths, and stone planters.

The tour highlight, of course, is ascending Hawk Tower, the three-story, 40-foot stone spire Jeffers built as a monument to his love for Una. Four years of devotion and sweat went into this labor of love, and the results are nothing short of enchanting. From the below-ground "dungeon" to the observation deck with its spectacular ocean view, Hawk Tower is a joy to explore. The hidden winding staircase up to Una's sanctuary is a tight fit, but a delightful adventure for all but the most claustrophobic.

Tor House is open to the public Friday and Saturday only. (Jeffers's daughter-in-law still lives in the newer east wing of the home, so please respect her privacy.)

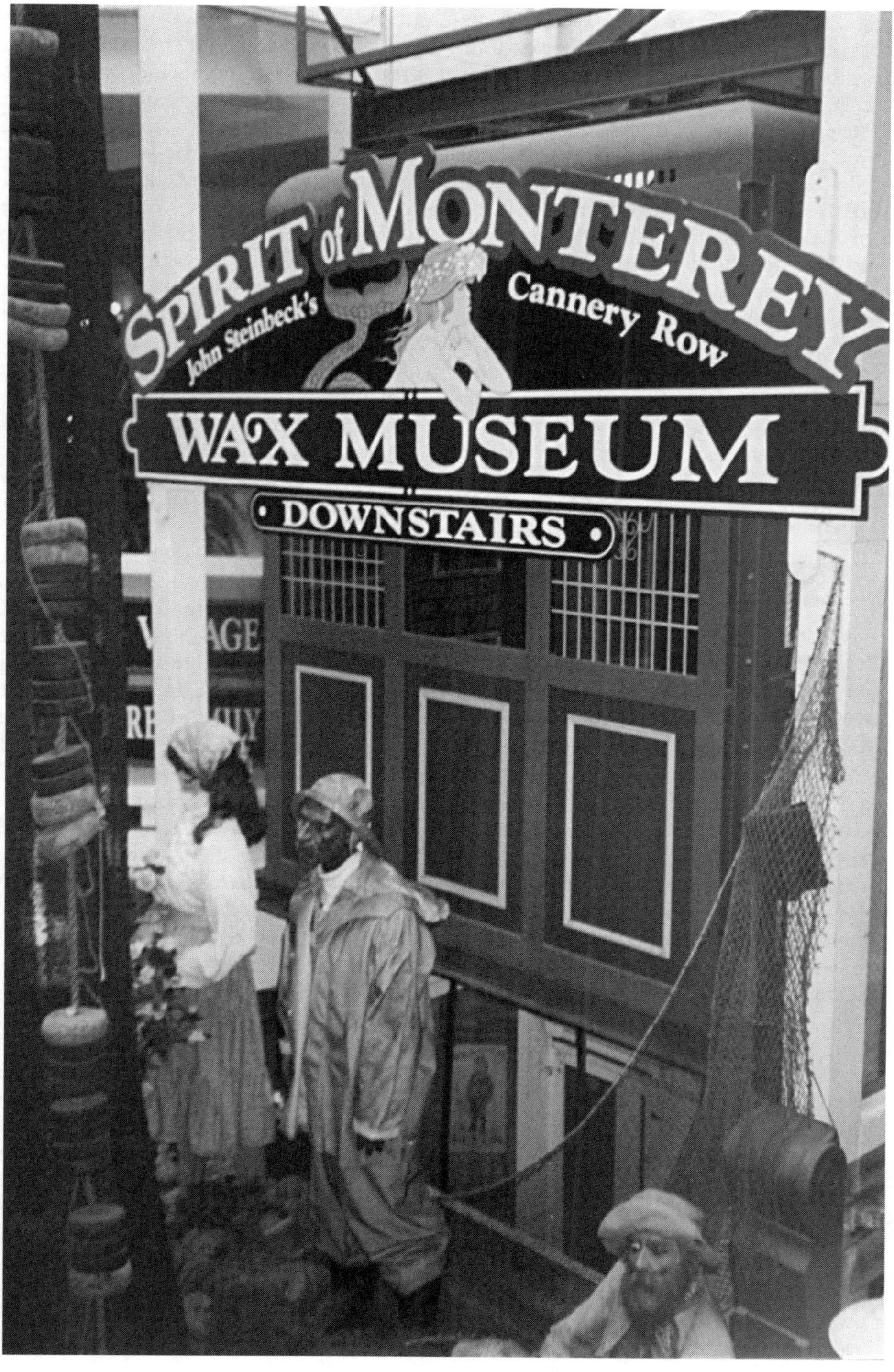

Steinbeck's Spirit of Monterey Wax Museum on Cannery Row is part history lesson, part kitsch, and pure fun. PHOTO: TOM OWENS

Docent-led tours are given on the hour beginning at 10:00 A.M., with the last tour conducted at 3:00 P.M. Tours are limited to six people and are by appointment only. The cost is $7.00 for adults, $4.00 for full-time college students, and $2.00 for high school and middle school students. Children must be age 12 or older to visit. Be sure to wear comfortable walking or hiking shoes for the climb up Hawk Tower.

The best way to find Tor House is to take Ocean Avenue south through downtown Carmel to Scenic Drive and turn left. From Scenic Drive, turn left on Bay View Avenue and then make a right turn onto Ocean View Avenue. Tor House will be on the right-hand side of Ocean View before you reach Stewart Way. Limited off-street parking is available.

Pebble Beach

17-Mile Drive
Pebble Beach
(831) 625–8530, (800) 654–9300,
www.pebblebeach.com/17miledrive.html

Since the 1880s, guests at the elegant Hotel Del Monte in Monterey, now part of the Naval Postgraduate School, were given the opportunity to enjoy the natural wonders of the Monterey Peninsula via horse-drawn carriage and later automobile. The tour, called the "Circle of Enchantment," wound through Pacific Grove and into the dense Del Monte Forest, made up largely of native Monterey pines and Monterey cypress. The hotel tours often included extravagant picnics on the pebbled beaches of the Pacific Ocean and Carmel Bay. The scenic round-trip excursion along the winding gravel road was about 17 miles in length.

Today, you can enjoy a similar scenic route through the 5,000-acre forest by the sea that comprises the area known as Pebble Beach. This breathtaking route is simply called 17-Mile Drive, even though the round-trip loop measures about 12 miles. Five guarded gates provide entrance into Pebble Beach, which is not an incorporated city but a private community owned largely by the Pebble Beach Company. An entrance fee of $8.00 per vehicle is charged for admittance. (The fee is reimbursed to guests staying at any of the resorts within the gates.) Admittance includes a map that points out the major highlights of the tour.

You can begin your tour at any of the five gates. Signs and the red and yellow stripes painted on the pavement guide your way along the drive. Your best choice of gates depends on your starting point. From Carmel, you can enter the Carmel gate near the south end of Ocean Avenue. From Highway 1, use the Highway 1 Gate at the top of Carmel Hill. From Highway 68, there's the Samuel F. B. Morse Gate near the Pacific Grove city line. And from Pacific Grove or Monterey, you can choose the Pacific Grove Gate off Sunset Drive near Asilomar State Beach or the Country Club Gate at Congress Avenue and Forest Lodge Road.

We'll start our tour at the Pacific Grove Gate, which provides the closest access to the beach route from the Monterey side of the Peninsula. Upon entering the gate at 17-Mile Drive and Sunset Drive, you'll immediately pass **The Inn and Links at Spanish Bay.** This is the newest of the famous resorts in Pebble Beach. Named 1996's No. 1 Mainland Resort in the *Condé Nast Traveler* Readers Choice Awards, this luxury resort features 270 guest rooms and an authentic Scottish linksland golf course designed by Robert Trent Jones. Visitors can enjoy a casual lunch with a great view at Roy's at Pebble Beach in the main inn (see our Hotels and Motels and Restaurants chapters).

Past the Inn at Spanish Bay, turn right, following the signs to the 17-Mile Drive Beach route. You'll wind to the coast at **Spanish Bay** itself, where explorer Juan Portolá camped in 1769 while trying to locate the entrance to Monterey harbor. A parking lot and picnic area are available.

Just a few minutes farther down the Drive, a rare ocean phenomenon occurs off the coast at **Point Joe.** "The Restless Sea," as it is called, is a convergence of two ocean currents that cause the sea to boil and bubble even on the calmest of days. Waves, white caps, and spray will often be evident here while the sea in both directions can be glassy calm. As poet Robinson Jeffers wrote, "Point Joe has teeth and has

Pacific Grove is an over-wintering site for the Monarch butterfly, which arrives annually from as far away as Canada and Alaska. PHOTO: MONTEREY PENINSULA VCB

torn ships; it has fierce and solitary beauty." Indeed, there is a long history of shipwrecks here, as seamen unfamiliar with the area often mistook Point Joe for Point Pinos, which marks the entrance into Monterey Bay. In case you're curious, Point Joe was named after a Chinese fisherman who for many years lived here in a small lean-to shack, tending goats and selling trinkets to tourists.

On the inland side of 17-Mile Drive is the ocean course of the **Monterey Peninsula Country Club.** Out on the course you'll see an outcropping of stone called China Rock, also named in honor of the Chinese who settled here and formed an active fishing village. Farther down the coast, you'll spot **Bird Rock** and **Seal Rock.** These offshore nursery and breeding grounds are home to black cormorants, sea gulls, and other shoreline birds as well as herds of sea lions, leopard seals, and harbor seals. During the heyday of the sardine industry, many of the birds that nested here flew out from these rocks to meet fishing boats and returned in great numbers at sunset. The Seal Rock picnic area along the coast provides a great vantage point for observing the marine life. Directly inland from this spot is the **Bird Rock Hunt Course.** Home to world-class equestrian events, this course was used prior to World War II for 11th Calvary riding and saber practice.

Continuing onward, we pass **Spyglass Hill Golf Course.** A turn up Spyglass Hill Road takes you along the course to **The Grill,** a pleasant lunch spot right off the ninth green. Returning to the coast, we come next to **Fanshell Beach** and its gleaming white sands. The beach gets its name from the shells of immature giant rock scallops that appear when the tides and seasons are just right. **Note:** During the spring, temporary fencing may block beach access and obscure the view. This is

CLOSE-UP

The California Missions

San Carlos Borromeo de Carmelo, or Carmel Mission (see the listing in this chapter), was the second of the 21 Franciscan missions built in California by the Spanish. Founded between 1769 and 1823, the missions were part of an attempt by Spanish King Charles III to secure the land north of Mexico before either the Russians, advancing south from the Bering Sea, or the English, moving west from what is now the United States and Canada, could lay claim to it.

As father of the mission system, Padre Junipero Serra oversaw the founding of the first nine missions, including Carmel Mission where he is buried. Today, the missions that stretch from San Diego in the south to Sonoma in the north are in varying states of restoration.

Counting Carmel Mission, 10 of the missions are located between San Luis Obispo and San Francisco along U.S. 101. This route largely follows El Camino Real, the original "King's Road" that connected the missions. There are nine other missions within a few hours of the Monterey Peninsula you might want to visit. We've organized them from south to north.

San Luis Obispo de Tolosa, the fifth mission, was established in 1772. It is noted as being the first mission to use in large scale the red-clay roof tiles now associated with California's Spanish architectural style. The padres in San Luis Obispo found that the tile roofs held up much better to flaming arrows from disgruntled local tribes than the thatched tule roofs that had been used previously. Today, despite some rather horrendous remodeling over the years, there is a pleasant Mission Plaza and a quality museum and gift store to visit. Mission San Luis Obispo is at the corner of Monterey and Chorro Streets, approximately two hours and 40 minutes (145 miles) south of Monterey. Call (805) 543–6850 for tour information.

San Miguel Arcangel, the 16th mission, was built in 1797 approximately 8 miles north of Paso Robles. The church interior is considered one of the best examples of mission art, featuring colorful and ornate work of Native Americans under the direction of renowned artist Estevan Munras. Of special note is the "Eye of God" tilework behind the altar. The mission is approximately two hours and 10 minutes (110 miles) south of Monterey. Call (805) 467–3256 for tour information.

San Antonio de Padua, the third mission, was constructed in 1771 about 6 miles west of the town of Jolon. It retains one of the most idyllic settings of the missions, especially during the height of the spring wildflower season. Some of the grounds still occupied by Franciscan monks are off-limits to the public, but the mission has a nice museum that is well worth the visit. Off U.S. 101 on the small, winding County Highway G-14, San Antonio de Padua is approximately two hours (85 miles) south of Monterey. Call (831) 385–4478 for tour information.

Nuestra Señora de la Soledad, the 13th mission, was built in 1791, 3 miles northwest of today's town of Soledad. One of the most desolate and least popular of the missions during the 19th century, it is also one of the last to go through restoration. Still, a small museum that chronicles the history of triumphs and misfortunes makes Soledad Mission an interesting attraction. The mission is on Fort Romie Road, approximately one hour (45 miles) south of Monterey. Call (831) 678–2586 for tour information.

San Juan Bautista, the 15th mission, was founded in 1797 and has been in continual use as a parish church ever since. This, the largest mission church, is part of a tranquil State Historic Park that includes a hotel, stable, and two adobe houses. A museum includes fascinating musical instruments and transcripts, reflecting the mission's peaceful past. Located alongside the very visible San Andreas Fault line, San Juan Bautista is 35 minutes (30 miles) north of Monterey on Highway 156. Call (831) 623–4881 for tour information.

Santa Cruz, the 12th mission, has suffered a series of disasters since it was built in 1791. Plundered by vagabonds, rocked by earthquakes, and undermined by a tidal wave, the original mission was finally leveled in 1857. Today a small-scale replica of the original church, with a modest museum is all that remains at the site at Emmett and High Streets in Santa Cruz. The mission is approximately 45 minutes up Highway 1 (40 miles) north of Monterey. Call (831) 279–3732 for tour information.

The Carmel Mission is one of 21 California missions built by the Franciscans. PHOTO: ROSS ANDRÉSON

Santa Clara de Asís, the eighth mission, was founded in 1777 and boasted the greatest number of Native American baptisms, more than 8,500. The church that stands today is actually a replica built in 1929. It is faithful to the original 1825 church, including three-dimensional concrete renderings of painter Agustin Davila's original designs. On the campus of the University of Santa Clara, the mission is approximately one hour and 20 minutes (75 miles) north of Monterey off of U.S. 101. For tour information, call (408) 554–4023.

San Jose, the 14th mission, was constructed in 1797. One of the most prosperous of the missions, it featured a large military presence to combat local hostile tribes. Today there is little left of the mission but a small museum housing a few artifacts. In the city of Fremont, San Jose Mission is approximately one hour and 40 minutes (85 miles) north of Monterey at Highway 238 and Washington Boulevard. Call (510) 657–1797 for tour information.

San Francisco de Asís, the sixth mission, was built in 1776. Commonly referred to today as Mission Dolores, it was founded by Juan Bautista de Anza, who led 240 settlers on an amazing journey from Sonora Mexico to Monterey and eventually San Francisco to claim this strategic Bay for Spain. The present church was completed in 1791 and has changed little since then, still featuring original Native American-designed chevrons on the ceiling beams. The mission was never very prosperous due to the cold, foggy weather, which contributed to illness and epidemics. Located at 16th and Dolores Streets in San Francisco, the mission is a little more than two hours (120 miles) north of Monterey. For tour information, call (415) 292–1770.

> **Insiders' Tip**
>
> The Monterey Peninsula Recreation Trail connects Cannery Row and Fisherman's Wharf. So park the car and enjoy both attractions on foot.

necessary to protect the harbor seals that return to this spot each year to bear and raise their young.

As the Drive begins to wind up around **Cypress Point,** we enter one of the most beautiful spots of the entire Peninsula. Large ancient Monterey cypress create a beautiful canopy above a rugged stretch of coast. Sunny or foggy, the effect can be spectacular. Take advantage of the Cypress Point Lookout to stretch your legs and take in this spectacular view. As you wind around Cypress Point and the private Cypress Point Golf Course, the forest grows thicker and darker. You've entered **Crocker Grove,** a natural preserve encompassing 13 acres of some of the largest and oldest Monterey cypress in **Del Monte Forest.** This is one of only two naturally growing stands of *Cupressus macrocarpa* in the world. The other is south of Carmel Bay at Point Lobos State Preserve. A picnic area provides a great setting for lunch.

Farther along this magnificent coast, you'll observe some of the most splendid of the villas and estates of Pebble Beach. And it is here that you'll find Pebble Beach's most famous landmark, the **Lone Cypress.** This ancient tree clings stubbornly to a granite headland above the rugged shoreline, defiantly surviving the seemingly inhospitable environment of rock, wind, and salty sea spray. Its spirit and beauty have made it an inspiration for photographers and painters worldwide.

Another famous tree resides a bit farther down the coast just before Pescadero Point. It's the **Ghost Tree,** so named for its bleached-white trunk and gnarly, twisted limbs. It is near here, too, that the legendary ghost of Maria del Carmen Garcia Barreto Madariaga, who once owned all of Rancho El Pescadero (now Pebble Beach), is said to wander through the fog-shrouded forest late at night.

Past **Pescadero Point,** 17-Mile Drive turns north, winding above Stillwater Cove. Just ahead is the world-famous **Lodge at Pebble Beach.** Since 1919, The Lodge at Pebble Beach has offered luxurious accommodations and challenging golf to visitors from around the globe (see our Hotels and Motels and Golf chapters). But even if you're not staying at The Lodge or playing a round at Pebble Beach Golf Links, it's still worth a visit. You can enjoy the manicured grounds, the fine shops, and a choice of dining options, from casual to elegant. **The Gallery,** a popular golfers bar and grill, is perfect for an informal breakfast or lunch overlooking the putting greens and first tee at Pebble. In the evening, **The Tap Room** provides a warm and friendly pub filled with golf memorabilia from past Pebble Beach tournaments. The **Stillwater Bar and Grill** is noted for its fresh seafood, Friday night clambakes, and Sunday brunches, while **Club XIX** offers award-winning French cuisine (see our Restaurants chapter). Another option is the **Pebble Beach Market,** which offers gourmet picnic fare, coffees, and pastries for the road as well as fine wines and cheeses for a romantic evening.

Stillwater Cove Beach behind The Lodge makes for an excellent stroll when the weather is pleasant. This protected cove is a favorite safe harbor for sailors and was the site of a Chinese fishing village from the 1860s until 1912. Access to the beach is provided through the Beach & Tennis Club, but advanced visitor parking reservations are needed. You can call (831) 625-8507 up to two weeks in advance to reserve your spot.

The 17-Mile Drive continues along the Pebble Beach Golf Links and among homes of the rich and famous. Soon you will come across a turnoff to the Carmel Gate entrance of Pebble Beach, and you'll have a decision to make. You can exit here and enjoy the rest of the day or evening in Carmel. Or you can continue on the 17-Mile Drive loop, which will lead you back to the Pacific Grove Gate.

This trip from Pacific Grove to Carmel along the coast has included most of the major sites the Drive is known for. The return trip travels up away from the coast through the Del Monte Forest. It features some beautiful vistas from Shepard's Knoll and Huckleberry Hill as well as a peek at Poppy Hills Golf Course.

Kidstuff

- **Aquarium**
- **Arcade**
- **Beaches**
- **Biking**
- **Boating**
- **Bowling**
- **Camps**
- **Golf**
- **Horseback Riding**
- **Kite Flying**
- **Libraries**
- **Museums**
- **Playgrounds**
- **Restaurants**
- **Skating and Skateboarding**
- **Shopping**
- **Swimming**
- **Theater**
- **Whale Watching**
- **Youth Centers**

Kids love the Monterey Peninsula. Whether it's combing the beaches for seashells and driftwood, searching the tide pools for creepy crawly creatures, or getting up close and personal with a California gray whale, children will have amazing tales to tell all the friends back home. In this chapter, we deviate from our usual geographic headings so you and the kids can more easily find your favorite types of fun-filled activities available on the Monterey Peninsula. Some of the attractions, restaurants, and shops mentioned here will be covered in greater length in other chapters of this book, so check elsewhere for added details. Here, we'll focus solely on their kidstuff possibilities. Pull out your pen, pencil, or crayon and get ready to circle the activities of choice for the kids of all ages in your family.

Aquarium

Monterey Bay Aquarium
866 Cannery Row, Monterey
(831) 648–4800, www.mbayaq.org

The Monterey Bay Aquarium amazes young and old alike. Kids will be especially pleased to find that it includes exhibits specifically designed for them. Among these exhibits, the hands-down favorite is the Touch Pool filled with prickly, slimy, bumpy, lumpy moving creatures of the sea. Here, wide-eyed kids pick up and examine sea stars, abalone, chitons, and other strange but gentle ocean inhabitants. Right next door to the Touch Pool is a supercool pool for the young daredevil in the family—the Bat Ray Pool. Go ahead kids: Lean over the ledge, dip your hand into the shallow pool, and pet the slithery rays as they glide by. We dare ya!

"Flippers, Flukes and Fun" is a lively children's exhibit in the Outer Bay Wing. Designed for youngsters aged four to seven, it's an interactive exhibit where kids and parents can learn about the similarities and differences between people and marine mammals. You'll discover what marine mammals eat, how they care for their young, how they swim and navigate through the oceans, and how they communicate. Kids also enjoy exploring with the microscopes, telescopes, and viewer-guided underwater video cameras throughout the aquarium exhibits. Splash Zone, the aquarium's premiere kid-space, features more than 50 species specially selected for their kid appeal. Among them, you'll find penguins, eels, sharks, and a colorfest of corals. There are hands-on displays, videos, and other educational exhibits, so Mom and Dad will probably learn just as much as Junior and Sissy. See our Attractions chapter for information on hours and prices.

Arcade

Edgewater Packing Company
640 Wave Street, Monterey
(831) 649–1899

On your trip to Cannery Row, save an hour or so for family fun at the Edgewater

Kids love anchovies without the pizza at the Monterey Bay Aquarium. PHOTO: ROB LEWINE/MONTEREY VCB

Packing Company. Located along the Monterey Peninsula Recreation Trail at Prescott Avenue, this former cannery warehouse provides old-fashioned amusements right alongside the latest in video games. A delightful turn-of-the-century carousel is the hallmark of the arcade. Its bright colors, whirling lights, and spirited music are inviting to parents as well as the kids. So don't be shy, take a whirl! Other yesteryear amusements include a horseracing arcade and the Old Time Photo Emporium, where you can pose for a sepia-tone family photo in one of many Wild West settings. They've even reinstalled the skeetball alleys for your bowling pleasure.

If kids are suffering from video-game withdrawal, they'll love the wide selection of popular arcade games. In addition to the usual shoot-em-ups, you'll find virtual snow skiing, Indy car driving, motorcycle racing, and baseball batting cages that test your virtual athletic skills. Lower-tech pinball machines, air hockey, and basketball shoot-outs will delight the arcade traditionalist. Edgewater Packing Company opens at 10:30 A.M. daily. It stays open until 11:00 P.M. Sunday through Thursday and until 1:00 A.M. Friday and Saturday.

Beaches

The Monterey Peninsula is awash with beaches, so your options are aplenty. For kids who enjoy the traditional beach-blanket outing, complete with sand pail, lunch, and wading in the surf, try the sandy Monterey State Beach just east of the Municipal Wharf in Monterey. Other good choices are Carmel Beach at the end of Ocean Avenue in Carmel and Lovers Point Beach in Pacific Grove. If Rover and Spot are coming along, check out Moss Beach at Spanish Bay just south of Asilomar between Pacific Grove and Pebble Beach. While this spot is canine friendly, doggie-do cleanup is a must, so please use plastic bags or other scooping devices. Free plastic bags and trash cans are located at the trailhead at the beginning of the boardwalk, just across Sunset Drive from the Asilomar Conference Center. Smaller sandy coves amid rocks and tide pools are located all along Ocean View Avenue, from just south of the Monterey Bay Aquarium to Sunset Drive in Pacific Grove. A similar terrain continues along the coast through Pebble Beach. Walking trails and wooden boardwalks make beach access easy.

Two important words of caution to pass on to kids:

First, Monterey Peninsula beaches can be extremely dangerous, with riptide currents, large waves, slippery rocks, and cold, cold water. Going into the water is highly discouraged except for the most experienced swimmers, and only along the sandy, rock-free beaches mentioned above. Children should never be left unattended wading at the water's edge or climbing on the shoreline rocks, no matter how safe it may seem. Sea conditions change rapidly, and the big wave can be next in line. Typically, the safest, most protected spot for swimming or wading is Lovers Point Beach in Pacific Grove. But even there, caution is a must!

Second, kids should be instructed that the Monterey Bay is a National Marine Sanctuary. Never disturb wildlife and don't try to personally aid baby seals or other creatures that may appear abandoned or injured. Check beach ordinances before removing shells, driftwood, or other natural objects. And, please, let's all leave the shoreline as clean or cleaner than we found it.

For more about our beaches, see our In and Around the Water chapter.

Biking

Young bike riders enjoy the long expanse of the Monterey Peninsula recreational trail, which stretches from Lovers Point in Pacific Grove all the way to the northern border of Monterey and beyond. Kids can pedal to their hearts' delight as long as common-sense safety rules are followed. In California, bicycle helmets are mandatory for all minors 17 and younger, and the helmet law is strictly enforced. Also, the recreational trail is shared by cyclists, in-line skaters, skateboarders, joggers, and walkers, many of whom are more intent on observing the local scenery than paying attention to where they are going. Bike defensively, and stay on the right side of the path. Be especially careful where the trail crosses streets since the local scenery can distract drivers too.

While bicycling is permitted on most city streets, caution is advised. Again, drivers unfamiliar with the area may be so intent on trying to follow a map, find their hotel room, or enjoy the spectacular scenery that they fail to look out for cyclists. Obey the laws, avoid busy thoroughfares, and use appropriate hand signals. Also wear bright clothing or reflectors to make yourself as visible as possible, especially after sunset. Kids and parents can rent bikes at shops along the recreation trail.

Adventures by the Sea
299 Cannery Row, Monterey
201 Alvarado Mall, Monterey
The Beach at Lovers Point, Pacific Grove
(831) 372–1807, www.adventuresbythesea.com

Mountain and hybrid bikes are available starting at $6.00 per hour, $18.00 for four hours and $24.00 per day. Overnight rentals are $30.00. Locks and helmets are provided, and bike tours are available. You can also rent trailers for the toddlers and in-line skates. Adventures by the Sea offers some free pick up and delivery, so call for details.

Bay Bikes Rentals & Tours
640 Wave Street, Monterey
(831) 646–9090

Bay Bikes, located in front of the Edgewater Packing Company above Cannery Row, offers bike rentals for $10.00 for the first two hours and $4.00 per additional hour. You can rent for a full day for $24 and not have to return the bike until the following day. Child trailers and baby seats are available. Bay Bikes also rents the four-wheel surreys you'll see all along the recreation trail. For $18 to $28 per hour, the whole family can pedal together!

Boating

A high-sea adventure may be just the ticket for your hearty buccaneers. Motorboats and sailboats provide Monterey Bay tours of various lengths from Fisherman's Wharf (see our In and Around the Water chapter for details). Here are a couple of low-key boating options kids will enjoy.

A B Seas Kayaks
32 Cannery Row #5, Monterey
(831) 647–0191, (888) 371–6035,
www.montereykayak.com

For the more adventurous kids, how about paddling a kayak out on Monterey Bay? A B Seas Kayaks offers a guided tour for novice kayakers, which consists of a two- to three-hour excursion along the shoreline of Monterey Bay. Plus, if you and the kids haven't gotten your fill, you can continue kayaking for the rest of the day, all for $50 per person. If you are experienced kayakers, forego the tour and venture out on your own for $30 per person. These are stable, sit-on-top kayaks and you are equipped with paddles, seat back, wet suit, dry bag, and instruction. On calm days, the Bay waters are very gentle, but you should probably avoid taking younger kids out for the first time if the swells are high or strong winds are kicking up the white caps.

Glass Bottom Boat Tours
Fisherman's Wharf, Monterey
(831) 372–7150

If you or your little ones aren't quite ready for the open sea, consider a half-hour harbor excursion on the Glass Bottom Boat Tours, which depart from Fisherman's Wharf. It's a gentle, relaxing way to enjoy the waters and get an up-close look at sea lions, starfish, crabs, and other harbor inhabitants. The cost is $6.00 for adults and $5.00 for children 12 and younger. During the peak summer season, boats leave daily every half-hour between 10:00 A.M. and 6:00 P.M.

El Estero Boating
Lake El Estero, Monterey
(831) 375–1484

For leisurely freshwater boating, there's the popular El Estero Boating on Del Monte Boulevard at the corner of Camino El Estero. This company rents paddle boats, kayaks, and canoes. The whole family can paddle or pedal around the gentle city lake, enjoying the many waterfowl and the tranquil park setting. Boats rent for $8.00 per half-hour or $13.00 per hour. Paddle boats seat up to four people; canoes and kayaks seat two. Be sure to enjoy an ice cream, soda, popcorn, or hot dog from the snack bar. El Estero Boating is open seven days a week from 10:00 A.M. until dusk, weather permitting.

Bowling

Monterey Lanes
2161 N. Fremont Street, Monterey
(831) 373–1553

If bowling is your kid's cup of tea, visit Monterey Lanes. The lanes are open seven days a week, starting at 9:00 A.M. Saturday morning junior leagues are available from 9:15 to 11:00 A.M. for children ages six through 12. Call for rates and details regarding public lane availability. Ask about the popular glow-in-the-dark "Galactic Bowling" on Friday nights and the Saturday night "Rock and Bowl" program for teens.

Camps

Children who spend a substantial part of their summers on the Peninsula, whether as residents or visitors, might relish the thought of a fun-filled summer-camp experience. There is a range of options, from simple summer day camps to complete live-in academic and training programs. Check out the choices below as well as city recreation programs, which offer additional summer-camp options.

Insiders' Tip

Holy Willy Wonka! In neighboring Seaside, you can take a free chocolate factory tour that includes samples. The Chocolate Factory is at 1291 Fremont Boulevard. Call (831) 899-7963.

Camp Carmel
Location varies, Carmel
(831) 625–3321

Camp Carmel offers one- and two-week day-camp sessions from late June through early August for children ages three to 12. "Cub Camp," a combination of planned recreation and free play for preschoolers, features games, songs, stories, skits, crafts, water play, and small animal care. Camp Cubs can attend all full days, all half-days, or any combination that fits your schedule. Camp Carmel for the older kids features full days of sporting activities such as archery, tennis, soccer, softball, Frisbee golf, basketball, and swimming as well as dance, art, nature study, hiking, trail marking, and film making. Campers select their activities of interest and are grouped according to age to heighten enjoyment and social interaction. Camp Carmel is held at the Carmel High School or the Carmel Middle School campus. One-week sessions cost $150; two-week sessions are $260.

Carmel Valley Tennis Camp
20805 Cachagua Road, Carmel Valley
(831) 659–2615,
www.carmelvalleytenniscamp.com

Tennis anyone? Carmel Valley Tennis Ranch was recently selected as one of the top junior tennis camps in the country. It's located more than 20 miles out Carmel Valley Road in rural Cachagua, but that only adds to the adventure. Husband-and-wife owners Steve Proulx and Susan Reeder, both noted coaches and players in their own right, hold one- and two- week sessions from June through August for kids ages 10 to 17. It's a well-planned program of tennis instruction and competition, but the fun doesn't end there. It's a real camp, with campfires, cookouts, arts and crafts, swimming, hot-tubbing, table tennis, Foosball, volleyball, hiking, dancing, and even movies. The cost is $850 for one-week sessions; $1595 for two weeks.

Robert Louis Stevenson Camp
3152 Forest Lake Road, Pebble Beach
(831) 626–5300

Robert Louis Stevenson Camp, within the Del Monte Forest in Pebble Beach, is open to boys and girls ages 10 to 15. The five-week sessions, which begin the last week of June and continue through mid-July, are offered on both a day-camp and resident-camp basis. Resident campers live in school dormitories under full-time supervision with hot meals served in a large dining hall. Morning workshops include academic programs in math, English, and biology as well as art classes in ceramics, drama, music, and photography. Afternoons are reserved for sporting activities such as swimming, biking, archery, fencing, tennis, and golf. Sailing is offered on the school's sailboats in nearby Stillwater Cove. Each weekend, resident campers go on overnight hiking trips in the local Los Padres National Forest, with an occasional trip to the High Sierras. Tuition for day students is $1,800; for resident students it's $3,200.

Santa Catalina Summer Camp
1500 Mark Thomas Drive, Monterey
(831) 655–9386, www.santacatalina.org

This residential and day camp at the 35-acre Santa Catalina School campus is for girls from age eight to 14. Both five-week and 2½-week sessions are offered, typically beginning in late June. College-age women counselors live in the dormitories with resident students to organize evening and weekend activities in and around the Monterey Peninsula. The wide variety of activities to choose from include musical theater, drama, jazz dance, tap, ballet, art, painting and sketching, ceramics, crafts, fashion design, creative writing, photography, computers, marine biology, cooking, sewing, swimming, tennis, riding, golf, and team sports. Students can choose six of these activities as part of the school's General Program or specialize in musical theater, horseback riding, marine biology, or tennis. Tuition for the 2-week camp is $2,100 for resident camp and $1,100 for day camp. For the five-week session, it's $3,700 for residents and $2,200 for day camp. There are additional fees for riding and golf programs. Day camp hours are 9:00 A.M. to 4:30 P.M.

Golf

As strange as it may seem in this golf mecca, there are no miniature golf courses on the Monterey Peninsula. However, there is a golden opportunity to take your budding Tiger Woods for a memorable outing at Pebble Beach.

Peter Hay Golf Course
17-Mile Drive at Stevenson Drive, Pebble Beach
(831) 625–8518, (800) 654–9300,
www.pebblebeach.com

Adjacent to the world-famous Pebble Beach Golf Links, Peter Hay Golf Course was designed by former Pebble Beach professional Peter Hay. It's a nine-hole, par 3, 819-yard course that provides a fun and affordable round of golf for players of all ages. Best of all, children younger than 12 play for free when accompanied by a parent. Golfers 13 to 17 pay a very reasonable $5.00, while those 18 and up pay $20.00. Each foursome must include at least one adult. Call for reservations. For residents of the Monterey Peninsula, the AT&T Pebble Beach Junior Golf Association provides free lessons and other programs for kids age seven to 17. Call (831) 625–1555 for details.

The turn-of-the-century carousel at the Edgewater Packing Company is a delight for kids of all ages.
PHOTO: TOM OWENS

Horseback Riding

Pebble Beach Equestrian Center
Portola Road at Alva Lane
Pebble Beach
(831) 624–2756, www.ridepebblebeach.com

Pebble Beach Equestrian Center presents a wide range of options for both novice and experienced horseback riders. Pony rides will thrill kids as young as three, while children seven to 12 can enjoy escorted walking trail rides along some of the 34 miles of winding paths through Del Monte Forest. Those 12 and older can partake in the hour-plus beach ride, which takes travelers through the forests, across the sand dunes, and down to the water's edge on an expanse of sandy beach. Group and private lessons are also available for both English and Western riding. The Pebble Beach Equestrian Center is about a half-mile from The Lodge at Pebble Beach. Rides range from $20 (pony) to $47 per person. Group lessons start at $25 per hour and private lessons start at $47 per hour. Summer and holiday camp programs are also available.

Kite Flying

Kite flying is a popular beach activity, and the Peninsula features some fantastic shops that will fix you up with just the right kite or windsock. Favorite kite-flying areas for participants and spectators are the sands just north of the Monterey Beach Hotel in Monterey and Carmel Beach at the foot of Ocean Avenue in Carmel. But any long stretch of sand and sky will do. So what are you waiting for? Go fly a kite!

Windborne Fun
125 Ocean View Boulevard, Pacific Grove
(831) 375–0851, (877) 272–5483

Windborne Fun brings the latest in kites, banners, spinners, and windsocks to The American Tin Cannery near Cannery Row, with a nice selection for young beginners. All kites are unconditionally guaranteed, and Windborne has a liberal return and refund policy. Expert repairs are also provided.

Libraries

For a little quiet time, visit any of the local public libraries, which are understandably proud of their children's programs.

City of Monterey Public Library
625 Pacific Street, Monterey
(831) 646–3932, www.monterey.org/library

The Monterey Public Library Storytime for Kids program includes Pajama Storytime for youngsters age three to seven the last Tuesday of every month at 7:00 P.M. Baby and Me Rhymetime for babies up to age two and toddlers ages two to five is presented the last Friday of each month at 10:00 A.M. Toddler Storytime for children age two is held Wednesday mornings at 10:00 A.M. Preschool Storytime is held Tuesday and Wednesday mornings at 11:00 A.M. for kids ages three to five. Pajama Storytime for kids age three and up is offered the last Tuesday of each month at 7:00 P.M. Special seasonal storytime programs are also scheduled. Call (831) 646–3934 for details on all children's programs.

Pacific Grove Public Library
550 Central Avenue, Pacific Grove
(831) 648–3160, www.pacificgrove.lib.ca.us

Pacific Grove Public Library has a storytime program for kids of various ages. Baby Time presents stories, songs, and other play activities for children age two and younger. Preschool Storytime for two- and three-year-olds is held Wednesday at 10:30 A.M. After-school Storytime for four- to eight-year-olds takes place Wednesday at 3:30 P.M. Junior Friends of the Library is a club for fourth and fifth graders who meet Tuesdays at 3:30 P.M., September through April, for crafts, field trips, and other activities. Children's Librarian Lisa Maddalena will be happy to provide information on all children's library programs.

Harrison Memorial
Public Library, Park Branch
6th Avenue and Mission Street, Carmel
(831) 624–4664, www.hm-lib.org

Harrison Memorial Public Library's special Park Branch caters to kids. Storytime programs include Lap-Sit Storytime for babies and toddlers on Friday at 10:30 A.M., Preschool Storytime on Tuesday and Wednesday at 10:30 A.M. and Pajama Storytime on Tuesday at 7:00 P.M. The library also features six computers specifically for kids, with more than a dozen different educational computer games and programs. Children's librarian Susan Jones says she loves to have kids and parents from outside the Peninsula drop by to visit.

Museums

It used to be that museums and active kids didn't necessarily mix. But these days, more and more museums are featuring exhibits specifically for the younger set. In fact, Monterey has one special museum designed exclusively for children younger than 10. For other museums, see our Attractions and Arts and Galleries chapters.

Monterey County Youth (MY) Museum
601 Wave Street, Monterey
(831) 649–6444, www.mymuseum.org

Monterey County Youth Museum, or "MY Museum" for short, is on the third level of the Cannery Row Parking Garage. MY Museum is a place where young kids and parents can explore, create, and share in a fun-filled learning environment. Educating and entertaining, the museum's exhibits of exciting sights and sounds are designed to stimulate curiosity and learn-

Rental bikes and four-wheel surreys are popular forms of transportation along the Recreational Trail that stretches from Fisherman's Wharf through Cannery Row and along the shoreline to Pacific Grove's Lovers Point. PHOTO: TOM OWENS

ing among the younger set. Kids will discover The Row, a hands-on, interactive replica of Cannery Row. They can fish from a boat, buy food and supplies, and cook up meals at MY Grill. Then there is MY Theater, where puppet shows and costume plays bring out the real ham in everyone. At Creation Station, kids explore all forms of art, including a giant loom for making their own weavings. Plus, there is MY Health Center, MY Classroom, and MY Build-A-House for hours of imaginative and creative play. There is also a birthday room that can be reserved for up to 12 kiddies. You bring the cake, juice, snacks, and presents and MY Museum provides the party favors and loads for fun things to do. MY Museum is open from 10:00 A.M. to 5:00 P.M. every day except Sunday, when it's open noon to 5:00 P.M., and Wednesday, when it's closed. Admission for each child and adult is $5.50, and wee ones younger than two play for free.

Maritime Museum of Monterey
5 Custom House Plaza, Monterey
(831) 372–2608,
www.mntmh.org/maritime.htm

The Maritime Museum of Monterey has designed a treasure hunt that keeps the young ones entertained while mom and dad enjoy the historic artifacts. Complete the treasure hunt, and ring the big ship bell (see our complete listing in the Attractions chapter).

Pacific Grove Museum
of Natural History
Forest and Central Avenues, Pacific Grove
(831) 648–3116, www.pgmuseum.org

This award-winning natural history museum maintains special hands-on exhibits for kids. Plus, there's the ever-popular Sandy the Whale, an outdoor life-size sculpture that just loves to be climbed upon. Call for details on additional children's programs (see our Attractions chapter for more information).

Playgrounds

In addition to the many splendid beaches and parks on and around the Monterey Peninsula, there are some great playgrounds for kids to enjoy. Also see our Parks and Recreation chapter.

Dennis the Menace Park
Pearl Street at Lake El Estero, Monterey
(831) 646–3860

The biggest and most famous Peninsula playground for kids is Dennis the Menace Park, located in downtown Monterey adjacent to Lake El Estero. Acclaimed for its unique design, the park opened in 1956 amidst much fanfare. Cartoonist Hank Ketcham, creator of Dennis the Menace, and local sculptor Arch Gardner dreamed up some of the wildest playground equipment ever seen. Salt air and years of rugged use proved too much for some of the original equipment. Fortunately, the park was completely renovated in 1988 and once again provides a great place for kids to burn energy. Featured attractions include a real train steam engine, a swinging rope bridge, a roller slide, and a hedge maze. A snack bar is right outside the playground entrance in the parking lot on Pearl Street, between Camino Aguajito and Camino El Estero. Dennis the Menace Park is open daily from 10:00 A.M. until sunset.

The mouth of the lion awaits thirsty park-goers at Dennis the Menace Park in Monterey. PHOTO: ROSS ANDRÉSON

Caledonia Park
Caledonia Street and Central Avenue, Pacific Grove
(831) 648–3130

There are small Peninsula playgrounds for kids that, while not on the grand scale of Dennis the Menace Park, provide pleasant spots for fun and exercise. Among the favorites of Pacific Grove youngsters is Caledonia Park, bounded by U-shape Caledonia Street and Central Avenue, directly behind the Pacific Grove Post Office. You'll find the usual slides and swings, plus a submarine-shaped jungle gym, baseball field, and basketball court. (**Note:** The south end of Pacific Grove's George Washington Park, which also includes a Butterfly Tree Grove, has swings, slides, and other equipment along Sinex Avenue.)

Forest Hills Park
Scenic Road and Camino del Monte, Carmel
(831) 624–3543

In Carmel, Forest Hills Park features a pleasant forest setting. You'll find horseshoe and shuffleboard facilities as well as an enjoyable playground area. (As an alternative, Mission Trails Park off of Rio Road near the Carmel Mission is a good spot for an adventurous hike.)

Restaurants

As in most upscale resort areas, there are restaurants where kids are warmly welcomed, and there are restaurants where, at best, they are tolerated. It's always advisable to check with the restaurant when kid-friendliness is in question, especially at the higher-end establishments that cater to the formally dressed or specialize in quiet romantic evenings. That being said, there are plenty of restaurants where kids can feel free to let loose and have a grand old time.

Monterey

Abalonetti Seafood Trattoria
57 Fisherman's Wharf, Monterey
(831) 373–1851

Abalonetti is a great spot to introduce the young ones to calamari. (Wait till after the meal to tell them they just ate squid!) You'll also find great brick-oven-baked pepperoni pizza, fish and chips, burgers, and spaghetti.

Bagel Bakery
452 Alvarado Street, Monterey
(831) 649–1714
539 Carmel Rancho Shopping Center, Carmel
(831) 625–5180
1132 Forest Avenue,
Pacific Grove
(831) 649–6272

Young bagel lovers will relish the many choices at the Bagel Bakery, a local icon for breakfast or lunch. Fresh boiled and baked bagels come with a choice of toppings. Even kids who don't like the usual bagel with cream cheese will enjoy the pizza bagel or a toasted cinnamon-raisin bagel with honey-butter.

Bubba Gump Shrimp Company Restaurant and Market
720 Cannery Row, Monterey
(831) 373–1884

On Cannery Row, Bubba Gump Shrimp is the choice of young *Forrest Gump* fans. They can have their picture taken on the famous bench with a box of chocolates and then go inside for a kid-size portion of shrimp. Burgers, pizza, and corn dogs are also on the menu for ocean-view lunch and dinner.

Chef Lee's Mandarin House
2031 N. Fremont Boulevard, Monterey
(831) 375–9551

For good Chinese food for lunch and dinner in a family environment, try Chef Lee's in Monterey. Ask to sit in Sun's section because she loves kids. Chef Lee's is on Fremont Boulevard just east of Highway 1.

Del Monte Express
2329 N. Fremont Boulevard, Monterey
(831) 655–1941

This is the place for juicy, drippy burgers for the whole family. Kids really like the alphabet-shaped fries, and the turkey and cheese sandwiches are favorites too. Train decor and The Del Monte Express circling the restaurant keep kids entertained. Traditional breakfasts also served.

El Torito Mexican Restaurant
600 Cannery Row, Monterey
(831) 373–0611

If Mexican food is a family favorite, try El Torito on Cannery Row. Tacos, tostados, burritos, chicken fingers, and other selections all come in children's portions, with or without rice and beans. El Torito has one of the best ocean views in town.

Gianni's Pizza
725 Lighthouse Avenue, Monterey
(831) 649–1500

Pizza-loving kids won't complain at Gianni's Pizza in New Monterey. They have hand-tossed dough and good fresh toppings and will make any combination the kids want. This noisy, action-packed pizzeria is great for lunch or dinner with large family groups. It's a perfect spot for picking up a pizza to take back to the motel room too.

Jamba Juice
398 Alvarado Street, Monterey
(831) 655–9696, www.jambajuice.com

If the kids are into fresh juices and smoothies, Jamba Juice is just the ticket. It features a wide choice of fruit smoothies, fresh squeezed juices, and hearty soups. They're great energy boosts for walks around town and strolls down the beach.

Rappa's Seafood Restaurant
101 Fisherman's Wharf, Monterey
(831) 372–7562, www.rappas.com

Located at the end of the wharf, Rappa's welcomes children of all ages. The children's menu features hamburgers, fish and chips, shrimp and chips, and spaghetti. An outdoor observation deck

Caledonia Park is a great place to take kids on a sunny warm day in Pacific Grove. PHOTO: ROSS ANDRÉSON

and great harbor views of boats, sea lions, and sea gulls provide entertainment for lunch or dinner.

Pacific Grove

First Awakenings
125 Ocean View Boulevard, Pacific Grove
(831) 372–1125

For a hearty breakfast before your trip down Cannery Row, stop by First Awakenings in the American Tin Cannery. You'll find eggs fixed any way the kids like them as well as pancakes, waffles, hot cocoa, juices, cereals, and other morning favorites. Outdoor seating is available.

Fishwife Seafood Restaurant
1996 Sunset Drive, Pacific Grove
(831) 375–7107

The Fishwife caters to kids for lunch and dinner, featuring a large fish tank, crayons to color the paper table cloths, and good fish and chips with incredible air fries. After dessert, take the kids on a family stroll down nearby Asilomar State Beach.

Shnarley's Bronx Pizza
650 Lighthouse Avenue, Pacific Grove
(831) 375–2002, www.shnarleys.com
688 Cannery Row, Monterey
(831) 373–8463

Here's a local pizzeria with a New York flair. Mom and dad will enjoy a fine selection of beers and wines as well. Buyers beware: The large pizza is truly LARGE. Check out the sizes before ordering, and then be prepared to sink your teeth into a really great pizza pie.

Tinnery at the Beach
Ocean View Boulevard at 17th Street, Pacific Grove
(831) 646–1040

A great view of the Bay from Lovers Point in Pacific Grove is the perfect setting for a quality breakfast, lunch, dinner, or in-between at a reasonable price. Special children's breakfasts are good deals.

Toasties Cafe
702 Lighthouse Avenue, Pacific Grove
(831) 373–7543

In downtown Pacific Grove, Toasties Cafe is a local favorite for a delicious home-style breakfast. Kids like the pancakes and the hot chocolate stacked with whipped cream, and mom and dad will enjoy the peaceful Pacific Grove ambiance. Lunch and dinner are also served.

Carmel

Chevy's Mexican Restaurant
123 Crossroads Boulevard, Carmel
(831) 626–0945, www.chevys.com

In the Crossroads Shopping Center, Chevy's is very kid-friendly, with lots of complimentary chips. There's a good children's menu of Mexican food favorites.

Em Le's Old Carmel Restaurant
Dolores Street and 5th Avenue, Carmel
(831) 625–6780

A great Carmel breakfast or lunch spot is Em Le's, with its award-winning French toast and vintage soda fountain. The cozy setting and fireplace make for great memories.

General Store/
Forge in the Forest Restaurant
5th and Junipero Avenues, Carmel
(831) 624–2233, www.forgeintheforest.com

This is an ideal choice for sharing the true Carmel experience with the kids. The heated patio with outdoor fireplaces makes for a great place to unwind on a pleasant Peninsula night. Good California cuisine lunches are also served.

Plaza Cafe and Grill
Carmel Plaza on Ocean Avenue, Carmel
(831) 624–4433

Try a late breakfast of pancakes or waffles at the Plaza Cafe and Grill. The heated patio is nice for a family lunch or dinner as well.

Skating and Skateboarding

In-line skating is a most popular activity on the Monterey Peninsula Recreation Trail. If you forgot to pack your kids' own skates and protective gear, you can rent them at spots along the recreation trail. Plus, a skate park was added in 1999 at El Estero Park and became an instant hit with skaters and skateboarders.

Adventures by the Sea
299 Cannery Row, Monterey
(831) 372–1807
201 Alvarado Mall, Monterey
(831) 648–7235, www.adventuresbythesea.com

Adventures by the Sea has two in-line skate rental locations, one on the Monterey Peninsula Recreation Trail and the other downtown near the DoubleTree Hotel. Rates are $12 for two hours, $18 for four hours and $24 all day. Safety gear is included.

Monterey Bay SK8 Station
1855 East Avenue, Sand City
(831) 899–SK8S

Monterey Bay SK8 Station is the Peninsula's premier indoor skate park. Off California Street near Costco in Sand City (just north of Monterey along Del Monte Boulevard), SK8 Station features a vert ramp, Bauer box, corner bowl, quarter-pipes, and more. (Don't worry, Mom and Dad, your kids will know what that means.) It's open Monday through Thursday from 3:30 to 8:00 P.M., Friday from 3:30 to 10:00 P.M., Saturday noon to 10:00 P.M. and Sunday noon to 8:00 P.M. The price of entry is $12.

Del Monte Gardens
2020 Del Monte Avenue, Monterey
(831) 375–3202

Del Monte Gardens is the traditional roller-skating rink in Monterey. Both roller skates and in-line skates are allowed on the indoor oval rink. The doors open to the public Thursday through Monday. Matinees are 2:00 to 4:00 P.M. on Saturday ($5.00), Sunday ($5.00), and Monday ($4.00). The rest of the schedule looks like this: Thursday nights from 7:00 to 9:00 P.M. is $4.00. Friday evening has sessions from 6:30 to 8:30 P.M. or from 8:00 to 10:00 P.M. for $5.00 each or $7.00 combined. Saturday sessions include a 3:30 to 5:30 P.M. afternoon skate ($4.00) and evening sessions at 5:00 to 7:00 P.M. ($4.00), 6:30 to 8:30 P.M. ($5.00), and 8:00 to 10:00 P.M. ($5.00), with double sessions

A skate park designed with the guidance of local youth is a popular gathering spot at El Estero Park, right next to Dennis the Menace Park. PHOTO: JANA MORBA

costing an extra $2.00. Skate Sunday evening from 7:00 to 9:00 P.M. for $4.00. Roller skates rent for $1.00, in-line skates for $3.00. You can use your own skates if they pass rink inspection. Roller hockey games are held through local leagues and Saturday lessons are provided for $18 a month.

Shopping

The Monterey Peninsula is world famous as a shopper's paradise. That holds true for kids as well as for adults. Check out our Shopping chapter for a wider selection, but here's a quick rundown of places kids like.

Monterey

Del Monte Shopping Center
Highway 1 at Munras Avenue, Monterey
(831) 373–2705

In Monterey, the Del Monte Shopping Center has an array of clothing, toy, and gift shops for the kiddies. Major chains as well as local shops make up the more than 100 stores, restaurants, and services. Favorite shops for kids include Gap Kids, Gymboree, Thinker Toys, Games & Things, and KB Toys.

Fuzybops Toys
700 Cannery Row, Monterey
(831) 643–2342

Fuzybops. Funny name, funny store. It's a great place to pick up a little treat for the kids after a well-behaved day of touring Cannery Row. There are lots of humor and joke toys, kites, die-cast toys, lunch boxes, and many types of collectibles, including Hello Kitty and other Sanrio toys.

Pacific Grove

Chatter Baux Children's Shoppe
157 Fountain Avenue, Pacific Grove
(831) 647–8701

Chatter Baux Children's Shoppe carries new and used clothing, toys, books, and accessories for the wee ones through high schoolers. You can find great deals on reconditioned high chairs, car seats, playpens, and other kid equipment. A choice of European strollers too.

Learning Depot
168 Central Avenue, Pacific Grove
(831) 372–8697

Learning Depot in Pacific Grove specializes in educational toys and supplies. This is a good choice for preschool-age children who enjoy imaginative puzzles and games.

Peek A Boo
303 Grand Avenue, Pacific Grove
(831) 643–1121

Peek A Boo is a quaint little shop that carries new and used clothing, toys, and equipment. It's a convenient and affordable place to pick up that sweater, raincoat, or pair of shorts you forgot to pack.

Tessuti Zoo
171 Forest Avenue, Pacific Grove
(831) 648–1725

This colorful, one-of-a-kind shop features wild handmade dolls, animals, and otherworldly creatures along with tin windup toys, great kids' books, crazy clocks, and cute clothing. While the kids check out the creatures, mom can discover the wearable art of the Playful Spirit clothing line. You'll find Tessuti Zoo across the street from Peppers Mexican Cafe.

Carmel

Bib 'N Tucker
Ocean Avenue and Dolores Street, Carmel
(831) 624–2185

Bib 'N Tucker is the place for the baby set in Carmel. You'll find a nice selection of clothing and toys for infants as well as for young children through preschool age.

Nana's for Remarkable Kids
26366 Carmel Rancho Lane, Carmel
(831) 625–6262

For American and French-made children's clothing, check out Nana's for Remarkable Kids. You'll discover a unique collection for girls age infant to 14 and boys age infant to seven years. Handmade rockers, blankets, and other gift items are a browser's delight.

Sandcastles by the Sea
3722 The Barnyard, Carmel
(831) 626–8361

Sandcastles by the Sea in The Barnyard features an amazing display of wooden toys. You'll also find a good selection of beach toys, games, and crafts and a charming collection of dress-up clothes.

Thinker Toys
7th Avenue and San Carlos Street, Carmel
(831) 624–0441, www.thinkertoys.com

Thinker Toys is the largest toy store on the Peninsula and has tons of new brand-name merchandise. Train sets are a store specialty, and you'll enjoy the great display. There's now a second area location at the Del Monte Shopping Center in Monterey, (831) 643-0534.

Toys In the Attic
Carmel Plaza, Carmel
(831) 622–9011

For stuffed animals and dolls, classics to collectibles, try Toys In the Attic. From Teddy Bears to Beanie Babies, your child is sure to find a perfect friend. This shop also features a fine selection of metal cars, trucks, and windup toys.

Swimming

We can't emphasize enough the unpredictable nature of the ocean around the Monterey Peninsula. Ocean swimming is best left to experienced adults and only on the sandy beaches, away from the rocky shores. For kids, stick to the hotel or motel pools or visit the Monterey Sports Center.

Monterey Sports Center
301 Franklin Street, Monterey
(831) 646–3700, www.monterey.org/sportscenter

Located across Del Monte Avenue from Fisherman's Wharf, The Monterey Sports Center features two indoor pools that can accommodate kids of all ages. The main pool is kept at a comfortable 82 degrees. Older kids will love the 112-foot corkscrew water slide that twists and turns you on a wild ride from high above the pool, then dumps you unceremoniously into the warm water. The second smaller pool at the Sports Center is a cozy 6 meters by 25 yards and ranges in depth from 1 to 5 feet. A ramp makes the pool accessible to the disabled, and the water is kept at a bath-like 90 degrees. The Monterey Sports Center is open Monday through Friday from 6:00 A.M. to 9:30 P.M., Saturday from 8:00 A.M. to 5:00 P.M. and Sunday from noon to 5:00 P.M. Admission for out-of-town visitors is $1.75 for children age five and younger, $3.50 for youths six to 17, $5.50 for adults 18 to 54, and $4.00 for seniors 55 and older. Monterey residents receive reduced rates. Showers, lockers, towel service, and baby-sitting are available. Call for recreational swimming hours.

Theater

There is a strong contingent of local theater groups on the Monterey Peninsula that produce shows by and for children. Check out the local papers to see which theater and dance productions might suit your little one's tastes. Here are a few to keep an eye on. For other cultural entertainment options, see our Arts and Galleries chapter.

Children's Experimental Theater
Indoor Forest Theatre,
Santa Rita Street and Mountain View Avenue, Carmel
(831) 624–1531

Since 1960, this group has presented opportunities for local kids to perform on stage. Inquire into special programs and children's theater productions.

The Forest Theater Guild
Indoor Forest Theatre, Santa Rita Street and Mountain View Avenue, Carmel
(831) 626–1681

Bring the kids and a picnic and enjoy theater under the stars. With this Carmel tradition, you can experience live theater and films outdoors during the summer months. A big bonfire helps fight off the evening chill.

California's First Theatre
336 Pacific Street, Monterey
(831) 375–4916

The old-time comedies and melodramas at California's First Theatre in Monterey are kid favorites. Hear them laugh out loud, boo the villains, and cheer the heroes. You'll enjoy the ambiance of the state's first theater, built in 1844.

Whale Watching

"I saw a whale! I saw a whale!" Those shrieks of joy are repeated by children from around the world, in many languages, upon return from a whale-watching expedition in Monterey Bay. Peak California gray whale-watching season is from December through March, with one- to two-hour excursions leaving hourly off of Monterey's Fisherman's Wharf. Prices average $15 for adults and $10 for children, but call for current rates and schedules. Remember: Boat trips on the Bay can be cold, windy, and wet. Bring multiple layers of clothing, waterproof gear, and motion-sickness relief (see also our In and Around the Water chapter).

Chris' Fishing Trips
Fisherman's Wharf, Monterey
(831) 375–5951

Chris' offers whale-watching boats every hour from 9:00 A.M. until dusk from December through April. Six-hour summer charter cruises in search of sea mammals are also available for large groups.

Monterey Sportfishing and Cruises
Fisherman's Wharf, Monterey
(831) 372–2203

December through March, 1½- to two-hour cruises go out to sea to follow the migration of the California gray whales. From June through September, three- and four-hour cruises head for deep waters in search of blue whales, orcas, humpbacks, minkes, and dolphins.

Randy's Fishing Trips
Fisherman's Wharf, Monterey
(831) 372–7440

With whale-watching trips from mid-December through March, Randy's Fishing Trips feature fully narrated two-hour excursions. Boats leave every two hours on weekdays and every hour on weekends from 9:30 A.M. until 3:30 P.M.

Youth Centers

City youth centers, recreation departments, and other community activities for kids abound on the Peninsula. While many programs are limited to city residents, some centers have summertime programs open to visitors. The best way to discover the scope of activities available is to request a written activity guide from the organizations.

Monterey Youth Center
777 Pearl Street, Monterey
(831) 646–3873

Next to Dennis the Menace Park, the Monterey Youth Center provides games and activities for youth of all ages. Call for visitor programs.

Carmel Youth Center
Torres Street and 4th Avenue, Carmel
(831) 624–3285

Founded by Bing Crosby nearly 50 years ago, Carmel Youth Center is geared toward teens ages 12 to 19. Activities include sports, live music, pool tables, and games. Visitors are welcome.

Pacific Grove Youth Center
302 16th Street, Pacific Grove
(831) 648–3134

This recently constructed facility provides a wealth of activities for teens in grades six through 12 who reside within the Pacific Grove Unified School District boundaries. Ping-Pong, pool, dances, karaoke, and movies are just some of the activities. Call for visitor programs.

Actor Bill Murray is a favorite celebrity player at the annual AT&T Pebble Beach National Pro-Am Golf Tournament. PHOTO: © KELLI ULDALL

Annual Events

The scenic beauty and rich cultural history of the Monterey Peninsula are continually celebrated in a multitude of yearly events and festivals. Several of our events are held outside and focus on our natural resources. The annual Whale Festival is a three-month celebration honoring gray whales' migration from Alaska to Baja California and back. Other aquatic-related events, such as the Sardine Festival, gather locals and visitors to enjoy the bounty of the Monterey Bay. Pebble Beach and Laguna Raceway entice car buffs with several international auto shows and races, while history enthusiasts will enjoy the many opportunities to participate in the events of historical significance. In this chapter you will discover the hometown celebrations of Pacific Grove, events that bring people together in a spirit of cooperation and good old-fashioned fun. Pacific Grove's Good Old Days, where local police officers compete in a motorcycle race, and the Butterfly Parade, when school children dress up as butterflies and walk through town welcoming back the Monarchs that spend the winter here, are town favorites.

Monterey has been known for its festivals since the early days of Spanish settlement, when fiestas were a common occurrence. Alvarado Street, in the historic district of Old Monterey, is perfectly designed for holding street festivals. Numerous times during the year the entire street is blocked off for celebrations. Among them is the Sidewalk Fine Arts Festival, when Alvarado Street becomes a huge gallery. This event is like a sidewalk sale for various painters, photographers, and other artists.

Carmel events tend to focus around food and the arts. The annual Masters of Food and Wine Festival at the Highlands Inn draws an international crowd each February. The Carmel Bach Festival, held in July and August, is also world-renowned and has been well attended for more than 60 years. Each year the Carmel Music Society hosts a series of concerts featuring internationally acclaimed pianists, vocalists, violinists, and ensembles who perform classical compositions.

Pebble Beach has its share of events, too, with the Concours d'Elegance classic car show, the widely acclaimed AT&T Pro-Am golf tournament, and horse-jumping events at the Pebble Beach Equestrian Center. The AT&T is one of the largest events on the Peninsula, bringing in thousands of out-of-towners who love golf and hobnobbing with pro golfers and celebrities like local resident Clint Eastwood.

Events are listed in the month in which they are held. The events we've listed occur annually, but in all cases it is best to confirm the dates, times, and fees by calling the phone number indicated or visiting the Web site.

January

AT&T Pebble Beach National Pro-Am
Various golf courses, Pebble Beach
(800) 541–9091, www.attpbgolf.com

The AT&T golf tournament is a 72-hole PGA Tour Championship Tournament hosted by Spyglass Hill, Pebble Beach, and Poppy Hill golf courses. Professionals compete for a $4 million purse and are paired with amateurs in two-man teams competing for a $100,000 purse. Foursomes rotate to each of the three courses on Thursday through Saturday. The famous cut is made Saturday night, and the 25 low Pro-Am teams play the Pebble Beach Golf Links on Sunday for the championship. If there is a playoff, sudden death starts on the 18th hole. Celebrities and pro golfers who have played in past tournaments include Clint Eastwood, Kevin Costner, Tiger Woods, Bryant Gumbel, Bill Murray, Fuzzy Zoeller, Huey Lewis, and Jack Lemmon, to name only a few. The weeklong event usually occurs at the end of January. For tickets there are basically three options, daily tickets, a season badge, or a grandstand badge. Daily tickets cost around $40 for practice Monday to Wednesday and $40 per day for tournament rounds. The season badge and the grandstand badge cost $95 to $110 and get you in for all seven days, but the grandstand badge includes seating. The AT&T brings thousands of golf enthusiasts to the Monterey Peninsula over the week of the tournament.

Monterey Swingfest
Hyatt Regency, 1 Old Golf Course Road, Monterey
(805) 937–1574

This annual event held in mid-January offers swing dance workshops with past and present world and national champions, a swing dance contest, and over 40 hours of open dancing. West Coast swing dancing is emphasized with a concentration on rhythm and blues music. Advance tickets are $75. Call for specific event registration and schedule.

Rio Resolution Run
Crossroads Shopping Center,
Highway 1 at Rio Road, Carmel
(831) 644–2427,
www.riogrillsresolutionrun.com

This annual 6.8-mile run and 3-mile family fun run/walk, a benefit for the Suicide Prevention Center, is always held on the first day of the new year. The cross-country course is mapped out to travel from the Crossroads Shopping Center into Carmel, ending at the Carmel Mission. Here's your chance to start the new year off right by getting plenty of exercise and helping out a local charity at the same time. Entry fee for participants is $25 for adults, $17 for ages 12 and younger.

February

Cannery Row John Steinbeck Birthday Party & Symposium
Cannery Row, Monterey
(831) 372–8512

This annual celebration honors the author who gave Cannery Row worldwide recognition. Free birthday cake is served at the rail car on the recreation trail below the Edgewater Packing Company building. Events include a sardine-eating contest, musical entertainment, and nostalgic exhibits on Steinbeck. Walking tours are held at Cannery Row and Doc Ricketts' Lab (for a fee of around $10 to $15 per tour). A bus tour to Steinbeck country in Salinas is also offered. Free lectures are held at the Monterey Bay Aquarium auditorium. The festivities take place at the end of February.

Day of Romance in Old Monterey
Various historical locations, Monterey
(831) 647–6204, www.mbay.net/~mshp

Held in mid-February, this event is an opportunity to see musicians, dancers, and a living history pageant featuring actors in period clothing telling romantic stories of Old Monterey in the actual homes where the stories took place. Food is available. This is a very popular event, so get your tickets early! Ticket price is approximately $15; tickets are available at Bay Books and the Cooper Museum Store.

International Cat Show
Monterey Fairgrounds,
2004 Fairgrounds Road, Monterey
(831) 372–7018

More than 175 cats are in the limelight at this two-day event that is reportedly more fun than a dog show. Cat breeds are confirmed and judged by weight, grooming, and personality. There are 10 shows, each with a judge. Each cat is carried up in its cage; no leashes are allowed. Owners then point out the characteristics and personality of their cats. Exhibitors, including veterinarians and groomers, are on hand. There are also vendors selling pet food, pet-care products, and all manner of feline paraphernalia. The show is usually held the last week of February. Call for dates and ticket prices.

The Masters of Food and Wine
Highlands Inn, Highway 1, Carmel
(831) 624–3801

This annual weeklong celebration features an international gathering of chefs and master winemakers in several locations around the Peninsula, including the

Monterey Conference Center, Rancho San Carlos, and the Highlands Inn. Winery tours and tastings, cooking demonstrations, a wild mushroom hunt, and fabulous gourmet lunches and dinners highlight the event. Event prices range from $85 to $495 and typically include the Opening Night Extravaganza and lunchtime demos by world-famous chefs. Reservations are highly recommended. Events take place from the end of February to the beginning of March.

Steinbeck's Birthday Weekend
National Steinbeck Center, Salinas
(831) 796–3833, www.steinbeck.org

The last weekend in February is set aside to honor the life and times of the internationally acclaimed author, John Steinbeck. Celebrate Steinbeck's birthday with tours, speakers, luncheon at the Steinbeck House, and a visit to the new National Steinbeck Center interactive museum. Many events are free to the public; others include admission charges which vary according to the individual event. Call for specific information.

March

Cutting Day
Friendly Plaza, corner of Pacific and Jefferson Streets next to Colton Hall, Monterey
(831) 646–3860, www.monterey.org

This is an excellent opportunity to exchange cuttings and plants. All Monterey Peninsula gardening buffs are invited to this popular event to exchange softwood cutting materials, seedling plants, bulbs, potted plants, and so on. The Parks Division has free seedling trees available for the public. Participants are encouraged to bring cuttings and plants for the exchanges. This event is free and takes place on a Saturday in March. For exact date and time, contact the Parks Division.

Dixieland Monterey
Various locations around the Peninsula
(831) 443–5260

This annual event consists of a weekend of traditional Dixieland jazz. National and international bands appear in various cabaret locations and at the Monterey Convention Center. Previous headliners have included The Bob Crosby Bob Cats, Generic Swing Orchestra, Night Blooming Jazz Men, and the Frisco Jazz Band. The event also features youth bands, jam sessions, a parade, and parties. Dixieland Monterey usually takes place the first week of March. Admission prices are $20 to $45 depending on days of attendance and seating preference.

Sea Otter Classic
Laguna Seca Recreation Area,
1021 Monterey-Salinas Highway, Monterey
(650) 306–1414, www.seaotterclassic.com

The Sea Otter Classic, the premier cycling festival in the U.S., has been deemed "the hippest cross-platform happening in two-wheeled racing." This sports festival also features mountain bike races, roller hockey, and in-line skating events. Sports enthusiasts will enjoy the nonstop action, food courts, and vendors at this three-day event, usually held at the end of March. Admission charge is under $10 per person.

April

Annual Adobe Tour
Historic Adobes, Monterey
(831) 372–2608

The Annual Adobe Tour features the gardens of Monterey's many historic adobes and includes garden-related activities for both adults and children. Living history programs and performances are also on the schedule. The Sensory Garden area is a showstopper with floral displays by local merchants and growers. Antique gardening tools are on display at the Doud House. Children's gardening workshops are held at the Stevenson House, Cooper-Molera Adobe, and the Monterey Museum of Art. The Historic Fashion Gallery presents a 1920s Garden Party, and a Famous Author Book Signing is held at the Mayo Hayes O'Donnell Library. The event is held at the end of April. Call for exact dates and ticket prices.

Annual Easter Egg Hunt
Frank Sollecito Ballpark,
777 Pearl Street, Monterey
(831) 646–3866, www.monterey.org

Children love this special event, held for preschoolers through third graders. More than 5,000 eggs and 100 golden prize eggs are hidden in four age-designated hunt areas. Parents are asked to bring a basket for their kids to collect the Easter eggs. The free event takes place the Saturday before Easter Sunday.

Annual Wildflower Show
Pacific Grove Museum of Natural History,
Forest and Central Avenues, Pacific Grove
(831) 648–3116, www.pgmuseum.org

The museum hosts its annual display of more than 600 varieties of wildflowers, many at the height of their blooming cycle. The flowers are either potted or in vases and are displayed in the museum. Visitors may wander through the exhibit and admire specimens. The event takes place in mid-April. There is no admission fee.

Big Sur International Marathon
Highway 1, Carmel
(831) 625–6226, www.bsim.org

The Big Sur International Marathon is known as the "World's Most Beautiful Marathon." Entrants run along the gorgeous California coastline from Big Sur to Carmel, cheered on by extra-enthusiastic volunteers and classical musicians at choice locations. A 5K run/walk and the marathon are held concurrently. A carbo-loading party is held the evening before the race. Held at the end of April, the race has an entry fee of $65 for runners/walkers. There is no charge for spectators.

Breakfast with Bunny
Devendorf Park,
Ocean Avenue between Junipero and Mission Streets, Carmel
(831) 626–1255

Bring the entire family to the park for a $3.00 pancake breakfast. Then join Mr. Bunny in a personal appearance at Eggland, where face-painting, cookie decorating, carnival games, and other fun activities are held to celebrate Easter. The event takes place on Easter weekend. Entrance to Eggland costs about $5.00.

Bunnies and Horses
Redwings Horse Sanctuary, Highway 1, Carmel
(831) 624–8464, www.redwings.org

Enjoy a pancake breakfast and Easter egg hunt at Redwings Horse Sanctuary, across from Point Lobos State Park in Carmel. Activities include face-painting, horse-grooming demonstrations, and photo opportunities with the horses. The event takes place on the Saturday before Easter. Admission typically is $10.00 for adults and $5.00 for children younger than 12.

A Garden Affair
3618 The Barnyard, Highway 1, Carmel
(831) 624–8886, www.thebarnyard.com

The Barnyard, a premier shopping center in several historic barns, hosts its annual garden tour and festival featuring gardening demos, food tastings, entertainment, and gorgeous spring flowers. The event takes place at the end of April. A portion of the small admission charge goes to benefit the Friends of the Hospice Foundation.

Good Old Days Celebration
Lighthouse Avenue, Pacific Grove
(800) 656–6650, www.pacificgrove.org

PG's annual celebration of the late 1800s includes a parade, more than 200 exhibitors at an arts and crafts fair/street bazaar, an antique fashion show, and a police officers' motorcycle competition and drill team. There are also pie-eating contests, a quilt show, live entertainment, a golf tournament, and more. The event takes place early April.

Monterey Bay Spring Faire
Custom House Plaza, Monterey
(831) 622–0100, www.pacrep.org

One hundred West Coast artists and craftspeople sell original, handmade creations, including jewelry (beadwork and precious metals), wearable art (clothing and hats), wooden toys, birdhouses, pottery, and metalwork sculptures.

Monterey Wine Festival
Monterey Conference Center, 1 Portola Plaza, Monterey
(800) 656–4282, www.montereywine.com

The state's original wine festival brings together more than 150 California vintners presenting more than 800 different wines. The Scholarship Wine Auction features private reserves, artist series, and oversized, decorative, and unique bottles of wine. Events include winery tours, winemaker dinners, workshops/seminars, cooking demos, gourmet tastings, entertainment, and the festive finale brunch. The four-day Wine Festival takes place in mid-April each year. The events are held at various locations with tickets starting around $30.

Old Monterey Seafood and Music Festival
Custom House Plaza and Alvarado Street, Monterey
(831) 655–8070

This event celebrates seafood, including shrimp, abalone, squid, and more. There are crafts, music, and food all wrapped into one street festival staged in historic downtown Monterey. There is continuous musical entertainment featuring several local musicians on two outdoor stages. The free event takes place during mid-April.

Spring Horse Show
Pebble Beach Equestrian Center, Alva Road and Portola Lane, Pebble Beach
(831) 624–2756, www.ridepebblebeach.com

This is the annual spring equestrian competition held in early April at the Pebble Beach Equestrian Center. You'll see horse-jumping events and finely groomed horses. There are pony rides for the kids, food tents, and vendors selling items appealing to horse lovers. There is no admission fee.

Spring Trade Fair and Expo
Monterey Conference Center, 1 Portola Plaza, Monterey
(831) 648–5356, www.mpcc.com

The Monterey Peninsula Chamber of Commerce sponsors this annual event featuring chamber members touting their goods and services. The expo is an excellent opportunity to acquaint yourself with local businesses, pick up some useful giveaways, taste the gourmet spreads of various restaurants, and enter contests for free prizes. The Expo, held at the end of April, has a nominal admission fee.

May

24 Hours of Adrenaline
Laguna Seca Recreation Area
(905) 944–9436, www.24hoursofadrenaline.com

Called the "Woodstock of Mountain Biking," 24 Hours is a relay race with the objective of completing as many laps as possible during a 24-hour period. Riders of all levels, shapes, and sizes are invited to participate, and categories are available for the serious racer as well as the casual rider.

Castroville Artichoke Festival
Various locations in Castroville
(831) 633–2465, www.artichoke–festival.org

Held the third weekend of May, the famous and fun Artichoke Festival features a parade, 10K run, classic car show, and, of course, artichokes prepared in every conceivable manner. A Marilyn Monroe look-alike contest celebrates the fact that the actress was named Artichoke Queen in the 1950s.

Garden Day at Cooper-Molera Adobe
Cooper-Molera Adobe, 525 Polk Street, Monterey
(831) 649–7118, www.mbay.net/~mshp

Spring brings out the best in the native plants at the gardens of the historic Cooper-Molera Adobe. This annual event provides the chance for visitors to see and purchase cuttings from the adobe's garden. The cuttings vary from year to year depending on which plants have grown well. Usually there are old-fashioned plants like lavender and veronica. Refreshments for the free event, usually held mid-May, are provided by the Carmel-by-the-Sea Garden Club.

The Human Race
Lake El Estero, Monterey to Lovers Point, Pacific Grove
(800) 776–9176, www.yesillhelp.org

An 8.5 and 10K run/walk, sponsored by several local businesses, allows participants to designate pledged funds to the charity of their choice. The course starts at Lake El Estero and follows the recreation trail to Lovers Point and back. The early morning Pacesetter's Breakfast starts the day off right, and T-shirts are given to participants. The event usually occurs mid-May. Participants can collect pledges or pay a $25 entry fee.

Marina Festival of the Winds
Various locations in Marina
(887) 973–2233, www.marinafestival.com

Kites, hot-air balloons, hang gliding, and paragliding races—if it uses the wind, it's at the Festival of the Winds. Also included are competitions, live music, international foods, and much more.

Monster Truck Jam
Salinas Sports Complex
(831) 775–3105, www.ushra.com

Every year, over 1.5 million fans in the United States experience the phenomenon known as Monster Trucks. The third Sunday of May sees the likes of Bigfoot, Gravedigger, Gunslinger, Eradicator, and Blue Thunder invade the Salinas Sports Complex. Admission charge.

National Chamber Music Competition
Sunset Center, San Carlos Street between 8th and 9th Avenues, Carmel
(831) 625–2212

The Chamber Music Society of the Monterey Peninsula hosts this prestigious annual student competition at the Sunset Center in Carmel. Ten groups of students playing piano and stringed instruments compete for scholarships. The age limit for entrants is 26. A winners' concert is held the following Sunday. The free event takes place the first week of May.

June

Grand Prix of Monterey
Mazda Raceway at Laguna Seca
(800) 327–7322, www.laguna-seca.com

Fans of open-wheel auto racing from around the world converge at Laguna Seca to watch drivers like Mario Andretti, Christian Fittipaldi, and Jimmy Vasser battle for top honors. Also featured are the Shell 300, the CART FedEx Championship Series, and the Shelby Cobra Challenge Senior Racing Series. Various admission packages and camping are available.

Monterey Bay Blues Festival
Monterey Fairgrounds,
2004 Fairgrounds Road, Monterey
(831) 394–2652, www.montereyblues.com

The annual Monterey Bay Blues Festival is dedicated to preserving blues as an American art form. Three separate shows are held on three stages. Two shows, each featuring numerous acts, are held each day. Past lineups have included artists such as Etta James, Frankie Lee, and Clarence Carter. More than 30 veteran blues artists and several newcomers are showcased in this weekend event held at the end of June. There are also food, merchandise, and exhibit booths on the grounds. Ticket prices are from $15 to $70 (for a two-day pass).

Monterey Bay TheatreFest
Custom House Plaza, Monterey
(831) 622–0100, www.pacrep.org

The TheatreFest features live music on stage, a Human Chess Game, and fairy tale classics in the open air. The Pacific Repertory Theatre players produce the plays and the Human Chess Game, which has a yearly theme. Bleacher seating is set up near a stage at the Plaza. Pacific Repertory players march onto the Custom House Plaza and carry out full-scale chess game war on the chess board stage. The TheatreFest is held at the end of June, and performances are free to the public.

Sardine Festival
Cannery Row, Monterey
(831) 372–2259, www.cannery.row.com

This free one-day event, sponsored by and benefiting the Cannery Row Foundation in cooperation with the Cannery Row Marketing Council and Cannery Row Association, is held in mid-June. Activities include a frog-jumping challenge and multicultural presentations with music, dancing, and singing. Local chefs conduct

Insiders' Tip

Pacific Grove residents know that in order to get a front-row seat for the Feast of Lanterns, you can stake out your territory at Lovers Point early in the day by leaving a blanket on the ground along the recreation trail.

cooking demos on preparing foods made with sardines and allow you to taste their creations. Ever wonder how many sardines you can eat in one minute? For $1.00 you can enter the sardine-eating contest. There is also a reunion of people who worked at the Cannery Row sardine canneries.

Spirit West Coast
Laguna Seca Recreation Area
(831) 443–5399, www.spiritwestcoast.org

Over 60,000 people attend this three-day Christian music festival, the only one of its kind in the Western U.S. The nonprofit event features concerts by more than 50 of the top performers in Christian music on six stages as well as speakers, camping, sports, and recreation.

July

California Rodeo Salinas
Salinas Sports Complex, 1034 N. Main, Salinas
(831) 775–3100, www.carodeo.com

See world champion cowboys compete at the biggest Rodeo in California. While PRCA cowboys compete in the main arena, trick riders, clowns, and horse races take place on the track. Put on your boots and hat, eat your fill of barbecue from the many food vendors, listen to some cowboy poetry, and have a true Western experience. The annual Rodeo is usually scheduled the second or third weekend in July. Admission fees start around $10.

Carmel Bach Festival
Various locations on the Peninsula
(831) 624–2046, www.bachfestival.org

This internationally known event has featured world-class baroque music for more than 60 years. The season presents concerts, recitals, master classes, open rehearsals, and a children's concert. Recitals, about an hour and a half long, are held prior to each performance. There are two or three evening concerts held each week. Each concert is repeated several times over the three-week period, allowing a greater number of people to attend the concerts. The Bach Festival begins in mid-July. Prices vary according to the event. Attending the recitals is the least expensive way to go. Call or visit the Web site for a schedule and information.

Carmel Shakespeare Festival
Various theaters, Carmel
(831) 622–0100, www.pacrep.org

The Forest, Golden Bough, and Circle theaters host this annual event with professional and community actors in a selection of works from Shakespeare. The season includes a total of four productions. On the weekends, two plays run simultaneously on separate stages for the first half of the season, followed by the second pair. The event is held late July through mid-October. Tickets are $15 for adults, $10 for seniors and students. Call or visit the Web site for venues and ticket information.

Equestrian Classic
Pebble Beach Equestrian Center,
corner of Alva Road and Portola Lane,
Pebble Beach
(831) 624–2756, www.ridepebblebeach.com

More than 500 ponies and thoroughbreds compete in equestrian events, including hunter and jumper events, at the Equestrian Classic. Children's classes are held, and the $25,000 Grand Prix Jumping contest is a big draw. Many people like to attend the jumper events because it is more colorful and bold. The Children's Fun Fair features a petting zoo, and there are also food booths. The event takes place over a two-week period at the end of July. Horses that qualify will compete in the Grand Prix Jumping event for prize

Each summer, the Carmel Bach Festival draws musicians and music lovers from all over the world.
PHOTO: MONTEREY COUNTY CONVENTION & VISITORS BUREAU

money. Admission is free except for the entrance fee at the Pebble Beach gate.

Feast of Lanterns
Various locations, Pacific Grove
(831) 373–7625

Feast of Lanterns, an annual Pacific Grove community celebration, includes street dancing, a pet parade, a pageant at Lovers Point Beach, and a fireworks display. The weeklong event takes place during the last week of July. There is no admission charge.

Fourth of July
Locations throughout Monterey Bay
(831) 646–3996, www.monterey.org

A morning parade on Alvarado Street in downtown Monterey includes bands, community groups, and floats kicking off the July 4th celebration. In the evening, fireworks synchronized with patriotic music are presented over the Monterey Bay. Good locations to see the free fireworks show are Monterey State Beach and Fisherman's Wharf.

Garlic Festival
Christmas Hill Park, Miller Avenue, and Santa Theresa Boulevard, Gilroy
(831) 842–1625,
www.gilroygarlicfestival.com

Gilroy, the Garlic Capital of the World, loves to celebrate garlic, the beloved "stinking rose." Numerous food booths feature garlic dishes from a variety of ethnic backgrounds. Celebrity chefs are on hand to demonstrate the preparation of various dishes made with garlic. You'll want to sample delicacies such as garlic ice cream (seriously, it's delicious) and gator tail and ostrich cooked with garlic. Vendors sell fine arts and crafts and other items such as garlic braids and wreaths. There is continuous musical entertainment, including rock, country, reggae, and jazz. Admission for this popular annual event, held the last full weekend of July, is $8.00 for adults, $4.00 for seniors and children younger than 12.

Moss Landing Antique Street Fair
Off Highway 1, Moss Landing
(831) 633–4501

More than 100 vendors showcase their antiques and collectibles and sell everything imaginable at this shoppers' heaven. You'll find Victorian furniture, vintage linens, toys, glassware, tableware, books, and other paper products. The quantity and variety of antiques is staggering. We suggest that serious shoppers wear sunglasses, layers of clothing (it can get hot around midday), and comfortable shoes. The event usually takes place the last Sunday of July. A nominal admission fee includes parking.

Obon Festival
Buddhist Temple,
1155 Noche Buena, Seaside
(831) 394–0119

The Monterey Peninsula Buddhist Temple hosts this annual event that celebrates an international Buddhist tradition. The local festivities feature bonsai dwarfed-tree exhibits, delicious Asian foods (such as teriyaki and tempura), tea ceremonies, crafts, and spectacular Obon Dance performances. This lively bazaar is held in early July.

United States World Superbike Championship
Mazda Raceway Laguna Seca
1021 Monterey-Salinas Highway, Monterey
(800) 327–7322, www.lagunaseca.com

This international motorcycle event brings champion riders from more than 10 countries to this Monterey County track for the eight-race series. The race times vary for categories, including motorcycles like Supersport, Pro Thunder, Big Twins, Triumphs, and Harley-Davidsons. The only World Superbike event in North America takes place over a two-week period and usually occurs mid-July. Tickets are $10 to $40 per day, depending on seating preference.

August

BlackHawk Collection Exposition Sale
Classic Cars
Peter Hay Golf Course, Pebble Beach
(510) 736–3444,
www.blackhawkcollection.com

More than 75 rare, vintage, classic, and one-of-a-kind automobiles are displayed and offered for individual sale at the Peter Hay Golf Course on 17-Mile Drive near The Lodge at Pebble Beach. The event is held mid-August each year as part of the Concours d'Elegance. There is no admission fee to view the automobiles, but you must pay the $7.00 gate fee to enter Pebble Beach.

Carmel Bach Festival
Various locations on the Peninsula
(831) 624–2046, www.bachfestival.org

The Bach Festival, held over a three-week period beginning in mid-July, has events featuring world-class concerts, recitals, master classes, open rehearsals, and a children's concert. See our July entry for more details.

Carmel Shakespeare Festival
Various theaters, Carmel
(831) 622–0100, www.pacrep.org

Several local theaters host this annual event with professional and community actors starring in works by Shakespeare. The event starts in the end of July and is held through mid-October. See our July entry for more information.

Concorso Italiano
Quail Lodge Resort and Golf Club
8205 Valley Greens Drive, Carmel Valley
(425) 688–1903, www.concorso.com

The Quail Lodge Resort and Golf Club, with the beautiful Santa Lucia Mountain Range as a backdrop, hosts this world-renowned show. Attendees from around the world come to view an impressive display of more than 400 classic Italian automobiles and motorcycles on the expansive lawns of Quail Lodge. Individual auto makes, such as Porsche, BMW, Viper, and Lamborghini, are set up in separate areas. The annual event, held in conjunction with the Concours d'Elegance, occurs in mid-August each year. Ticket prices are $40, which includes a parking pass.

Concours d'Elegance
The Lodge at Pebble Beach
(831) 659–0663,
www.pebblebeachconcours.net

For over 50 years this internationally recognized premier showcase of more than 100 classic automobiles has graced the lawn at The Lodge. With the breathtaking 18th green and the rugged coastline as the backdrop, this is an automobile extravaganza one will never forget. Pre- and post-war marquees feature an exclusive selection of classic autos. In addition to the cars, many people come to see the stars. Celebrities such as comedian Jay Leno and clothing designer Ralph Lauren have both entered cars in past events. Proceeds from the event, held in mid-August, benefit local organizations including United Way of Monterey County. Tickets cost $50 and include the program and shuttle service.

Jewish Food Festival
Congregation Beth Israel,
5716 Carmel Valley Road, Carmel Valley
(831) 624–2015

The Concours d'Elegance is the world's premier concours event. Each year, vintage auto enthusiasts from all over the world are drawn to Pebble Beach to view exquisitely restored classic automobiles.
PHOTO: JULIE ARMSTRONG/MONTEREY COUNTY CONVENTION & VISITORS BUREAU

This festive event on the first or second Sunday in August features a crafts fair, Jewish food, dance, music, and entertainment and a village market with costumed vendors. Nosh on traditional Jewish fare like kugel and latkes. There are also wandering storytellers, pushcart peddlers, strolling musicians, Israeli dance lessons, synagogue tours, and more. Admission to the event is free.

Monterey County Fair
Monterey County Fairgrounds,
2004 Fairgrounds Road, Monterey
(831) 372–5863,
www.montereycountyfair.com

Who doesn't love the fair? The Monterey County Fair is an exciting blend of carnival rides, craft and food booths, produce and flower displays, art and photography, livestock, contests, demonstrations, 4-H club exhibits, and lively entertainment. The event is held at the end of August each year. Admission is $6.00 for adults, $5.00 for seniors, $3.00 for children ages six to 12, and free for children younger than five.

Monterey Historic Automobile Races
Mazda Raceway Laguna Seca
1021 Monterey-Salinas Highway, Monterey
(800) 327–7322, www.lagunaseca.com

The "Historics" are yet another opportunity to see vintage cars during the Concours d'Elegance festivities. Watch Mustangs, Cobras, Corvettes, and other rare autos race around the Laguna Seca Raceway. Races are for seven groups, from pre-1928 sport and racing cars through 1981 championship cars. Tickets range from $25 to $40 depending on seating preference.

Rick Cole Sports and Classic Car Auction
Monterey Conference Center, 1 Portola Plaza, Monterey
(818) 506–6533

Another world-famous auto event, the two-day auction is held in conjunction with the Concours d'Elegance. A preview of the vintage sports cars and classic automobiles, including Corvettes, Porsches, Formula 1 race cars, Cobras, and MGs, takes place in the Custom House Plaza prior to the sale. The event is held mid-August each year. Tickets are normally $20.

Scottish and Irish Festival and Highland Games
Toro County Park
Monterey-Salinas Highway, Salinas
(831) 647–6311,
www.montereyscotgames.com

This is a giant three-day event, held in early August, with bagpipe bands, dancing, athletic events, competitions, clans, kilts, blarney, and killarney. A Caber parade takes place, in which brawny lads wearing kilts toss around an object that looks like a telephone pole. Other competitions include shot put and a hammer throw. All the judges for the competitive events are themselves teachers of the sports. About 150 dancers from as far away as Canada compete individually in Highland step dances. Items such as kilts, sweaters, and handmade crafts are for sale by vendors. Ticket prices in recent years were $11 to $50 depending upon days of attendance and seating preference.

Steinbeck Festival
Various locations in Salinas
(831) 775–4720, www.steinbeck.org

Four full days of activity with speakers, presenters, films, and tours highlight the annual festival honoring John Steinbeck. A bus tour features historic ranches, views, scenes, and readings from Steinbeck's novels and short stories that take place in the Salinas Valley. You'll also visit the site where Steinbeck was laid to rest. A walking tour of historic Salinas points out the new Steinbeck Center and restored buildings in Old Town Salinas. You may also tour the Steinbeck Archives for a look at the 30,000 items in the vault. The events, which usually take place in early August, have various ticket prices ranging from $5.00 to $30.00. Call for reservations and information.

The Monterey Historic Automobile Races at Mazda Speedway Laguna Seca features vintage racing cars such as Mustangs, Cobras, and Corvettes. PHOTO: ROSS ANDRÉSON

CLOSE-UP

Classic Car Weekend

For one weekend in August, the eyes of the world's automotive cognoscenti are on the Monterey Peninsula. For days preceding the events, huge trucks carrying scores of the most pampered, polished, primped—and pricey—automobiles on the planet begin to arrive. Just watching them unload causes jaws to drop all over town.

They are bound for one of the world-famous events that comprise the Classic Car Weekend on the Monterey Peninsula.

The premier affair, and the event that started it all, is the Pebble Beach Concours d'Elegance. Arguably the world's most prestigious automotive concours ("contest" in French), the Pebble Beach Concours is a gathering for wonderfully restored, historically accurate, and rare or unusual examples of the automotive maker's art. It takes place on the 18th fairway of the Pebble Beach Golf Links, adjacent to the Pacific coastline, in the shadow of The Lodge at Pebble Beach. This one-day affair attracts the rich and famous as well as the merely awestruck.

Collectible car auctions are also part of the festivities. The two-day Rick Cole Auction takes place at the Monterey Conference Center and includes vintage sports and racecars and marques such as Ferrari, Porsche, Cobra, and MG. A preview of the offerings takes place at Custom House Plaza. One of the highlights is watching the cars

The finely-tuned engines of Italy's finest sports cars can be heard at Concorso Italiano in Carmel Valley.

PHOTO: MATT STONE/CONCORSO ITALIANO © 2001

being fired up and driven to the auction, where bidding quickly reaches the stratosphere. Admission includes entrance to both the preview and the sale itself.

The BlackHawk Collection Exposition and Sale of Classic Cars is held at Peter Hay Golf Course in Pebble Beach. It was here that a record $5 million was paid for a classic Ferrari in 2000. Admission to this event is free, but you must pay the gate fee for entrance to Pebble Beach.

Speaking of Ferraris, the Concorso Italiano showcases more than 600 examples of sleek Italian motorcraft. In addition to the famous red cars from Modena, Lamborghini, Alfa Romeo, Fiat, and Pantera as well as exotic, lesser-known makers Iso, Abarth, and DeTomasso are featured. The Concorso is held at Quail Lodge in Carmel Valley.

Mazda Raceway Laguna Seca is home to the Monterey Historic Automobile Races. Those not satisfied with ogling static displays of vintage racecars watch lovingly restored Maseratis, Jaguars, Ferraris, Bugattis, and MGs return to competition. There are fourteen race groups, held over two days, classed by year of manufacture, engine size, and type of racing. Although vintage racecars are not as fast as modern cars, the nostalgia at the event is as thick as the blue smoke hanging over the track. Weekend tickets as well as single-day passes are available, and camping is possible at Laguna Seca.

If gazing at rare, classic automobiles isn't your thing, come for the stargazing. Celebrities the likes of Jerry Seinfeld, Jay Leno, Nicholas Cage, and many others, come to admire and acquire the vintage vehicles during the Classic Car Weekend.

Winemaker's Celebration
Custom House Plaza, Monterey
(831) 375–9400,
www.montereywinecountry.org

The Winemaker's Celebration features more than 25 Monterey County winemakers and local restaurants presenting wine tasting, food sampling, and wine-education events at the end of August each year. Jugglers, musicians, barrel-building demos, viticulture displays, and entertainment make this an exciting and informative event. Tickets are $15 in advance, $18 the day of event. The price includes a souvenir glass and wine-tasting tickets. Children enter for free.

September

Big Sur Ride
(831) 373–1839, www.cypressgroup.org

The Big Sur Ride is a spectacular two-day, 170-mile bicycle ride that includes 11,100 feet of climbing. The ride begins and finishes in Carmel Valley Village. The route runs along the rugged Big Sur coastline, through the beautiful Salinas Valley, and into the dramatic rolling hills of Carmel Valley.

Carmel Mission Fiesta
Carmel Mission, Rio Road, Carmel
(831) 626–9272

The free annual Carmel Mission Fiesta includes mariachis, dancing, and more than 55 vendors selling food and crafts. Mexican, Irish, and country and western style dancing take place. Foods served include barbecue chicken, tri-tip sandwiches, and tacos. Handmade crafts for sale include paintings, clothing, and holiday ornaments. The fiesta is always held the last Sunday in September.

Carmel Shakespeare Festival
Various theaters, Carmel
(831) 622–0100, www.pacrep.org

Several local theaters host this annual event with professional and community actors starring in works by Shakespeare. The event starts in the end of July and is held through mid-October. See our July entry for more information.

Carmel TomatoFest
Quail Lodge Resort, Carmel
No phone, www.tomatofest.com

Tired of the tasteless, hard-as-the-ketchup-bottle varieties found in grocery stores, the founders of TomatoFest began to raise "heirloom" tomatoes, hybrids lost to time through commercial agriculture's search for the perfect fruit. Over time, what began as a group of friends sharing recipes and a good time has evolved into a charity event that last year donated almost $50,000 to local causes. More than 200 tomato varieties are showcased in recipes by 50 of California's finest chefs. A Best of the Fest Tomato Salsa Contest, wine and olive oil tasting, live music, and dancing are also part of this joyous celebration. Very popular with locals and visitors, this event always sells out. Tickets and more information are available on the Web site.

Cherries Jubilee
Laguna Seca Recreation Area, 1021 Monterey-Salinas Highway, Monterey
(831) 759–1836

Cherries Jubilee is a car show and festival featuring parties, dancing, food booths, and vendors selling everything from T-shirts and jewelry to handcrafted items. Beautifully restored street rods from 1972 and earlier cruise Alvarado Street in downtown Monterey on Thursday, the first day of the event, followed by an After the Cruise party. Official Cherries Jubilee memorabilia, such as hats, T-shirts, and buttons are for sale at the events. On Saturday night there are dances held at various locations in downtown Monterey.

At the Mazda Raceway Laguna Seca Midway, two food vendors tempt race fans with delicious dishes. Pride of Monterey is an upscale food area in a relaxed, smartly decorated environment. Chefs at open-style cooking stations prepare culinary delights such as stir-fry, seafood or artichoke pasta, steamed artichokes, carne asada or chile verde burritos, and clam chowder. Dale's Diner is a food concession tent with an entrance resembling a '50s-style diner. Favorite diner foods like hamburgers, hot dogs, chili dogs, burritos, and salads are served in this casual setting.

This annual event takes place at the end of September and benefits the Salinas Valley Memorial Hospital Foundation. Expect to pay about $8.00 for teens and adults, $2.00 for children ages six to 12, and nothing for children younger than six.

Festa Italia/Santa Rosalia Festival
Custom House Plaza, Monterey
(831) 649–6544, (831) 655–8070

Nearing its seventh decade, this annual Italian celebration includes a parade, the National Bocce Ball Tournament with 60 teams (with a $3,000 prize), and food booths. There is continuous musical entertainment on stage with favorite Italian songs sung in English and Italian. The adventurous will want to enter the "O Sole Mio" singing contest; the prize is usually a salami. You'll find around 50 arts and crafts booths, most with handmade items such as jewelry, pottery, and the like. The free festival takes place on a weekend in mid-September.

Great Sand Castle Contest
Carmel Beach at the end of Ocean Avenue, Carmel
(831) 626–1255

This annual event begins early in the morning, and judging takes place in the early afternoon. Each entrant has designated boundaries for her or his creation. Each year there is a theme; the castles must represent the theme in some way, but the interpretation is entirely up to the artists. Bribing of judges, especially with food and drink, is absolutely permitted (no cash, though). Begging is also an effective means of winning. Award-winning entrants receive trophies made by the City of Carmel Recreation Department and the Monterey Bay Chapter of American Institute of Architects, who cosponsor the event. The date of the event, never announced until just before it occurs, is usually at the end of September. There is no registration or entrance fee required.

Monterey Bay ReggaeFest
Monterey Fairgrounds
(831) 394–6543, www.mbayreggaefest

Jamaica's most famous export is celebrated each Labor Day weekend. Reggae stars and fans from all over the world come to dance, sing, and revel in the joy of their favorite music. Admission charge.

Monterey Jazz Festival
Monterey County Fairgrounds,
2004 Fairgrounds Road, Monterey
(831) 373–3366,
www.montereyjazzfestival.org

The Monterey Jazz Festival, an annual tradition for more than 40 years, is the oldest continually held jazz festival in the world. Artists and attendees from around the country come to celebrate jazz. Each year fans are entertained by famous and up-and-coming artists such as Sonny Rollins, David Sanborn, Diana Krall, Wynton Marsalis, Dave Holland, Herbie Hancock, Taj Mahal, Thomas Chapin, Jim Hall, Charlie Hadan, Ivan Lins, and many others. High school all-star bands from around the country are also featured. Continuous entertainment takes place on three stages at this heavily attended three-day festival. Food, drink, and merchandise vendors are also on the grounds. Prices for one-day grounds passes and season tickets can be found on the Web site or by calling.

Monterey Sports Car Championships/
American Le Mans Series
Mazda Raceway Laguna Seca
(800) 327–7322, www.laguna–seca.com

Patterned after the famous 24 Hours of Le Mans, the American Le Mans Series gives fans a taste of the French event. Spectators get a chance to see the cars in the paddock area and to get autographs from their favorite drivers.

October

Butterfly Parade
Lighthouse Avenue, Pacific Grove
(831) 373–3304, www2.ci.pacific.grove.ca.us

Each year from October to mid-February thousands of Monarch butterflies spend the winter in Pacific Grove. It's not unusual to see hundreds of butterflies flying from flower to flower on a sunny day.

Every year since 1958, the world-famous Monterey Jazz Festival has showcased top jazz performers at the Monterey Fairgrounds. PHOTO: CHARLENE ALDINGER/MONTEREY COUNTY CONVENTION & VISITORS BUREAU

To pay tribute to this phenomenon, Pacific Grove children make their own costumes and parade down Lighthouse Avenue. The parade is held in early October. This free annual event is followed by a street bazaar in downtown Pacific Grove. Also as homage to the butterflies, the town of Pacific Grove commissioned the sculpture by the late Christopher Bell that's in front of the post office. The sculpture has a small boy and girl dressed in Monarch costumes.

California Constitution Day Reenactment
Colton Hall, Monterey
(831) 646–5640, www.monterey.org

Be transported back to 1849 as actors in period costume re-create the scene of the debates and signing of California's first constitution, which led to statehood. Reservations are required for this free event.

California International Airshow
Salinas Airport, 30 Mortensen Avenue, Salinas
(831) 754–1983, www.salinasairshow.com

One of the premier aviation events on the West Coast begins the last week in September and continues through the first few days of October. Pyrotechnics (including the Wall of Fire), air acts, and ground acts by military and civilian teams are the highlights of this annual event. Previous performers include the Blue Angels, the Thunderbirds, and the Canadian Snowbirds.

Carmel Performing Arts Festival
Various locations in Carmel
(831) 624–7675, www.carmelfest.org

The annual Carmel Performing Arts Festival is a three-week community cultural event that highlights regional and distinguished guest performing artists. Beginning in mid-October and continuing until early November, theater, dance, and music performances for all ages occur in intimate venues in and around Carmel. Call or visit the Web site for admission prices.

Carmel Shakespeare Festival
Various theaters, Carmel
(831) 622–0100, www.pacrep.org

Several local theaters host this annual event with professional and community

The Monarch Butterfly Parade in Pacific Grove celebrates the return of the Monarch butterfly to town. Local schoolchildren have been dressing as butterflies in the parade for decades. PHOTO: JULIE ARMSTRONG/ MONTEREY COUNTY CONVENTION & VISITORS BUREAU

actors starring in works by Shakespeare. The event starts at the end of July and is held through mid-October. See our July entry for more information.

Historic Home Tour
Various locations in Pacific Grove
(831) 373–3304

Cosponsored by the Pacific Grove Chamber of Commerce, the Pacific Grove Art Center, and the Heritage Society, this tour takes you inside many of the town's immaculately restored Victorian homes and businesses. The number of houses varies from year to year, depending upon the residents and innkeepers who wish to participate. A committee selects participants based on the home's historic value and the quality of restoration done on the property. Docents dressed in period costume conduct the tours and give information about each home or inn. The event occurs in early to mid-October each year. Tickets are $12.

Old Monterey Historic Festival & Faire
Custom House Plaza, Monterey
(831) 655–8070

The Old Monterey Historic Festival & Faire is a celebration of arts, crafts, and food that takes place at the end of Alvarado Street at the Old Custom House Plaza. It's held on a weekend in early to mid-October. You'll find handmade items such as pottery, jewelry, wood products, metal work, and wearable art in the form of clothing and hats. Musical entertainment is also provided at this free event.

November

Christmas Tree Lighting Ceremony
Steinbeck Plaza on Cannery Row, Monterey
(831) 649–6690

The holidays officially begin on Cannery Row with caroling by what remains of the old canneries, the arrival of Santa, and the lighting of the Christmas tree, a huge Douglas fir. It all happens at the end of November.

Great Wine Escape Weekend
Various locations
(831) 375–9400, www.montereywines.org

This event features over 25 wineries at 15 locations, with narrated bus tours or self-guided tours. Other events throughout the weekend include: The Great Wine Escape Golf Tournament; The Monterey Wine Auction & Gala; Winemaker Dinners by world-renowned chefs; a Wine Symposium featuring a panel of Monterey County vintners; an evening jazz concert; and The Great Wine Escape Finale with more than 30 Monterey County wineries pouring their world-class wines.

Monterey Bay Holiday Gift Faire
Custom House Plaza, Monterey
(831) 622–0100

Each year the Custom House Plaza becomes a shopping destination for those seeking the handmade wares of artists and craftspeople. You'll discover jewelry made from beads and precious metals, pottery, wooden toys, wearable art, weather vanes, and birdhouses. The artists themselves sell their goods. The free event takes place in late November, right around the time you're looking for the perfect holiday gifts.

Monterey Book Festival
Monterey Fairgrounds,
2004 Fairgrounds Road, Monterey
(831) 624–1803, www.mbib.org

This one-day festival features a huge selection of new, used, and antique books. Storybook characters and a host of prominent authors are on hand, and you'll find children's events and a bookmobile. Proceeds from the event, sponsored by the Monterey Bay Independent Booksellers, benefit the Reading is Fundamental program. The event takes place mid to late November. A small donation is requested.

Robert Louis Stevenson's Un-Birthday Week
Stevenson House, 530 Houston Street, Monterey
(831) 649–6204

The Stevenson House honors the famous author and poet with tours and un-birthday

Christmas in the Adobes offers tours of Monterey's historic adobe buildings. Each is festively decorated for the season. PHOTO: MARTIN BROWN/MONTEREY COUNTY CONVENTION & VISITORS BUREAU cake. The event, hosted for school children, has costumed docents and an actor playing Robert Louis Stevenson. It celebrates Stevenson's gift of his birthday to a young friend who was born on Christmas Day. Stevenson thought that no one should have to share his or her birthday with Christ. The free annual event is sponsored by the California Parks Department and the Old Monterey Preservation Society. It's held mid-November each year. There is also a gala reception open house, which costs $25.

Thanksgiving Community Dinner
Monterey County Fairgrounds,
2004 Fairgrounds Road, Monterey
(831) 372–5863

For more than 20 years, the Kiwanis of Monterey and volunteers have been putting together this very special community dinner for anyone who doesn't want to spend the holiday alone. Clothing and toiletry items are available for those in need, and the event continues to grow in popularity and numbers each year. All the food and supplies are donated by various people in the community. There is no charge for the event, which always takes place on Thanksgiving Day.

December

Carmel Lights Up the Season
Devendorf Park, Ocean Avenue between Junipero and Mission Streets, Carmel
(831) 624–0137

The official Carmel Christmas tree, situated at the intersection of Ocean Avenue and Junipero Street, is lighted during the first week of December. An open house follows at Carmel Plaza. The event is free.

Christmas at the Inns
Various locations in Pacific Grove
(831) 373–3304

Seven of Pacific Grove's bed and breakfast inns dress up in Victorian holiday splendor for this self-guided tour. Docents in period costumes, live entertainment, and refreshments add to the ambiance of this festive event, held on a Tuesday in early December. Tickets are $10 and can also be used to receive a discount at several Pacific Grove restaurants and shops.

Christmas in the Adobes
Various locations in Monterey
(831) 647–6226

Candlelight walking tours and visits to 20 beautifully decorated Monterey adobes are hosted by the Old Monterey Preservation Society and Monterey State Historic Parks. The annual event takes place mid-December. Tickets are $12.00 for adults (18 and older), $2.00 for kids (ages six to 17), and free for children younger than six.

Christmas Community Dinner
Monterey County Fairgrounds,
2004 Fairgrounds Road, Monterey
(831) 372–5863

The Christmas Community Dinner is a celebratory meal for those in need of giving or receiving. Volunteers are always welcome to participate at this long-standing event. The free dinner, open to all, is always held on Christmas Day. The dinner is sponsored by businesses and individuals in the community.

Dolls' Tea Party
1491 Contra Costa, Seaside
(831) 899–4911

For more than 20 years the Salvation Army Community Center has hosted a tea party with refreshments. Dolls, teddy bears, handmade doll furniture, craft items, and cookies are for sale. Funds are used to buy toys for needy children and for distribution to local programs for children and seniors. The free event is held in early December.

First Night Monterey
Various locations in Monterey
(831) 373–4778

Celebrate the start of the New Year at this family-oriented event which provides an alcohol-free environment. An outstanding line-up of local artists and musicians furnishes music, entertainment, dancing, food, arts and crafts, and hands-on projects for all ages. Join the "Auld Lang Syne" gathering at 11:30 P.M. in Custom House Plaza to ring in the New Year. The under-

Cannery Row gets into the spirit of the season. PHOTO: JANE MORBA

$10 fee includes shuttle service from Monterey Peninsula College, 980 Fremont Boulevard in Monterey.

Hospice Foundation Trees of Life
DoubleTree Hotel, 2 Portola Plaza, Monterey
(831) 642–2035

Each light on this tree represents a donation in memory of a loved one. Music and refreshments are also part of the ceremony. The free event takes place at the beginning of December.

La Posada
Monterey Conference Center,
2 Portola Plaza, Monterey
(831) 646–3866

A candlelight procession, mariachi bands, piñatas, and food are the focus of this free annual event, held on a Friday in early December. Participants are asked to bring a candle to join in the awe-inspiring candlelight procession as it meanders through the adobes in Old Town Monterey. The event is a reenactment of Christmas night, with costumed actors posing as Joseph and Mary. Participants sing carols during the procession. It terminates at the conference center, where a piñata party is held and refreshments are served.

Monterey Cowboy Poetry and Music Festival
Monterey Conference Center
(800) 722–9652, www.montereycowboy.com

The largest event of its kind in Northern California, this festival draws the finest practitioners of the uniquely American art form that is cowboy poetry. The festival also features cowboy troubadours and artisans showcasing Western crafts. Admission charge.

Monterey Tree Lighting Ceremony
Colton Hall Museum,
351 Pacific Avenue, Monterey
(831) 646–3866

Choral groups and bands perform while the 35-foot fir Christmas tree on the front lawn at Colton Hall is lighted. Participants are asked to light a candle in the ceremony. Apple cider and refreshments are served afterwards. The free event takes place the first week of December.

Pacific Grove Tree Lighting Ceremony
Jewell Park, Central Avenue between Grand and Forest Avenues, Pacific Grove
(831) 373–3304

Pacific Grove opens the holiday season with a tree lighting, live entertainment by school bands, caroling, and a visit from Santa. The evening also heralds the Pacific Grove Hometown Holidays with a window-decorating contest among the downtown merchants. The free event takes place at the beginning of December.

Streets of Bethlehem
First Baptist Church
1130 San Vincente Street, Salinas
(831) 422–9872, www.1stbaptist.net/streets

A cast of 200 volunteers reenacts the sights and sounds of Bethlehem at the time of the birth of Jesus. Period costumes, live animals, and beautiful sets enliven the scene. A production of the First Baptist Church in Salinas, Streets of Bethlehem has been presented every December since 1992.

The Arts and Galleries

The arts have long held a special place in the hearts of Monterey Peninsula residents. From the Bohemian artists of Carmel to the jazz lovers of Monterey, locals embrace culture with great vigor. Why the fascination with the arts? It could be the spectacular natural scenery in this area that draws artists and stirs the passion for things beautiful. Maybe it was the influx of writers, painters, and musicians who migrated here from San Francisco following the great 1906 earthquake and fire. Perhaps it's because many creative talents who can choose to live virtually anywhere choose to live here. In truth, it's a combination of these three reasons and more. Regardless of the reasons, arts and culture continue to thrive in this bountiful community.

In this chapter we'll take a look at the various art forms prevalent on the Peninsula, with a special focus on the area's famous art galleries. As one of the oldest art colonies in the country, Carmel remains the cultural center of Peninsula life. And in Carmel, the Sunset Cultural Center between San Carlos and Mission streets at 9th Avenue is the cultural heart of the village. It's home to the Sunset Center Theatre, where you'll see symphonies, dance, drama, and other artistic performances. Also inside the center are smaller workshops and studios that give rise to tomorrow's top performers.

We'll now take a quick look at some of the local institutions and organizations that make up the art and culture scene on the Monterey Peninsula. Also be sure to check out our Annual Events chapter, which lists many of the most popular yearly cultural events in the area. While in town, check out the *Go!* section of the Thursday *Monterey County Herald* and the recent issue of *Coast Weekly* for the listings of current art and culture activities (see our Media chapter for more information about these publications).

Visual Arts

Galleries

Painters and photographers play a very important part in the history of the Monterey Peninsula. Since the towns of Carmel, Monterey, and Pacific Grove sprang up, artists have been drawn to and inspired by the area's rugged beauty. Carmel, in particular, is an artist's haven. Its history is filled with the Bohemian influences of artists such as Robinson Jeffers, Edward Weston, Henry Miller, and Armin Hansen. That influence lives on today, as new generations of painters, photographers, and other artists continue to rise on the scene and make a name for themselves worldwide.

In this section, we have provided a sampling of the art galleries you can enjoy on the Peninsula. Most are in Carmel, but we mention a few in Monterey, Pacific Grove, and Pebble Beach as well. Our goal is not to try to provide a list of the "best" galleries. Because tastes in art vary so widely, that designation would be too subjective and presumptuous. Instead, we have attempted to provide a good mix of galleries and artistic styles that will appeal to a variety of tastes. The Carmel galleries have done a fine job of organizing themselves and providing walking tour maps, which are available in many of the galleries. Our suggestion is to pick up these maps while in town and enjoy breakfast or lunch while planning your own art walk route through the village based on your personal interests and tastes. Fortunately, most of the Carmel galleries are within a few square blocks. Your best bet is to focus on San Carlos and Dolores Streets between 5th and 7th avenues. Also, 6th Avenue between Lincoln and Mission Streets has some of the most wonderfully unique galleries. If you have the time, don't hesitate to venture beyond these limits to discover your own personal favorites.

Monterey

California Views
469 Pacific Street, Monterey
(831) 373–3811, www.caviews.com

Discover a visual treasure of Monterey Peninsula history at California Views, a fascinating photographic gallery of 19th- and 20th-century Monterey Peninsula images. In downtown Monterey, this is an internationally known collection of historic photos archived by Pat Hathaway. He has catalogued more than 80,000 images from 1870 to the present and can provide off-the-shelf or custom-made prints. Also for sale are negatives, stereo views, postcards and photo albums. California Views is open Tuesday through Saturday.

Cardinal Gallery
711 Cannery Row, Monterey
(831) 657–0297

Relatively new to the Monterey Peninsula gallery scene is Cardinal Gallery on Cannery Row. Two world-renowned Italian artists are featured here, Bruno Paoli and Andrea Stella. Paoli, born in Florence, is a modern master often compared to Paul Gauguin. Stella uses an original technique of fusing 24-karat gold to copper to create incredible colors on canvas. Both are worth seeing during your visit to The Row.

Kinkade Family Galleries
685 Cannery Row, Monterey
(831) 657–2365, www.kinkadecenter.com
Monterey Plaza, 400 Cannery Row, Monterey
(831) 657–2350
Del Monte Shopping Center, Munras Ave at Highway 1, Monterey
(831) 657–1210

Thomas Kinkade Museum and Cultural Center
590 Calle Principal, Monterey
(831) 655–1477

Following in the tradition of 19th-century American Luminists, Thomas Kinkade has developed a worldwide reputation as a "Painter of Light." In addition to offering his beautiful oils through four galleries in Carmel (see separate write-up), the prolific Kinkade has four Monterey locations. Two are in the Cannery Row area, one is in the Del Monte Shopping Center, and the Thomas Kinkade Museum & Cultural Center is in historic downtown Monterey.

Pacific Grove

Claypoole-Freese Gallery
216 Grand Avenue, Pacific Grove
(831) 373–7179

This small Pacific Grove gallery features the work of Barry Masteller, a local artist whose work has been shown extensively in museum and gallery exhibitions from coast to coast. His oil landscapes and seascapes present soft dreamlike images. Other artists include Carolyn Berry, Rose Johnson, Erastes Cindaedi, Chris Winfield, Martha Cazane, and Canadian sculptor Bruce Garner. Claypoole-Freese Gallery is open Thursday through Saturday and by appointment Sunday through Wednesday.

Hauk Fine Arts
206 Fountain Avenue, Pacific Grove
(831) 373–6007, (800) 393–HAUK,
www.artnet.com/hauk.html

Hauk Fine Arts specializes in California art from the 19th and 20th centuries. Early painters include Armin Hansen, whose dramatic seascapes express the power of nature, as well as William Ritschel, Maynard Dixon, and Mary DeNeale Morgan. Contemporary painters include Carmel artist and author Belle Yang, whose depictions of Chinese life through whimsical paintings and books are a joy. Other contemporary artists include Jay Hannah, William Saroyan, Kate Carew, and Judith Deim. Hauk Fine Arts is open Wednesday through Saturday.

Pacific Grove Art Center
568 Lighthouse Avenue, Pacific Grove
(831) 375–2208, www.pgartcenter.org

In the heart of downtown P.G., the Pacific Grove Art Center has been a gathering spot for Butterfly Town's local artists since 1969. About a dozen artists maintain their studios in the center, and most are glad to let you peek in at their works. Exhibitions of works by famous and not so famous local artists are held in the center's David Henry Gill Gallery, Elmarie Dyke Gallery, Boyer Gallery, and Photography Gallery. The Pacific Grove Art Center is closed Monday and Tuesday.

Tessuti Zoo
171 Forest Avenue, Pacific Grove
(831) 648–1725

"Tessuti" is Italian for fabrics and that is precisely what you'll find at Pacific Grove's Tessuti Zoo. Emily Owens, the artist formerly known as Emily Ann Originals, uses fabric as her canvas and palette, and scissors, thread, and needle as her brush to create wild and wonderful artwork for the home. Her line of fantasy creatures and dolls attract children and adults alike, while her wall hangings and quilts are magic. Tessuti Zoo partner Mary Troup developed a loyal clientele for her fashionable wearable art clothing at her former gallery, Playful Spirit. She is equally talented in creating hand-painted furniture and other designer decor. You'll find this intensely colorful gallery on Forest Avenue below Lighthouse Avenue, right across the street from the popular Peppers Mexicali Cafe. Tessuti Zoo is open Monday through Saturday.

Carmel

Atelier
Dolores Street and 5th Avenue, Carmel
(831) 625–3168, www.ateliercarmel.com

The 17th- through 20th-century artwork available at Atelier is nothing short of museum quality. Ray Ramsey has gathered a breath-taking collection of high-end art that includes Renoir, Degas, Picasso, Pissaro, Monet, Cézanne, and Gauguin. Early California artists include Gay, Gile, Braun, and Payne. This is history, folks, a can't-miss adventure worthy of your time and attention. The Atelier galleries are a bit back off the street on Del Dono Court at Dolores and 5th, so look carefully. It's well worth it.

Bleich Gallery
Dolores Street and Ocean Avenue, Carmel
(831) 624–9447, www.bleich4art.com

Set your eye on a George Bleich seascape, and you sense his deep understanding of the subject (he was a seaman since the age of 15). Gaze at his impressionist gardens, and you feel his kinship with Monet, Gauguin, and Renoir. Bleich Gallery, established in 1969, features an array of works from this noted Carmel artist, including paintings from Monet's gardens in Giverny and Provence and landscapes and seascapes from the Monterey Peninsula. His paintings hang in homes and museums worldwide, including the White House. Bleich has a unique approach to commissioned paintings and other works. He allows family members to apply a portion of the underpainting and thus become closer to the art. Limited-edition prints and drawings are also available. Drop in on a Saturday, and there's a good chance you'll meet the artist himself, sharing stories and possibly strumming his own compositions on guitar. Bleich Gallery is open daily.

Lilliana Braico Gallery
6th Avenue and Dolores Street, Carmel
(831) 624–2512,
www.lillianabraicogallery.com

Lilliana Braico has been making a name for herself locally and internationally since she first moved to Carmel in the 1960s. Her brightly colored oil and acrylic florals, Mediterranean seascapes, portraits, and abstracts have a light and serene quality that reflect her experiences living on the Isle of Capri and in Paris and London. Her festive studio is up a narrow path off 6th Avenue near Dolores Street. Prints and calendars of her work are also available.

Chapman Gallery
7th Avenue and San Carlos Street, Carmel
(831) 626–1766, www.chapmangallery.com

At a time when a few Carmel galleries are starting to look a bit too trendy for the old village, it's nice to experience one that gives a feel of Bohemian Carmel. Dean and Joanna Chapman have captured that feel in this historic spot on 7th Avenue between San Carlos and Mission Streets. The Chapman Gallery's emphasis is on regional California artists, with many from the Monterey Peninsula. Featured are S.C. Yuan, Reed Farrington, Gail Howdin Reeves, and cartoonist Hank Ketcham (of *Dennis the Menace* fame). The gallery is closed Mondays.

The Digital Giraffe
Dolores Street and 8th Avenue, Carmel
(831) 624–1833, www.giraffe.com

There's a whole new wave of art in Carmel. The Digital Giraffe, a.k.a. Corrine Whitaker, brings digital painting to the quaint village of Carmel. Whitaker is known worldwide as a groundbreaker in her field. She has shown her computer-generated works in more than 70 solo exhibitions and has taken part in 200 group exhibitions. Her most famous series, "Jane and Dick Revisited," was exhibited in India at the Centre for Photography as an Art Form as the first ever digital fine art exhibit in the country. She has also been commissioned to produce work for the Kennedy Space Center and the American Embassy in Minsk, Belarus. The works are output as digital dye prints on paper, canvas, Plexiglas, glass, and other surfaces. Her newest ventures are in digitally designed sculptures. It's worth the trip down Dolores Street between 7th and 8th Avenues to see this unique and friendly gallery.

Nancy Dodds Gallery
Hampton Court, 7th Avenue and San Carlos Street, Carmel
(831) 624–0346,
www.nancydoddsgallery.com

Nancy Dodds is a contemporary art gallery that features works of California artists in a variety of mediums. You'll find innovative watercolors, oils on paper, lithographs, monotypes, and etchings from artists such as Bruce Botts, David Smith-Harrison, Alicia Meheen, Leslie Toms, Randall Sexton, Carol Chapman, Carolyn Lord, Gail Packer, Kipp Stewart, and Anita Toney. Drop in and meet Nancy and Topper, her cocker spaniel. Nancy Dodds Gallery is closed on Tuesdays except by appointment.

Galerie Plein Aire
Dolores Street and 6th Avenue, Carmel
(831) 625–5686
www.galeriepleinaire.com

They are called "The Informalists," this group of local Carmel artists who operate Galerie Plein Aire and create colorful landscapes of the place they live and love. Meet Johnny Apodaca, Mark Farina, Barry John Raybould, Jeff Daniel Smith, Richmond P. Woodson, Gerard Martin, and gallery founder Cyndra Bradword. They work and play at Galerie Plein Aire so you are indeed likely to meet one or more of them, and perhaps Jake the dog, when you walk inside the gallery's bright blue door. The gallery is located behind Highland Sculpture, so don't miss it. The Informalists are open every day but Tuesday.

Gallerie Amsterdam
Dolores Street and 6th Avenue, Carmel
(831) 624–4355, www.amsterdamfineart.com

If European art of the 18th, 19th, and 20th centuries holds a special place in your heart, visit Gallerie Amsterdam. This elegant gallery is one of the largest in Carmel and displays the works of more than 70 artists. Featured are Hungarian ultrarealist Vida Gabor, impressionist Anatoli Belakoni, Netherlands plein-air artist Jacobus Baas, Russian-born painter Alexander Volkov, and Vietnamese sculptor Tuan. Whether your pleasure is still life, plein-air, landscapes, seascapes, portraits, or figuratives, Gallerie Amsterdam provides a relaxing stroll through European and other art.

Gallery Twenty-One
Dolores Street and Ocean Avenue, Carmel
(831) 626–2700, www.gallery21.com

Gallery Twenty-One is home to the paintings, serigraphs, and sculptures of the late modern artist and Carmel resident

Galerie Plein Aire on Dolores Street is home to "The Informalists," a group of local Carmel artists who create colorful landscapes. PHOTO: TOM OWENS

Eyvind Earle. Once referred to as "the artist of the 21st century," Earle painted introspective and mysterious landscapes from a deep inner world that convey drama and wonder in the balance of darkness and light. Lovers of modern art will not want to miss this exceptional gallery north of Ocean Avenue on Dolores Street. Available are books of Earle's graphic art, Christmas card art, and his words and poetry.

Highlands Sculpture Gallery
Dolores Street and 5th Avenue, Carmel
(831) 624–0535

Hands on! There aren't many galleries where the staff greets you with an encouragement to place your fingers on the art. But that's the case at Highlands Sculpture Gallery, a 100 percent contemporary sculpture gallery. The pieces themselves are remarkable, with beryllium and bronze sounding sculptures that ring like bells when stroked, and bronze, metal, stone, ceramic, glass, and wood sculptures for indoors and out. Artists include amazing Bulgarian sculptor Ana Daltchev as well as Ken Matsumoto, Carolyn Cole, Winni Brueggemann, Norma Lewis, David Herschler, Eileen Hill, and Robert Holmes. You'll surely enjoy the brightly colored mobiles of Lauront Davidson and the equally vibrant fused-glass hangings of Yolanda Adra. So take the time to look, touch, and feel at Highlands Sculpture Gallery.

It's Cactus
Court of the Fountains, Mission Street and Ocean Avenue, Carmel
(831) 626–4213, www.itscactus.com

If folk art rather than fine art is your cup of tea, don't miss It's Cactus on Mission Street between Ocean and 7th Avenues. Owner Casey Eastman collects folk art from around the world and puts together an eclectic display of carvings, weavings, paintings, and other forms of indigenous folk art. You'll find a definite Central and South American theme at It's Cactus, but pieces from Asia, Africa, and other environs (including the good old USA) are also present. If you've been looking for a Bolivian chumpas to add to your sweater collection or a folk art nativity scene for the holidays, this is definitely the place to be. It's Cactus is open daily.

Kinkade Family Galleries
Ocean Avenue and Dolores Street, Carmel
(831) 626–1927
Paseo San Carlos and 7th Avenue, Carmel
(831) 622–1136
The Barnyard, Highway 1, Carmel
(831) 622–0939
The Tuck Box, Dolores Street and Ocean Avenue, Carmel
(831) 622–1133, www.kinkadecentral.com

One of the most commercially astute and successful artists of the day, Thomas Kinkade is known appropriately as the "Painter of Light." Working with advanced techniques developed by a group of 19th-century American painters known as Luminists, Kinkade produces paintings that seemingly emit light from his landscapes, cityscapes, and country cottages. A prolific artist, Kinkade now runs seven separate galleries on the Monterey Peninsula, including the four here in Carmel, two on Cannery Row, and one at Del Monte Shopping Center in Monterey. His Ocean Avenue gallery down Del Ling Lane between Lincoln and Dolores Streets is the best for first-timers, while the gift gallery in the Tuck Box Tea Room on Dolores Street features smaller Kinkade collectibles.

Martin LaBorde Gallery
6th Avenue and Lincoln, Carmel
(831) 620–1150,
www.martinlabordegallery.com

Meet Bodo. He's a little magician in a brightly colored robe, a childlike figure with an old-world soul. He comes from the imagination of artist Martin LaBorde and is the focal point of a series of spirited paintings by the New Orleans painter. The dreamer in all of us will enjoy the whimsy of the robed one, which led to LaBorde winning the prestigious Pushkin Medal of Honor from the Hermitage Museum in Leningrad. Russian artists are also featured, including Vladimir Vitkovsky, as well as local favorite Paxton. Jazz aficionados will appreciate the paintings of musical legends by Don Ransom and Elizabeth Palmer. Friday nights often feature presentations by musicians, poets, and other performance artists from 7:00 to 9:00 P.M.

Richard MacDonald Galleries
San Carlos Street and 6th Avenue, Carmel
(831) 624–8200, (800) 972–5528,
www.richardmacdonald.com

Perhaps you saw Richard McDonald's *The Flair*, a 24-foot bronze monument of a gymnast that was part of the 1996 Summer Olympics in Atlanta. Or maybe you visited the monument at Pebble Beach commemorating the 100th U.S. Open Championship in 2000. If so, then you have a hint of the true artistry that McDonald sculpts from clay and casts in bronze. If you enjoy the beauty and emotion of the human form, enter here. McDonald's depictions of dance, mime, mythology, and simple childhood moments have a delicate, whimsical charm. Other figurative forms, like *The Flair*, express power and strength. You'll also find McDonald's dramatic drawings, lithographs, and serigraphs. Richard MacDonald Galleries now has a second location at The Shops at the Lodge in Pebble Beach.

New Masters Gallery
Dolores Street and Ocean Avenue, Carmel
(831) 625–1511, www.newmastersgallery.com

For more than 25 years, New Masters Gallery has been bringing fine paintings and sculpture to Carmel. Today this large Dolores Street gallery between Ocean and 7th Avenues houses an extensive collection representing international artists such as DeWitt Whistler Jayne, Andre Balyon, Mou-Sien Tseng, Tinyan, Stephen Stavast, Gerald Brommer, June Carey, Pino Daeni, Kurt Ard, Ovanes Berberian, Ou Chu Jian, and Yi-Fu Zhao. Fans of marquetry inlaid woodwork will marvel at the works of Jean-Charles Spindler. Also featured is Carmel favorite Will Bullas, a local watercolorist who specializes in whimsical depictions of geese and barnyard critters. In fact, New Masters Gallery owners Bill and Jennifer Hill also run the Will Bullas Fun Art Gallery on San Carlos Street between Ocean and 7th Avenues. With paintings, books, stuffed animals, clothing, and greeting cards all reflecting the Will Bullas touch, this new gallery is sure to be a favorite of children of all ages.

Pitzer's of Carmel
Dolores Street and 6th Avenue, Carmel
(831) 625–2288, www.pitzersart.com

Representing more than 60 artists, Pitzer's is a large, bright gallery that offers traditional paintings, sculptures, and limited edition prints, from realism to impressionism. You'll immediately notice that sculpture is a Pitzer's specialty. The gallery displays an array of bronze works both large and small, for indoors and the garden. Among the paintings, the bold beachscapes of William Berra are sure to catch your eye. Nelson Boren's western themes, Simon Bull's floral and landscape acrylics, and James Kramer's watercolors are other favorites.

Rodrigue Studio
6th Avenue and Lincoln Street, Carmel
(831) 626–4444, www.bluedogart.com

Everywhere you look, you see those haunting yellow eyes of that soulful Blue Dog. There's Blue Dog with Elvis, Blue Dog with crocodile, and Blue Dog as vampire. If you aren't familiar with Louisiana Cajun artist George Rodrigue and his more than 500 bold and bright "Naïve Surrealism" Blue Dog paintings, you owe it to yourself to get acquainted at Rodrigue Studio (formerly Galerie Blue Dog) on 6th Avenue between Dolores and Lincoln Streets. First created in 1984, Blue Dog is based on the mythical "loup garou," a French-Cajun ghost dog, and Tiffany, Rodrigue's own pooch who had passed away a few years prior to the notoriety. Since then, Rodrigue, already an internationally acclaimed painter, has taken Blue Dog on a fanciful journey, with the moon-eyed rascal showing up in some of the most unusual places, with some of the most unusual characters. Don't miss this one. The gallery is open daily.

Loran Speck Gallery
6th Avenue and Dolores Street, Carmel
(831) 624–3707, www.loranspeck.com

Is still life your cup of tea, or your bowl of cherries? Then Loran Speck is your man when visiting the galleries of Carmel. You'll find a wide selection of original paintings reminiscent of the Dutch Masters, as well as limited-edition Giclee prints, photoprints, and signed posters from this prolific local artist. Speck has been showing his original oils, watercolor contés, charcoals, and etchings in Carmel for more than 25 years. He also makes exquisite frames and mirrors, most gilded in 22-carat gold leaf or metal leaf and handcarved in his own studio. Loran Speck Gallery is open daily.

Richard Thomas Galleries
Dolores Street, at 5th and 6th Avenues, Carmel
(831) 625–5636, (800) 243–7600,
www.richardthomasgalleries.com

One of the most spacious galleries in Carmel with two locations on the same block of Dolores, the Richard Thomas Gallery has an impressive collection of American and international art covering a wide range of styles, with an emphasis on contemporary realism. From the Romantic Renaissance of mixed media artist Csaba Markus to the emotional acrylic portraits of Michael Wilkinson to the peaceful landscapes of Henry Peeters, visitors are bound to find a favorite among this large and impressive collection. Other featured artists include Aldo Luongo and Alexander Volkov.

Weston Gallery
6th Avenue and Dolores Street, Carmel
(831) 624–4453, www.westongallery.com

The Monterey Peninsula and Big Sur coastline have been home to some of the greatest 19th- and 20th-century photographers in the world. Ansel Adams, Edward Weston, and their contemporaries found the rugged coastline and mountains a stunning subject for their art. Weston Gallery on 6th Avenue between Dolores and Lincoln Streets is a virtual museum of this area's photographic art history. Works by the masters Adams and Weston as well as the following generation of Weston photographers, Cole and Brett, grace the walls. Yousuf Karsh's portraits of celebrities from Albert Einstein to Brigitte Bardot to Winston

Churchill are especially fascinating. Photographs of other contemporary artists such as Michael Kenna and Jeffrey Becom of Maya Color fame are featured. Portfolios, books, posters, and great greeting cards are available for purchase.

Zantman Art Galleries
6th Avenue and Mission Street, Carmel
(831) 624–8314, www.zantmangalleries.com

No listing of Carmel galleries is complete without a mention of Zantman Art Galleries. Established in 1959, Zantman has grown to be one of largest and most popular galleries in the village. It continues to display high-quality paintings and sculptures as it celebrates its 40th year. Current featured artists include sculptor Dennis Smith as well as painters Ted Goerschner, Marilyn Simandle, Richard Murray, Lucio Sollazzi, Cynthia Britain, Gilles Archambault, Dorothy Fitzgerald, Wilson Chu, Frank Ashley, and George Hamilton.

Pebble Beach

Ansel Adams Gallery
The Inn at Spanish Bay, Pebble Beach
(831) 375–7215, www.anseladams.com

The Ansel Adams Gallery offers a large collection of works by the noted nature photographer. The black and white images of Yosemite, Big Sur, and other California natural treasures are stunning in their dramatic beauty. The gallery represents other fine art photography as well as Native American crafts and jewelry, books, and other gift items.

6th Avenue in Carmel between Dolores and Lincoln Streets is home to marvelous galleries including Rodrigue Studio (home of the Blue Dog), Loran Speck Gallery, Lilliana Braico Gallery, and Weston Gallery. PHOTO: TOM OWENS

Museums

Small in number but large in stature and charm, the art museums on the Peninsula include two museums operated by the city of Monterey.

Monterey Museum of Art at Civic Center
559 Pacific Street, Monterey
(831) 372–5477, www.montereyart.org

Once called "the best small-town museum in the United States," the Monterey Museum of Art at Civic Center offers a great collection of California art, photography, Asian art, and international folk art. Featured artists include painter Armin Hansen and photographers Edward Weston and Ansel Adams. The museum's education department hosts a variety of classes and workshops. Admission to the museum is $5.00 for nonmembers. The Monterey Museum of Art at Civic Center is closed Monday and Tuesday.

Monterey Museum of Art at La Mirada
720 Via Mirada, Monterey
(831) 372–3689, www.montereyart.org

At the Monterey Museum of Art at La Mirada, the setting of the museum and grounds, across Fremont Street from Lake El Estero, is as spectacular as the art itself. Originally an elegant adobe home, it still features exquisite furnishings and spectacular gardens of roses and rhododendrons. The Dart Wing of the museum houses four contemporary galleries featuring a fine permanent collection, including folk and Asian art, and changing exhibitions. The Monterey Museum of Art at La Mirada is closed Monday and Tuesday. Admission is $5.00 for nonmembers.

Performing Arts

Dance

World-renowned dancers of all genres periodically grace the stages of the Peninsula for special engagements, with Carmel's Sunset Center Theater the most likely venue for top-name stars. The bulk of the dance activity on the Peninsula, however, centers on local groups—both adult and children, professional and amateur—who study the art and provide entertaining performances for appreciative audiences. Call the Sunset Center Theatre, (831) 624–3996, or check the local entertainment calendars for the schedule of upcoming headliners. On the local dance scene, for both performances and instruction, check out these fine studios.

Carmel Ballet Academy
Mission Street and 8th Avenue, Carmel
(831) 624–3729,
www.carmelballetacademy.com

Since 1954 the Carmel Ballet Academy has been providing instruction and performances for generations of Peninsula families. The Academy provides instruction in ballet, jazz, tap, pointe, modern, hip-hop, drama, voice, and musical comedy for children as young as age 2½ as well as adults. Dance and theater camps are held each summer, and Carmel Ballet Academy performs an annual showcase each June.

Dance Kids Inc.
Mission Street and 8th Avenue, Carmel
(831) 626–2980

Featuring ballet and other forms of dance, Dance Kids Inc. provides instruction for children as young as four years of age as well as for adults. In conjunction with the Carmel Ballet Academy it performs regular annual events, including a spring musical, a summer performing arts camp and a winter presentation of *The Nutcracker.*

Monterey Peninsula Dance Association
71 Soledad Drive, Monterey
(831) 648–8725

This is the place in Monterey to learn a wide variety of dance steps, including ballroom, nightclub, country and western, waltz, fox trot, tango, rumba, cha cha, swing, samba, salsa, and disco. Youths, singles, and couples are welcome. Lessons are provided Monday through Friday, with a dance party held every Friday and Saturday night. The Monterey Peninsula Dance Association is a member of the Imperial Society of Teachers of Dancing in England.

Peninsula Ballet Center
568 Lighthouse Avenue, Pacific Grove
(831) 372–0388, www.balletfantastique.org

Kira Ivanovsky, formerly of Ballet Russe, and Milou Ivanovsky codirect the Peninsula Ballet Center out of the Pacific Grove Art Center in downtown Pacific Grove. Classes are offered for beginners through to professionals, from children age five to adults. The Center is home of Ballet Fantastique, a nonprofit dance company of professional, semiprofessional, and student dancers. Founded in 1974 it performs a repertoire of classical, ethnic, and interpretive dance, including *The Nutcracker,* spring gala performances, and summer ballet festivals.

The many exceptional music events on the Peninsula bring innovative performers like the Sharon Shannon Band. PHOTO: JANA MORBA

Literary Arts

As home to Robinson Jeffers, Robert Louis Stevenson, and other well-known writers, the Monterey Peninsula remains an active literary community. Poetry is in the limelight these days, but songwriters and spoken-word artists also share their craft at local coffeehouses, bookstores, and other small venues.

The best-known literary event in the area is Carmel's Poetry on the Beach, held on Carmel Beach at sunset on the last Saturday of every month, weather permitting. Take Scenic Drive to the beach at 13th Avenue and look for the bonfire. Feel free to bring along a poem or story as well as a blanket, a potluck dish to share, a bottle of wine, and some firewood.

Other spots to hear or share the spoken word include the following.

Borders Books, Music and Cafe
2080 California Avenue, Sand City
(831) 899–6643, www.bordersstores.com

Borders bookstore and cafe presents poetry and literary readings, as well as musical and other events, most evenings. Call for the current schedule of events or drop by and pick up a free monthly calendar.

Juice and Java
599 Lighthouse Avenue, Pacific Grove
(831) 373–8652

Friday is open-mike night at Juice and Java in Pacific Grove. Poets, authors, and songwriters should sign up at 7:00 P.M. for the 7:30 P.M. presentation.

Sally Griffin Senior Center
700 Jewell Avenue, Pacific Grove
(831) 373–5602

Seniors share their wit and wisdom at open poetry readings at the Sally Griffin Senior Center, home to Meals on Wheels in Pacific Grove. Open poetry readings are held the fourth Thursday of each month at 3:00 P.M.

Thunderbird Bookshop Cafe
3600 The Barnyard Shopping Center, Carmel
(831) 624–1803, www.thunderbirdbooks.com

Readings, lectures, writing workshops, and book signings are almost a nightly event at this, the largest independent and family-owned bookstore and cafe on the Peninsula. Call for information or pick up a monthly calendar of events.

Music

The Monterey Peninsula has long been noted for its exceptional music festivals, including the Monterey Jazz Festival (September), the Carmel Bach Festival (July and August), and the Monterey Bay Blues Festival (June). These events are included in our Annual Events chapter. In addition, the Peninsula offers a nice blend of professional and amateur music groups that provide performances across the Peninsula.

Carmel Music Society
Sunset Center Theatre,
San Carlos Street and 9th Avenue, Carmel
(831) 625–9938, www.carmelmusic.org

Each year, the Carmel Music Society presents a world-class series featuring top-flight artists from September through April. Internationally known pianists, vocalists, violinists, and ensembles perform classical compositions in concerts and competitions. Season tickets and individual performance tickets, when available, can be purchased.

Monterey Symphony
Sunset Center Theatre,
San Carlos Street and 9th Avenue, Carmel
(831) 624–8511,
www.montereysymphony.org

Since its first performance in Carmel in 1947, Monterey Symphony has been providing a fully professional orchestra for locals and visitors alike. The symphony performs a series of seven concerts from October through May, performing at the Sunset Center Sunday afternoons at 3:00 P.M. and Monday nights at 8:00 P.M. Tuesday night concerts are held at the Sherwood Hall in Salinas, 940 North Main Street. Kate Tamarkin is the symphony's 10th—and first woman—conductor.

Mozart Society of California
(831) 625–3637

The Mozart Society of California hosts a series of five concerts featuring the compositions of this brilliant Austrian composer. The concerts are held October through May at the Sunset Center Theatre in Carmel, at San Carlos Street and 9th Avenue. The Mozart Society is an affiliate of the International Mozart Foundation in Salzburg, with members receiving season concert tickets, admission to lecture demonstrations, and other foundation benefits.

Youth Music Monterey
2911 Garden Road, Suite C-175, Monterey
(831) 375–1992,
www.youthmusicmonterey.org

Youth Music Monterey offers performance opportunities through its Youth and Honors Orchestras, which hold formal and collaborative concerts with the Monterey County Symphony and the Santa Cruz County Youth Symphony. In addition, the South County Strings Program offers entry-level students in the Salinas Valley to train and perform on the violin, viola, and cello. Youth Music Monterey presents an annual playathon each December at Del Monte Center, collecting pledges from the community. Participating students audition for placement in an orchestra and participate in a fall weekend residential retreat.

Theater

As with dance, the Monterey Peninsula theater scene is primarily made up of fairly modest productions by local, mainly amateur, performers. But that doesn't mean you are not likely to find high-quality dramas, comedies, and musicals by very talented actors, singers, and dancers. Many of the local theater groups have long-running traditions and pride themselves in bringing quality theater to the Peninsula. Check out the following theater groups for their schedule of performances.

The Ali Khan Band performs at Monterey's World Music Festival. PHOTO: JANA MORBA

Bruce Ariss Memorial Wharf Theater
Fisherman's Wharf, Monterey
(831) 372–1373

Not many visitors to Monterey are aware there is a theater right on Fisherman's Wharf. The Bruce Ariss Memorial Wharf Theater presents four shows a year, primarily musicals, with each show running anywhere from five to 10 weeks. This is primarily amateur theater that holds open auditions for each show. It's a great place for newcomers to break into the local theater scene.

California's First Theatre
Pacific Street and Scott Street, Monterey
(831) 375–4916

The oldest theater in the state of California still holds authentic melodramas and comedies from the 19th century. The Troupers of the Gold Coast (California's oldest continually performing theatrical company) stage performances each Friday and Saturday night from September through June and each Thursday through Saturday night from July through Labor Day Weekend. The curtain goes up at 8:00 P.M. You'll have a ball cheering the heroes and heroines and hissing the villains.

CSUMB World Theater
100 Campus Center, Building 28, Seaside
(831) 582–4580
www.worldtheater.csumb.edu/

The World Theater at California State University Monterey Bay is the most technologically sophisticated theater in the area. It was renovated from a historic 900-seat movie theater built more than 50 years ago for the soldiers stationed at the U.S. Army's Fort Ord. In the late 1990s, the building was radically remodeled as a multiuse theater and opened in 1999 with a seating capacity of 540. It is used for theater, music, dance, and other functions sponsored by the University.

The Forest Theater Guild
Mountain View and Santa Rita Streets, Carmel
(831) 626–1681

Chartered in 1949, the Forest Theater Guild provides community theater and films in Carmel's historic Outdoor Forest Theater. The Guild welcomes participation by all interested parties and is dedicated to providing quality theater at affordable prices. The Forest Theater Guild productions, which include classics, comedies, and musicals, are held outdoors during summer nights. Locals often show up well before the performance starts with a picnic dinner, wine, hot coffee, and plenty of warm coats and blankets. It's a local tradition and one any Insider shouldn't miss.

Magic Circle Center
8 El Camino Road, Carmel Valley
(831) 659–1108

This small theater company debuted in 1994 and has been pleasing local audiences with its contemporary and thought-provoking plays ever since. A children's theater group has been recently added, and musical events are now also held at the Magic Circle Center's Carmel Valley Village location.

Monterey Peninsula College Theatre Company
980 Fremont Street, Monterey
(831) 646–4213, www.mpc.edu

MPC, the Peninsula's community college, has a solid reputation for its drama department and fine theater presentations. Drama, comedy, and musicals are presented in its 350-seat main house and 50-seat studio, and in the Carl Cherry Center for the Arts in Carmel. The works of O. Henry, Neil Simon, Arthur Miller, Cole Porter, and Shakespeare have recently graced the stage.

Pacific Repertory Theatre
Golden Bough Playhouse,
Circle Theater,
Casanova Street and 9th Avenue, Carmel
(831) 622–0100, www.pacrep.org

Founded in 1982, Pacific Repertory Theatre presents its annual Great Play Series of productions and participates in community outreach programs such as the free Monterey Bay TheatreFest, a summer weekend series at Monterey's Custom Plaza. Pacific Repertory Theatre also holds The Carmel Shakespeare Festival, with performances held from August through October at Carmel's Outdoor Forest Theater. In 1994, the group purchased the historic Golden Bough Playhouse in Carmel and has renovated it into a fine two-venue theater. Performances are held in the 305-seat Golden Bough and the 99-seat Circle Theatre year-round.

Staff Players Repertory Company
Mountain View and Santa Rita Streets, Carmel
(831) 624–1531

Founded in 1969, Staff Players Repertory Company is the oldest continually producing theater company in Carmel. It produces both ancient and modern theater classics. The repertory company is a major supporter of the Children's Experimental Theatre, (831) 624-1531, a local training program for kids ages six through 18. The Staff Players and the Children's Experimental Theatre perform at the Indoor Forest Theatre, Santa Rita and Mountain View Streets, in Carmel.

Unicorn Theatre
320 Hoffman Avenue, Monterey
(831) 649–0259,
www.redshift.com/~unicornthetr

One of the most active theaters on the Peninsula, the Unicorn Theatre presents a wide range of performances for all ages. Children delight in the afternoon presentations, while adults can enjoy contemporary plays and the classics evenings at 8:00 P.M. (7:00 P.M. Sundays). Then there are the late-night performances that often feature the unusual, the sensual, or the macabre.

Support Organizations

The arts are widely supported by Peninsula residents, who volunteer their time and provide financial assistance to promote the many creative endeavors they enjoy. The artists, gallery owners, and others within their own community also volunteer much time and effort to promote their avocations. Below are a few of the local organizations that help keep the arts alive on the Peninsula.

Carmel Art Association
Dolores Street and 5th Avenue, Carmel
(831) 624–6176, www.carmelart.org

Started in 1927 by a group of local artists, the Carmel Art Association is still an active and vibrant force in the community. Members have included such dignitaries as Armin Hansen, William Ritschel, Arthur Hill Gilbert, Paul Dougherty, Francis McComas, and John O'Shea. Made up of several gallery rooms exhibiting the works of some of the more than 120 artist members, the Carmel Art Association deserves a spot on your gallery tours. Exhibits change monthly, and lectures, demonstrations, and openings are often open to the public. Call for details about special programs.

Carmel Gallery Alliance
(831) 642–2503, www.carmelartfestival.com

A standing committee of the Carmel Business Association, this alliance of Carmel art galleries works to showcase the art of member galleries and to perpetuate the city's long-standing tradition as a fine arts village. Each spring the nonprofit organization hosts the Carmel Art Festival, and during the summer months it holds a 6:00 to 9:00 P.M. Friday night Artwalk in which member galleries open their doors and provide exhibits and demonstrations. The Carmel Gallery Alliance also publishes a great gallery guide, *Art In Carmel*, that profiles its members.

Center for Photographic Art
Sunset Center, San Carlos Street and 9th Avenue, Carmel
(831) 625–5181, www.photoctr.mbaynet.com

As a California nonprofit public benefit corporation, the Center for Photographic Art encourages an awareness and appreciation of photography as a fine art form. Supported by memberships, grants, and gifts, the center provides an ongoing program of exhibitions (six to eight annually) and workshops featuring the works of both established and new photographers. The center is closed on Mondays.

Cultural Council for Monterey County
(831) 622–9060, www.culturalmonterey.org

Founded in 1982, the Cultural Council for Monterey County promotes and financially supports education, appreciation, and excellence in the arts. As the county's partner with the California Arts Council, CCMC is a networking organization for the many cultural entities of Monterey County.

Monterey Jazz Festival
2000 Fairgrounds Road, Monterey
(831) 373–3366,
www.montereyjazzfestival.org

There's more to the Monterey Jazz Festival than the world-famous Monterey Jazz Festival event held each September. It is a major supporter of music education throughout Monterey County and the state of California. Over the years it has raised more than $2 million for music education through scholarships, the California High School Jazz Competition (held each April and free of charge to attend), and the Jazz Education Fund. This unique fund pays for music instruments, sheet music, and clinician training for Monterey County Middle and High School jazz bands. The festival also funds a tour of Japan by the California High School All Star Jazz Band.

Parks and Recreation

The natural beauty of the Monterey Bay, our pine forests, clean air, and nearly perfect weather provide the ideal setting for all types of recreation. Walking, biking, in-line skating, camping, and hiking top the list of favorite activities for both locals and visitors.

The number of parks in our area is impressive. We've listed a few of the city, county, state, and regional parks to get you started, but don't hesitate to stop at any one of our open spaces to enjoy gorgeous views of the Bay, the rocky coastline, or our magnificent forests.

In most cases, turnout areas are available at scenic spots for parking. Always use these areas rather than park illegally. Legal parking is strictly enforced and the fines can be hefty.

Some useful recreation-oriented phone numbers are highlighted in the Close-up in this chapter. These numbers are invaluable to those who have specific questions or want more information.

Several recreational opportunities are covered in depth in other chapters of this book. See our In and Around the Water chapter for scuba diving, fishing, beaches, and all other water-related activities. The Peninsula's many golf courses, some of which are world-famous, are written up in our Golf chapter. You'll find bicycle and surrey rentals in the chapter called Getting Here, Getting Around.

Parks

City Parks

Monterey
www.monterey.org

El Estero Park Complex
Camino El Estero, Monterey
(831) 646–3866

The complex is a 45-acre park in the center of Monterey. It incorporates Lake El Estero, making it a popular place for fishing, paddleboating, picnics on the lawn, and feeding ducks. You can circle around the entire lake, a pleasant moderate walk, by following the designated path. El Estero Park is the site of an imaginative play area, Dennis the Menace children's playground, designed with the help of Hank Ketcham, creator of the popular comic strip. There is also a youth center, a multiuse field with a lighted baseball diamond, a skate park, a dance studio, and a boating concession with pedal-powered paddle boats. The park has areas for group barbecue picnics, a 17-station fitness course, and restrooms. There is no entrance fee for admission, but you need to call ahead to reserve the group areas. With the exception of the ball field, park hours are from dawn to dusk daily.

Fisherman's Shoreline Park
Cannery Row, Monterey
(831) 646–3866

This five-acre coastline park borders the recreation trail and has a grassy lawn and seating areas with Bay views. The park is between Fisherman's Wharf and the Coast Guard pier. There is no entrance fee. The park is open every day from dawn to dusk.

Hilltop Park and Hilltop Park Center
871 Jessie Street, Monterey
(831) 646–3975

This 2.8-acre neighborhood park has a grassy area, a picnic area with barbecues, play equipment, a tennis court, a basketball court, baseball backstop, and a multipurpose facility. There is no entrance fee, and the park is open from dawn to dusk every day.

San Carlos Beach Park
Cannery Row, Monterey
(831) 646–3866

This 2.87-acre coastline park at the foot of Reeside Avenue has a landscaped grassy lawn, paved walkways, beach access, outdoor showers for divers, and restrooms. Seating areas provide close up views of Monterey Bay. In-line or roller skates and skateboards are not allowed. There is no entrance fee, and the park is open every day during daylight hours.

Veterans Memorial Park
Jefferson Street and Skyline Drive, Monterey
(831) 646–3865

This 50-acre city park offers 40 sites for RV and group camping, hiking trails, picnic areas, restrooms, and playing fields. Camping sites are around $15 per night. The sites have no hookups and are available on a first-come, first-served basis. Group picnic areas can be reserved in advance. The park also provides access to the Huckleberry Hill Nature Preserve, an 81-acre park with numerous, well-established hiking trails that offer wonderful bay views.

Pacific Grove
www.pacificgroverecreation.org

Berwick Park
Ocean View Boulevard, Pacific Grove
(831) 648–3130

This one-acre park at 10th Street and the coastal side of Ocean View Boulevard offers a well-manicured lawn, the perfect spot to enjoy superb views of Monterey Bay and the surrounding coastline. This park is a popular place for outdoor weddings. There is no entrance fee, but use permits begin at around $25, depending on the size of the group. The park is open every day from dawn to dusk.

Caledonia Park
Caledonia Street, Pacific Grove
(831) 648–3130

This open space, located on the corner of Central and Caledonia Streets, contains a children's play area, baseball field, basketball court, climbing equipment, and picnic tables. There is no entrance fee, but group use permit fees start at $25. The park is open every day during daylight hours.

George Washington Park
Sinex Street, Pacific Grove
(831) 648–3130

This six-block, forested park, the largest in Pacific Grove, is at the corner of Sinex and Alder Streets. Most of the park is left in a natural state on unimproved forest land that provides a habitat for wildlife. Monarch butterflies reside here from October to March. The park has a full-size baseball field, picnic tables, barbecue grills, a play area, and restrooms. There is no entrance fee; however, a use permit is required for large groups (the minimum group fee is $25). The park is open every day during daylight hours.

Jewell Park
Central Avenue, Pacific Grove
(831) 648–3130

Jewell Park, located at the corner of Central and Forest Avenues, is next to the library and across from the natural history museum. A nice lawn area makes it an ideal place to bring young children. The park has a small meeting room with a kitchen and a gazebo that is sheltered by trees. A fee and a use permit are required for the gazebo. The "Little House" meeting room has a rental fee and a use permit is required. Use permits start at $25 depending upon the size of the group. There is no entrance fee, but you must apply in person at the Pacific Grove Recreation Department (515 Junipero Street) to reserve either the gazebo or the meeting room. The park is open every day from dawn to dusk.

Lovers Point Park
Ocean View Boulevard, Pacific Grove
(831) 648–3130

This beautiful oceanside, landscaped park is at the foot of 17th Street. The park's amenities include a large green lawn area, a sand volleyball court, a toddler's swimming pool, two small sandy beaches, rocky outcrops, a concrete pier structure, a snack bar, and restrooms. The park is a popular place for family gatherings, picnics, fishing, sunning, swimming, watersports, diving, and surfing. There is no entrance fee, but you must obtain a permit for weddings or large group gatherings. Use fees vary according to group size, the minimum fee is $25. Daylight hours are observed, and the park is open every day.

Monarch Butterfly Sanctuary
Grove Acre, Pacific Grove
(831) 373–7047

This park, between Short Street and Lighthouse Avenue, was purchased by the city of Pacific Grove in 1992. It is protected as an open space and butterfly habitat and is one of the original winter locations for the beautiful Monarch butterfly. Docent-led tours are available by appointment. The park has no entrance fee and is open daily from dawn to dusk (see our Attractions chapter for more detailed information).

Carmel
www.carmelcityhall.com

Mission Trail Park
Rio Road, Carmel
(831) 624–3543

Park visitors can follow in the footsteps of Father Junipero Serra and the Indians on the same trail they used when traveling from the mission to Monterey. Three main trails form a walking loop around the park. The terrain, with a stream in the winter months and a few hills, is a fairly easy walk. Benches are set up along the way where one can sit and admire the variety of trees such as willow, oak, pine, and eucalyptus. In spring, California poppies, lupine, honeysuckle, and other colorful flowers are in full bloom.

The origins of its name are the subject of debate, but all agree that Pacific Grove's Lovers Point Park is one of the most picturesque locales on the Peninsula. Locals and visitors gather here for picnics, swimming, sunning, and taking in the spectacular views. PHOTO: JANE MORBA

Within the park is the Rowntree Arboretum, a native garden worth exploring. Lester Rowntree started a career as an independent naturalist at the age of 53. She (yes, she) delighted in harvesting seeds from native plants and began planting them in this garden setting. The plants in the arboretum are at their peak of beauty in spring. To reach the arboretum, take the Doolittle trail. The park entrance is on Rio Road across from the mission. There is no fee, and the park is open every day during daylight hours.

County Parks
www.co.monterey.ca/parks

Jacks Peak Park
25020 Jacks Peak Park Road, Monterey
(831) 484–1108

Located off Highway 68, this 525-acre mountain-top park is a natural reserve offering more than 10 miles of hiking and equestrian trails through cathedral-like pine and oak forests to breathtaking ridge-top vistas of the Monterey Peninsula. The Skyline Self-Guided Nature Trail has vistas of Carmel and Point Lobos. The park has restrooms, picnic areas, barbecues, and a group site that can accommodate up to 50 people. A paved road goes almost to the top of Jacks Peak. At 1,068 feet, the peak is the highest point on the Monterey Peninsula. There is a nominal fee for cars entering the park. Parking is just outside the gates with an easy walk to the trailheads. Park hours are from 10:30 A.M. to 6:30 P.M. daily.

Laguna Seca Recreation Area
1025 Monterey-Salinas Highway, Monterey
(831) 484–1108

This county recreation area has over 180 campsites for RVs or tents. There are hiking trails, bike trails, picnic areas, restrooms, and areas to watch wildlife. Laguna Seca is the home of the Mazda Raceway Laguna Seca, which hosts frequent automotive and motorcycle races. There is also an outdoor amphitheater for music concerts and a rifle/pistol shooting range. The shooting range is open Friday through Monday from 11:30 A.M. to 4:30 P.M. and on weekends from 9:00 A.M. to 4:30 P.M. For information about the shooting range, call (831) 757–6317. The day-use fee for Laguna Seca is around $5.00 per car.

Regional Parks

Frog Pond Natural Area
Canyon Del Rey Road, Del Rey Oaks
(831) 372–3196

This 16.88-acre nature reserve is off Canyon Del Rey across from the Via Verde intersection. A seasonal freshwater marsh, acquired by the Monterey Peninsula Regional Park District in 1977, provides a habitat for the rare Pacific tree frog and is also a wetland habitat for bird-watching. A short trail passes through willow, oak, and redwood trees as it circles the property. Free parking is available across from the entrance to the park at City Hall, where you can pick up a brochure. Numbered posts in the reserve correspond with descriptions found in the brochure. There is no entrance fee, and the park is open every day from dawn to dusk.

Garland Regional Park
700 W. Carmel Valley Road, Carmel Valley
(831) 659–4488

Miles of hiking and equestrian trails are the focal point of this 4,462-acre park that rises from the Carmel River to the slopes of the Santa Lucia Mountains. Viewing wildlife, hiking, horseback riding, walking, and nature study are among the popular activities at Garland Park. The park has picnic areas and restrooms. You can call ahead to arrange ranger-guided walks and lectures. Information on the species of birds, mammals, and plants found in the park is available at the visitor center located at the entrance of the park. The park is open every day from early morning to sunset. There is no entrance fee.

Laguna Grande Regional Park
Canyon Del Rey Boulevard, Seaside
(831) 899–6236

This 34-acre park is at the corner of Canyon Del Rey Road and Del Monte Avenue. The park, surrounding a freshwater marsh and lake, borders the cities of Seaside and Monterey. It features two picnic areas, bicycling and pedestrian paths, and two children's playgrounds. On Sundays in the summer months, free jazz concerts are held on the hillside area. A picturesque Russian Orthodox Church sits between the two picnic areas. The park has no entrance fee and is open every day during daylight hours.

Toro Park
501 Monterey-Salinas Highway, Salinas
(831) 647-7799

Off the Monterey-Salinas Highway just 13 miles east of Monterey, Toro Park is a pastoral setting with more than 20 miles of well-maintained hiking trails. It's an expansive site with 4,756 acres of rolling grassland, wooded canyons, and hills rising to 2,000 feet. From March to May the area is filled with wildflowers. The park has playgrounds, softball fields, a volleyball court, horseshoe pits, and restrooms. Several picnic areas suitable for large groups have barbecue pits, tables, electrical outlets, and water. To reserve the group area, call (888) 588-2267. A map can be obtained at the entrance to the park and should be used when hiking. Bring your own drinking water when hiking, as there are no safe sources of water. Parking is free, but there is a small entrance fee to the park. The park is open every day from 8:00 A.M. to 7:00 P.M.

State Parks
www.parks.ca.gov

Asilomar State Beach
800 Asilomar Avenue, Pacific Grove
(831) 372-4076

This beach park is at the border of Pacific Grove and Pebble Beach overlooking the ocean. The name Asilomar means "refuge by the sea" and was chosen by the YWCA, which founded the retreat in 1913. It's a beautiful park with fishing, surfing, wildlife viewing, food service, lodging, picnic areas, exhibits and programs, and hiking trails that provide wheelchair access. There are several historical buildings, sand dunes, the Pacific shoreline, and a Monterey pine forest filled with wildlife. Park rangers are available to lead cultural and natural history walks, but you must call ahead to schedule.

The Asilomar Conference Grounds offer a full-service facility of year-round meeting rooms, overnight lodging, dining, and a park store. Adjacent to the conference grounds is the dune boardwalk, which meanders through a restored sand-dune area. The boardwalk follows a self-guided nature walk where visitors can learn more about this unique ecosystem.

If you feel inclined to take a walk on the beach, there are several choice spots. A long strip of unbroken beach, which meets a rocky shoreline sheltering several sandy coves, is perfect for exploring. You'll often see harbor seals, California sea lion, and sea otters swimming offshore. There is no entrance fee. The beach is open every day from dawn to dusk.

Garrapata State Park
Highway 1, Carmel
(831) 624-4909

This 2,879-acre park with 4 miles of coastline is about 10 miles south of Carmel. Parking is available in one of several highway turnouts near Sobernales Point. The undeveloped park has no entrance signs or exclusive parking areas. Hiking trails are diverse and include trails to ocean beaches, a steep ascent to a hilltop with amazing views of Pacific horizons, and trails through cacti and dense redwood groves.

Monterey State Historical Park
Visitor Center in the Stanton Center, Monterey
(831) 649-7118, www.mbay.net/~mshp

The starting place for guided tours of the park is the visitor center, where a free history film is shown every 20 minutes or so. Pick up a brochure for the walking tour, which guides you to Monterey's adobes, historic sites, and unique gardens. The visitor center is open daily. Guided tours are available for a nominal fee (see the Monterey Path of History write-up in our Attractions chapter for more information).

Point Lobos State Park
Highway 1, Carmel
(831) 624-4909

Some of the Peninsula's most dramatic, scenic, and memorable ocean panoramas are located at Point Lobos. This 1,200-acre reserve, located 3 miles south of Carmel, features 7 miles of hiking on 14 intersecting trails that meander through pine forests and spectacular coastal scenery. The reserve is a popular spot for scuba diving (by reservation only) and viewing wildlife, such as sea otters, harbor seals, sea lions, pelicans, and gulls. Picnic areas and restrooms are available. The reserve offers guided tours, exhibits, and programs. The entrance fee is under $10 and provides same-day entrance to other area state parks. The reserve is open every day from 9:00 A.M. to 7:00 P.M. (5:00 P.M. during the winter months).

National Parks

Los Padres National Forest
406 South Mildred Avenue, King City
(831) 385–5434,
www.r5.fs.us/10s/padres/index.html

The Monterey Ranger District of the Los Padres National Forest, the rugged northern part of the Santa Lucia Mountains, extends south from Carmel Valley to the northern part of San Luis Obispo County near San Simeon. On the east its boundary is the Salinas Valley and to the west, the Pacific Ocean.

At its highest point, 5,000 feet, a coastal ridge plunges dramatically to the rocky shore below. The mountains are rugged with narrow coastal canyons, picturesque cliffs, and waterfalls. The upper ridges of the mountains are mostly covered with brush and can be accessed only where trails have been cut through the undergrowth. Hiking in the park is advisable only for the experienced hiker, due to the rigorous wilderness conditions.

Those who do visit will notice a wide range of plant life. Flowers found in the woods tend to be less noticeable, while the fields showcase golden California poppies, deep pink owl's clover, Johnny jump-ups, shooting stars, blue hound's tongue, and Douglas' iris. Redwood canyons harbor a wide variety of ferns and shade-loving plants such as woodwardia, maidenhair, and five-finger ferns. You will also see wood sorrel, huckleberry, and wood rose.

Redwoods, tanbark oak, red and white alder, big-leaf maple, and several varieties of willow are scattered throughout the low areas. Higher up, you'll find coast live oak, black oak, interior live oak, and pines such as Coulter, ponderosa, and sugar. Chaparral, an impenetrable brush, is found throughout the forest, forming fragrant flowering shrubs that bloom throughout the year.

An abundance of wildlife allows hikers and campers to observe a full spectrum of birds and animals. Predators such as mountain lion, coyote, and bobcat present little problem to hikers. Raccoons, known as camp bandits, can be a problem for campers who leave their food supplies out in the open. Wild pigs are sometimes seen, but unless they're wounded or cornered, they mostly avoid humans. The most familiar birds in the forest are hawks, eagles, turkey vultures, and a wide variety of owls. The Ventana Wilderness Sanctuary programs include the California Condor Recovery Program and the monitoring of bald eagle territories.

The Monterey Ranger District encompasses more than 300,000 acres. Over 200,000 acres make up the Ventana Wilderness, and more than 14,000 acres comprise the Silver Peak Wilderness. Hikers must check with the Forest Service, (831) 385–5434, for prevailing conditions such as weather, fire, landslides, and vegetation growths when planning hikes or camping trips.

For those interested, the Ventana Chapter of the Sierra Club has published the Trail Guide to Los Padres National Forest for the Monterey Ranger District; the book offers guidelines and information to both the Ventana and Silver Peak Wilderness areas. The book is available at the Sierra Club Bookstore, located in Carmel on the south side of Ocean Avenue between San Carlos and Dolores Streets, on the second floor. Bookstore hours are 12:30 to 4:30 P.M., Monday to Saturday. Put on your hiking boots and make the ascent! For more information call (831) 626–1588.

A campfire permit is required (at no charge) from May 1 through December 31. An Adventure Pass is required to gain entrance to the park. The passes can be purchased by mail from Los Padres National Forest, 6755 Hollister Avenue, Suite 150, Goleta, CA 93117. Passes can also be purchased at the following locations:

Big Sur Multi-Agency Facility
Big Sur Station #1, Big Sur
(831) 667–2315

Zen Mountain Center
39171 Tassajara Road, Carmel Valley
(831) 659–9961

Lynn's Liquors
601 Broadway, King City
(831) 385–6715

Big 5
1300 Del Monte Shopping Center, Monterey
(831) 375–8800

Big 5
1000 Northridge Shopping Center, Salinas
(831) 449–6768

Adventure Passes are $5.00 per visit or $30.00 for an annual pass.

Recreation

Recreation Centers

Monterey Sports Center
301 Franklin Street, Monterey
(831) 646–3700, www.monterey.org

The sports center sits on a 3.2-acre site at the corner of Washington and Franklin Streets. You'll find a 30-meter swimming pool, a 6-meter therapeutic pool, three cross-court gyms, a weight room, cardiovascular room, aerobic room, kids' activity room, restrooms, locker rooms, a sundeck, baby-sitting services, and a snack bar. In addition to facility use, the Sports Center also offers instruction in tennis, jujitsu, and karate and has basketball leagues, too. There is a small admission fee for nonmembers and nonresidents. The fee includes use of locker and shower rooms, both pools and the waterslide, gymnasium, weight room, cardiovascular room, and sundeck. The Sports Center is open every day. Call for daily hours.

Patullo Swim Center
1148 Wheeler Street, Seaside
(831) 899–6272,
bbs.ci.seaside.ca.us/patulloswim

To reach the swim center, follow Fremont Street north to Kimball Street. Turn right on Kimball then left on Wheeler, and you'll see the swim center on the right. The center offers adult lap swims, water aerobics, senior swims, and recreation swims as well as adult and youth lessons. The center is open daily from early morning until late in the evening. Prices range from $2.50 (nonresidents) for lap swims to $37.50 for a 25-visit swim card. Fees for residents are lower. Some recreational and senior swims are free. Schedules vary so call or visit the Web site for current information.

Baseball/Softball

Cages
414 Adams Street, Monterey
(831) 375–1800, www.cagesindoorbatting.com

Cages is located in downtown Monterey across from the Sports Center. Billed as a family entertainment center, it has indoor baseball and softball batting. In addition to batting, you'll find other entertainment such as skeeball, a video arcade, a pool table, and air hockey. Call or visit the Web site for hours and prices.

Frank E. Sollecito Jr. Ballpark
Camino El Estero, Monterey
(831) 646–3969, www.monterey.org

Although a multiuse field, the ballpark has a standard baseball diamond with night lighting, bleachers, and restrooms. The field is used for adult and kid leagues so call ahead for availability. Picnic kits are available from the Monterey Recreation Department, 546 Dutra Street. A kit contains recreational equipment including baseballs, bats, etc. Rental costs vary. For reservations, call (831) 646–3866.

Jack's Ballpark
Franklin Street at Figueroa Street, Monterey
(831) 646-3969, www.monterey.org

This 3.7-acre multiuse municipal sports park is at Franklin and Figueroa Streets in downtown Monterey. It has a ball field with night lighting and bleachers, a play area with a sand pit and climbing structures, and restrooms. The field is used for adult and kid leagues; call the ballpark for specific scheduling. Picnic kits, including baseball, bats, and other related equipment are available from the Monterey Recreation Department, 546 Dutra Street. The kits rent for $25 for Monterey residents, $33 for all others, and can be reserved by calling (831) 646-3866.

Pacific Grove Municipal Ballpark
17-Mile Drive, Pacific Grove
(831) 648–5730
The ballpark is located at the corner of 17-Mile Drive and Pico Street. The park is used for adult softball/soccer/slow-pitch leagues, pony baseball/softball, and high school softball. Permits are required for use of the ballpark and may be obtained at the Pacific Grove Recreation Department, 515 Junipero Avenue. Permit prices depend on the number of people attending the event. For a fee of around $20, you can rent a kit containing recreational equipment including baseballs, bats, bases, etc. Reservations are necessary, so call the Pacific Grove Recreation Department at the number above to schedule a field or to reserve a kit.

Basketball

Public courts are available throughout the Peninsula. For more information see the listings for Caledonia, Hilltop, and Veterans Memorial parks in the "City Parks" section of this chapter. Picnic kits, available from the Monterey Recreation Department, 546 Dutra Street, contain recreational equipment including basketballs. The kit rental fees are $25 for Monterey residents and $33 for nonresidents. Reserve a kit by calling (831) 646-3866.

Picnic kits are also available from the Pacific Grove Recreation Department at 515 Junipero Avenue, (831) 648-5730. A $20 fee covers the rental cost of a kit containing recreational equipment including basketballs.

Bowling

Monterey Lanes
2161 N. Fremont Street, Monterey
(831) 373–1553
The bowling alley has 24 lanes. Open daily. Call for hours. Leagues play evenings Monday through Friday so the facility is not open to the public during that time.

CLOSE-UP

Parks and Recreation Departments

Carmel Recreation Department, San Carlos between 8th and 9th, Carmel, (831) 626–1255

City of Monterey Recreation and Community Services Department, 546 Dutra Street, Monterey, (831) 646–3866

Monterey Parks Division Office, 23 Ryan Ranch Road, Monterey, (831) 646–3860

Monterey County Parks Department, 855 E. Laurel Street, Salinas, (831) 647–7799 (reservations), (831) 385–1484 (tourist information)

Pacific Grove Recreation Department, 515 Junipero Avenue, Pacific Grove, (831) 648–3130

Seaside Recreation Department, 896 Hilby Street, Seaside, (831) 899–6270

State Parks & Recreation Department District Office, 2211 Garden Road, Monterey, (831) 649–2836

Camping

In addition to the Laguna Seca Recreation Area (see our listing in the County Parks section of this chapter), there are two state parks and one National Forest near the Peninsula where camping is permitted. Reservations for campsites are always necessary in California, especially during the spring and summer months. (A few campgrounds are available only on a first-come, first-served basis.)

Julia Pfeiffer Burns State Park
Highway 1, Big Sur
(831) 667–2315
This state park is 37 miles south of Carmel and encompasses nearly 4,000 acres stretching from the Pacific coastline to the 5,682-foot Junipero Serra Peak, the highest point in the Santa Lucia range. An environmental camp has a hike-in distance of one-quarter mile. No drinking water is available. Two cypress-shaded campsites accommodate up to eight people. You must register at the Pfeiffer Big Sur Station. Dramatic coastal vistas and the only major coastal California waterfall, McWay Falls, which tumbles into the Pacific Ocean, are two highlights of this camp area. No dogs are allowed at the environmental camp.

Los Padres National Forest
406 Mildred Avenue, King City
(831) 385–5434
The Monterey Ranger District of the Los Padres National Forest, the rugged northern part of the Santa Lucia Mountains, extends south from Carmel Valley to the northern part of San Luis Obispo County near San Simeon. On the east its boundary is the Salinas Valley and to the west, the Pacific Ocean.

Most of the developed campgrounds on the Monterey Ranger District are open year round. Family units are all on a first-come, first-served basis. Each campsite has a table and stove, and the campground has restrooms and potable water. Although designed for tent camping, some of the units can accommodate recreational vehicles (self-contained) up to 30 feet long. There are no hookups or electricity. Camping within the campground is limited to a maximum of eight people and two vehicles per group. See our "National Parks" section in this chapter for reservation information. There are nine developed campgrounds in the Los Padres National Forest, three of which are fairly close to the Monterey Peninsula.

Botchers Gap is 8 miles east of Highway 1 on Palo Colorado Road. The intersection of Highway 1 and Palo Colorado Road is approximately 15 miles north of Big Sur and 11 miles south of Carmel. The campground, at an elevation of 2,100 feet, is situated among oaks and madrone, featuring an excellent view of the Ventana Double Cones in the Santa Lucia Mountains. There is trailhead parking for the Ventana Wilderness. The campground has 11 units with no water. The fee is around $10 per day.

China Camp and White Oaks Campgrounds are along the unsurfaced Jamesburg-Tassajara Road. Access is by Cachagua Road off Carmel Valley Road, approximately 23 miles from the junction of Carmel Valley Road and Highway 1. China Camp is a departure point for the Ventana Wilderness. The road is not recommended for trailers during winter. China Camp sits at an elevation of 4,500 feet and has only six units. White Oaks is at 4,000 feet and has seven units. Neither campground has potable water at this time.

Pfeiffer Big Sur State Park
Hwy. 1, Big Sur
(831) 667–2315
This 218-site campground, 31 miles from Carmel, is open year-round. Established in 1933, the park offers hikes through redwood canyons as well as glorious views of the Big Sur coastline. Amenities include restrooms, hot showers, laundry facilities, and a camp store. The park is open to trailers (maximum length of 27 feet) and motor homes (maximum length of 32 feet). Rates range from $12 to $26 depending on time of year, site size, and location.

Chess

Monterey Chess and Dart Center
430 Alvarado Street, Monterey
(831) 646–8730

The Chess and Dart Center is open to the public and charges a daily fee of $2.50 or a monthly fee of $15 (students $12). The monthly pass allows limited guest privileges. Lessons are also available for $10 an hour at the Center or $20 an hour at your home. Tournaments are held about once a month on Sundays and once a week on Wednesdays at 7:00 P.M. The Center is open Tuesday through Friday from 4:30 to 10:00 P.M. and on weekends from 2:00 to 10:00 P.M.

Climbing

Sanctuary Rock Gym
1855-A East Avenue, Sand City
(831) 899–2595, www.rockgym.com

For a different kind of workout, visit Monterey County's first rock-climbing gym. The gym contains more than 5,600 square feet of molded, sculpted terrain with extensive bouldering that provides a challenge and also includes a padded floor to protect against injury. Classes and lessons are offered. The daily rate of $12 is discounted with the purchase of five- and ten-visit punch cards. A full rental package containing shoes, a harness, and a chalk bag rents for under $10. Call or visit the Web site for hours and costs.

Cycling, Running, Walking

Don Dahvee Greenbelt
Munras Avenue, Monterey

This greenbelt is a 35.8-acre recreation area that lies adjacent to Munras Avenue in Monterey between El Dorado Street and Del Monte Shopping Center. There are miles of trails to explore and tables for picnic lunches. The park is open daily from dawn to dusk, and there's no entrance fee.

Monterey Peninsula Recreational Trail

This 9-mile paved recreation trail stretches from Pacific Grove's Lovers Point nearly to Marina. The trail, laid out along the water's edge, is a popular place to bike, walk, and inline skate. It passes Lovers Point, the Aquarium, Cannery Row, and Fisherman's Wharf. The trail is always open and is free to the public.

Hang Gliding

Western Hang Gliders
Hwy. 1 at Reservation Road, Marina
(831) 384–2622

Western Hang Gliders is "a place where people have found freedom in flight." As a member of the United States Hang Gliding Association, this company offers the highest quality instruction available in beginning to advanced courses. A three-hour course, the place where everyone starts, includes classroom time, ground school, and at least five flights for around $100. Western Hang Gliders is open every day, weather permitting. Reservations are advised.

Hiking

Don Dahvee Greenbelt
Munras Avenue, Monterey

This 35.8-acre recreation area lies adjacent to Munras Avenue in Monterey, between El Dorado Street and Del Monte Shopping Center. Hikers can explore miles of trails, and tables are available for picnic lunches. The park is open daily from dawn to dusk, and there is no entrance fee.

Garland Regional Park
700 W. Carmel Valley Road, Carmel Valley
(831) 659–4488

Varied hiking trails are the focal point of this 4,462-acre park, which rises from the Carmel River to the slopes of the Santa Lucia Range. Amenities include picnic areas and restrooms. Call ahead to arrange ranger-guided walks or ask for information at the visitors center, which is at the park's entrance. Garland Park has no entrance fee and is open every day from 8:30 A.M. to sunset.

Carmel River Station
Nason Road, Carmel
(831) 659–2612

The upper ridges of the mountains here are mostly covered with brush and can be accessed only where trails have been cut through the undergrowth. Hiking in the park is recommended for well-conditioned, experienced hikers familiar with wilderness hiking. Daily and annual park passes are available for purchase.

Point Lobos State Park
Hwy. 1, Carmel
(831) 624–4909, www.parks.ca.gov

Point Lobos, a 1,200-acre reserve 3 miles south of Rio Road on Highway 1, Carmel, is a spectacular area to hike. It has 7 miles of hiking on 14 intersecting trails that meander through pine forests and spectacular coastal scenery. A map of the specific trails is given to you when you pay the entrance fee to the park. The entrance fee is under $10 and provides same-day entrance to other area state parks. The reserve is open daily from 9:00 A.M. to 7:00 P.M. It closes at 5:00 P.M. during winter months.

Horseback Riding

Pebble Beach Equestrian Center
Portola Road and Alva Lane, Pebble Beach
(831) 624–2756, www.ridepebblebeach.com

The experienced instructors at the Pebble Beach Equestrian Center welcome all levels of riders for trail rides in the forest or on the beach. They work with individuals and private groups. Trail rides can be arranged for picnics or special events. Guided trail rides are offered four times daily. Call or visit the Web site for times and cost. Reservations are necessary.

Public Swimming Pools

See Recreation Centers.

Skating

Del Monte Garden Skating Arena
2020 Del Monte Avenue, Monterey
(831) 375–3202

This traditional public roller rink is popular Thursday through Sunday for the older in-line skate and rollerskate crowd. Monday through Wednesday is booked for private groups. Call for exact hours, skate rental fees, and skating fee.

Monterey Bay SK8 Station
1855 East Avenue, Sand City
(831) 899–8588, www.teamphoenix.org

Skateboarding at the SK8, an indoor in-line skate and skateboard park, features a death box, vert ramp, corner bowl, fun box, quarterpipes, and a full street course to challenge your skills. The SK8 Station is open daily. Call or visit the Web site for hours and costs.

Skydiving

Skydive Monterey Bay
3261 Imjin Road, Marina
(831) 384–3483, www.skydivemontereybay.com

Just 10 minutes away from Monterey, Skydive Monterey Bay offers tandem, accelerated freefall, and static-line training programs. All training programs meet the requirements necessary for membership in the U.S. Parachute Association. Groups are welcome. Family and friends can observe your landing at the airport's drop zone. Rates for a tandem jump begin at $199. Video or still photography is available to commemorate the occasion. Reservations are recommended on weekends and necessary on weekdays. The facility is open daily, weather permitting.

Tennis Courts

Monterey Tennis Center
401 Pearl Street, Monterey
(831) 646–3881,
www.montereytenniscenter.com

The center, at the corner of Pearl and Adams streets, has six lighted courts and a pro shop. An extensive lesson program, directed by certified and experienced members of the U.S. Professional Tennis Association, is offered for all ages and abilities. A "Buddies List" has the names of people who are looking for a match. The Monterey Tennis Center is open daily. Call or visit the Web site for lesson fees, court use fees, and hours.

Morris Dill Tennis Court
515 Junipero Avenue, Pacific Grove
(831) 648–3129

Racquet stringing is available at the fully stocked pro shop here. A comprehensive program of lessons and leagues is offered to include any age and level. Racquet and ball-machine rentals are available. There is a nominal fee per person per hour for court use. Reservations are accepted for court times. Open daily from 9:00 A.M. until dusk.

Volleyball

Del Monte Beach
Del Monte Avenue, Monterey
(831) 646–3866, www.monterery.org

Del Monte Beach, adjacent to Tide Avenue and Surf Way in Monterey, has one sand volleyball court. Picnic kits, available from the Monterey Recreation Department, 546 Dutra Street, contain recreational equipment including volleyballs and nets. There is a rental fee, reduced for Monterey residents. Reservations are necessary. The beach is open during daylight hours.

Lovers Point Park
Ocean View Boulevard, Pacific Grove
(831) 648–3130,
www.pacificgroverecreation.com

This beautifully landscaped, oceanside park is at the foot of 17th Street. The park has one sand volleyball court, a snack bar, and restrooms. Picnic kits containing volleyballs and nets are available from the Pacific Grove Recreation Department, 515 Junipero Avenue, for a $20 rental fee. There is no entrance fee, but you must call ahead to reserve the court. The park is open every day from dawn to dusk.

Monterey Bay Park
Del Monte Avenue, Monterey
(831) 646–3866

This 3.9-acre park is adjacent to the beach and has five sand volleyball courts. Picnic kits, available from the Monterey Recreation Department at 546 Dutra Street, contain recreational equipment including volleyballs and nets. The kits rent for around $25 for Monterey residents and $33 for nonresidents. Reservations are necessary. The park is open every day during daylight hours.

> **Insiders' Tip**
>
> There is an ever-growing selection of centers teaching the martial arts on the Monterey Peninsula. Check the local Yellow Pages for a current list of places to train in karate, jujitsu, tae kwon do, judo, kick boxing, and more.

Yoga

Yoga Center of Carmel
San Carlos Street, Carmel
(831) 624–4949, www.yogacentercarmel.org

The Yoga Center, founded in 1989, is at the corner of 10th and San Carlos Streets, in the Sunset Center (cottage No. 17). Beginner classes are offered Tuesday mornings and Thursday mornings and evenings. Intermediate classes are held Monday through Friday. Classes are also held on Saturday and Sunday. Drop-in class fees are under $10 and multiple-class passes are available at a discount. Call or visit the Web site to double check class schedules.

In and around the Water

The mesmerizing waters of Monterey Bay have provided inspiration and sustenance for many individuals beginning with the first Native American inhabitants of the area. The incredible power and beauty of the Pacific Ocean in our section of California are key factors in the decision to visit or live here. From commercial and recreational fishing and tour boat operations to restaurants, real estate, art, and photography, the lives of local residents are very much linked to this body of water. As one of the richest, most diverse marine environments in the world, the varied physical aspects of the Bay—its rocky coasts, sandy beaches, and deep marine canyons—create many different habitats for a vast array of plant, animal, and marine life. In 1992, Monterey Bay became a National Marine Sanctuary.

In this chapter we explore the various beaches and the activities made possible by our proximity to the magnificent Monterey Bay. Boating, fishing, surfing, diving, and the ever popular walk along the water's edge are a few of the recreational possibilities available in and around the water.

Beaches

Visitors captivated by the sights of scenic coastal vistas often are unaware of the potential hazards contained in the deceptively tame waters. Although there is the temptation to think of Monterey Bay as protected waters, it is always advisable to use caution when boating, swimming, surfing, wading, or walking along the beach or rocky headlands. Because of the expanse of the Bay and its submarine canyons, every precaution taken in the open ocean should apply to the Bay. Dangerous undertows and riptides exist at nearly every beach, so extreme caution and strict attention to posted regulations are necessary. Walking out on rocky outcrops during low tide should be done, if at all, with utmost care and awareness of the incoming tides.

Tides in the Monterey Bay have a variance of 7½ feet. This means the tides will vary around 3½ feet above or below the shoreline base. A range of about 8½ feet can occur on days of maximum tides. The water level throughout the harbor is almost always a minimum of 8 to 10 feet. For your own safety, check the tide tables each day in the local newspaper or pick up a tide book, available wherever fishing tackle is sold.

Asilomar State Beach
End of Highway 68, Pacific Grove
(831) 372–4076, www.parks.ca.gov

Asilomar has a long sandy stretch of beach perfect for walks and watching sunsets. It's also a great surfing beach. Located at the border of Pacific Grove and Pebble Beach, Asilomar has steady, offshore breezes making it ideal for kite flying. There are several choice spots for walking on the beach. At one spot, a long strip of unbroken beach meets a rocky shoreline, sheltering several sandy coves perfect for wading in tide pools. Another alternative is to follow the wooden boardwalk as it weaves along the rocky shoreline and through extensive restored dune areas where you'll see native plants in their natural environment. You'll often see and hear harbor seals, California sea lions, and sea otters swimming offshore. There is no entrance fee, and the beach is open every day from dawn to dusk.

Carmel Beach
West end of Ocean Avenue, Carmel
(831) 624–3543, www.carmelcityhall.com

Carmel Beach is quite possibly one of the most beautiful beaches in the world and certainly one of California's most famous. As you stand at the main entrance to the beach, at the end of Ocean Avenue, you can see the spectacular Pebble Beach Golf courses on your right. On your left, the view is just as amazing, with the picturesque Point Lobos State Reserve visible. The beach is surrounded by bluffs and has white sand, native cypress trees, and spectacular scenery. It is excellent for long walks, surfing, sunning, and picnics. To be on this beach and watch the sun sink into the Pacific at sunset, especially on a clear day, is an experience you won't soon forget.

Carmel River State Beach
Carmelo Road, Carmel
(831) 649–2836, www.parks.ca.gov

To get to this beach (1 mile south of Ocean Avenue), head south on Highway 1. Turn right on Rio Road, then left on Carmelo Road and into the parking lot. The beach has hiking trails, areas for viewing wildlife, a lagoon, and restrooms. Stewart's Cove, tucked into the northern tip of the ocean basin, is frequently uncrowded. It's a good place to view the ocean, especially on stormy days when the waves crash into the boulders along the shore. Climbing on the rocks, swimming, and wading are prohibited due to unpredictable wave patterns and a lethal undertow. Dogs are permitted if they are kept on a leash. The beach has no entrance fee and is open every day from 7:00 A.M. until 10:00 P.M. The parking lot closes at sunset.

China Cove and Gibson Beach
Point Lobos State Reserve, Highway 1, Carmel
(831) 624–4909, www.parks.ca.gov

Four miles south of Ocean Avenue, these pristine, photogenic beaches are at the southern end of the Point Lobos State Reserve. China Cove, accessible from a steep stairway along the cliff, is a tiny beach with white sand leading into emerald-green water. Otters and other marine life can be seen from this fascinating hideaway. China Cove once inspired Robert Louis Stevenson, who used the setting in his popular book *Treasure Island*. If the tide is out, explore the small cave at the water's edge.

After ascending the steps, take the path along the top of the cliff to a second staircase, which descends to Gibson Beach. Down below, gigantic rocks are found in interesting formations along the narrow beach. Solitude, save for the seabirds circling overhead, is one of the highlights of this small beach.

The entrance fee to the reserve is under $10 and covers same-day access to other area state parks. The reserve is open every day.

Lovers Point Beach
Ocean View Boulevard, Pacific Grove
(831) 648–5730, www.pacificgrove.com

This beautiful beach and landscaped park is at the foot of 17th Street, below the Old Bath House Restaurant. There are two small sandy beaches, rocky outcrops, and a concrete pier structure. The park's amenities include a large green lawn area, a sand volleyball court, a toddlers' swimming pool, a snack bar, and restrooms. The protected cove at Lovers Point makes it a popular place for family gatherings, picnics, fishing, sunning, swimming, scuba diving, and surfing. It's open every day during daylight hours, and it is free to the public.

Monastery Beach
Highway 1, Carmel
(831) 624–4909, www.parks.ca.gov

Monastery Beach, about 1.5 miles south of Ocean Avenue across from the Carmelite Monastery, is a great spot for scuba diving, but only for the very experienced. A sharp drop-off and a dangerous undertow make the beach unsafe for swimming or wading. The "sand" is actually coarse-grained rocks that can be very hard on bare feet. Be sure to wear suitable shoes for walking. The beach has no entrance fee and is open every day from 7:00 A.M. to 10:00 P.M.

Monterey State Beach
Canyon Del Rey Road, Monterey and Seaside
(831) 649–2836, www.parks.ca.gov

Shared by the cities of Monterey and Seaside, Monterey State Beach is actually three separate beaches about a mile apart. It stretches along Del Monte Avenue from the Monterey Municipal Wharf up the coast to Seaside. An easy access to the beach is found at the west end of Canyon Del Rey Road. At the southern end, the beach has lots of rocks, rounded smooth by the surf. Dune restoration is currently underway at the northern end of the beach. Hiking trails provide wheelchair access. Other activities include bike trails, fishing, scuba diving, kayaking, swimming, volleyball, and kite flying. There is no entrance fee to the beach. It's open from dawn to sunset.

San Carlos Beach
Cannery Row, Monterey
(831) 646–3866, www.monterey.org

An almost 3-acre park with a grassy area lines the beachfront at San Carlos. Seating areas provide a chance to stop and enjoy the view. Access to the beach is easy, and there are safe currents due to the protection of Breakwater Cove. Restrooms and picnic tables are available. There is no entrance fee, and the park is open during daylight hours.

Estuary

Elkhorn Slough National Estuarine Research Reserve
1700 Elkhorn Road, Moss Landing
(831) 728–2822, www.elkhornslough.org

The Elkhorn Slough Reserve is about 20 miles north of Monterey, northeast of Moss Landing and 2 miles north of Dolan Road and is one of the few undeveloped coastal wetland areas in California. The estuary area has 5 miles of walking trails. The reserve is a nursery area for many fish, sharks, and rays and is home to more than 200 species of birds. Docent-led tours are available on weekends. The reserve is open Wednesday through Sunday from 9:00 A.M. to 5:00 P.M. There is a nominal admission fee for adults and children 16 and older.

Lake

Lake El Estero
Del Monte Avenue, Monterey
(831) 646–3866, www.monterey.org

Lake El Estero is in the Lake El Estero Park Complex at the corner of Del Monte Avenue and Camino El Estero. Fishing is allowed in designated areas, mainly the two piers on Pearl Street. The lake is stocked with rainbow trout, Sacramento perch, Sacramento blackfish, Sacramento hitch, carp, tule perch, and yellow bullhead. Anyone 16 years and older is required to have a fishing license (see our "Fishing" section in this chapter for more on licenses).

Boating

Regulations and Equipment

Recreational vessels are required to carry specified safety equipment, the amount and type of which varies according to type of propulsion, construction, number of people aboard, and the area and time of use. All Coast Guard-approved equipment must be kept in good, serviceable condition, readily accessible, and must be the proper type and/or size. For equipment purposes, sailboats, canoes, rowboats, and inflatable rafts equipped with motors are considered motorboats.

Sailboats and manually propelled vessels must carry personal flotation devices (PFDs), navigation lights, sound signaling devices, and visual distress signals. Motorboats less than 16 feet in length must carry personal flotation devices, a fire extinguisher, a backfire flame arrestor, muffling system, ventilation system, sound signaling devices, visual distress signals, and navigation lights. Required equipment for motorboats more than 16 feet in length varies. For more information contact the Department of Boating and Waterways, 1629 South Street, Sacramento, California, (916) 445-6281.

State law requires that all children age six or younger wear a Type I, II, or III life jacket while on board a moving vessel that is 26 feet or less in length. The only exceptions are on a sailboat if the child is restrained by a harness tethered to the sailboat or in an enclosed cabin.

The number and type of U.S. Coast Guard-approved PFDs required on a vessel depends on the length of the craft and the number of persons on board. All boats, canoes, and kayaks of any length must carry at least one personal flotation device for each person on board.

All boats 16 feet or longer, except canoes and kayaks of any length, must carry one wearable PFD (Type I, II, III) of the appropriate size for each person on board and one throwable (Type IV) device in each boat.

PFD Types I, II, and III must be readily accessible, meaning they may not be kept inside a plastic bag or protective covering. They must be easy to reach and stowed with the straps untied. All throwable PFDs (Type IV) must be immediately available. The law requires them to be kept in an open area where persons aboard can reach them quickly in an emergency.

It is recommended that vessels in semi-protected waters carry the following additional equipment: anchor and cable; bailing device; boat hook; a bucket; compass; depth-sounding device; emergency drinking water; fenders; first-aid kit with manual; flashlight and spare batteries; heaving line; local charts; a mirror for signaling; mooring lines; an extra supply of motor oil and grease; spare set of oars; spare parts; radio direction finder; radio/telephone; additional ring buoys; shear pins if used; current tables; tide tables; and tools.

Registering Your Boat

California law requires current registration of most vessels, including moored vessels whether used or not. All vessels must be registered and numbered with the exception of sailboards, boats that are manually propelled, sailboats of 8 feet or less propelled solely by sail, or vessels having valid registration in the state of principal use and not remaining in California for more than 90 consecutive days.

Applications to register a vessel can be made at the Department of Motor Vehicles (DMV), 1180 Canyon Del Rey Road, Monterey, (831) 649-2935. The DMV will issue a Certificate of Number, a Certificate of Ownership, and a set of registration stickers. The stickers must be displayed on each side of the forward half of the vessel so that enforcement officers do not have to board the boat to determine if the vessel is currently registered.

Transient boaters should report to the harbor office at the head of the Wharf #2 for berth assignments. The harbormaster can be contacted on VHF channel 5 or 16. Quarantine, customs, and immigration services are handled by representatives from San Francisco, (831) 373-1155.

Navigation

Monterey Bay, located between Point Pinos and Point Santa Cruz, is a 20-mile-wide open roadstead practically free of dangers. The shores are low with sand beaches backed by dunes or low sand bluffs. A 10-fathom curve lies at an average distance of .7 of a mile offshore. The Submarine Monterey Canyon (with a depth of more than 50 fathoms) heads near the middle of the Bay about a half-mile from the beach near Moss Landing.

Point Pinos, on the south side of Monterey Bay, is low and round with visible rocks extending offshore for less than .3 of a mile. The point is bare for about .2 of a mile back from the beach, beyond is covered with pines. The light at the Point Pinos Lighthouse (36° 38.0' N, 121° 56.0' W), 89 feet above the water, is shown from a 43-foot white tower on a dwelling near the north end of the point. A radio beacon is at the light, and a fog signal is 450 yards northwest.

The breakwater at the head of the harbor is about 1,700 feet long, affording protection in northwesterly weather. The outer end of the breakwater is marked with a light and a fog signal. You will hear the barking sea lions when approaching the breakwater.

The Monterey Harbor (36° 37'N, 121° 53'W), 3 miles southeast of Point Pinos is a compact resort harbor with some commercial activity and fishing. Depths of more than 20 feet are available in the outer harbor and the entrance and 6 to 10 feet in the small-boat basin. There are many sportfishing landings, and the small-craft basin provides good shelter for about 500 boats. Prominent features include the Presidio Monument on the brow of a barren hill and a radio tower .6 of a mile north of the monument. The speed limit in the harbor is three knots.

Municipal Wharf #2 (East Municipal Wharf) is 1,600 feet long and 86 feet wide at the outer end. Depths alongside the outer east and west sides are 24 feet. Freight and supplies are trucked directly onto the wharf. A 2-ton hoist is available. Municipal Wharf #1, also called Fisherman's Wharf, 300 yards west, is lined with restaurants and shops. A crane hoist lifts boats, up to 8 tons, for ordinary repairs.

For safe navigation, the U.S. Department of Transportation and the U.S. Coast Guard mark all waters by the lateral system of buoyage. California's waterway-marking system employs buoys and signs with distinctive standard shapes to show regulatory or advisory information. These markers are white with black letters and orange borders. They signify speed zones, restricted areas, danger areas, or general information. Hanging on to a beacon or tying up to any navigation buoy (except mooring buoys) is prohibited.

Red buoys, always even numbered, are kept to the starboard (right) side when proceeding from the open sea into port. Likewise, green buoys, always odd numbered, are kept to the port (left) side. Conversely, when proceeding toward the sea or leaving port, red buoys are kept to the port side and green buoys to the starboard side.

Port-hand buoys are painted green with fixed or flashing green lights. Starboard-hand buoys are painted red, with fixed or flashing red lights. Safe-water buoys, also called midchannel or fairway buoys, and approach buoys are painted with red and white vertical stripes and have flashing lights. Preferred channel, or junction, buoys are painted with red and green horizontal bands and have flashing lights. Special markers (traffic separation, anchorage areas, dredging, fishnet areas, etc.) are painted yellow and have a fixed or flashing light (if lighted).

Public Boat Ramps and Marinas

Monterey Marina
Commercial Wharf #2, Monterey
(831) 646–3950, www.monterey.org

Monterey Marina, open year-round, is between Fisherman's Wharf and Wharf #2. There are two concrete public ramps with two lanes each, an anchorage and buoying area, and more than 400 slips with dockside electricity. The wharf at the marina also has restrooms and benches. Fishing licenses, rod rentals, bait and tackle, marine supplies, boat maintenance, boat and motor rentals, motor parts, and repairs can all be obtained at the marina.

Breakwater Cove Marina
32 Cannery Row, Monterey
(831) 373–7857,
www.montereybayboatworks.com

This modern, well-maintained facility is open daily from 8:00 A.M. to 5:00 P.M. There are 75 slips complete with power, water, and telephone hookups. Guest berthing is available for vessels of up to 120 feet. Restrooms, hot showers, laundry facilities, and mail and fax services are also available. The fuel dock has both gasoline and diesel oil. Monterey Bay Boatworks at the marina provides expert repair in wood, metal, fibreglass, or cement. Paint jobs and engine repairs are additional services offered. A 70-ton travel lift or strapless-keel lift system, a launching ramp, and marine supplies are available. You'll find a convenience store and a picnic area as well. Breakwater Cove Marina monitors VHF channels 16 and 67.

Marine Supply Stores

The Compass Boating
and Fishing Supplies
Commercial Wharf #2, Monterey
(831) 647–9222

This convenient store at the foot of the harbor carries boating supplies and equipment including hardware, spare parts, engines, pump hoses, rope, and cordage. It also carries everything you'll need for fishing.

Quarter Deck Marine Supply
32 Cannery Row, Monterey
(831) 375–6754,
www.montereybayboatworks.com

At Breakwater Cove, this full-service marine chandlery serves both the pleasure and commercial boating community. It provides complete painting, electrical, plumbing, and rigging systems. The Quarter Deck is an authorized dealer for Interlux and Z-Spar paints; Perko, Jabsco, and Rule pumps; Samson Line; and many other marine supplies. If it's not on the shelf, they can usually have it by noon the next day.

Boat Sales, Repairs, and Fuel

Gateway Outboard Service
490 Orange Avenue, Sand City
(831) 394–0126

Established in 1969, Gateway sells marine hardware, parts, and accessories. It is an authorized dealer for Johnson, OMC, and MerCruiser. Electronics can be special ordered and usually arrive within two days. Gateway also offers outboard sales and service for Yamaha, Mercury, Honda, and Mariner motors.

Monterey Bay Boatworks
32 Cannery Row, Monterey
(831) 375–6921,
www.montereybayboatworks.com

This facility at Breakwater Cove offers full-service haul outs and boat repair. It offers restoration and repairs for both motor and sailing vessels weighing up to 70 tons. A special keel lift is available for wood vessels. Services include sandblasting, spray painting, fiberglass repair, welding, and fabrication. A clean concrete yard has power, water, and compressed air in all work areas.

Monterey Mariner In Board-Out Board
Coast Guard Pier, 32 Cannery Row, Monterey
(831) 655–3207

Specializing in small and large diesel engines, this company offers sales and service of Mariner, MerCruiser, and Volvo Penta powered inboard/outboard engines.

In Case of Emergency on the Water

Recognized distress signals include a continuously sounding fog horn, a gun fired at one-minute intervals, Mayday by radio, radiotelegraph alarm, or a radiotelephone alarm. You could also hold your arms out and wave them up and down if you are within sight of another vessel.

One danger signal to remember is the sound of five or more short blasts sounded in rapid succession. This indicates a risk of collision or the intent of the other vessel is not understood. A short blast is one second in length.

The nonemergency phone number for the U.S. Coast Guard is (831) 647–7300.

Insiders' Tip

To get a copy of the free California Home Study Boating Safety Course, write to the California Department of Boating and Waterways, Publications, 2000 Evergreen Street, Suite 100, Sacramento, CA 95815-3888, or visit www.ca.gov. The course can be completed at your own pace, and a state certificate is sent once the optional examination is taken.

Fishing

Recreational fishing is a popular activity on Monterey Bay. You have the choice of spearfishing, hook-and-line fishing from wharves and the shore, or chartering a boat and fishing offshore. Bottom-fishing is very popular because it is a relatively simple method of angling, and a variety of fish will take bait on or near the bottom. For those who would rather fish by ocean trolling, group charters are available from Fisherman's Wharf, so you can try your luck reeling in salmon, rockfish, mackerel, perch, or lingcod. Fishing hours on the Monterey Bay are from one hour before sunrise to one hour after sunset.

Licenses

Anyone older than 16 years of age must have a fishing license to fish from the shore or offshore from a boat. Fishing from a California ocean pier, such as Municipal Wharf #2, is excepted; pier fishing in California does not require a license.

You can get an annual or single-day fishing license from the following stores. Call the store or visit www.dfg.ca.gov for license fees. Licenses can also be purchased on-line.

The Compass Boating and Fishing Supply, Monterey Marina, (831) 647–9222

Longs Drugs, 686 Lighthouse Avenue, Monterey, (831) 655–5404
2170 North Fremont Street, Monterey, (831) 373–6134
6 Crossroads Mall, Carmel, (831) 624–0915

K-mart, 1590 Canyon Del Rey Road, Monterey, (831) 394–6523

Big-5, 1300 Del Monte Shopping Center, Monterey, (831) 375–8800

Department of Fish and Game, 20 Lower Ragsdale Road, Suite 100, Monterey, (831) 649–2870

Sportfishing Regulations

In general, one person can take up to 20 finfish in any combination of species, with not more than 10 of any one species. When fishing offshore, and filleting your catch, please note that unless otherwise indicated in the regulations book, each fillet must have a one-inch square patch of skin remaining. For detailed information about sportfishing regulations, the publication "California Sport Fishing Regulations" is provided when you purchase your fishing license. You can also request one in advance by writing the California Department of Fish and Game, 1416 Ninth Street, Sacramento, CA 95814, by visiting www.dfg.ca.gov, or by calling (916) 653–7664.

Guides and Charters

Chris' Sport Fishing
48 Fisherman's Wharf #1, Monterey
(831) 375–5951, www.chrissfishing.com

Chris' has four large craft used for daily fishing trips: the 70-foot *New Holiday,* 58-foot *Check Mate,* 56-foot *Tornado,* and 55-foot *Holiday.* These diesel-powered, government-inspected vessels are equipped with fish finders, ship-to-shore radios, radar, and comfortable deck lounges. Chris' rents rods, offers fish cleaning, sells one-day fishing licenses, and provides free bait and ice. Individual ticket prices range from $30 to $100 depending on the specific tour (cod, salmon, and albacore fishing trips are featured). Group charters for up to 20 people are offered, call or visit the Web site for exact rates and reservation information.

Monterey Sport Fishing and Whale Watching Cruises
96 Fisherman's Wharf #1, Monterey
(831) 372–2203

Guaranteed uncrowded fishing trips are promised aboard the 75-foot *Magnum Force* or 70-foot *Top Gun.* The wide boats have enclosed lounges, snack bar, and state-of-the-art electronics and are U.S. Coast Guard inspected. The captains are Coast Guard licensed. Private group charters are available by appointment only. The boats can accommodate both large and small groups on fishing trips for salmon, albacore, lingcod, snapper, or rock cod. Individual fare for a total package (rod rental, tackle, a one-day fishing license, and a fish bag) is around $40 per person on weekdays and a few dollars more on weekends. Box lunches are available upon request. You can order a videotape or still photograph to capture the moment you land the big one. Services provided include fish cleaning and freezing. Reservations are recommended.

Randy's Fishing and Whale Watching Trips
66 Fisherman's Wharf #1, Monterey
(831) 372–7440

Randy's three, fully insured and Coast Guard–approved boats are available for fishing trips and private charters. Rates for a deep-sea cod fishing trip on a 65-foot boat for an adult are $35 weekdays or weekends. Children age 16 and younger pay $20. Daily salmon fishing trips cost $45. Group charters for cod-fishing trips for up to 17 people start at $525. Salmon-fishing trips for up to 13 people start at $630. Randy's rents fishing rods and tackle and offers fish cleaning. It also sells fishing licenses, bait, sack lunches, and ice.

Sam's Sportfishing
Fisherman's Wharf #1, Monterey
(831) 372–0577

Sam's offers deep-sea fishing trips aboard three Coast Guard-Certified and approved boats. It has fishing rods for rent, tackle, fish bags, bait, fishing licenses, and free ice. Fish cleaning is also available. Sam's can accommodate any size group up to 50 people. All-day, deep-sea cod-fishing trips on the *Star of Monterey* are $28 for adults on weekdays and $32 on weekends. Children age 12 and younger pay $15 on weekdays and $20 on weekends. Salmon and albacore fishing trips are also available in season. Sam's welcomes beginning anglers.

Outfitters and Bait and Tackle Shops

Big 5 Sporting Goods
1300 Del Monte Center, Monterey
(831) 375–8800

This national chain carries a variety of tackle, lures, fishing licenses, and related fishing equipment and supplies.

The Compass Boating and Fishing Supply
Commercial Wharf #2, Monterey
(831) 647–9222

The Compass is a one-stop shop for all your fishing needs. It sells fishing licenses, lures, and bait (anchovies and squid) and rents poles and tackle.

Gone Fishin'
1675 Contra Costa Street, Sand City
(831) 899–1111

An unlikely location—upstairs from an auto repair shop in landlocked Sand City—is home to one of the best fishing supply stores on the Monterey Peninsula. Rods and reels for fresh and saltwater fishing from top manufacturers are available along with lures, tackle, and accessories. And Gone Fishin' is a great place to swap stories about "the one that got away."

Sailing

Charters

Carrera Sailing
66 Fisherman's Wharf #1, Monterey
(831) 375–0648

Monterey Bay Sanctuary sailing and nature excursions in the Monterey Bay are offered at $25 per person for a two-hour sail. Sunset cruises, offered April through October, cost the same. Private charters suited to your needs can also be arranged for special occasions. All charters are aboard the 30-foot custom Capo 30 sloop *Carrera,* a fast offshore cruiser racer. Reservations are required.

***Chardonnay II* Bay Cruises**
790 Mariner Park Way, Dock FF, Santa Cruz
(831) 423–1213, www.chardonnay.com

The *Chardonnay II* is a beautiful 70-foot sailing yacht available for cruises or private charter. Accommodating up to 49 passengers, the boat sails out of the Santa Cruz Yacht Harbor. There are many regularly scheduled theme cruises to choose from including whale-watching, astrology, winetasting, brewmaster, and more. Reservations can be made by phone or on-line.

Sailing Courses

Carrera Sailing School
66 Fisherman's Wharf #1, Monterey
(831) 375-0648

Since 1994 Carrera has been providing basic to advanced sailing school programs. The U.S. Sailing Keelboat Certification is also offered. Practice cruises are made to Moss Landing or Santa Cruz.

Monterey Peninsula Yacht Club
Municipal Wharf #2, Monterey
(831) 372-9686, www.mpyc.com

This yacht club offers a junior sailing program during the summer months. It also has sailing leagues throughout the year for high school students.

Whale-Watching and Harbor Tours

Chris' Sport Fishing
48 Fisherman's Wharf #1, Monterey
(831) 375-5951

Chris' offers daily whale-watching cruises from December through March. Two-hour narrated trips, Monterey Bay Marine Sanctuary tours, and private group charters are available. Call ahead for reservations and rates.

Glass Bottom Boat Tours
90 Fisherman's Wharf #1, Monterey
(831) 372-7150

This company offers calm-water cruises in a fully enclosed glass-bottom boat around Monterey Bay Harbor. Cruises depart frequently throughout the day from Fisherman's Wharf. Observe sea lions, seals, fish, otters, and other marine life in their natural habitat. The fully narrated, 25-minute tours are under $7.00 for adults and under $5.00 for children younger than 12. Individual, group, or private parties are welcome. They also offer whale-watching, marine mammal, and Bay tours. Call for availability, reservations, and rates.

Monterey Bay Whale Watch
84 Fisherman's Wharf #1, Monterey
(831) 375-4658,
www.montereybaywhalewatching.com

These whale-watching trips depart from Sam's Sportsfishing on Fisherman's Wharf. During the six-hour trips you'll observe a variety of marine mammals and seabirds, while you're accompanied by a marine biologist who narrates and answers questions during the excursion. Common sightings include both humpback and blue whales; Pacific white-sided, Risso's, bottlenosed, and common dolphins; and harbor and Dall's porpoise. Trips are offered May through November on Tuesday, Thursday, and Sunday. Winter and spring trips (December to April) are three-and-a-half hours in length. Call or visit the Web site for fares and departure times.

Monterey Sport Fishing and Whale Watching Cruises
96 Fisherman's Wharf #1, Monterey
(831) 372-2203

Climb aboard and enjoy a two-hour whale-watching cruise during the migration of California gray whales. There are seven departures daily, December through April. Tours cost under $20 for adults, less for children age 12 and younger. Enjoy a three- to four-hour cruise during the summer (June through September) in the search for blue whales, orcas, humpbacks, minkes, dolphins, marine birds, and more. Three cruises depart daily. Rates are higher during the summer. Call for exact rates and departure times.

Randy's Fishing and Whale Watching Trips
66 Fisherman's Wharf #1, Monterey
(831) 372-7440

The fully narrated two-hour cruise provides a chance to see the magnificent California gray whale. Six daily departures on weekends (four on weekdays) are available from December through March. Tours start around $15 for adults, $12 for children age 12 and younger. Four-hour and all-day group charters are also available. Call for rates and availability.

Sanctuary Cruises
"A" Dock, Moss Landing Harbor
(831) 643–0128, www.sanctuarycruises.com

Operating out of Moss Landing Harbor, Sanctuary Cruises is owned and operated by dedicated whale and ocean preservationists. The *Princess of Whales,* a comfortable, 149-passenger power catamaran departs Tuesday through Sunday for four- to five-hour cruises year-round. She has a full galley with freshly prepared hot foods and beverages. The *Sanctuary* is a more intimate boat, carrying 39 passengers. Detailed narratives and marine mammal orientations are presented on each trip, with an emphasis on conservation and preservation. Bookings can be made on-line or by phone.

Sea Life Tours/*Baywatch* Cruises
90 Fisherman's Wharf #1, Monterey
(831) 372–7151, www.sealifetours.com

Sea-life tours of the Monterey Bay Marine Sanctuary and seasonal (December through March) whale-watching cruises are narrated by marine biologists on the distinctive yellow-and-red *Baywatch.* In the high season, there are up to eight departures per day. Reservations can be made on-line or by phone.

Diving and Snorkeling

The Monterey Bay is a world-renowned diving spot. Giant kelp forests, sea otters, sea lions, and an abundance of other marine life make the Monterey Bay a fascinating place for diving. If an emergency arises, the region's only hyperbaric chamber is on the Peninsula.

Dive Sites

Divers can swim out from several beaches along the shoreline or launch from a dive boat in the Bay. One of the best spots for beginners (or for those taking their first dive in the Monterey Bay) is the breakwater at **San Carlos Beach,** adjacent to the Coast Guard Pier in Monterey. The beach's safe currents allow for easy entry and exit. Diving here you'll see huge boulders; a variety of fish, anemones, starfish; and maybe an otter or sea lion.

Lovers Point Beach in Pacific Grove is another popular spot with easy beach access and lots of parking.

Divers of all levels will find Point Lobos one of the best diving spots. **Whaler's Cove** and **Bluefish Cove** provide plenty of chances to view sea otters and sea lions. Only a limited number of divers are allowed into the reserve each day. To make reservations, call (831) 624–8413 or visit www.pointlobos.com.

Carmel's **Monastery Beach** is one of the region's most popular dive sites. It is a good place to hook up with a dive buddy. However, the deep water, a steep drop-off, and severe undertow make this an area limited to the very experienced diver (see our "Beaches" section in this chapter).

Dive Centers

Aquarius Dive Shop
2040 Del Monte Avenue, Monterey
(831) 375–1933
32 Cannery Row, Monterey
(831) 375–6605, www.aquariusdivers.com

Open since 1970, Aquarius is one of the locals' favorites. The shop is an authorized dealer for Scubapro, USD, and Body Glove merchandise. A full scuba kit, which includes all gear and one air tank, rents for around $60, with consecutive days at half-price. Rental gear for snorkeling is $35, with consecutive days at half-price.

Bamboo Reef
614 Lighthouse Avenue, Monterey
(831) 372–1685

Bamboo Reef is diving-equipment headquarters for sales, rentals, service, and instruction. It has the West Coast's largest compressor so there's no waiting in line for air refills. It also offers scuba tours and a certified diving school. All gear is available for rental individually, or a full scuba kit, including one tank of air, rents for about $65 per day. Snorkeling gear costs about $30 per day.

Monterey Bay Dive Center
225 Cannery Row, Monterey
(800) 607–2822

598 Foam Street, Monterey
(831) 655-1818, www.mbdc.to

The Dive Center has a retail shop at the Cannery Row location and a training facility on Foam Street. It provides equipment rentals including a full scuba kit ($60 per day) and a full snorkeling kit ($35 per day). It also offers instruction with 16 different classes. It can handle equipment repairs too.

The Dive Center offers guided underwater tours for up to four divers, night dives, and guided snorkeling tours. Tours can be scheduled any day of the week, and a 24-hour advance notice is appreciated. Call or visit the Web site for costs.

Dive Boats

Monterey Express
Operates from the City of Monterey Marina
(888) 422-2999, www.montereyexpress.com

Rates vary depending on the number of divers and length of dive. Call or visit the Web site for booking information.

Surfing

The most popular surfing spots in the Monterey area are **Asilomar** and **Lovers Point,** both in Pacific Grove. Both beaches have easy access to the water and plenty of parking. **Carmel Beach** gets its fair share of surfers, too, but parking is limited, especially during the summer months. See the listings for these beaches at the beginning of this chapter. The following retail shop provides all the necessary equipment for riding the perfect wave.

Sunshine Freestyle Surf and Sport
443 Lighthouse Avenue, Monterey
(831) 375-5015

Surfboards, swimwear, and wet suits are all in stock at Sunshine Freestyle. Service and rentals of surfing gear are offered as well.

Swimming

The water temperature is typically a chilly 55 degrees in the Monterey Bay. If you're willing to experience the invigoratingly cold waters, the best swimming beaches are in the protected cove at **Lovers Point** and along the shoreline of **Monterey State Beach.** See the listings for these beaches at the beginning of this chapter. Wet suits are highly recommended! See the diving and surfing listings for wet-suit sales and rentals.

Kayaking

If an up-close and personal view of marine life along the coastline sounds like your kind of adventure, you'll rate kayaking on the Monterey Bay as one of the area's most enjoyable attractions. The rugged coastline and chance meetings with aquatic birds, whales, sea lions, sea otters, and other inhabitants of the kelp beds provide a unique opportunity for exploration.

Adventures by the Sea
299 Cannery Row, Monterey
(831) 373-1807
201 Alvarado Mall, Monterey
(831) 648-7253
Lovers Point Beach, Pacific Grove
(831) 373-1807

Explore the wonders of Monterey Bay in ocean kayaks. Kayak tours include all the necessary gear, paddling instruction, and a marine wildlife orientation. The docent-led two- to three-hour tours are $45, with an option to use the equipment after the tour is finished. All-day kayak rentals including gear and instruction are $25.

Monterey Bay Kayaks
693 Del Monte Avenue, Monterey
(800) 649-5357
2390 Highway 1, Moss Landing
(800) 649-5357, www.montereybaykayaks.com

Natural history tours with professional naturalists and marine biologists are recommended for novices. The interpretive tours provide an introduction to the various ecosystems of Monterey Bay. Tours last three and a half hours and are available (by reservation) on weekdays and weekends for around $50.

Personal classes are offered to develop your skills in paddling techniques, boat

Asilomar State Beach and Lovers Point Park are favorite surfing areas. PHOTO: JANE MORBA

control, rescues, surf zone, etc. Classes are offered every first and third Saturday by reservation only. Basic Skills 1 and 2 classes are offered in closed-deck single kayaks. Each class is around $90.

Rental of open kayaks for good swimmers requires no paddling experience. Closed-deck kayak rental requires the basic skills two-day sea kayaking class (or equivalent). The rate per person for open kayaks, including all gear and a wet suit, is around $30. The fiberglass boat (closed-deck kayak) rate is about $35 per person.

Monterey Bay Kayaks is one of the area's largest outfitters in sea kayaking. It carries more than 50 different kayak models, a wide range of accessories, clothing, and hardware. The facility includes an on-the-beach location, plenty of parking, changing rooms, and outside hot showers.

Paddle Boating and Canoeing

El Estero Boating
Lake El Estero, Monterey
(831) 375-1484

Paddle around Lake El Estero aboard a paddleboat, kayak, or canoe. El Estero Boating rents boats for under $10 per half-hour, a little more than $10 per hour. You'll see ducks, coots, sea gulls, and a variety of other seabirds as you tour the lake by boat.

Motorized Personal Watercraft

A motorized personal watercraft is defined as any motorized vessel less than 15 feet in length that can exceed 17 miles per hour and can hold up to two people. The term includes, but is not limited to, JetSkis, wet bikes, surf jets, miniature speed boats, air boats, and hovercraft.

To help protect the sensitive marine life and its habitats of the Monterey Bay Marine Sanctuary (the entire Monterey Bay), it is unlawful to operate motorized personal watercraft outside the access route and the designated zone. Launching is permitted only at the Monterey Harbor, and you must proceed directly to the operating zone. Look for signs posted at the harbor launch explaining where you can go and the bright yellow buoys and navigation aids marking the area.

As a personal watercraft rider, you are also considered a boater (these craft are defined as Class A inboard boats by the U.S. Coast Guard) and are required to follow most boating regulations.

Speeding can be dangerous to marine life and people. Avoid areas concentrated with wildlife, such as large gatherings of seabirds resting on the water or groups of marine animals. Minimize disturbance by riding slowly near sensitive habitats such as kelp forests.

Protecting the Bay

Pollution

California state law prohibits dumping garbage into navigable waters or loading garbage on a vessel with intent of dumping it. It is illegal to dump plastic, paper, rags, glass, food, metal, crockery, lining, or packing materials that float into the Bay.

Plastic in particular is a hazard to marine life. Birds, fish, and even sea lions will die when a six-pack holder gets stuck around their necks and bodies. Some animals will eat plastic, which makes them feel full, causing them to slowly starve to death. Plastic debris in the water can cause life-threatening situations for boaters by fouling propellers and clogging engine-intake systems. This can result in disabled vessels and expensive repairs.

Plastic pollution has become an international issue. So prevalent, in fact, that the International Treaty to Prevent Pollution from Ships was created to address the plastic-pollution problem. The treaty prohibits the dumping of plastic into the water. All boats longer than 26 feet must display, in a prominent place where the crew and passengers can read it, an informational placard on the subject of these prohibitions. The placards can be purchased at marine supply dealers or can be requested free of charge from the Department of Boating and Waterways, 1629 S Street, Sacramento, CA 95814, or on-line at www.ca.gov.

As a boater you can become a part of the solution to marine pollution by helping to keep our bay and its beaches clean. Develop a simple vessel trash plan by separating plastics and storing trash on board. Dispose of it in dumpsters at port, recycling whenever possible. You can further help by always using care when fueling, changing oil, or repairing your boat.

Residents of Monterey County take pride in their Bay. Since the mid-1980s, an annual coastal cleanup has taken place around the Monterey Bay. This data collection effort supports legislation protecting our ocean and dunes. The event is sponsored by numerous local businesses, and all necessary materials are provided to volunteers.

Environmental Service Organizations

Friends of the Sea Otter
2150 Garden Road, Monterey
(831) 373–2747, www.seaotters.org

This organization is dedicated to the rare and threatened southern sea otter as well as sea otters throughout the north Pacific range and all sea otter habitats. It provides educational materials and gives presentations to schools and community groups. See our Close-up in the Shopping chapter for more information about the Friends of the Sea Otter Education Retail Center and Friends of the Sea Otter Foundation.

Save Our Shores
2222 East Cliff Drive, Suite 5A, Santa Cruz
(831) 462–5660, www.saveourshores.org

Save Our Shores is dedicated to the preservation of the environmental integrity of the Monterey Bay Marine Sanctuary through education, policy research, and citizen action. It provides volunteer opportunities through a Sanctuary Stewards Program, The Sanctuary Watch, and a used oil-pad program. Volunteering as a Sanctuary Steward involves an extensive training program, but the positions require only enthusiasm and a willingness to serve.

Golf

Courses
Driving Range
Golf Shops

Many visitors to the Monterey Peninsula have only one thing in mind: golf. Sure, they'll enjoy the scenery, the world-class restaurants, and the historic attractions. But not far from their center of attention at all times are those little white balls and long expanses of green.

It's no secret that the Monterey Peninsula is a golf mecca. Names like Pebble Beach, Old Del Monte, Spyglass Hill, and Spanish Bay are whispered with reverence. Many players wait their whole lives for a chance to play Pebble. Nongolfers may think it's crazy to spend hundreds of dollars for the experience of chasing a little white ball around the sand dunes and through the woods, but for devotees Pebble is a dream come true that spawns a lifetime of memories. And afterwards the shots get longer, the putts truer, and the course more challenging and spectacular with each telling of the tale.

In this chapter we'll look at a host of public and semiprivate courses in and around the Monterey Peninsula. Some of the area's most familiar names, such as Cypress Point and Pasadera, aren't listed here because if you're not a member, chances are you won't be able to play. But in this chapter you're likely to find one or two unfamiliar names that offer an exciting and challenging round of golf during your stay on the Peninsula.

Before we start touring the courses, let's go over a few ground rules. Yardage for each course listed is from the men's white tees whenever they're available. The fees we list include the price for 18 holes and the cost of a cart. In most cases, carts are optional, and you can shave $15 to $30 off the price if you're willing to hoof it around the course on foot.

Green fees, ratings, and course conditions, of course, are subject to change. It is recommended that you schedule your tee times a week in advance, though you might be able to get on the less notable courses the day you decide to hit the links. For the Pebble Beach courses, make your plans as early as possible since prime times can be booked months in advance.

As a rule, the elements of nature will have a big impact on your golf game, particularly on the coastal courses. The rainy season will add a few water hazards, but most courses remain playable through the winter. Wind can be a huge factor year-round. You'll notice that a number of courses offer discount twilight fees, often as early as 1:00 P.M. But be aware that the wind typically picks up in the afternoon and can send your drives soaring and diving in unexpected directions on blustery days. For the best conditions, locals recommend an early or midmorning start. That being said, let's tee up the ball and get going. Here are the popular Peninsula courses to choose from.

Courses

Monterey

Bayonet and Blackhorse Golf Courses
1 McClure Way, Seaside
(831) 899–7271, www.bayonetblackhorse.com

These two 18-hole courses at the former Fort Ord north of Monterey on Highway 1 are open to the public, providing a great alternative for local and visiting golfers. The two courses are set among the sandy hills and dunes overlooking Monterey Bay so they have excellent drainage and are open and very playable every day, rain or shine. Bayonet in particular is proving to be a local favorite. The par 72, 6496-yard course provides an excellent challenge. The long 631-yard, par 5 fourth hole and the 462-yard, par 4 fifth, with its uphill approach to a well-guarded green, present a skill-testing one-two punch. A round of golf costs $70 Monday through

Thursday and $95 Friday through Sunday. Carts are mandatory on Saturdays and Sundays before noon. Ask about reduced twilight rates.

Blackhorse is a 6175-yard, par 72 course. While Bayonet has the reputation as the better course, Blackhorse is one of the Peninsula's best-kept secrets for an affordable and enjoyable round. The views from the hills overlooking the Bay are spectacular, and the course presents a series of short but tough par 4 doglegs. Fees are $70 Monday through Thursday and $95 Friday through Sunday, with carts mandatory on weekends before noon.

Bayonet and Blackhorse share a driving range ($2.00 per bucket), a well-stocked pro shop, and the Bayonet Bar & Grill. Al Luna is the course pro, and golf lessons are available.

Del Monte Golf Course
1300 Sylvan Road, Monterey
(831) 373–270, www.pebblebeach.com

Now more than a century old, the Del Monte Golf Course behind the Monterey Hyatt is the oldest continuously operating golf course west of the Mississippi. And it's a classic, too, designed by Charles Maud in 1897. Owned by Pebble Beach Company, Del Monte plays 6069 yards of wide fairways lined with pine, oak, and cypress trees that make for a demanding par 72. The back nine features the 502-yard, par 5 13th hole with a tee shot over a deep ravine, followed immediately by the great 217-yard, par 3 14th with the green securely guarded by two imposing bunkers. Fees for Hyatt and Pebble Beach Resort guests are $80; nonguests can play for $90. Reduced twilight fees are available, so inquire about seasonal rates and hours. Carts are always optional. Neal Allen is the course pro, and group or individual lessons are available through the Pebble Beach Golf Academy. The Del Monte Golf Shop has great gift ideas for the duffers back home, and the Del Monte Grill serves great breakfasts and lunches in a beautiful setting. Locals will want to know about the annual membership plan, which provides reduced greens fees and tournament fun for a yearly fee.

Laguna Seca Golf Club
10520 York Road, Monterey
(831) 373–3701, www.lagunasecagolf.com

Known as the Peninsula's "Sunshine Course," Laguna Seca is a few miles inland from Monterey along the Monterey-Salinas Highway (Highway 68). Designed by the team of Robert Trent Jones Sr. and Jr., the 5726-yard, par 71 layout is noted for its strategic bunkering. You'll need every club in the bag and every trick in the book to master this oak-studded and hilly course. Most challenging is the 511-yard, par 5 15th hole. It's a dogleg right, often straight into a stiff wind, with water hazards to the left, right, and front of the green. Fees are $65 daily with a twilight rate of $35 after 1:00 P.M. Carts are optional. The course pro is Jeff Hardy, and golf instruction is available. The clubhouse features a nice golf shop and a large restaurant with a full bar. Locals should ask about the many membership plans available that include privileges at Rancho Cañada in Carmel Valley.

Monterey Pines Golf Course
1250 Garden Road, Monterey
(831) 656–2167

Formerly known as the U.S. Navy Golf Course, this well-maintained course is open to the public. Next to the Monterey Fairgrounds on Garden Road, it's right in town and provides a great golf value, especially for active and retired military personnel. The par 69, 5675-yard course makes for a relatively pleasant, low-stress round. But before you conclude it's too gentle, get through the 18th hole, a four-handicap, 540-yard par 5 that may leave you heading to the clubhouse a little humbled. Active or retired military can play weekdays (Monday through Thursday) for $12 and weekends (Friday through Sunday) for $14. For Department of Defense personnel, the fees are $14 weekdays and $18 weekends. For you civilians, it's $20 weekdays and $28 weekends. Carts are optional. The course pro is David Arancio, and lessons are available. There's a driving range ($1.50 and $3.00 buckets), a snack bar that serves generous freshly made sandwiches, and a small golf shop.

Pacific Grove

Pacific Grove Municipal Golf Links
77 Asilomar Boulevard, Pacific Grove
(831) 648–5777, www2.ci.pacific-grove.ca.us

Known affectionately as "the poor man's Pebble Beach," Pacific Grove Municipal Golf Course is right on the northern edge of the Peninsula, under the watchful eye of the Point Pinos Lighthouse. This 5571-yard, par 70 course is actually two distinctly different sets of nines. The front nine is inland and offers nice green fairways, a few towering pines and oaks, and an achievable par on a solid day of driving and putting. But then it's time to cross Asilomar Boulevard and face the often-brutal coastal back nine. The 10th hole teases you with a short and easy par 3, but then 11 heads directly seaward toward sand dunes, ice plant, thin fairways, and, if you're really lucky, howling gusts off the Pacific. You battle the bare elements of Point Pinos through the 16th and then have the pleasure of teeing off on the 17th over a small lake to a sloped green framed by thick cypress trees. A gently uphill par 4 finishes the course as you head back to the clubhouse. Greens fees are $32 Monday through Thursday and $38 Friday through Sunday. Twilight rates after 3:00 P.M. are $20. Junior rates of $15 are available Monday through Thursday for golfers age 17 and under. Carts are optional. Reservations can be made a maximum of seven days in advance. The course pro is Peter Vitarisi, and the pro shop and snack bar are conveniently situated between the first and ninth holes. A driving range is available, with balls at $3.00 a bucket.

Carmel

Carmel Valley Ranch
1 Old Ranch Road, Carmel
(831) 626–2510

Carmel Valley Ranch is a semiprivate course for members and guests of the Carmel Valley Resort, with an extensive reciprocal program for members of other clubs worldwide. The 5563-yard, par 70 course is situated in the usually sunny Carmel Valley. The valley and hill terrain offer some great challenges, including the

A small lake in front and a grove of cypress trees to the rear guard the 17th green at the Pacific Grove Municipal Golf Links. PHOTO: TOM OWENS

402-yard, par 4 11th hole, with a 500-foot elevation tee looking down to a choice of two landing areas. Then you have to guide your approach shot to a small green protected by a pair of nasty bunkers. The short 138-yard, par 3 13th also has an elevated tee, but this time it's a blind tee shot to a green hidden below a grove of oak trees. Guests of the resort play for $150, while nonguests pay $180. Carts are required and included in the greens fee. Mike Fish is the course pro, and five instructors provide lessons. A driving range is available to players free of charge. A nice pro shop and a great club grill are also on site.

The Golf Club at Quail Lodge
8205 Valley Greens Drive, Carmel
(831) 624–2779

The semiprivate Golf Club at Quail Lodge is open to members, resort guests, and members of other resorts that share a reciprocal program. The 6140-yard, par 71 course is set it a beautiful location just 3.5 miles inland from the mouth of Carmel Valley. Among the favorite holes is the 161-yard, par 3 17th hole (which, by the way, provides a great view of Doris Day's home). All you need to do is hit an hourglass-shaped green surrounded on three sides by water and guarded by two mean front bunkers. Try it, you'll like it. Both the front and back nine come back to the clubhouse, where you find a nice pro shop and snack bar. Greens fees for guests of Quail Lodge are $115. Reciprocal club members can play for $125 on Monday through Thursday and $150 on weekends. Twilight rates apply after 3:00 P.M. All fees include the cart, which is mandatory. The fee also includes a small basket of balls for the driving range. Extra baskets of various sizes are also available for a small charge. The driving range offers buckets of balls for $5.00 and $9.00 to those just practicing. The course pro is Dave Anderson, and Quail Lodge is the home of world-renowned teaching pro Ben Doyle.

Rancho Cañada Golf Club
Carmel Valley Road, Carmel
(831) 624–0111, (800) 536–9459,
www.carmel-golf.com

Rancho Cañada Golf Club in Carmel Valley offers 36 holes of truly championship golf designed by Robert Dean Putman. The 6006-yard, par 71 West Course is a

The golf course at Carmel Valley Ranch presents majestic views and challenging holes. PHOTO: ROSS ANDRÉSON

beautiful and challenging layout. The extremely tight and narrow fairway on the 372-yard, par 4 15th hole is indicative of the challenges that await you. (As Sam Snead once quipped about the 15th, "I didn't know we'd have to play that hole single file.") Greens fees for the West Course are $80 daily, with a 1:00 P.M. twilight rate of $45. The 5832-yard East Course may play second fiddle to the West, but it still provides an extremely challenging round, particularly on the back nine. You cross the Carmel River no fewer than five times completing this par 71 course. Of particular note is the 192-yard, par 3 13th hole that features a daring elevated tee shot across the river to the green below. Greens fees for the East Course are $65 and $35 for twilight hours. Carts are optional at both courses. If you plan on playing Rancho Cañada as few as five or six times a year, there are a number of annual membership packages that reduce the per-round cost significantly for play at either course as well as Laguna Seca in Monterey. Rancho Cañada has a nice driving range ($5.00 per bucket), an extensive golf shop, and a comfortable restaurant. Mark Stoddard is the course pro, and lessons are available.

Pebble Beach

The Links at Spanish Bay
2700 17–Mile Drive, Pebble Beach
(831) 647–7495, (800) 654–9300,
www.pebblebeach.com

Those of you who dream of the challenge of an authentic Scottish links course will love The Links at Spanish Bay. Robert Trent Jones Jr., Tom Watson, and Sandy Tatum designed the 6078-yard, par 72 course. This is a demanding course with 20-foot dunes, rugged native vegetation, and sand, sand, sand. Memorable holes include the 571-yard 14th, with a spectacular coastline view from the elevated tee, and the 414-yard 17th, which follows the gorgeous shoreline. On 17, you're tested with a 180-yard drive to an island fairway surrounded by trouble. Make that shot, and you approach the green over hilly dunes and six awaiting bunkers.

Fees are $210 with complimentary cart for Pebble Beach Resort guests and $235 for nonguests. Pebble Beach and Spanish Bay residents and club members pay $210. Carts are optional. Be sure to ask about the special twilight rate. The 24,000-square-foot clubhouse is the home of The Links pro shop, locker rooms, and a restaurant that overlooks the first fairway and serves breakfast and lunch. The course pro is Rich Cosand, and the Pebble Beach Golf Academy provides individual and group lessons.

Pebble Beach Golf Links
17-Mile Drive, Pebble Beach
(831) 624–6611, (800) 654–9300,
www.pebblebeach.com

Welcome to golf heaven. There's probably not much we have to say to the serious golf nut about Pebble Beach Golf Links except "go play." Anyone who's ever watched the then–Crosby Clambake, now the AT&T Pebble Beach National Pro-Am, knows all about this world-famous course. But let's cover a few basics anyway. Designed by Jack Neville and Douglas Grant (and first played in 1919), it's a 6357-yard, par 72 course. But the numbers don't come close to telling it all. How do you describe the feeling of standing on the seventh tee? You're looking down 100 yards, seaward, to a postage-stamp-size, trapped-framed green perched on a rocky point that, depending on the wind, might take either a wedge or a 4-iron to reach. How do you measure the thrill of standing on a cliff above the Pacific Ocean ready to launch an approach shot 190 yards over the sea itself to the small eighth green surrounded by traps on three sides? Or of teeing up on the 209-yard, par 3 17th hole at Stillwater Cove, home to two of the most famous shots in U.S. Open history? (We're talking about Jack Nicklaus's famous tee shot in 1972 and Tom Watson's amazing chip-in from the rough in 1982.) How do you describe the view of the sea and The Lodge as you navigate the 548-yard, par 5 18th?

Now, for a few other numbers. Pebble Beach Resort guests pay $350 (with complimentary cart), while nonguests fork over $375 for this lifelong memory. Pebble

Beach residents and club members pay $350. Caddies ($50 a bag plus gratuity) are highly recommended to help you get the most from your game. The driving range for Pebble Beach is off The Lodge grounds near the Pebble Beach Equestrian Center at Stevenson Road. The Lodge has a choice of shops, including The Golf Shop, and restaurants. The course pro is Chuck Dunbar, and the Pebble Beach Golf Academy provides public and private lessons. Make your tee time as soon as your visit to the Peninsula is firmed up. Otherwise, you may be in for a big disappointment.

Peter Hay Par Three
17-Mile Drive, Pebble Beach
(831) 624–3811, www.pebblebeach.com

Pebble Beach for $20 a round? Yes, it's true at the Peter Hay nine-hole, par 27, 819-yard course. It's not exactly the Pebble Beach Golf Links, but this compact course near The Lodge provides an inexpensive, approach-pitch-and-putt warm-up, or an enjoyable diversion all its own for the budget-minded. This is an especially good choice for newcomers to the game and for young ones learning the game. In fact, kids younger than 12 play for free when accompanied by an adult. Teens up to age 17 play for $5.00. And for adults it's only $20 a round. Former Pebble Beach pro Peter Hay designed the course.

Poppy Hills
3200 Lopez Road, Pebble Beach
(831) 625–2035, www.ncga.org

Deep in the Del Monte Forest, Poppy Hills is possibly the least known of the public courses in Pebble Beach. But this 6210-yard, par 72, heavily wooded beauty is both breathtaking and heartbreaking, with its long, narrow fairways and difficult approaches. Designed by Robert Trent Jones Jr., Poppy Hills is the home of the Northern California Golf Association (NCGA). You begin with a bang, a difficult 413-yard, par 4 with a thick grove of trees to the left that seems to act as a ball magnet. And the back nine starts with one of the best holes of all of Pebble Beach. The par 5, 472-yard 10th green is guarded by a beautiful lake strategically located to the front left, which just dares the best of golfers to try to make the green in two shots.

NCGA members play for $40. Public greens fees are $125 weekdays and $150 weekends and holidays. Carts are optional. There is a driving range with $3.00 buckets and a well-stocked pro shop but no restaurant. The pro is Richard Nauck, and the John Jacob School offers its topnotch training courses at Poppy Hills from May through November.

Spyglass Hill Golf Course
Spyglass Hill Road and Stevenson Drive, Pebble Beach
(831) 625–8563, (800) 654–9300, www.pebblebeach.com

Pebble Beach Golf Links gets top billing, but Spyglass Hill gives it a great run for the money as the top Peninsula course. Trying to pick the most popular hole on this par 72, 6346 yard Robert Trent Jones Sr.-designed course with great ocean and forest views is difficult. You start on the first hole with a great 600-yard downhill to the Treasure Island green surrounded completely by sand. Then there's the demanding 468-yard Black Dog 16th hole, a par 4 dogleg. (All of the holes are named after a Treasure Island character or theme.) But talk to most golfers about the toughest hole at Spyglass, and they'll recall the eighth, Signal Hill, with its severe uphill climb to a sloped green protected by large bunkers. In fact, Signal Hill is rated among the PGA's Top 18 Toughest holes.

Greens fees for Pebble Beach Resort guests are $250, including complimentary cart. Nonguests pay $275, and carts are optional. Ask about seasonal twilight rates. The course pro is Bill Sendell, and Pebble Beach Golf Academy offers lessons.

Driving Range

Del Rey Oaks Driving Range
899 Rosita Road, Del Rey Oaks
(831) 394–8660

In addition to the driving ranges listed with the golf courses above, Del Rey Oaks

Driving Range provides a great place to practice day or night, rain or shine. It features covered as well as grass tees, bright lights for nighttime driving, practice bunkers, and an artificial green. A discount pro shop and snack bar are on site. PGA professionals offer individual and group lessons. Buckets of balls cost from $4.00 to $7.00, and the driving range is open seven days a week until 9:00 P.M.

Insiders' Tip

Just because you didn't pack your clubs, doesn't mean you can't play. Many courses and golf shops provide rental equipment.

Golf Shops

All of the golf courses listed in this chapter have their own pro shops that carry equipment, accessories, and apparel of varying quantities, qualities, and prices. Below are a few more local choices, ranging from discount golf stores to custom club designers. You might also want to check out the area's large discount stores (such as Kmart) and sporting goods shops (like Big 5) for bargain prices.

The Golf Mart
2040 Fremont Boulevard, Seaside
(831) 583–1000, www.thegolfmart.com

The area's newest discount golf store is also its largest. The Golf Mart boasts of 12,000 square feet of retail space, including an indoor driving range and the largest indoor putting green on the Peninsula. You'll find a wide selection of top brands at very decent prices.

Nevada Bob's Golf
399 Lighthouse Avenue, Monterey
(831) 372–5516

Nevada Bob's is a discount golf store chain that carries a full line of golf equipment and accessories. If you need it, Nevada Bob's probably has it for a pretty low price. It's open seven days a week.

Orlimar-Travaux
San Carlos Street and 5th Avenue, Carmel
(831) 625–7115

For 38 years this has been home to Orlimar custom fitted clubs. You'll also find a full line of custom men's clothing carrying such labels as Nicklaus, Norman, and Pebble Beach. Orlimar-Travaux is open seven days a week.

Pro Golf Discount
296 Lighthouse Avenue, Monterey
(831) 372–4653

Pro Golf Discount carries a complete line of golf equipment, clothing, and accessories as part of a large 190-store national chain. Brand names include Hogan, Callaway, Ping, and Wilson. Pro Golf accepts trade-ins and provides club repair and rentals. It is open seven days a week.

Riley Golf
2 Harris Court, Monterey
(831) 373–8855

Since 1980, Riley Golf has been designing and manufacturing personally fitted woods, irons, and putters for professionals and amateurs alike. Its new shop in the Ryan Ranch business park also sells bags, instructional videos, and a line of apparel carrying the Riley logo. Riley Golf is open seven days a week.

Village Golf Shop
601 Wave Street, Monterey
(831) 375–8340
Ocean Avenue and Lincoln Street, Carmel
(831) 624–9551

Known as "The Knickers Place," Village Golf Shop is the place to go to get your fashionable knickers and plus-fours. You'll also find accessories such as balls, bags, putters, shirts, gloves, hats, and shoes. Village Golf Shop is open seven days at both locations.

OREGON
CALIFORNIA
NEVADA
NEVADA
CALIFORNIA
Lake Tahoe
SACRAMENTO
Santa Rosa
SAN FRANCISCO
Oakland
San Jose
Santa Cruz
Castroville
Pacific Grove
Monterey
Pebble Beach
Salinas
Carmel
YOSEMITE NATIONAL PARK
Fresno
Big Sur
LOS PADRES NATIONAL FOREST
San Simeon
Cambria
Morro Bay
San Luis Obispo
Pacific Ocean
LOS ANGELES
1
80
5
101
99
33
10
N
0
100
Kilometer
0
Mile
100

DAYTRIPS

Daytrips

Highway 1 South through Big Sur
Highway 1 North to San Francisco
Salinas Valley
Carmel Valley

This book is focused pretty firmly on the Monterey Peninsula, a small block of land of fewer than 30 square miles surrounded on three sides by the Pacific Ocean. That geographic fact is the primary reason people are drawn here. It's what accounts for the beauty of this chunk of forest-and-beach-covered rock jutting out into the sea. But turn around, away from the Peninsula, and the entire "Central Coast" of California (the semiofficial name for this part of the state) offers equally majestic scenery and equally pleasant diversions. Look south, and there is Point Lobos and Big Sur beyond. If a walk or even a drive through that section of God's green earth on a sunny day doesn't move you, maybe you're dead. Head east and you run into two distinct but very Californian valleys—the agricultural splendor of Salinas Valley and the wild west of Carmel Valley. And what lies north? Only a California beach-hugging trip through the fun and exciting metropolises of Santa Cruz and San Francisco as well as all the charming coastal communities and parks in between.

Daytripping is a favorite pastime of Monterey Peninsula locals, and all visitors of more than two days should partake in a jaunt around the region. Whether your pleasure is exploring the rugged beauty of Big Sur, experiencing the extreme pleasure of Monterey County wine tasting, riding a historic wooden roller coaster right on the beach, taking a steam-driven train through California redwood forests, or splurging on a day of shopping and dining in San Francisco, one of these daytrips is just right for you. Let us present Highway 1 South through Big Sur, Highway 1 North to San Francisco, the Salinas Valley, and Carmel Valley.

Highway 1 South through Big Sur

In 1966 Lady Bird Johnson stood on a stretch of Highway 1 south of the Monterey Peninsula and, as the nation's first lady, dedicated it as California's first scenic highway. And little wonder why. The ribbon of asphalt and concrete that twists and turns approximately 130 miles from Carmel to San Luis Obispo winds through some of the most breathtaking scenery in the world.

Completed in 1937 after 16 years of backbreaking and dangerous labor, this stretch of Highway 1 is, at points, literally cut into the side of 1,000-foot cliffs. At other points, it sweeps down across tranquil coastal valleys only 50 feet above the surf. The numerous, sometimes mammoth bridges spanning the many creeks and rivers that dump into the Pacific are marvels of engineering. Yet they can't hold a candle to the natural splendor that waits around virtually every curve.

Anyone and everyone who comes to visit the Monterey Peninsula for more than a day or two owes it to themselves to visit the Big Sur coast. The approximately 27-mile drive from Carmel into the Big Sur River Valley takes less than an hour and is well worth the effort, even if it's only for a quick lunch or an immediate U-turn back to the Peninsula. The drive south on Highway 1 can be slow and treacherous or quick and carefree, depending on weather and traffic.

Rules of the Road

There are a few rules of the road we should point out before you begin your southbound journey. First of all, don't hurry, be happy! Enjoy getting there, and don't worry about the destination. A slow recreation vehicle lumbering up ahead or an impatient tailgater to the rear can easily get your blood pressure rising, if you let it. The great majority of this length of highway is a no-passing zone, and for good reason. Blind curves, steep grades, and heavy fog create hazards that turn ill-advised passing attempts into tragedies. Fortunately, there is no shortage of turnouts along the highway's edge. Use them! If Teddy Tailgater won't get off your butt, pull off to the side, enjoy the view for a few minutes and let the impatient idiot go bother someone else. Similarly, if the 15-miles-per-hour, refuses-to-pull-over motor home up ahead is filling up your entire windshield, destroying the view and your nerves, maybe it's time to pull over, get out of the car, and deeply breathe in this magnificent piece of paradise. Take it easy, drive defensively, and keep your eyes on the road. Our suggestion is to share the driving chores so that everyone gets a chance to gaze out the window at the majestic mountains, the crashing surf, and the deep blue sea beyond.

In this section, we've indicated the distance (to the nearest half-mile) to the major points of interest down the coast. Our mileage markers are measured from the intersection of Highway 1 and Rio Road near the mouth of Carmel Valley. Set your mileage indicator to zero at the intersection, and the mileage marks noted here should be fairly accurate.

Ready for the ride of a lifetime? Don't forget to bring along some comfortable walking or hiking shoes, at least a windbreaker jacket, some drinking water and light snacks, your camera and plenty of film, disks, or tape, and, if you're susceptible to car sickness on winding roads, a big plastic bag and your favorite tummy remedy.

Carmel to Big Sur Valley

From Rio Road, our trip begins across a rather new bridge that spans the Carmel River. The old bridge was washed out only a few winters ago during major flooding, stranding those south of the river for weeks until a temporary crossing could be built.

At approximately the 1-mile mark of our journey on the coast side of the highway is Carmel Bay School, a preschool that's been attended by generations of Big Sur and Carmel children. Highway 1 then swoops down the hill to spectacular **Monastery Beach** (mile 1.5), part of Carmel River Beach. This is a very popular spot with experienced scuba divers, surfers, and beachcombers, not to mention myriad shorebirds. Please be aware that Monastery Beach has a severe drop-off. The surf, undertow, and riptides can be extremely hazardous. (This caution applies to virtually all of the open beaches along this coastline and will be repeated often in this chapter.) All but the best swimmers and divers are cautioned to enjoy the scenery from a safe distance.

Why is this stretch of sand and surf called Monastery Beach? The answer lies directly across the highway: the **Monastery of Our Lady and St. Theresa**. This monastery was built in the 1920s and continues to be home to an order of Carmelite nuns. There are no regular visitor hours, though the monastery occasionally opens for significant holiday services. A bit farther past the monastery at Riley Ranch Road is the **Redwings Horse Sanctuary,** a nonprofit organization that rescues abused or unwanted horses and lets the animals live out their final days in the safety of this idyllic setting. Visitors are welcome daily, except Sunday, from 10:00 A.M. to 3:30 P.M. as well as during special weekend events. Weekday group tours can also be arranged in advance. Call (831) 624-8464 or visit www.redwings.org for details.

At mile 2 of our journey lies what has been called the greatest meeting of land and sea in the world. **Point Lobos State Park** is a 1,275-acre preserve, more than half of which is below the sea. In fact, it is the first undersea preserve in the United States. Simply put, Point Lobos is one of the most beautiful spots you'll hope to see, with more than 300 species of plants and 250 species of birds and animals populating a spectacular pristine coastline. Highlights include **Whaler's Cove,** with its 1860 Portuguese whaling station, and **China Cove,** an almost fluorescent aqua-colored bay on the south end of the park that's perfect for a picnic or, in warm mild weather, a quick dip in the cold crystal water. During whale-watching season

Springtime is a wonderful time for hiking among the wildflowers at Sobranes Point, between Carmel and Big Sur Valley. PHOTO: ROSS ANDRÉSON

(November through February), the **Cypress Grove Trail** to **Pinnacle Cove** makes for a great hike. Point Lobos is open daily from 9:00 A.M. to 7:00 P.M. (5:00 P.M. during winter months), with a $3.00 entrance fee per car ($2.00 with a senior). Bicyclists and pedestrians enter for free. For general information, call (831) 624-4909 or visit http://pt-lobos.parks.state.ca/us; for scuba information, (831) 624-8413 (see our Parks and Recreation chapter for additional details).

Beyond Point Lobos near the 3-mile mark is Carmel Highlands, an exclusive enclave of hillside homes and a scattering of small businesses like the **Sculpture**

House and Gardens Gallery, Highway 1 and Fern Canyon Road, (831) 624–2476, www.sculpturecarmel.com, with its unique garden, indoor, and water sculptures. About 1.5 miles later is the coastal Yankee Point neighborhood (see our Real Estate chapter). This beautiful area is home to two of the Peninsula's finest hotels, The Highlands Inn and The Tickle Pink Inn (see our Hotels and Motels chapter).

Once past Yankee Point and across Malpaso Creek Bridge (mile 5), the coastline opens up into a panoramic wonder. In clear weather you can view miles of rugged shoreline stretching as far as the eye can see. This is the image of the Big Sur coast most people are familiar with, and it's your first chance to see the magnitude of the unspoiled splendor that still exists.

The next spot of note is a line of cypress trees clumped along the inland side of the highway at **Sobranes Point,** approximately the 7-mile point. This area is the starting point for the **Sobranes Canyon Trail,** which provides for a leisurely 1.5-mile hike to redwood groves along Sobranes Creek, affording nice views back to the coast. Farther up the canyon, the angle of ascent increases, creating a more rigorous hike. On the coast side of the highway are a few trailheads that lead down to the coast at Sobranes Point. Some trails can be quite steep, so caution is advised. This area is a favorite spot for local anglers and is also the northern point of the **California Sea Otter Refuge,** which stretches down to Point Sur.

Easier beach access is afforded farther south at **Garrapata State Park** (mile 9.5), (831) 624–4909. This is a great spot for beachcombing or a romantic sunset walk along the rugged coastline. Again, the surf is extremely dangerous, and surfing, swimming, and wading are highly discouraged. Inland you'll find hiking trails up to redwood groves among the park's more than 2,800 acres. About another 1.5 miles past Garrapata is your first great chance for a few creature comforts in this rugged country: **Rocky Point Restaurant** (mile 11). Here, you can enjoy a great breakfast, lunch, or dinner seven days a week from a wonderful vantage point overlooking the Big Sur Coast. A full menu of seafood and traditional American meals are served, and there's a full bar. Call (831) 624–2933 or visit www.rocky-point.com for hours and reservations, which are recommended for dinner (see also our Restaurants chapter).

At mile 11.5 is an inland turn to **Palo Colorado Canyon.** This road winds through a shady Big Sur residential area for the first few miles, then ascends sharply up the canyon to **Bottcher's Gap,** the site of a campground and several trailheads into the **Ventana Wilderness.** A popular day hike among the physically fit is a scenic 8-mile jaunt to the vistas of **Devil's Peak** and back. Spring and fall hikes are recommended, as winter rains and summer heat can make the trek very rigorous.

Approximately 2 miles beyond Palo Colorado Canyon and Rocky Creek Bridge (mile 12.5) is one of the most photographed and recognizable bridges in

Insiders' Tip

Highway 1 and other roadways and hiking trails along the Big Sur coastline are subject to severe washouts and rockslides during the rainy months, particularly January through March. Always check weather conditions before embarking on your trip south on Highway 1. Likewise, check with the U.S. Forest Service Office at (831) 667-2423 before embarking on long hikes or overnight trips. Trails can wash out during a harsh winter, and forest fires can make some areas downright inhospitable.

Spectacular views await around every curve along the rugged Big Sur coastline south of the Monterey Peninsula. PHOTO: MONTEREY PENINSULA VCB

America. **Bixby Bridge** (mile 13.5) was built in 1932 as one of the longest concrete arch span bridges in the world, with an arch of 320 feet and standing more than 250 feet above Bixby Creek. You probably recognize it from one of the seemingly hundreds of car commercials and movie scenes filmed here. For a real treat, park your car at the pullout just before the bridge and walk out to one of the observation alcoves that were built to take in the spectacular view. Pay attention to traffic, as the pedestrian path to the alcoves is quite narrow.

From Bixby Bridge, Highway 1 continues south around steep and winding **Hurricane Point,** one of the windiest sections of the Big Sur coast. Navigate around this treacherous point and feast your eyes on **Point Sur State Historic Park** in the distance, a huge outcropping of volcanic rock with the **Point Sur Lighthouse** (mile 19) perched some 360 feet above the water. Point Sur Lighthouse, built in 1889, is now open for public tours on Saturdays at 10:00 A.M. and 2:00 P.M., Sundays at 10:00 A.M., Wednesdays at 10:00 A.M. and 2:00 P.M. (April through October) and Thursdays at 10:00 A.M. (July and August). Monthly moonlight tours are also available from April through October. All tours are subject to cancellation due to inclement weather. Reservations are highly recommended, so call (831) 625–4419 or visit www.point sur.org in advance of your trip. Meet your docent in the parking lot at the base of Point Sur's giant moro rock formation. The cost of the tour is $5.00 for adults, $3.00 for kids ages 13 to 17, and $2.00 for ages five to 12. Children younger than five get in free, but strollers are not permitted. Tours last three hours and include a rather steep half-mile hike with a rise in elevation of 360 feet.

The entrance to **Andrew Molera State Park,** (831) 667–2315, the area's largest state park at more than 4,800 acres, is at the 22-mile mark of our journey. This is a great spot for day hikes, with miles of trails along the 4 miles of coastline and up to 2 miles inland along the Big Sur River. There is walk-in, rustic camping on a first-come, first-served basis (no reservations accepted). The day use fee is $2.00. If you're staying overnight, there's a $1.00 per-person, per-night charge for up to three nights. Horseback riding is available from April until January through **Molera Horseback Tours,** (831) 625–5486,

Point Sur Lighthouse is a well-known landmark on the Big Sur coast. PHOTO: ROSS ANDRÉSON

(800) 942-5486. Walk-ins are welcome, with rides starting at $25.

Adjacent to Andrew Molera State Park is the old **Coast Road,** an unpaved, sometimes narrow road that loops up through the woods and joins back to Highway 1 North at Bixby Bridge. The adventuresome with good tires and shocks on a sturdy vehicle will enjoy this alternate route back toward the Monterey Peninsula, but it's best to avoid it during the muddy rainy season (usually November through April). There is also a trailhead to the Little Sur River's south fork about 3.8 miles up the Coast Road from the southern entrance at Andrew Molera.

Big Sur Valley

Continuing south, Highway 1 now leaves the coastline and enters Big Sur Valley. The scenery changes dramatically from rugged coastline to idyllic forests of coastal redwoods, pines, sycamores, cottonwoods, maples, alders, and willows. The highway follows the Big Sur River as it meanders through the forest, and signs of civilization begin to appear on both sides of the road. Approximately half of the population along the entire Big Sur coastline resides in the Big Sur Valley. This area is also home to most of the area restaurants, inns, campgrounds, shops, and stores.

The first major establishment you'll come upon is the **Big Sur River Inn** (mile 24.5). Since the 1930s this venerable landmark has served as a popular meeting place for generations of locals and visitors. Today it offers lodging for overnight guests and a very popular restaurant for breakfast, lunch, or dinner. There's also an outdoor pool, and nighttime entertainment is provided on some weekend evenings. A favorite pastime on warm summer days is to enjoy a tall cold one and some delicious appetizers right in the middle of the Big Sur River. That's right: The Big Sur River Inn has outdoor seating smack dab in the middle of the docile river. Cool your tootsies and enjoy the scenery from the best seats in the house. For information, call (831) 667-2700, or visit www.bigsurriverinn.com.

Another spot worth mentioning if you're considering turning your daytrip into an overnighter is the **Ripplewood Resort** (mile 25). Here you'll find 17 quaint cabins, nine of them right along the Big Sur River under a canopy of redwoods. Rates are reasonable (most are less than $100), and the serenity is unmatchable. Call (831) 667–2242 or visit www.ripplewoodresort.com for details.

Nearby are two other Big Sur landmarks: the **Big Sur Grange Hall** that serves as the community's town meeting hall and **St. Francis of the Redwoods Chapel,** with a unique glass wall that opens up to allow for religious services out under the redwoods.

Our next stop is **Pfeiffer Big Sur State Park,** (831) 667–2315. This 810-acre park provides a recreational haven for hikers, swimmers, sunbathers, anglers, and picnickers. The **Big Sur Lodge,** (831) 667–3100, (800) 424–4787, www.bigsurlodge.com, provides 61 guestrooms and a swimming pool, cafe (for breakfast, lunch, and dinner), gift shop, and country store. There are also more than 200 campsites and a large day-use picnic area with grills and tables. Giant coastal redwoods (reaching circumferences of up to 27 feet) provide a cool and sheltering canopy over the majority of the park, which provides miles of hiking trails. A favorite hike is the 0.7-mile trek from the lodge through the redwoods along Pfeiffer Redwood Creek up to 60-foot **Pfeiffer Falls.** Then follow the half-mile trail from the foot of the falls to the **Valley View Overlook,** which affords spectacular views of Big Sur Valley. The mostly downhill return trip from the overlook to the lodge is approximately 1 mile. You can encounter a variety of wildlife including squirrels, deer, quail, raccoon, fox, bobcat, wild boar, hawks, woodpeckers, and kingfishers. Call the park regarding fishing regulations for steelhead and rainbow trout. During the summer, the water temperature of the Big Sur River is often above 60 degrees, so bring your bathing suits. The U.S. Forest Service Office is within the park and provides the wilderness permits required for overnight backpacking into **Ventana Wilderness** and **Los Padres National Forest.** For park information call (831) 667–3100 or (800) 424–4787.

Farther south at about the 28.5-mile mark, you'll notice a rather nondescript, poorly marked road that dips down off to the coast side of the highway. This is Sycamore Canyon Road, the route to **Pfeiffer Beach,** the most popular day-use beach in the Big Sur Valley area. This mostly single-lane road of a little more than 2 miles leads to a parking lot and a 150-yard path to a spectacular stretch of sandy coastline with dramatic rocks, arches, and caves. You might recognize it as the beach Richard Burton and Elizabeth Taylor cavorted on in *The Sandpiper.* Although Dick and Liz are gone, you will find surfers, anglers, tidepoolers, and probably lovers enjoying the scenic vistas. Beach access costs $5.00 and the park is open daily 9:00 A.M. to 8:00 P.M. (**Note:** You're likely to meet oncoming traffic on this narrow road. In California, uphill traffic has the right of way; downhillers must yield or back up to allow passing. Also, parking is limited to 65 vehicles.)

Meanwhile, back on Highway 1, it's time to check the gas gauge. If you're planning on continuing to the southern end of our journey, the service station at the **Cactus Cafe** is your last chance for petrol for 35 miles. We now approach two of the most luxurious resorts in Big Sur, practically across the road from each other at the 29.5-mile mark. On the ocean side, **Post Ranch Inn,** (831) 667–2200, (800) 527–2200, www.postranchinn.com, has been receiving rave reviews as one of the ultimate resort spots in the world since its heralded opening in 1992. The unique stone, glass, and wood architecture blends

Insiders' Tip

For overnight campground reservations at the California State Parks along Highway 1, call ReserveAmerica at (800) 444-7275, or go to www.reserveamerica.com.

Water rushes through a tunnel in the rock at Pfeiffer State Beach. PHOTO: ROSS ANDRÉSON

in with the spectacular scenery from a bluff high above the Pacific Ocean. The altitude of the room prices nearly matches the altitude of the bluff, but who's to say the experience isn't worth it? The **Sierra Mar** restaurant is seemingly perched on the edge of the world. When seating is available, a limited number of visitors can join the guests for a delicious continental Californian dinner. Call the Post Ranch

Inn for reservations. The **Post Ranch Mercantile** offers a variety of one-of-a-kind clothing, jewelry, and gift items.

Inland, **Ventana Resort,** (831) 667-2331, (800) 628-6500, www.ventanainn.com, is a local favorite, both for its luxurious accommodations (including fabulous clothing-optional Japanese hot baths) and its popular restaurant and bar with imaginative California cuisine for lunch and dinner (see our Restaurants chapter for more). The gift shop and boutique has a surprising selection of high-end goods for such a rustic location.

At the 30-mile mark, you'll find **Nepenthe,** (831) 667-2345, www.nepenthebigsur.com. This legendary restaurant, built on a bluff 800 feet above the ocean in 1944 as a getaway cottage for Orson Welles and Rita Hayworth, is perhaps the most popular of all eateries among Big Sur daytrippers. The coastline views on a bright sunny day or during the evening sunset are nothing short of stunning. There's ample outdoor seating to enjoy the vistas, and the food is downright tasty. The Ambrosia Burger with the homemade bean salad and basket of hot fries has been known to cause bliss, and vegetarians will be delighted with the menu too (also see our Restaurants chapter).

Just below Nepenthe at the parking lot is **The Phoenix Shop,** (831) 667-2347, with a great selection of gifts made by local artists. And directly over The Phoenix is **Cafe Kevah,** (831) 667-2344, a great choice for a quick pastry and coffee or soup and sandwich.

Heading south of Big Sur Valley, shortly past Nepenthe, Highway 1 leaves Big Sur Valley and again returns to the coast. Nestled at the mouth of Graves Canyon on the inland side of Highway 1 is the **Henry Miller Library** (mile 31). Miller lived, wrote, and painted in Big Sur from 1944 to 1962, and his story of the region is contained in *Big Sur and the Oranges of Hieronymous Bosch.* The library was founded by Miller's longtime friend Emil White and features a fascinating collection of Miller's books, photographs, letters, art, and other memorabilia. The library is open Wednesday through Sunday from 11:00 A.M. to 6:00 P.M. (Friday through Sunday 11:00 A.M. to 5:00 P.M. in the winter) and schedules various exhibits, readings, concerts, and other special events year-round. Call (831) 667-2574 or visit www.henrymiller.org for details.

At 31.5 miles is **Deetjens Big Sur Inn,** (831) 667-2377, a bed and breakfast inn with great rustic charm. Pioneers Helmuth and Helen Deetjen, immigrants from Norway, homesteaded this spot at Castro Canyon in the early 1930s and welcomed overnight guests traveling the coastal wagon road (prior to Highway 1). That tradition continues today as the Norwegian-style inn built with locally milled scavenged redwood is operated by the nonprofit Deetjen's Big Sur Inn Preservation Foundation. Breakfast and dinner are served for nonguests by reservation; call (831) 667-2378.

Two miles south of Deetjens is **Coast Gallery & Café,** (831) 667-2301, www.bigsurgallery.com, the best known of the Big Sur art galleries. Housed in two giant, empty redwood water tanks, the gallery specializes in the work of local painters, sculptors, woodworkers, and other artisans. Around back is the **Henry Miller Gallery,** featuring a selection of watercolors, lithographs, books, and photos by the famous Big Sur citizen. There's also a great candle shop where you can watch a master candlemaker wax poetic.

Back on Highway 1, we continue south to a majestic stretch of coastline. At about mile 36.5 is beach access to **Partington Cove.** Look for an old dirt road that slopes directly to the beach and features some great secluded coves and tunnels. This spot was once an important shipping point for tanbark and timber. At the 38 mile mark is **Julia Pfeiffer Burns State Park,** a fabulous spot for quick and easy walks to some beautiful spots along the Big Sur coast. The most popular walk is along the trail that disappears into a tunnel under Highway 1 and emerges at **McWay Cove.** Here you'll find a splendid view of **McWay Falls** which, at 80 feet, is said to be the tallest waterfall in California that drops directly into the Pacific. (Actually, it hits the sandy beach at low tide, but who's to nitpick?) The trail to the view of McWay Falls ends at a great little outlook that provides an unbelievable panorama of the coast back northward. It's a great spot for whale watching during December and January. You'll also notice ruins from the **Waterfall House,** which was home to Lathrop and Helen Hooper Brown, close friends of Julia Pfeiffer of the Big Sur pioneer Pfeiffer family. Inland at **Julia Pfeiffer Burns State Park** are nice trails through the redwoods, along McWay Creek, and up into the Santa Lucia Mountains. There are also picnic tables and restrooms for a nice luncheon stop.

South of Julia Pfeiffer Burns State Park, it gets a bit windier on Highway 1, and Big Sur becomes less populated. But there are still many highlights for those venturing onward. The first point of interest at mile 41 is the **Esalen Institute,** (831) 667-3000, www.esalen.org, one of the most notable venues of the "human potential movement" of the 1960s. Today Esalen offers many workshops and spa activities (it is on the site of the former Old Slate Hot Springs). Unfortunately, the El Niño storms in the winter of 1998 destroyed the outdoor baths available for public use. An ambitious rebuilding effort is currently underway, so check with Esalen regarding the reopening.

Ten miles farther at the 51-mile mark is Lucia, home of the **Lucia Lodge,** (831) 667-2391. The restaurant and cabins here are absolutely fantastic for those wanting to get away from it all. The cabins line a bluff overlooking a picturesque bay hundreds of feet below. The cabin farthest out on the point is particularly nice for a romantic evening for two overlooking Lucia Cove and the Pacific.

At mile 52 is **Limekiln State Park,** (831) 667-2403. In addition to a fascinating half-mile hike up to the historic late 19th-century kilns of the Rockland Cement Company and a pretty waterfall along Limekiln Creek, the park provides coastal access to a beautiful beach. A pleasant picnic area and campsites are also available. The entrance fee is $3.00.

About a mile past Limekiln (mile 53 on our trip) is the **Immaculate Heart New Camaldoli Hermitage,** (831) 667-2456, www.contemplation.com, the first branch of the Benedictine order of monks in America. There's a gift shop that sells religious artifacts, books, and the Hermitage's famous brandied fruitcake and date-nut cake. (For those of you who don't make the trip this far south, these goods are also sold at Hermitage Shop in Carmel.)

Nacimiento-Fergusson Road

At mile 55 near Kirk Creek, you have your first opportunity since you passed Carmel Valley Road to leave Highway 1 and cross the Santa Lucia Range to the Salinas Valley. Nacimiento-Fergusson Road travels east over the 4,000-foot Nacimiento Summit before winding down the eastern slope through the **Fort Hunter Liggett Military Reservation** and onward to **Mission San Antonio de Padua,** the town of Jolon, and finally U.S. 101 at King City. The total trek from Highway 1 to U.S. 101 is 55 miles. Plan for about a one-and-a-half to two-hour drive over this narrow but paved road, which provides some great vistas back toward the coast, within the Santa Lucia Range, and overlooking the Salinas Valley. There are campgrounds with restrooms about 8.5 miles up the road from Highway 1 if you want to take a detour back into the Santa Lucias for a scenic vista and then return to the coast.

Continuing south on Highway 1 to mile 59 brings you to the quaint community of **Pacific Valley.** In addition to having a restaurant, market, and shop, Pacific Valley is home to the **Big Sur Jade Co. and Museum,** (805) 927-8655, which features some fine examples of the native jade. At mile 60 is **Sand Dollar Beach,** a favorite among beachcombers, scuba divers, surfers, picnickers, hikers, and hang gliders. This expansive stretch of sand makes for an enjoyable day in itself. A couple miles farther south is **Jade Cove,** reportedly the only known source of certain types of California nephrite and Pacific Blue Jade. Rockhounds and divers owe it to themselves to make this little side trip to the water's edge.

The town of **Gorda** at mile 65 is your last best chance for diesel, gas, snacks, or a meal before continuing on down south about 25 more miles to perhaps the best known attraction of the southern Big Coast, Hearst Castle. The name Gorda comes from the Spanish term for "fat woman," which was the name given to the large shapely rock just off the coast.

The **Whalewatcher Cafe,** (805) 927-3918, is a favorite among Highway 1 regulars. Traditional American breakfasts, lunches, and dinners are accompanied by some fresh seafood dishes. Continue south past Soda Springs, Salmon Creek, and Ragged Point (all good scenic and hiking spots) and beyond the **Piedras Blancas** (white rocks) **Lighthouse** (in operation since 1874) to about mile 91 at **San Simeon.** That places you directly at the entrance to Hearst Castle. This is the ultimate destination for many visitors and a must-see for anyone interested in the style, architecture, and opulence of California's gilded age gone by.

Hearst Castle

Hearst Castle, (800) 444-4445, www.hearstcastle.org, was the summer home of publisher William Randolph Hearst, who began construction at what he commonly called "The Ranch" in 1919. The designer was famous San Francisco architect Julia Morgan, whose talents and patience were both severely tested on this monumental project. For nearly three decades, as the home expanded into its current 165 rooms (including 41 baths) and more than 125 acres of manicured gardens, terraces, paths, and pools, it was visited by the most famous names in world and Hollywood affairs. Especially impressive are the interior decor, antiques, and the many classic statues. Most of these largely European treasures in the house were unloaded from ships docked at San Simeon Pier and hauled up the hill to the castle. Today, there are a variety of tours of Hearst's La Cuesta Encantada (The Enchanted Hill), each offering a unique view of the estate. Tour 1 is certainly the best for first-time visitors, providing access to the first floor of Casa Grande (the main house) with its famous Moorish twin towers, the spectacular gardens, and one of the three guesthouses. Tour 2 goes through the upper levels of Casa Grande (including the magnificent library), while Tour 3 takes you through the north wing of the main house and the Casa del Mar guesthouse. Tour 4 is an extended visit to the gardens and terraces and provides interesting peeks into the wine cellar and the dressing rooms of the Neptune Pool. All of the tours visit both the 104-foot-long, 345,000-gallon outdoor Neptune Pool and the 205,000-gallon, Venetian-glass-tiled indoor Roman Pool. Tours begin at 8:20 A.M., take approximately 100 minutes, and require plenty of walking, so wear those comfy shoes. Wheelchair-accessible tours can be arranged by calling (805) 927-2020 at least 10 days in advance of your visit. Entrance fees per tour are $10.00 to $14.00 for adults and $5.00 to $7.00 for youth ages 6 to 17. An evening tour with docents in 1930s period costumes is available in the spring and fall; it runs $20 for adults and $10 for children.

The coastline below Hearst Castle is a worthy destination all its own. There's **William Randolph Hearst Memorial State Beach,** (805) 927-2068, with swimming, fishing, picnic areas, and great views; the old **San Simeon Pier;** and **Sebastian's General Store,** a State Historical Landmark in the small town of San Simeon.

Cambria

Continuing south on Highway 1 to about the 101-mile mark you reach the town of **Cambria,** originally settled in the 1860s by Welsh miners looking for copper and quicksilver. Often referred to as a more rustic version of Carmel, today's Cambria is a charming artist community made up of three distinct villages. The **East Village** is a quaint town of late 19th-century Victorian architecture, now home to restaurants, shops, galleries, and lodging. The **West Village** around Main Street also has enjoyable shops, galleries, and restaurants and is home to the Cambria Chamber of Commerce, (805) 927-3624, which provides valuable visitor information. Finally, **Moonstone Beach** hugs the coast paralleling Highway 1 and is home to many bed and breakfast inns and other accommodations as well as great picnic spots at Leffingwell Landing and Shamel Park.

Others spots of interest include **Nit Wit Ridge,** a "found-material" mansion built by a local eccentric and now a historical landmark, on Hillcrest Drive north of Main Street, and the old **Cambria Jail House** on Main Street.

Inland from Cambria on Highway 46 are local wineries and tasting rooms. Highway 46 connects to U.S. 101 for a straighter and faster route back north to Salinas and (via Highway 68 West) the Monterey Peninsula.

Morro Bay to San Luis Obispo

Twenty miles farther south on Highway 1 is the town of **Morro Bay** (mile 121), situated at the heart of Estero Bay between the smaller towns of Cayucos and Los Osos. Morro Bay Harbor lies inside a 3-mile long sandspit that provides protection for a thriving fishing community and recreational boaters. And standing like a guardian over the bay is 576-foot tall **Morro Rock,** one of the Nine Sisters volcano peaks that run toward San Luis Obispo. Today, this "Gibraltar of the Pacific" is a protected home for endangered peregrine falcons.

Morro Bay Estuary is a 2,300-acre tidal wetland park that provides for great hiking and wildlife watching. On the southeastern shore of Morro Bay is the **Elfin Forest,** an ecologically diverse parkland that is home to about 150 species of birds, mammals, and reptiles. There are also interesting middens throughout the parkland, evidence of the Chumash tribe that populated the area at one time. Nearby **Montana De Oro State Park** is 8,000 acres of shoreline and inland beauty with picnic tables and barbecue pits along the sandy beaches at Spooner's Cove. The active set will enjoy hiking, horseback riding, bicycling, hang gliding, fishing, tidepooling, or surfing in this park. The more citified visitors will appreciate the **Embarcadero,** a stretch of shops and restaurants along the harbor. From here you can visit a small aquarium or rent paddleboats to cruise the harbor.

From Morro Bay, we travel 14 miles inland to our final destination, the city of **San Luis Obispo** (mile 135). With a population of 45,000, this county seat is home to California Polytechnic State University and Mission San Luis Obispo de Tolosa. The downtown area is a lively, vibrant place with many outdoor cafes, coffeehouses, and specialty shops amid the picturesque Victorians and adobes. The Thursday night **Farmer's Market Street Fair** on Higuera Street is a local tradition with five city blocks of shops and booths selling fresh produce, flowers, arts and crafts, and great barbecued meats. The **Mission Plaza** area along San Luis Creek is home to a variety of special activities and festivals, so check out the local calendar of events available through the San Luis Obispo Chamber of Commerce and Visitors Center at 1039 Chorro Street, (805) 781-2777.

From San Luis Obispo, the quickest route back to the Monterey Peninsula is to take U.S. 101 North to Salinas and then Highway 68 West back to Monterey. It's typically a two-and-a-half to three-hour drive, but it's quicker than the return trip on Highway 1. If you're considering spending the night, there are many nice spots within the city of San Luis Obispo. Or for a real local experience, follow U.S. 101 to **The Madonna Inn,** 100 Madonna Road, (805) 543-3000, a landmark for more than 40 years. Each of the inn's more than 100 rooms is uniquely decorated, including all-rock rooms with waterfall showers. Seeing is believing.

Highway 1 North to San Francisco

North of the Monterey Peninsula, Highway 1 follows a storied and historic route along the scenic Pacific coast up to the grand city of San Francisco and beyond. Unlike Highway 1 South, which twists and turns like a pretzel through the rugged Santa Lucia Mountains of Big Sur, High-

Insiders' Tip

For up-to-date fishing and hunting information throughout the Santa Lucia Mountains, call the California Department of Fish and Game at (831) 649-2870 or visit www.dfg.ca.gov.

way 1 North is a relatively straight and gentle stretch of road. You pass through miles of flat agricultural fields, small villages and towns, historic cities, and gentle rolling coastlines.

The larger cities of Santa Cruz and San Francisco are in and of themselves substantial enough in history, charm, and splendor to warrant books all their own, and, indeed, many such books are available. So our quest here is not to provide you with all-inclusive, in-depth coverage of this long 100-mile-plus stretch of California Coast. Instead, we'll give you a general road map of points of interest on this splendid route and highlight some of our favorite spots along the way. Feel free to explore the many attractions and diversions we couldn't squeeze into this brief taste of Highway 1 north of the Monterey Peninsula.

To follow our approximate mileage markers, set your odometer on zero at the intersection of Highway 1 and Highway 68 East toward Salinas. Traveling north beyond Monterey and Seaside, you'll hit a stretch of tall sand dunes that obscure the view of the sea but provide a beauty all their own. This stretch of dunes is a favorite among hang gliders. At mile 4.5 we pass the entrance to the former Fort Ord and the current California State University at Monterey Bay.

Marina

Mile 7 down Highway 1 takes us to the bedroom community of **Marina,** population 25,000. Though not geared as a visitors' destination, there are a couple of potential diversions to point out. First is **Marina State Beach,** (831) 384-7695, a favorite spot among local surfers and hang gliders, at the west end of Reservation Road. Consistent wind and high sand dunes along the 170-acre park make for ideal hang gliding (or watching it), but swimming conditions can be dangerous due to a steep beach and heavy surf. A half-mile boardwalk provides for wheelchair access, and there is no entry fee.

Do you like to make a friendly wager on a game of cards? Marina is home to two small casinos that offer games of chance and cocktail lounges. **Marina Casino Club,** 204 Carmel Avenue, (831) 384-0925, and **Mortimer's,** 3100 Del Monte Boulevard, (831) 384-7667, offer poker, Texas Hold'em, California Lowball, 21st Century Blackjack, and Pai Gow Tiles. Finally, recreational vehicle fans should certainly consider **Marina Dunes RV Park,** 3330 Dunes Drive, (831) 384-6914, offering 75 sites (60 with full hookups) and easy beach access for those morning and evening strolls.

Castroville

Back on Highway 1, we drive north of Marina through wide-open spaces and agricultural fields. You'll likely notice large clumping plants with long serrated leaves and possibly big green thistle-like blossoms standing out on long stems. These beauties are artichokes, and they put our next destination on the map. The town of **Castroville** is known worldwide as The Artichoke Capital of the World. Virtually the entire commercial artichoke crop in the United States is grown right here. The annual Castroville Artichoke Festival, held one weekend each August, draws huge crowds of fans who love their "chokes" boiled, deep fried, barbecued, and every which way. Street vendors and restaurants serve up the thorny delicacies, while street parades and live music add to the festivities. To enter Castroville, take the Highway 156 exit at about mile 13 on our trip. Then exit immediately on Highway 183, also known at Merritt Street, the main drag through tiny Castroville. If it's not festival time, the town is pretty quiet, but there are a few restaurants worth noting. First, on the right as you enter town, is the **Giant Artichoke Restaurant,** Highway 1, (831) 633-3204, which serves the favorite thistle every which way but loose. Then there are two of the best greasy spoons in the area. **Bing's Diner,** 10961 Merritt Street, (831) 633-0400, offers great diner grub in an old streetcar. It's small and popular, so be prepared for a little wait. Then there is **Central Texan Barbecue,** 10500 Merritt Street, (831) 633-2285, many times voted the best barbecue in the area by local reader polls. You're also likely to notice a local gathering spot called **The Norma Jean Club,** named after the first Castroville Artichoke Festival Queen, who later adopted the screen name of Marilyn Monroe.

Past Castroville, Highway 1 narrows to a two-lane undivided road. Drive carefully with your headlights on through this 8-mile stretch, especially during foggy days and nights. There are plenty of slow-moving agricultural vehicles exiting and entering the highway, so be alert. At mile 16, enter the left turn lane to visit the charming fishing village of **Moss Landing.** A 90-degree left takes you to Potrero Road and the route to **Salinas River State Beach.** Here is where the Salinas River empties into the Pacific and where you'll find some great surf-fishing along the picturesque sand dunes. The park is open from sunrise to sunset daily with no entrance fee.

Moss Landing

By taking a 45-degree left from Highway 1 at mile 16, you enter Moss Landing Road, the route to the town of Moss Landing and its commercial fishing harbor. Moss Landing Road is a gold mine for junk store lovers and antiques shop aficionados. While unbelievable bargains are getting harder to find these days, you'll still discover some reasonably priced collectibles and fine antiques within some of the most rustically charming shops around these parts. Virtually any of the many stores in tiny Moss Landing can hold a hidden treasure, but some of our favorites include **Waterfront Antiques,** 7902 Sandholt Road, (831) 633-1112; **The Wood Shed,** a tiny shop next door to Waterfront with no listed phone; **Little Red Barn Antiques,** 8461 Moss Landing Road, (831) 633-5583; and **Moss Landing Antique and Trading Company,** Moss Landing Road, (831) 633-3988. When it's time to eat lunch or dinner, Moss Landing is home to some wonderful fresh seafood restaurants. For lunch, **Phil's Fish Market and Eatery,** Sandholt Road, (831) 633-2152, has marvelous fish and chips, chowder, and other simple seafood selections, with very casual indoor and outdoor seating. **The Whole Enchilada,** Highway 1 and Moss Landing Road, (831) 633-3038, does excellent Mexican seafood dishes (see also our Restaurants chapter). Farther north on Highway 1, at about mile 17.5, is **Maloney's Harbor Inn,** Highway 1, (831) 724-9371, with great seafood dinners in a scenic harbor setting. Near Maloney's on Highway 1 is a shop called **Little Baja,** (831) 633-2254, with a great selection of pottery and statuary from Mexico and elsewhere. Finally, Moss Landing is also home to the **Monterey Bay Aquarium Research Institute,** 7700 Sandholt Road, (831) 775-1773, which holds a fascinating open house for the public each spring.

Elkhorn Slough

At mile 17 on Highway 1 near the large power plant in Moss Landing is Dolan Road. Turn east (right) here and travel 3 miles to Elkhorn Road. Turn left (north) and drive 2 miles to reach **Elkhorn Slough National Estuarine Research Reserve,** 1700 Elkhorn Road, (831) 728-2822, www.elkhornslough.org. Elkhorn Slough is what's left of an ancient river valley located at the apex of the Monterey Submarine Canyon. Today, the main slough channel winds 7 miles inland and feeds more than 2,500 acres of rich marsh and tidal flats. This is home to hundreds of varieties of birds, including pelicans, herons, and egrets, as well as countless fish, sharks, crabs, rays, sea lions, otters, land mammals, and insects. You'll find an informative visitors center, interpretive displays, and miles of well-maintained trails. The Reserve is open Wednesday through Sunday from 9:00 A.M. to 5:00 P.M. Docent-led walks are available at 10:00 A.M. and 1:00 P.M. on weekends (also see our In and around the Water chapter). **Note: Elkhorn Slough Safari Nature Tours** offers 10-mile, two-hour guided tours of Elkhorn Slough on a 27-foot pontoon boat. Fares are $26 for adults and $19 for children age 14 and under. Call (831) 633-5555 or visit www.elkhornslough.com for seasonal schedules and reservations. The tour departs from the Harbor District parking lot off Sandholt Road in Moss Landing. Advance reservations required.

Back on Highway 1, mile 18.5 brings us to Geiberson Road, the turnoff to **Zmudowski State Beach,** (831) 384-7695. This is one of the most secluded and least-used beaches in the area. It is a great spot for surf fishing and taking long romantic walks along the sand. Horseback riding is allowed along the beach, but not among the long rows of sand dunes that parallel the shore. Zmudowski State Beach also has a protected nesting ground for the snowy plover. The park is open from 6:30 A.M. to 7:30 P.M., and entry is free of charge.

Watsonville

Leaving the Moss Landing area, Highway 1 stretches out through vast agriculture fields to the northern border of Monterey County. At mile 22, Highway 1 meets Salinas Road, an inland route to the Salinas Valley, and afterward widens back into a four-lane divided freeway. Here, we enter Santa Cruz County and the city of **Watsonville,** population 32,000. Watsonville is largely an industrial town serving the vast agricultural industry in the area, but it provides a few pleasant diversions for visitors. **Gizdich Ranch,** 55 Peckham Road, (831) 722-1056, www.gizdichranch.com, provides for a fun day of berry and apple picking. Load up with baskets of fresh strawberries, raspberries, olallieberries, or Watsonville's famous Pippin apples. Or, you can buy homemade jams and pies and fresh-pressed apple juice. Each Memorial Day weekend the Watsonville airport is home to the **West Coast Antique Fly-In and Air Show,** (831) 496-9559. Antique aircraft and hot-air balloons fill the skies, providing an exciting and colorful extravaganza.

At mile 23.5 on Highway 1 is San Andreas Road, the exit to **Sunset State Beach,** (831) 763-7062. This is a more developed state park than most in the area, with 90 sites for overnight trailers and campers as well as day-use picnic tables and barbecue pits. The 3 miles of flat beaches are some of the area's best for swimming, and a lifeguard is on duty during the summer. Surf fishing is also popular and, when conditions are right, beachcombers often find an ample supply of shells and sand dollars for their collections. Sunset State Beach is open from 8:00 A.M. to sunset, with a day use fee of $3.00 per vehicle. Call the California State Parks at (800) 444-7275 for overnight camping reservations (48 hours to seven months in advance).

Aptos

Mile 31 takes us to Larken Valley Road, the exit to **Seascape Resort,** 1 Seascape Resort Drive, Aptos, (831) 688-6800 or (800) 929-7727. Seascape is a luxury resort property that provides spacious accommodations, a great restaurant (Sanderlings), a splendid pool and spa, a tennis court, an exercise gym, and miles of scenic beaches. The **Aptos Seascape Golf Course** is adjacent to the resort. Daytrippers should definitely keep Seascape in mind for their next weekend getaway in this neck of the woods.

At mile 32.5 we enter the unincorporated town of **Aptos,** a population-19,000 bedroom community of Santa Cruz. Aptos is home to **Cabrillo College,** 6500 Soquel Drive, (831) 479-6100, a two-year community college; and the charming shopping districts of Historic Aptos Village and Seascape Village. Mile 34 in Aptos brings us to the Seacliff Beach exit. **Seacliff State Beach,** (831) 685-6442, is an 85-acre park with a fascinating pier, partly made from an old 430-foot concrete ship from the World War I era, the *Palo Alto.* The boat was towed here and sunk to the sea floor in shallow waters in 1929 to be used as an amusement and fishing ship. Although the amusement business went broke after two years, anglers still find the ship and an added pier an excellent spot to spend a day fishing for perch, sole, flounder, lingcod, and halibut. This is a popular and sometimes crowded swimming beach, and there are picnic facilities and 26 developed sites for trailers and campers. A lifeguard is on duty for the summer. There is a day-use fee of $3.00 per vehicle, and overnight spots for self-contained vehicles are $18.00 per night.

Capitola Village

Mile 37 brings us to the exit for **Capitola Village.** Known as California's oldest seaside resort (dating back to 1869), Capitola Village is a charming beach town in a protected cove between two sea bluffs, with the Soquel River meandering to the ocean. The wharf and riverside area are full of small shops, art galleries, and sidewalk cafes, reminiscent of a European seaport. Upriver lies the well-known **Shadowbrook Restaurant,** 1750 Wharf Road, (831) 475-1222, with a private tram that takes you down a steep hillside to the entrance. Two annual festivals held each September are worth a mention. First is the **Capitola National Begonia Festival,** (831) 476-3566, featuring flower-draped floats drifting down Soquel Creek and a festive sandcastle contest on the beach. The second event is the **Capitola Art & Wine Festival,** (831) 475-6522, with sidewalk art exhibitions, live music, tastings from local wineries, and food booths from area restaurants.

Santa Cruz

At mile 40 we enter **Santa Cruz,** at population 51,000 the largest city on the Central Coast. This town is a daytripper's delight, offering a wealth of recreational and relaxation opportunities for the entire family. The beaches themselves are wide-open expanses of white sand, relatively warm waters, and great surf. **Natural Bridges State Park,** W. Cliff Drive, (831) 423-4609, features awe-inspiring arches carved by wind and water from the soft sandstone as well as great spots for swimming, tidepooling, and picnicking. This is home each October to the **Welcome Back Monarch Butterfly Festival,** which, like Pacific Grove's Butterfly Festival on the Monterey Peninsula, greets the Monarch butterflies that arrive each fall to spend the winter in this area. Surfers will also want to visit the **Santa Cruz Surfing Museum** in the **Mark Abbott Lighthouse,** W. Cliff Drive, (831) 420-6281. The lighthouse overlooks the famous stretch of beach called **Steamer Lane,** the birthplace of mainland U.S. surfing.

Downtown shopping on the **Pacific Garden Mall,** renovated after the devastating Loma Prieta earthquake of 1989, provides for a great afternoon or evening. Restaurants offer every type of food imaginable. Among local favorites are **India Joze,** 1001 Center Street, (831) 427-3554, which serves a tasty lunch and dinner menu of Indian and California cuisine; the **Library at Chaminade,** 1 Chaminade Lane, (831) 475-5600, for elegant evening dining; **The Hindquarter Bar and Grille,** 303 Soquel Avenue, (831) 426-7770, for hearty steaks, ribs, and seafood; **Oswald's,** 1547 Pacific Avenue, (831) 423-7427, for a charming bistro atmosphere with European flair; **Ideal Bar & Grill,** 106 Beach Street at Santa Cruz Wharf, (831) 423-5271, for a casual beachside lunch or dinner; and **Miramar Fish Grotto,** 45 Municipal Wharf, (831) 423-4441, for fresh seafood and a fantastic view of Lighthouse Point. There are many, many more fine restaurants in Santa Cruz, so don't hesitate to explore and find your own favorite.

For fantastic family fun in Santa Cruz we have three attractions to recommend. Kids' favorite, bar none, is the **Santa Cruz Beach Boardwalk,** (831) 423-5590, www.beachboardwalk.com, California's oldest amusement park right on the sand. The crowning glory here is the Great Dipper, a 1920s wooden roller coaster with a 70-foot ascent and tummy-tickling drops and turns. The Great Dipper and the Beach Boardwalk's 1911 carousel are both National Historic Landmarks. Other fun attractions include the bumper cars, Logger's Revenge water slide ride, and Neptune's Kingdome arcade. Plan on a whole day here, and take advantage of the Unlimited Ride wristbands, which go for around $25.

For something really different, visit **The Mystery Spot,** 469 Mystery Spot Road, (831) 423-8897, www.mystery-spot.com, Santa Cruz's answer to the Twilight Zone. Magnetic forces and gravity seem to have gone awry in the 150-foot wide spot within a redwood grove in the hills about the city. Compasses go haywire. Things roll uphill. Optical illusions abound. The senses confound. Pure kitsch and pure fun, The Mystery Spot is a must-see for all of us who are a little off-center ourselves. Admission is $5.00 for adults, $3.00 for children age five to 11, and free for those younger than five.

Our third family fun spot is **Roaring Camp & Big Trees Narrow Gauge Railroad,** Graham Hill Road, (831) 335-4484, www.roaringcamprr.com, which is actually in the city of Felton in the Santa Cruz Mountains. This is a narrow gauge railway pulled by steam locomotives that chug through **Henry Cowell Redwood State Park,** down the San Lorenzo River Canyon and through Santa Cruz to the Beach Boardwalk. You can depart, spend some time at the Boardwalk, and return to Roaring Camp later in the afternoon. Chuckwagon barbecues are also offered. The cost of the ride to the Beach Boardwalk is $15 for adults and $10 for children. Round-trip rides within the Santa Cruz Mountains are also offered for $16.50 and $11.50. Call for seasonal schedules. To find Roaring Camp, take Highway 17 north out of Santa Cruz. Exit in Scotts Valley on Mt. Hermon Road and proceed 3.5 miles to Graham Hill Road. Go one-half mile, and it's on the right.

Navigating Highway 1 north through Santa Cruz can be a little tricky. When you reach the Highway 17 interchange (a commuter route to San Jose and the San Francisco Bay area) at mile 40.5, the Highway 1 freeway ends. As Highway 1 drops into the surface streets of Santa Cruz proper, follow the signs to "Beaches and Ocean Street" if you're going to the Beach Boardwalk, wharf, or other waterfront attractions. Follow the signs to Half Moon Bay and Highway 1 to proceed on our daytrip north toward San Francisco.

At mile 42, Highway 1 takes a right-hand turn onto Mission Street and continues through residential neighborhoods. (When you reach mile 43 at Laurel Street, notice the great farm-worker mural on the side of La Esperana Market). At mile 44 is Bay Street, where a right-hand turn will lead you to the **University of California at Santa Cruz,** (831) 459-4008, www.ucsc.edu, home of the UCSC Banana Slugs and one of the loveliest campuses you can hope to find. This University of California campus is known for its liberal curriculum and relaxed campus atmosphere.

Between Santa Cruz and Half Moon Bay

At mile 45, Highway 1 exits residential Santa Cruz and opens back up to beautiful coastal views. Mile 46 brings us to **Wilder Ranch State Park,** an interesting beach park that was once a 4,000-acre ranch. Many of the historic 1870 ranch buildings are still there. A visitor center offering group tours is on site; call (831) 426-0505 for information and reservations. On weekends, ranch hands dress in Victorian costume and demonstrate blacksmithing, doll making, and other 19th-century crafts. Wilder Ranch is also a popular spot among local surfers. The day use fee is $3.00 per car.

Mile 52 brings us to **Bonnie Doon Beach,** at the foot of Bonnie Doon Road. This area has traditionally been used by

Insiders' Tip

The Great Dipper, a 1920s wooden roller coaster at the Santa Cruz Beach Boardwalk is a National Historic Landmark. It's a must ride for coaster aficionados.

locals and UCSC students as a nude beach, so be prepared for sunbathers baring it all. Mile 53.5 brings us to charming **Davenport,** population 200. Originally a small company town built around the Pacific Cement and Aggregates plant, Davenport is now a quiet getaway spot that offers a great stop for Highway 1 daytrippers. The main attraction is the **New Davenport Cash Store, Restaurant and Bed & Breakfast Inn,** right on Highway 1, (831) 426-4122. At lunch the restaurant serves up great sandwiches made with delicious homemade bread. The hot dishes for breakfast, lunch, and dinner are also very fresh and tasty. The Cash Store inside the restaurant offers crafts from local artists as well as other interesting goods, while the bed and breakfast around back provides quiet and comfortable accommodations. Other stopping points in this tiny town include **Whale City Bakery Bar & Grill,** Highway 1, (831) 423-9803, for some croissants, cookies, or other baked goods for the road, and the **Pacific School Thrift Shop,** 81 Center Street, (831) 423-9338, where you just might find a great little bargain and vacation memento.

Leaving Davenport, Highway 1 hugs the coast, providing many spots for easy beach access. At mile 56, Scott Creek flows into the Pacific to create a freshwater marsh. The beaches have fascinating tide pools carved from sandstone, while the coastal bluffs are formed from ancient marine sedimentary rock that is 10 to 20 million years old. Waddel Creek and the "Skyline to the Sea" trailhead to **Big Basin Redwoods State Park,** (831) 338-8860, are at mile 61. You'll find a nature center and the beginning point of an 11-mile hike through the grassy Rancho Del Oso Canyon to the majestic redwood groves of Big Basin, California's oldest state park. It's a lengthy but moderate hike, with two trail camps along the way that can be reserved through Big Basin State Park headquarters. This canyon was explored by Captain Gaspar de Portolá back in 1769, and in 1862 it became home to what was to become the largest lumber mill in Santa Cruz County.

Insiders' Tip

Insiders know that Highway 1 is ideal for any trip from Monterey to San Francisco. Compared to nerve-wracking freeway travel up U.S. 101, the scenery is superb, traffic is generally light, and it typically adds only 15 to 20 minutes to the journey.

Año Nuevo State Reserve

At mile 62 we enter San Mateo County and at mile 63.5 reach **Año Nuevo State Reserve,** (650) 879-0227, (800) 444-4445, www.anonuevo.org. The 4,000-acre reserve is known worldwide by naturalists as an important birthing and mating ground for huge northern elephant seals who arrive each December and stay through March. The large males can be up to 16 feet long and weigh three tons. The smaller 1,200-pound females typically give birth to pups within a week of their arrival. The mating typically begins in late January, and ferocious turf wars often erupt as the large bulls fight for dominance. Visiting Año Nuevo during the mating and young-bearing season is allowed only through 3-mile guided tours led by park rangers each weekend. During the rest of the year, you are free to explore this peninsula and its fascinating tide pools, which are abundant with life. Unusual tube masses, created by the abundant tubeworms, are often visible at low tide. The area is also mating grounds for harbor seals and long-necked cormorants. Smaller groups of elephant seals may return to molt as well. Shell mounds and other remnants of the Ohlone Indians who lived for centuries near this area can also be found. There is a $5.00 parking fee and a $4.00 per-person charge for the guided tour. Call (800) 444-4445 for reservations.

At mile 66.5, you'll find one of the more recent additions to our daytrip options, the **Costanoa Coastal Lodge and Camp,** (650) 879-1100, (800) 738-7477, www.costanoa.com. This is a fabulous overnight excursion into the tranquility of a lovely stretch of California coast and mountain. Accommodations include a 40-room lodge, cabins (wood and canvas varieties), and RV and tent sites. It's a great setup for hikers, adjacent to four state parks and 30,000 acres crisscrossed with bountiful foot trails. And after a big day of hiking, you can visit the spa for a whole-body massage—Swedish or shiatsu, your choice. Two nights here with a visit to Año Nuevo in between makes for a memorable weekend.

Mile 68 of Highway 1 brings us to the entrance to **Butano State Park,** (650) 879-2044, one of the area's nicest campgrounds, with 21 developed sites and hiking and cycling trails among redwood and fir forests that are home to purple calypso orchids. There is a $3.00 vehicle fee and a $15.00 to $17.00 per-night camping fee.

Near here is **Gazos Creek** coastal access. This pleasant, secluded spot, among grassy sand bluffs, is favored by surf-fishers and beachcombers. From the highway, you also get your first view of **Pigeon Point Lighthouse,** at mile 70 of our drive. Built in 1872 by the Coast Guard, the lighthouse is now operated by the American Youth Hostel Association and accommodates up to 50 visitors per night. Call (650) 879-0633 or visit www.pigeonpointlighthouse.org for information about accommodations and call (650) 879-2120 for seasonal lighthouse tours, including newly offered night tours.

Mile 73 takes us to **Bean Hollow State Beach,** (650) 879-2170, a 44-acre beach known for its scenic vistas, secluded beaches, harbor seals, and lively tide pools. There is no entrance fee.

At mile 76.5 is the inland turnoff to **Pescadero,** a historic little town founded in the 1860s. About 2 miles up Highway 84, Pescadero makes for an enjoyable drive back into some idyllic countryside. For lunch, stop in at **Duarte's Tavern,** 202 Stage Road, (650) 879-0464, for its famous artichoke soup. Or stop by **Muzzi's Market,** 251 Stage Road, (650) 879-0410, to pick up some picnic fare for a drive on the back-country roads. **Memorial County Park,** (415) 363-4021, with its towering redwoods and scenic Pescadero Creek, makes for a great picnic spot. A limited number of campsites are also available.

Back on Highway 1, mile 77 brings us to **Pescadero State Beach,** (650) 726-8820. This 635-acre state park also provides for a nice picnic and tidepooling spot, with the **Pescadero Marsh Natural Preserve** right across the highway.

At mile 79, **Pomponio State Park,** (650) 879-2170, is yet another great lunch spot, especially if you are in need of some nice tables and barbecue pits. The sandy beach is also ideal for strolling and wading.

Mile 81 brings us to **San Gregorio State Beach,** (650) 879-2170, a 170-acre park where San Gregorio Creek empties into the Pacific. The estuary here is home to a variety of sea animals and birds.

Half Moon Bay

At mile 90 we reach civilization, the town of **Half Moon Bay,** population 10,600. Known as the Pumpkin Capital of the World, this is San Mateo County's oldest town, founded in 1846. It has a long history of agriculture due to its uniform mild climate and today is home to an abundance of both vegetable and flower growers. The big orange gourd, the pumpkin, remains king of the crops. Each October for the past quarter-century, this city has hosted the **Half Moon Bay Art & Pumpkin Festival.** The free-admission weekend event draws crowds from up and down the California coast, who enjoy the festivities on Main Street. Artist booths, live music, street performers, home-baked goods, and The Great Pumpkin Parade create a colorful scene. A giant pumpkin contest, a pumpkin-carving contest, and a haunted house are especially popular with the kids.

Half Moon Bay has visitor attractions during the rest of the year as well. At mile 92 near the Highway 92 East intersection is Kelly Avenue, the entrance to **Half Moon**

Bay State Beach, (650) 726-8819. This is an ideal spot for sunbathing, beachcombing, picnicking, and horseback riding. Nearby, **Sea Horse Ranch,** 1828 Coast Highway, (650) 726-9903, and **Friendly Acres Ranch,** 2150 Cabrillo Highway, (650) 726-9916, provides horses and ponies to ride among 12,000 acres and miles of scenic beaches and coastal trails.

Hungry? We've got a couple of interesting choices here in Half Moon Bay and environs. At mile 95, **The Miramar Beach Restaurant,** 131 Mirada Road, (650) 726-9053, is a great seafood establishment that was originally a Prohibition-era roadhouse and bordello. Try the famous clam chowder. Or for something really out of this world, go on to mile 98.5 and the **Moss Beach Distillery Restaurant,** (650) 728-5595, at 140 Beach Way. In addition to serving fine food, this establishment is known for a couple of tragic female ghosts who are occasionally spotted in or about the place. The Blue Lady, killed in an automobile accident back in the 1920s while on her way here to meet her lover, is said to be seen wandering the beach in her trademark blue dress. Another woman, who later threw herself off the cliffs and drowned herself in anguish over the same lover, has been spotted near the restaurant as well, dripping wet, covered with seaweed. The restaurant even holds special séance dinners in hopes of calling the two women from the other side. Bon appetit!

At mile 100 is **Montara State Beach,** (650) 726-8819. This area is known for its heavy surf and beautiful sandy beaches. While Montara is an experienced surfer's delight, beginning boarders and swimmers are advised to try a less hazardous spot. There is no entry fee.

At mile 101 of Highway 1, we reach a 3-mile stretch known as **Devil's Slide.** The winding, cliffside roadway is reminiscent of stretches of Highway 1 south at Big Sur, and, like Big Sur, is subject to landslides during the rainy season. In fact, during poor weather, it wouldn't be a bad idea to check with CalTrans, (800) 427-7623, and make sure this section of highway is open. If it's closed, take Highway 92 east back at Half Moon Bay to continue onward to San Francisco. Highway 92 crosses the Santa Cruz Mountains and hooks up with U.S. 280 North, which takes you directly into San Francisco.

San Francisco

We leave the Devil's Slide area at mile 104 and in a half-mile reach the town of **Pacifica,** a bedroom community of San Francisco. This tranquil little town is home to a few charming restaurants, including the cleverly named **Chez D Cafe,** 220 Paloma Avenue, (650) 355-2730, for coffee, baked goods, and light fare in the historic 1906 Anderson's Store building. Pacifica is also home to the Sanchez Adobe, 1000 Linda Mar Boulevard, (650) 359-1462. The oldest building in San Mateo County, it is now a fascinating museum that reveals local history and lore back to the local Native Americans and first Spanish settlers.

At mile 107, Highway 1 becomes a modern freeway for our ascent into San Francisco. As we enter the bustle of the city, Highway 1 merges temporarily with U.S. 280 North. As you enter San Francisco proper, Highway 1 then splits off to the left and takes you through Golden Gate Park, by the San Francisco Zoo, and over the Golden Gate Bridge to Marin and points north. U.S. 280 will take you to downtown San Francisco, the Bay Bridge, and over to Oakland and the East Bay.

To try and give justice to the city of San Francisco in this chapter would be an injustice. However, we would be remiss not to mention a few of the notable spots. For attractions, **Golden Gate Park,** Fell and Stanyon Streets, (415) 556-5801, and the **San Francisco Zoo,** Sloat Street and 45th Avenue, (415) 753-7080, are a real treat on a bright sunshiny day. **The Powell-Hyde Cable Car** line is a must, followed by a visit to the **Cable Car Barn and Museum** at 1201 Mason Street. **Chinatown** is a great eating and shopping experience, as are **Union Square** and **Ghirardelli Square.** A stroll through **North Beach** provides a real flavor for the city's Italian and Bohemian roots. **Coit Tower** has a spectacular view of the bay and marvelous interior murals. **Alcatraz Island,** of course, is a fascinating trip. Our list here could go on and on, and we haven't even mentioned the **Exploratorium** or the fabulous art museums.

If you're planning on spending the night, you have a wide range of choices. For the luxury of Nob Hill, it's hard to beat the **Mark Hopkins Inter-Continental,** 999 California Street, (415) 392-3434 or (800) 227-0200, with its spectacular Top of the Mark cocktail lounge; or the **Fairmont,** 950 Mason Street, (415) 772-5000 or (800) 527-4727. At Union Square there are the **St. Francis,** 335 Powell Street, (415) 397-7000; and the **Palace,** 2 New Montgomery Street, (415) 392-8600 or (800) 325-3535. For quaint bed and breakfast ambiance try the French country **Petitie Auberge,** 863 Bush Street, (415) 928-6000, and the swanky **English White Swan Inn,** 845 Bush Street, (415) 775-1755. Over near the Dragon Gates into Chinatown, the trendy **Hotel Triton,** 342 Grant Avenue, (415) 394-0500, is a marvelous stay. The **Holiday Inn at Fisherman's Wharf,** 1300 Columbus Avenue, (415) 771-9000, often has special rates, especially during the off-season.

For restaurants, it's hard to beat the City by the Bay. If the sky is the limit, **Masa's,** 648 Bush Street, (415) 989-7154, has appeared at the top of many top 10 lists, in both quality and price. There are many good Italian restaurants populating North Beach and other areas, including **Pane e Vino,** 3011 Steiner Street, (415) 346-2111, and **Acquerello,** 1722 Sacramento Street, (415) 567-5432. For French, both the fancy **La Folle,** 2316 Polk Street (415) 776-5577, and the more casual bistro-style **Fringale,** 570 Fourth Street, (415) 543-0573, come highly recommended. Other eclectic establishments in hip surroundings include **Flying Saucer,** 1000 Guerrero Street, (415) 641-9955, **Restaurant Lulu,** 816 Folsom Street, (415) 495-5775, and **Zuni Cafe & Grill,** 1658 Market Street, (415) 552-2522. And for Chinese, virtually any of the many restaurants in Chinatown serve good, authentic, and affordable food.

For your trip back to the Peninsula, your best bet is to take U.S. 280 South to Highway 85 South to Gilroy. Then take U.S. 101 South to Prunedale, Highway 156 west to Castroville, and Highway 1 South to the Monterey Peninsula. An alternate route that typically has heavier traffic is to take U.S. 101 south to Prunedale, Highway 156 to Castroville, and Highway 1 to the Monterey Peninsula. Or, read this chapter backwards and backtrack your way back on scenic Highway 1.

Salinas Valley

Steinbeck Country, Salad Bowl of the World, and the Other California Wine Country are a few of the names given to the Salinas Valley. This long expanse of rich agricultural farmland and fast-growing towns stretches about 100 miles along U.S. 101 from north of the city of Salinas to the San Luis Obispo County line. While not often considered a tourist destination on its own, the Salinas Valley offers some great daytripping activities for visitors and residents of the Monterey Peninsula.

The Valley is proud of its agricultural heritage and its important spot in California history as a major provider of food for a hungry state, nation, and world. By staging special events like September's **Salute to Agriculture,** an extensive program of tours and tastings, the Monterey County Agricultural Commission, Salinas Area Chamber of Commerce, and other local groups have made it a point to promote the Valley's key role in keeping America and the world stocked with fresh fruits and vegetables. Lettuce, broccoli, strawberries, tomatoes, sugar beets, spinach, and cabbage are only a few of the crops grown in this fertile valley. A group of wineries and vineyards that make up **Monterey Wine Country Associates,** (831) 375-9400, also plans tours and special events like the **August Winemaker's Celebration** and November's **The Great Wine Escape Weekend** to celebrate the expansive and growing wine industry. Check with the Salinas Area Chamber of Commerce, (831) 424-7611, for this year's schedule of special events and other daytripping opportunities.

In this section we've listed two great Salinas Valley daytrip options that can be enjoyed year-round—the National Steinbeck Center and a winery tour—in addition to recreational opportunities at Pinnacles National Monument.

The National Steinbeck Center

The National Steinbeck Center is a 37,000-square-foot, $10 million museum and community center honoring Nobel Prize-winning author and native son John Steinbeck. Located at 1 Main Street in historic Old Town Salinas (only 2 blocks from Steinbeck's birthplace), the center features a unique array of interactive, multisensory exhibits that lets you experience the sights, sounds, and smells of the time Steinbeck roamed the Salinas Valley and Monterey Peninsula. Text and graphic panels, film clips, and audiotapes provide detailed information on the author and his works. You'll also find the world's largest collection of Steinbeck artifacts, such as original manuscripts, correspondence, unpublished works, and even Rocinante, the camper that was Steinbeck's home on wheels during his *Travels with Charley*.

Among the permanent exhibits are: "The Valley of the World," portraying Steinbeck's early years in the Salinas Valley as depicted in *The Red Pony, East of Eden,* and *Of Mice and Men;* "Cannery Row," revealing the sights, sounds, and salty smells of The Row and Doc's Lab, as captured in *Cannery Row* and *Sweet Thursday;* "Hooverville," the agricultural labor camp of tents and cabins described in *The Grapes of Wrath* and *The Harvest Gypsies;* and "Mexican Plaza," demonstrating Steinbeck's fascination with and admiration for Mexico's history, as brought to light in *The Pearl, Viva Zapata,* and *The Forgotten Village.* A changing gallery highlights special temporary exhibits, including the work of other California artists influenced by Steinbeck's work. The National Steinbeck Center's library contains an incredible collection of first editions, manuscripts, notes, audiotapes, and photographs that attract researchers and scholars from

Salinas Valley is a major provider of fresh vegetables and is proud of its notoriety as the "Salad Bowl of the World." PHOTO: MARTIN BROWN/MONTEREY PENINSULA VCB

around the world. Visitors can view artifacts and gain access to Steinbeck's work at special CD-ROM stations in the Art of Writing room. A variety of special public programs keep the center fresh and alive for repeat visitors.

The **Steinbeck Festival,** held in early August every year, includes bus tours, lectures, films, and workshops. Call the center for information. The center holds numerous walking and bus tours to Steinbeck's birthplace and his gravesite at the Garden of Memories. It also hosts community events related to education, history, and the arts.

The National Steinbeck Center is an easy 20-minute drive from the Monterey Peninsula. Just take Highway 68 East to Salinas. The highway turns into Main Street in downtown Salinas. Proceed all the way to 1 Main Street in Old Town, and you're there. Steinbeck fans can expect to stay a good three hours viewing the multisensory exhibits. Admission is $8.00 for adults, $7.00 for seniors, $6.00 for youths 13 to 17, $4.00 for kids six to 12, and free for kids five and younger. Call (831) 753-6411 or visit www.steinbeck.org for details.

Wine-tasting Tour

Monterey County now produces more than 40,000 acres of grapes, with more than 40 wineries and vineyards. Both of these numbers are growing annually. The Salinas Valley is blessed with rich soil, ample water, sufficient sunlight, and mild temperatures. Plus, the Santa Lucia and Gabilan foothills and varying ocean influences create a wide variety of microclimates, each of which favors a certain type of grape. Thus Monterey County produces an extraordinary range of wine choices. The main varieties of white wines produced in the region include Chardonnay, Sauvignon Blanc, Riesling, White Riesling, Gewürztraminer, Pinot Blanc, White Zinfandel, and Chenin Blanc. Among the reds you'll find Pinot Noir, Cabernet Sauvignon, Cabernet Franc, Merlot, Vigonier, Syrah, Zinfandel, Malbec, Petit Verdot, and Meritage. You'll also find fine dessert wines like Port Souzoa and Late Harvest Pinot Noir and Riesling.

Of the dozens of wineries and vineyards in Salinas Valley, seven currently provide public tasting rooms and make for a great daytrip through the wine country. A couple more tasting rooms are in the planning stage. Tours of most of these winemaking facilities are also available but by appointment only, so call ahead. Bring along a picnic lunch for your Salinas Valley wine tour. Most of the wineries have nice picnic areas (Paraiso Springs in particular), and there are a few opportunities to purchase food along the way. For nice big sandwiches, try the Food Center Market at the corner of Highway 68 and Corral de Tierra.

To begin our wine-tasting tour from the Monterey Peninsula, head east on Highway 68 toward Salinas. The best time to depart is about 10:30 A.M. since most of the wineries open at 11:00 A.M. and you'll need an early start to fit in all seven on this tour by the general closing time of 5:00 P.M. Before reaching Salinas proper, take the off-ramp for River Road (G-17), which follows the Salinas River south along the foothills of the eastern edge of the Santa Lucia Mountains. For about 15 miles you'll follow River Road along acres and acres of agricultural fields of lettuce, broccoli, and other crops of the Salad Bowl of the World. (Note that at about mile 9, River Road jags off to the right: Don't follow the highway straight to the town of Chular.) Then, suddenly, the first vineyards begin to appear as you approach the start of the wine region near the town of Gonzales.

Insiders' Tip

For great information of virtually all Monterey County wineries, visit the Monterey County Vintners and Growers Association Web site at www.montereywines.com.

Monterey County now produces more than 40,000 acres of grapes, with more than 40 flourishing wineries and vineyards. PHOTO: MARTIN BROWN/MONTEREY PENINSULA VCB

At about mile 15 on River Road, the first large vineyard you'll pass is that of Morgan Winery, which produces some nice wines but unfortunately doesn't have a tasting room. Almost next door, however, is the first stop on our tasting tour. **Cloninger Cellars,** on your left at 1645 River Road in Salinas, is one of the newest and smallest wineries in Salinas Valley. This 51-acre vineyard officially opened in 1988 and has quickly gained a strong reputation for its Chardonnay, Pinot Noir, and Cabernet Sauvignon. The Chardonnay and Pinot Noir are grown right here in Salinas Valley, while the Cabernet comes from the Quinn Vineyard in warmer Carmel Valley. Cloninger Cellars has a small, pleasant tasting room with a nice view overlooking the Salinas Valley. Its wines are available at only a few select markets and shops, so your best bet is to purchase directly from the winery. Tasting hours are 11:00 A.M. to 4:00 P.M., Monday through Thursday, 11:00 A.M. to 5:00 P.M. Friday through Sunday. Reach them by calling (831) 675-9463 or visit www.usawines.com/cloninger.

From Cloninger Cellars, continue south on River Road. At approximately mile 17, the road will bend to the east at Gonzales Road, and you have to make a right turn at the elbow in order to continue south on River Road. At mile 20, notice the interesting farm of prickly pear cacti, grown for its flavorful fruit. At approximately mile 24, River Road ends. Take the right fork to Foothill Road and continue onward for another 3 miles. There you will find a signed dirt road, at 37700 Foothill Road in Soledad, that rises into the foothills to **Smith & Hook Winery,** (831) 678-2132, www.hahnestates.com. The dirt road meanders about 1.5 miles uphill through the Santa Lucia Highlands to the wine-tasting room and extensive gift shop. Smith & Hook Winery produces from five vineyards and bottles its wine under two labels. The Smith & Hook label features premium Cabernet Sauvignon, Merlot, and Viognier wines meant to be laid down in the cellar for a number of years to achieve peak drinkability. The 100 percent Viognier is particularly intriguing. Hahn Estates is the name of the label of Smith & Hook wines sold for immediate enjoyment. And for the money, they are some of the nicest wines available from Monterey County. You can enjoy a very pleasant Merlot, a light French-style Chardonnay, a smooth Cabernet Sauvignon or a blended Meritage. Also highly recommended is the Cabernet Franc, a spicy and robust wine that is a great picnic red and also goes marvelously with bittersweet chocolates. If you happen to be visiting the Monterey Peninsula in early December, check out the schedule for Smith & Hook's annual wreath-making party. Each year it draws up to 1,000 participants who make their holiday wreaths out of dried grape vines while sampling the splendid wines and enjoying a hearty barbecue. Tasting hours are 11:00 A.M. to 4:00 P.M. daily.

Continue south on Foothill Road about 2 miles to the entrance to **Paraiso Springs Vineyards,** 38060 Paraiso Spring Road, Soledad, (831) 678-0300, www.usawines.com/paraiso. This 400-acre estate affords excellent views of the Salinas Valley below and the Pinnacles in the Gabilan Mountains beyond. An outdoor deck with ample seating is an excellent spot to enjoy a picnic lunch along with your bottle of wine. And what a great selection of wine it is. Current releases include Chardonnay, Pinot Blanc, Pinot Noir, Baby Blush Rosé, and Riesling. The winemaker also bottles his own Cobblestone Chardonnay, a smooth, smoky wine aged in first-year French oak. Then there are the specialty selections like the Pinot Blanc Reserve, Syrah, Port Souzao, a Late Harvest Riesling, and, our personal favorite, a Late Harvest Pinot Noir. (This sweet dessert wine, available only at the tasting room, is excellent poured lightly over vanilla ice cream.) Tasting hours are noon to 4:00 P.M. Monday through Friday, 11:00 A.M. to 5:00 P.M. Saturday and Sunday.

As you leave Paraiso Springs, cross Foothill Road and continue east on Paraiso Springs Road approximately 1 mile to Arroyo Seco (G-17) and turn right (south). Follow Arroyo Seco for about 6.5 miles to the Arroyo Seco Gorge and turn left (east) on Elm Street. Turn right over the green bridge and travel about another 3 miles or so to 13th Street. Turn left on 13th and then make a right a few blocks down at Walnut Avenue. There on the left you'll find **Jekel Vineyards,** 40155 Walnut Avenue in Greenfield, (831) 674-5522, www.usawines.com/jekel. This winery has a national reputation for fine wines. In fact, Jekel wines were served exclusively at President Clinton's two inaugurations. It also holds the haughty title of "Official Wine of Pebble Beach." This notoriety is not without merit. Jekel produces quality whites and reds, including Chardonnay, Riesling (very crisp and refreshing), and Pinot Noir from its cool, windy Gravelstone vineyards. The Merlot, Cabernet Sauvignon, Cabernet Franc, and Meritage (a great blended table wine of Cabernet Sauvignon, Merlot, Malbec, Petit Verdot, and Cabernet Franc) come from the warmer Sanctuary Estate. A Late Harvest Riesling and Estate Petit Verdot are also offered (both are great). The tasting room is charming from the outside and comfortable inside, and the scenic grounds are worth a short stroll before returning to your car. Tasting hours are 10:00 A.M. to 5:00 P.M. daily.

From Jekel, continue east on Walnut Avenue 1 mile to U.S. 101. Proceed 3 miles south on U.S. 101 to Hobson Avenue and exit west (right) to **Scheid Vineyards** at 1972 Hobson Avenue, Greenfield, (831) 386-0316, www.scheidvineyards.com. There you'll find a converted 1920s-era barn that now serves as a modern tasting room. Scheid Vineyards was founded in 1972 and, with more than 6,000 acres under its ownership

Insiders' Tip

Don't forget the wine connoisseurs back home. Most of the wineries have nice gift shops featuring gift packs of wines, foods, apparel, and accessories.

Insiders' Tip

On wine-tasting tours, bring along a designated driver with the willpower to resist buttery Chardonnay and hearty Merlot. Treat him or her like royalty for the sacrifice. If everyone wants to taste, AgVenture Tours provides both agricultural and wine-tasting tours for parties of four to 14. Call (831) 643-WINE or visit www.whps.com/agtours for details and schedules.

or management, is among the country's largest independent producers of premium varietal wine grapes. But Scheid has only been selling wine to the public under its own label since 1997. And what a beautiful label it is, consisting of a series of colorful paintings by renowned artist Dominic Man-Kit Lam. The wines are actually produced at Storrs Winery in Santa Cruz under the Scheid label. More than 4,500 cases of high-quality Chardonnay, White Riesling, Merlot, Pinot Noir, Gewurztraminer, Sauvignon Blanc, and Cabernet Sauvignon are bottled each year. Ever think of owning your own vineyard? Well, you can now own a piece of Scheid, as the company went public in 1997 selling on the NASDAQ exchange under the SVIN symbol. You can pick up investor information at the Scheid tasting room, which is open 11:00 A.M. to 5:00 P.M. daily.

From Scheid, it's a long but beautiful journey to our next destination. Carefully cut back across U.S. 101 and continue east on Hobson Avenue to the end at Metz Road. Turn left (north) and follow Metz Road through the beautiful foothills of the Gabilan Mountains for approximately 6 miles until you reach Highway 146, the western entrance to Pinnacles National Monument (see our write-up later in this section). Turning right on Highway 146, you'll wind approximately 6 miles up a narrow canyon until you reach Stonewall Canyon Road. Turn left at the sign and continue about a mile to the tasting room of **Chalone Vineyard,** (831) 678-1717, www.chalonewinegroup.com. Chalone is open for public tasting 11:30 A.M. to 5:00 P.M. every weekend and on weekdays by appointment only, so call ahead Monday through Friday. It's a bit off the beaten path, but the scenic drive and fine wines are worth the effort. Chalone features a nice selection of Chardonnays (barrel fermented and aged), Pinot Noirs, Cabernet Sauvignon, Chenin Blanc, Syrah, Viognier, and Pinot Blanc. The Reserve Pinot Noir is deep and intense (if somewhat pricey) and the limited-quantity A-Frame Cabernet Sauvignon is a tasting room specialty bottled primarily for the winery principal's own pleasure.

For our final destination, proceed back east on Highway 146 to Metz Road and turn right (north). Go approximately 2.5 miles to the town of Soledad and turn left on East Street and then a quick right on Front Street. Front Street will take you back to U.S. 101, where you will proceed north for about 7 miles to the city of Gonzales. At Gonzales, exit on Alta Street and continue west less than a mile to **Riverland Vineyards,** 800 Alta Street, Gonzales, (831) 675-2481. This is the home of Mystic Cliffs Wines and the former home of the Monterey Vineyard. The expansive wine-tasting room is open daily from 11:00 A.M. to 4:00 P.M. The Mystic Cliffs wine portfolio includes Merlot, Cabernet Sauvignon, Chardonnay, Riesling, Syrah, and Pinot Noir.

You have two choices for your return trip to the Monterey Peninsula. Continue north on Alta Road, which hooks back up with U.S. 101, and proceed north on U.S. 101 to Highway 68 West, which leads you back to the Peninsula. Or, go north on Alta Road to Gonzales River Road and turn left. Gonzales Road will take you back to River Road near our first destination, Cloninger Cellars. Proceed on River Road north (right) to Highway 68 and then head west back to the Peninsula.

Pinnacles National Monument

About 35 miles southeast of Salinas lies Pinnacles National Monument, the remnants of an ancient volcano within the Gabilan Mountains along the eastern edge of the Salinas Valley. Hikers, rock climbers, cavers (spelunkers), and wildflower lovers will want to check out this unique geological and biological area. From the Monterey Peninsula, the quickest route to Pinnacles is to take Highway 68 East to U.S. 101 and then take U.S. 101 South to Highway 146 (about 25 miles south near Soledad). Follow Highway 146 East about 8 winding miles to the park's western entrance. (Pinnacles' eastern entrance, which is more hospitable to motor homes and trailers, is off of Highway 25. From Salinas, go north on U.S. 101 to Highway 156 and then east to Hollister. From Hollister, head south on Highway 25. There is no road connecting the east and west sides of the park.)

Pinnacles features spectacular 1,200 foot spires, a unique chaparral ecosystem, and more than 30 miles of hiking trails. Picnic and barbecue areas are also available. While open year-round, the best time to visit is the spring wildflower season between March and May and the fall months of October and November. The summer can also be pleasant, but temperatures can reach 100 degrees and higher during heat spells.

The Pinnacle's talus caves are especially fun to explore. From the west side, visit the **Balconies Caves,** about 0.7 miles from the Chaparral Ranger Station. From the east entrance, the **Bear Gulch Caves** are a similar distance from the visitor center. Bring your flashlight, which is required, or purchase one at the visitor center. Although the caves are relatively safe, caution is advised due to low ceilings, sudden drop-offs, and slippery-when-wet rocks.

Finally, rock-climbing at Pinnacles is best left to the pros with proper equipment.

The remnants of an ancient volcano, Pinnacles National Monument makes for a great daytrip of hiking, picnicking, rock climbing, and spelunking.
PHOTO: MARTIN BROWN/MONTEREY PENINSULA VCB

Rock climbers are asked to register at the visitor center and obey area closure signs posted at certain environmentally sensitive spots. For seasonal hours and road conditions, call Pinnacles National Monument at (831) 389-4485. Visit the Friends of Pinnacles Web site at www.pinnacles.org.

Carmel Valley

In his story *The Old Pacific Capital,* Robert Louis Stevenson describes Carmel Valley as "a True Californian Valley." That description continues to ring as true as a dinner bell, with Carmel Valley serving as a California country counterpart to the Peninsula's cozy coastal town and village atmosphere. This unincorporated area is home to more than 8,500 residents and a wide range of native flora and fauna.

Expect sunshine in these wide-open spaces as you drive down the main highway artery of Carmel Valley Road, more formally known as Monterey County Highway G-16. A spring or summer daytrip through the Valley is likely to provide views of brightly colored fields of wildflowers and rich green hillsides. Rich colors dominate the fall, as the sycamores, alders, and willows turn to golds and reds. Crisp blue skies with white fluffy clouds are a common sight during the chilly winter. You'll see ranches, farms, orchards, and vineyards as well as championship golf courses, rustic and regal resorts, and some great parks in which to enjoy the splendid setting. Drive some of the back roads and you may even encounter wild turkeys, California quail, gray foxes, and possibly a wild boar.

The lifeline of the Valley is the Carmel River, which flows 30 miles from the high canyons of the Santa Lucia Range out to the open sea. It is also the main source of drinking water for the entire Monterey Bay area, with reservoirs behind the Los Padres and San Clemente dams. The capacity of these dams is being severely tested by the area's ever-increasing population, and overpumping of the river aquifer has led to environmental damage. Controversy has reigned for years over the merits and curses of building larger dams with increased storage capacity to quench the area's growing thirst. But that's not our topic for today. Our goal is to provide an interesting, insightful, and relaxing tour of Carmel Valley.

We'll cover little more than 50 miles in our round-trip drive. Yet, at times you'll feel worlds apart from the Peninsula. Where Carmel Valley officially ends to the east is a matter of local debate. Some feel the Carmel Valley Village, about 14 miles inland, is the end of the trail. The approximately 64,000 acres that encompass the Valley from its mouth to the Village have been slowly and steadily divided into smaller and more populous segments since the 1830s, when large Spanish and Mexican land grants placed this entire wildland under private ownership, much to the dismay of the local Native Americans. Others feel that Carmel Valley's reach extends many miles farther east into the less populated canyons that eventually open up into the Salinas Valley near Greenfield. Regardless, our trip extends 23 miles out Carmel Valley Road and includes a scenic loop though the backcountry of Cachaqua Valley.

The Mouth of the Valley

We include general mile markers at major destinations along the way. Set your odometer at zero as you turn east onto Carmel Valley Road (G-16) from Highway 1 in Carmel. If you're traveling into the Valley during the summer months, be ready for some intense heat. Dress in layers, as the coastal mouth of the Valley can often be shrouded in chilly fog, while the inner Valley bakes under the hot sun. Ready?

From Highway 1 just south of Carmel proper, turn east on Carmel Valley Road. To the immediate right are Carmel Rancho Center, The Barnyard, and The Crossroads shopping centers. Here you can pick up those last-minute supplies you forgot to pack or get a ready-made lunch to take along on your trip. Two of our favorite choices for lunch or a snack are the **Bagel Bakery,** 539 Carmel Rancho Shopping Center, (831) 625-5180, and the **Power Juice and Food Company,** 173 The Crossroads, (831) 626-6577. Of course, once you see all the other specialty shops here at the mouth of the Valley, you just might forget about this whole idea of daytripping through the great outdoors and spend your entire day shopping.

Assuming you choose to continue on with your tour, you'll drive inland past open fields, Carmel Middle School, and three splendid golf courses. At approximately the 1-mile mark, you pass the two public Rancho Cañada Golf Club courses (see our Golf chapter). At about 2 miles, you reach Rancho San Carlos Road, the entrance to Carmel Valley Golf and Country Club, a private club for members and guests only. At the 3.5-mile mark is the Quail Lodge Resort (see our Hotels and Motels chapter), with its splendid accommodations and the award-winning Covey Restaurant (see our Restaurants chapter).

For those of you who left the golf clubs at home and are simply out for a leisurely drive, our first stop is at the Valley Hills Shopping Center, right next door to Quail Lodge past Valley Greens Drive. Hungry? For you morning folks, enjoy a great traditional country breakfast at **Katy 'n Harry's Wagon Wheel Coffee Shop,** (831) 624-8878. For 20 years, the Wagon Wheel has been serving hearty breakfasts of eggs, waffles, pancakes, french toast, and the like to a loyal following of locals and visitors. You might want to try the trout and eggs with a side of country potatoes or biscuits and homemade gravy. Lunch is served as well. If Mexican food is to your liking for lunch or dinner, the **Baja Cantina & Grill,** (831) 625-2252, with its outdoor fireplace deck and unusual automobile and filling station memorabilia is a bit farther back toward the rear of the shopping center. Walk off the hearty fare with a stroll through the **Tancredi & Morgen Country Store,** (831) 625-4477, and the other unique antiques and gift shops at the center.

Just past the Valley Hills Center, you'll find the **Earthbound Farms Produce Stand,** (831) 625-6219, featuring a nice selection of locally grown organic fruits and vegetables. This is a great stop for a few fresh car snacks or great salad mixes if you're preparing tonight's dinner. (During the summer and fall months, you'll likely find a number of fruit and vegetable stands along Carmel Valley Road, as local farmers sell their corn, pumpkins, melons, and other goods.)

Nearing the 4-mile mark at Cypress Lane is **Valley Hills Nursery,** (831) 624-3482. For you green thumbers, this is a great spot to pick up some beautiful begonias, fuchsias, azaleas, and those other luscious flowering plants that thrive in our cool coastal climate. At 4.5 miles, turn right (south) at Schulte Road and proceed about 1.5 miles to **Saddle Mountain Park,** (831) 624-1617, where you'll find some nice secluded campsites and picnic facilities as well as an outdoor swimming pool for day use. This is a good spot for kids who are itching to run, splash, and explore. Saddle Mountain has a challenging 3.5-mile trail that leads to a great view north over Monterey Bay toward Santa Cruz and south toward Big Sur. Right next door to Saddle Mountain is the **Riverside RV Park,** (831) 624-9329, in the event you're in need of a pleasant spot to park and hook up your recreational vehicle.

At the 5-mile mark you'll find the first of five wineries on our daytrip. **Chateau Julien Winery,** 8940 Carmel Valley Road, (831) 624-2600, www.chateaujulien.com, is in—what else—a French-style chateau. The wines are very pleasant and include some interesting Italian grapes you aren't likely to find elsewhere in the area. That includes Trebiano, Sangiovese, and a delicious, earthy Nebbiolo. Of course, you'll also enjoy the more traditional California selection of Chardonnay (all barrel fermented), Riesling, Gewurztraminer (a not-too-sweet delight), Sauvignon Blanc, Merlot, and Cabernet Sauvignon, as well as a unique Meritage white. For dessert, try the Carmel Cream Sherry or Aleatico. Wine tasting is offered daily, 8:00 A.M. to 5:00 P.M. Monday through Friday, 11:00 A.M. to 5:00 P.M. weekends, while tours are provided Monday through Saturday. When in town, inquire about the winery's special events, like the winemaker dinners and art festivals.

Mid-Valley

Next door to Chateau Julien is the **Flower Farm,** 9000 Carmel Valley Road, (831) 626-9191, where you can walk among the beautiful gardens and pick your own special bouquets. It's a memorable romantic treat for traveling twosomes. Six miles into our trip is the **Mid Valley Shopping Center,** another good supply stop for gasoline, picnic supplies—and a great cup of java at **The Carmel Coffee Roasting Company,** 319 Mid Valley Shopping Center, (831) 624-5934. They roast their own beans for a great taste and aroma. Immediately after the Mid Valley Center is Robinson Canyon Road. Turn right (south) to find **Carmel Valley Ranch Resort,** 1 Old Ranch Road, (831) 625-9500, with its championship private golf course for guests and members (see

Carmel Valley's Chateau Julien offers daily wine tastings and many special events. PHOTO: ROSS ANDRÉSON

our Golf chapter). This expansive resort also offers 100 luxury rooms amid the rural charm of the Valley. Of great interest to many daytrippers is **Carmel Valley Trail Rides,** (831) 625–9500, ext. 306, located right here at the Ranch Resort. Owned and operated by the Nason family, descendents of the Esselen Indian Tribe of Carmel Valley, Carmel Trail Rides offers one of the best opportunities to explore the Valley on horseback. Choose from a one-hour scenic ride, a two-hour ocean-view ride, a three-hour sunset ride, or a three-hour picnic lunch ride. Prices range from $40 to $85. All-day rides are also available for $150 per person. Reservations must be made in advance. Riders must be at least seven years old and should wear long, loose-fitting pants and sturdy shoes.

About a mile out Robinson Canyon Road is **Korean Buddhist Temple Sambosa,** or "Three Treasures," 28110 Robinson Canyon Road, (831) 624–3686. To find the temple, turn right up the drive immediately after crossing the small bridge over the Carmel River and follow the signs. The original lavender temple, a Carmel Valley landmark since 1973, tragically burned in 1987. The temple is now housed in a modern, rather nondescript hall that belies the beautiful altar that awaits within. A traditional Korean roof and temple bell are also on the grounds above the Carmel River. The public is invited to Sunday services beginning at 10:30 A.M.

For a beautiful meandering drive through oaks and redwoods, continue farther south out Robinson Canyon Road. At about 10 miles out, you might even spot the remnants of Robert Louis Stevenson's cabin, where the author lived for a short period while recovering from a horseback riding accident. The cabin is within the 20,000-acre Rancho San Carlos.

Garland Ranch

Meanwhile, back at mile 8.5 on Carmel Valley Road, is **Garland Ranch Regional Park,** more than 4,500 acres of beautiful scenery and great trails for hiking, horseback riding, and mountain biking. (You have to make your own arrangements for horses or bikes.) The Carmel River runs the length of the park, which ranges in altitude from 200 to 2,000 feet. A nice easy walk is the 1.4-mile Lupine Loop, a springtime favorite among wildflower lovers. The 2.9-mile hike along the waterfall trail and shaded Garzas Creek is another favorite among local hikers, ending in a secluded redwood canyon. In the park, you are likely to discover a wide range of wildlife, including California quail, great blue heron, red-shouldered hawk, wild turkey, blacktail deer, gray fox, brush rabbit, raccoon, bobcat, and the occasional mountain lion. (It's always a good idea to walk in groups and keep your eyes on the kids when venturing deep into the rugged hills and canyons.) The park is open year-round from sunrise until sunset, with docent-led nature hikes typically leaving from the visitor center at 9:00 A.M. Trail maps are also available at the visitor center inside the park. For information, call (831) 659-4488.

At the 10-mile mark of our trip, Laureles Grade Road intersects with Carmel Valley Road. By turning left (north) on Laureles Grade and driving 6 miles, you connect with Highway 68 near Laguna Seca, about midpoint between Monterey and Salinas. Just past Laureles Grade on the north side of Carmel Valley Road are a couple of great resorts that provide nice accommodations.

The first is **Bernardus Lodge,** 415 Carmel Valley Road, (831) 659-3131, www.bernardus.com, the latest high-end resort in the Valley. The lodge features 57 well-appointed rooms, a luxurious spa (ready for a grapeseed and red wine scrub?), swimming pool, tennis courts, croquet lawn, and a great restaurant with an amazing wine list.

Los Laureles Lodge, (831) 659-2233, www.loslaureles.com, is about a half-mile farther at 313 W. Carmel Valley Road. It's a quaint 1930s-style country inn with a lot of white picket fence charm. Sitting poolside brings you back to a California country atmosphere of days gone by. The poolside bar and food service add to the laid-back atmosphere. And the indoor Los Laureles Bar is a nice spot for an evening cocktail in a warm atmosphere. For $5.00, daytrippers can enjoy use of the swimming pool and bar, with an extensive lunch menu, while overnighters can enjoy relaxing accommodations and maybe a ride in the lodge's horse-drawn surrey.

An interesting slice of Carmel Valley history lies at about the 11.5 mark of our journey. Here you'll see the **Boronda Adobe,** built in 1840 by Don José Manual and Maria Juana Boronda. The story goes that after Don José was crippled in a bullfighting accident, Maria Juana Boronda began making cheese from an old family recipe in order to support the family. The cheese became very popular and, according to local lore, attracted the interest of noted Monterey businessman and dairy farmer David Jacks. Not one to miss a business opportunity, Jacks "borrowed" the recipe and soon began making his own "Monterey Jack Cheese." So, cheese lovers, here's the original home of that soft tasty white cheese made exclusively in California. (The adobe is still a private residence, so no tours are available.)

Looking for a secluded, affordable spot for a quiet overnight stay in Carmel Valley? At mile 12, turn left at Country Club Drive and head up 0.2 miles to **The Portofino Inn and Spa,** 10 Country Club Way, (831) 659-3486, (800) 568-6879, www.theportofinoinn.com. Formerly the Carmel Country Spa, this splendid retreat is currently being refurbished and converted from its former life as a "health farm." You'll still enjoy the huge swimming pool and Jacuzzi with deckside service, but the emphasis is now on relaxation rather than regimen. Daytrippers can enjoy a day of swimming and sunbathing for $8.00 per person.

Back on Carmel Valley Road, at mile 12.5 (across from Ford Road) is the renowned **John Gardner Tennis Ranch,** 114 Carmel Valley Road, (831) 659-2207, which has been providing tennis instruction and accompanying creature comforts to Carmel Valley for more than 40 years. There's not much here for daytrippers, but overnighters can enjoy the accommodations with private patios and fireplaces, the pool and spa, and the healthy gourmet cuisine—whether they play tennis or not. The tennis lessons themselves range from one-day instruction to three-week tennis camps. For schedules and details, call (800) 453-6225 or visit www.carmeltennis.com.

Right next door to the tennis ranch at Ford Road is **Hidden Valley Music and Dance Center,** which hosts a year-round series of musical and theater performances, dance instruction (ballet, tap, jazz, and ballroom), and music seminar programs featuring internationally known artists. Call (831) 659-7442 or (831) 659-3115 or visit www.hiddenvalleymusic.com for schedules. Our travels farther east bring us to the heart and soul of the Carmel Valley.

Carmel Valley Village

At about mile 13 is **Carmel Valley Village** (or alternately, Madonna of the Village), the center of community life for most of the local inhabitants. The charm and unique character of this little piece of the Wild West shines through to visitors as well. One interesting bit of trivia that gives you an inkling of the Village's character is that the Carmel Valley county library is now housed in the former Buckeye Bar. Daytrippers are encouraged to explore the Village and enjoy its wide range of shops, restaurants, and other attractions. We'll highlight a few of our favorite spots, but in no way should this list be considered all-inclusive. Explore!

Hungry? For breakfast, lunch, or dinner, there are a plethora of good restaurants throughout the Village. For real Carmel Valley cowboy character, try **The Running Iron,** 24 East Carmel Valley Drive, (831) 659-4633. It serves a hearty weekend brunch and daily lunch and dinner with a decidedly Western flair. Cowboy boots and other Wild West paraphernalia hang from the ceilings and rafters throughout the restaurant. Burgers and steaks are emphasized (many locals prefer the traditional Lonesome Burger), but good seafood, more than 25 different sandwiches, and other fare are offered. And The Running Iron bar is a great down-home place to stop in for a beer and jaw a spell with the locals.

Wills Fargo Dining House and Saloon, Carmel Valley Road, (831) 659-2774, is a guaranteed winner for a delicious and festive dinner in the Village. At 5:00 P.M. the antique etched glass doors swing open, and you enter a decidedly turn-of-

For a leisurely drive, try Carmel Valley Road, which affords many pastoral views. PHOTO: ROSS ANDRÉSON

Insiders' Tip

Carmel Valley is wild, rugged country with poison oak, rattlesnakes, mountain lions, and other dangers. Have fun, but keep an eye on the kids and proceed cautiously when visiting the backcountry.

the-century Victorian-era room full of chandeliers, carved mahogany, crystal goblets, and other touches of elegance. The saloon mixes an "honest drink," and the butcher shop's certified Angus beef is cut and cooked to your specification. This is a steak and potato lover's delight, but you'll also find lamb, seafood, pasta, and other entrees as well as an ample children's menu. Friday and Saturday nights feature live music. Reservations are advised.

If wine tasting is your pleasure, there are four great finds in Carmel Valley Village that are open daily. **Durney Vineyards,** 69 West Carmel Valley Road, (831) 659-6220, www.durneywines.com, produces some nice premium red and white wines produced entirely at its Carmel Valley Wine Estate in Cachagua Valley (where we'll visit a bit later). The grapes are grown with minimum irrigation thanks to ample hidden springs and without pesticides or herbicides other than sulphur dust. The white wines include Chenin Blanc, Chardonnay, Cuvée Gold, and a Late Harvest Johannisberg Reisling. The reds include Cabernet Sauvignon, Merlot, and Pinot Noir. The Village tasting room is small and modest, but the organically grown grapes result in premium wines that match up well with the best of Monterey County. Tasting hours are 11:00 A.M. to 5:00 P.M. Monday through Friday, 10:00 A.M. to 5:00 P.M. weekends.

Robert Talbott Vineyards, (831) 659-3515, www.talbottvineyards.com, opened its tasting room at 53 West Carmel Valley Road in 1999. The Talbott family offers five distinctly different Chardonnays, from freshly fruity to intensely complex, and two nice Pinot Noirs—one for extended aging and one to enjoy immediately. If you're curious, yes this is the same Robert Talbott that makes the splendid men's ties. In fact you'll find a Talbott Ties Factory Outlet just down the road at the Village Center. Tasting hours are 11:00 A.M. to 5:00 P.M. Thursday through Monday.

Bernardus Winery, 5 W. Carmel Valley Road, (831) 659-1400, (800) 223-2533, www.bernardus.com, is housed in a rather plain building that was once home to a major bank. Inside, however, the tasting room is nicely decorated, making for a pleasant spot to enjoy some fine wines. You'll discover the traditional selection of Monterey County Merlot, Cabernet Sauvignon, and Chardonnay (the white grapes are grown by Ventana Vineyards), each worthy of heartfelt praise. Be sure to sample the unique Marinus Bordeaux blend red table wine, a Bernardus specialty. The tasty Sauvignon Blanc, Pinot Noir, and Pinot Gris are made in limited quantities but definitely worth consideration when available.

Joullian Vineyards, 2 Village Drive, (831) 659-8100, www.joullian.com, opened its impressive tasting room in March of 2000. Joullian provides rich clonal selections of Chardonnay, Sauvignon Blanc, Cabernet Sauvignon, and Zinfandel, all grown exclusively in Carmel Valley's premium wine-growing region. The tasting room is open daily from 11:00 A.M. to 5:00 P.M.

Did you bring the whole family? The kids will undoubtedly enjoy some time at **Carmel Valley Village Park and Community Youth Center,** (831) 659-3983, along Carmel Valley Road east of Ford Road. Here you'll find large open spaces, picnic facilities, horseshoe pits, an activity house, a big outdoor swimming pool, and ample playground equipment, including an old red fire engine.

East of the Village

East of Carmel Valley Village, the canyons and the road narrow, and the density of civilization decreases substantially. But

CLOSE-UP

Tassajara Hot Springs Zen Mountain Center

The Hot Springs of Tassajara have been drawing visitors in search of physical and spiritual well-being for centuries. At the end of Tassajara Road near the edge of the Los Padres National Forest, the rich mineral springs were used extensively by generations of local Esselen Indians and later became a hot springs resort for California settlers in the 1860s. According to an 1875 handbook issued by Monterey County, the Smithsonian Institution tested a sample of the mineral spring water and declared it "the richest spring then known in the United States."

Since 1967, Tassajara has been home to a Zen Buddhist monastery. From September through April, the monastery is closed to the public. But from May to August, Tassajara opens for a series of retreats, workshops, and work practice programs, as well as overnight accommodations and day use of the facilities. Daytrippers can soak in the hot springs and bathhouse, swim in the warm-water pool, and stroll through the tranquil grounds between 10:00 A.M. and 9:00 P.M. daily. Reservations are mandatory. No food or towels are provided, so come prepared. The cost is $20 for adults and $10 for children. (For the full impact, it is suggested that you make your first trip to Tassajara sans kids.)

The trip to Tassajara is about a two-hour drive from Carmel Valley Village. The final 10-plus-mile leg up Tassajara Road is steep, winding, and bumpy—in fact, some passenger cars simply cannot make it. It is recommended, therefore, that you use The Stage, a Tassajara shuttle van that leaves the small town of Jamesburg each morning at 10:30 A.M. and returns at 4:00 P.M. each afternoon. The shuttle service costs $35 round-trip, and lunch is provided. For daytrip and shuttle reservations, call (831) 659–2229.

If you're planning an extended stay at Tassajara, overnight accommodations range from $80 per person for simple dorm rooms to $150 per person for suites. There is also a variety of work programs to consider. A Guest Practice Program of three or more days ($50 per day) allows you to join the students and monks for zazen meditation, morning service, temple cleaning, and breakfast,

Scenic beauty adds to the tranquility at Tassajara.
PHOTO: ROSS ANDRÉSON

followed by community work and lunch. The afternoons and evenings are then free for enjoying bathing, swimming, and hiking. Dinner is served in a common dining room. Work Practice Programs of five days or more ($70 for room and board for the first week) follow a daily schedule of meditation and work. And during the months of April and September, Work Periods provide the opportunity to receive free room and board in exchange for full working days of carpentry, painting, gardening, cooking, and general maintenance. Tassajara begins accepting reservations April 1. Call the San Francisco office of the Zen Buddhist monastery at (415) 865–1895 for reservations. Visit their Web site at www.sfzc.com.

Accommodations are comfortably rustic. There is no in-room electricity, and only a single phone line, so be prepared to be isolated from the outside world.

there are still plenty of reasons (besides the beautiful scenery) to keep driving onward. At approximately mile 15 of our journey, Holman Road appears to the left (north). Up the road lies **The Holman Ranch,** a 400-acre, 1920s-era private ranch that today serves as a popular equestrian center for both English- and Western-style lessons and recreational trail rides. One-hour rides through the oak-studded hills are $40 per person, while a two-hour ride up a scenic ridge is $60. Pony rides are available for youngsters age five to 10, starting at $30, and specially arranged day rides are offered to expert riders for $100 and more. The Holman Ranch also hosts special events and theme parties. This private ranch doesn't accept drop-ins, so be sure to call ahead for reservations at (831) 659–2640. Visit them on the Web at www.theholmanranch.com.

At mile 16 is **Stonepine Resort and Equestrian Center,** 150 E. Carmel Valley Road, (831) 659–2245, www.stonepinecalifornia.com, a former summer home of the famous Crocker banking family. Today, the 330-acre estate provides luxurious accommodations in the main house, Chateau Noel, and excellent equestrian facilities for guests.

Cachagua Valley

At mile 18, we leave Carmel Valley Road and turn right (south) on Cachagua (ka-shaw-wa) Road. Cachagua Road is about a 13-mile loop through the secluded Cachagua Valley that eventually reconnects with Carmel Valley Road about 7 miles farther east from our turnoff point.

After climbing over a ridge and passing a few residential neighborhoods, we enter Cachagua Valley. Our next stop at mile 23 is **Galante Vineyards,** 18181 Cachagua Road, (831) 659–2649 or 800–GALANTE. This is a spectacular little winery that's part of a 700-acre ranch (including cattle) and a huge garden of more than 12,000 rose bushes. The wines include tasty Sauvignon Blanc, Merlot, and premium Cabernet Sauvignon. Tastings are provided by appointment only, so call ahead. Galante Vineyards also holds a summer series of outdoor concerts (with music, wine, and food) and other special events. Call for the current schedule or visit www.galantevineyards.com.

At mile 24 you'll find the small town of **Cachagua.** This little enclave has a simple country atmosphere that seems closer to the Appalachians than to Pebble Beach. The town itself offers friendly residents; the small **Cachagua General Store,** 18840 Cachagua Road, (831) 659–1857; and **Princes Camp,** 37200 Nason Road, (831) 659–2678, the local watering hole. Cachagua serves as the entrance point to a popular visitor destination, **Los Padres Reservoir.** Follow the signs through town and drive a half-mile to a parking spot next to **Cachagua Community Park,** itself a pleasant picnic spot along the Carmel River. From the parking lot, it's a half-mile hike to the lake, where trout fishing, swimming, and rowboating are allowed. From the reservoir there is a variety of hiking trails that lead into the Los Padres National Forest and Ventana Wilderness. This is a popular starting point for overnight backpackers heading toward Big Sur. Overnight backpackers should sign in at the Rangers Station at China Camp out Tassajara Road (see subsequent directions). For daytrippers, a good day hike is along the Church Creek Trail above the dam.

Back at mile 24.5 on Cachagua Road is the COMSAT (Communications Satellite) Earth Station. This 34-ton, 10-story antenna dish is focused on a satellite more than 22,000 miles away and serves as a vital telecommunications link in North America. Guided tours of the facilities are provided from 1:00 to 3:00 P.M. on Wednesday. Call (831) 659-2293 for information and reservations.

Drive 2 miles to the 28.5-mile point and Cachagua Road reaches the Tassajara Road junction. Up Tassajara Road about a mile is the town of **Jamesburg.** Like Cachagua, it's a small settlement without a lot of visitor amenities, but it's a good spot to pick up a quick snack or beverage.

From Jamesburg, Tassajara Road winds about 6 miles to **Chews Ridge,** a popular spot for camping and hiking and one of the few places around the Peninsula where you're likely to find snow after a cold winter storm. Hikers will enjoy exploring caves, some decorated with drawings and writings by Esselen and, later, Costanoan Indians. Here you will also find the **Monterey Institute for Research in Astronomy** (MIRA) observatory, (831) 883-1000. It's not generally open to the pubic, but a few special nighttime open houses are provided throughout the year. Call for details. **China Camp,** which offers overnight camping facilities, is a short drive farther down Tassajara Road. There's also a Ranger Station here for more information about the local facilities, backpacking routes, and hiking trails.

Past China Camp, Tassajara Road becomes more rugged and difficult to transverse without a four-wheel drive vehicle. Daytrippers should likely avoid this section of the Valley unless they are specifically heading to the **Tassajara Hot Springs Zen Mountain Center** (see our Close-up in this chapter). Even visitors to the hot springs are advised to take advantage of the shuttle service offered to Tassajara.

From the Cachagua Road-Tassajara Road junction, it's just another 1.5 miles (mile 30) and you hook back to Carmel Valley Road. Turn left, and you have a 23-mile drive back to Highway 1 in Carmel. Turn right, and Carmel Valley Road takes you on a long and winding journey all the way to Salinas Valley near Greenfield. It's a lovely 30-mile drive but slow going with few signs of civilization until you reach Greenfield and U.S. 101. Assuming you're heading back to the Monterey Peninsula, wine lovers might want to consider going over Laureles Grade to Highway 68 and then proceeding west back toward Monterey. About 4.5 miles down Highway 68, you'll come to **Ventana Vineyards** tasting room, 2999 Monterey-Salinas Highway, (831) 372-7415, www.ventanawines.com. It's in the Old Stone House next to **Tarpey's Roadhouse Grill,** just past the junction of Highway 218. The wide selection of featured wines include Sauvignon Blanc, Pinot Blanc, Chardonnay, Gewürztraminer, Riesling, Muscat d'Orange, Chenin Blanc, Cabernet Sauvignon, Merlot, Cabernet Franc, and Syrah. The tasting room is open daily from 11:00 A.M. to 5:00 P.M.

If you forego the sidetrip over Laureles Grade, there is one more point of interest to mention, about 1.5 miles before you reach Highway 1. On the north side of Carmel Valley Road is a small monument to **El Encino del Descanso** (the Oak of Repose), where Native Americans stopped to rest on their burial processions up the valley. Today, you'll often find flowers left at a small shrine commemorating the dead.

Well, that's it for our daytrip. Be sure to check out the **Carmel Valley Chamber of Commerce,** upstairs at 71 W. Carmel Valley Road, (831) 659-4000, to discover the latest and greatest happenings in this always charming, sometimes wild and woolly neck of the Monterey Bay area.

Neighborhoods and Real Estate

When it comes to real estate on the Monterey Peninsula, the familiar adage rings true: location, location, location. With a unique perch on the scenic Central California coast, the Monterey Peninsula is and probably always will be premium real estate.

The gently rising terrain and native forests overlooking the Pacific Ocean provide spectacular views from virtually every corner of the landscape. With the dramatic rocky coastline and deep-blue sea vistas, ocean views are highly prized in this part of the country. In fact, property prices reflect both the quality and quantity of seaside scenic splendor that you can enjoy from your home and garden.

Then there are the homes themselves. Between its Pebble Beach estates, Monterey adobes, Pacific Grove Victorians, and Carmel cottages, the Monterey Peninsula offers a plethora of desirable architecture and lifestyles. And if it's wide-open space you yearn for, travel a few miles in any and all directions and you'll find it. From the Western ranch-style homes in Carmel Valley and the mountain-top cabins in Big Sur to the sprawling farmlands of the Salinas Valley, you'll discover plenty of room to roam. Though the focus of this chapter is the Monterey Peninsula itself, we cover the surrounding areas as well.

The highly desirable location and the inflexible laws of supply and demand have created a healthy real estate market that is annually near the top of the California scale in terms of price and appreciation. Even California's well-publicized, on-again-off-again economic problems over the last few decades and the midnineties departure of the area's largest single employer—the U.S. Army Base at Ford Ord—hardly put a dent in escalating real estate prices. These economic woes have brought temporary stalls and slight short-term dips, but those downturns seem to always be immediately followed by continued steady rises. Just when you think Peninsula prices can't get any higher, they do.

The reason for our healthy market is simple, really. There are only so many square feet on this relatively small headland surrounded on three sides by the Pacific Ocean. Plus, local conservation and preservation efforts, coupled with a limited supply of freshwater resources, have substantially checked the amount of new construction. Meanwhile, the desire to live on the Monterey Peninsula has only continued to grow as more and more areas of California fall victim to urban sprawl.

A recent phenomenon is the rapid influx of second-home buyers into the local real estate market. It is estimated that up to half of the home purchases in Carmel these days are by people buying a second home for a getaway retreat and eventual retirement spot. That trend has spread to Pacific Grove as well.

Lately, technology has also played a role in increased demand for real estate on the Peninsula. Over the past decades, employment opportunities outside the hospitality and agricultural industries have been fairly limited. But with the coming of telecommuting, more professionals whose skills are in high demand (many from neighboring Silicon Valley) have found they can live here and work for clients or employers elsewhere via modem, Internet, and fax.

In a nutshell, the combination of a great location, limited supply, and growing demand has created a residential real estate market where the price of entry begins at about $300,000 and rises from there to the multimillion dollar stratosphere.

What will $300,000 buy you in the area? Probably a plain-vanilla condominium or a modest one- or two-bedroom, one-bath home in need of repair. It's what local real estate agents call a "fixer-upper" or "charming starter home"—and it's likely off the Peninsula proper. Don't expect too much house or lot, but the views can sometimes make up for the lack of square-footage. Move up to the $400,000 range, and you've probably moved onto the Peninsula or added a third bedroom and/or second bath in the deal—or perhaps a better neighborhood or ocean view from your little bungalow. A price of $600,000 puts you in the range of a more substantial home and lot, including the many well-preserved Victorian or Monterey-style adobes, and $800,000 starts moving you into the most desirable areas of Monterey, Carmel, and Pacific Grove and within the lower range in Pebble Beach. Beyond that, you're entering the near-oceanfront market of Carmel and Pacific Grove. Million-dollar-plus homes move you into the Peninsula's elite.

The lament of most outsiders who begin home shopping on the Monterey Peninsula is that they just can't buy nearly as much house here as they can back home. Unless you're moving from San Francisco, Manhattan, or some other high-priced locale, that's probably true. But what balances the cost equation is the natural splendor that lies outside your new front door.

Neighborhoods

In this section we'll provide a bit of insight into the neighborhoods that make up the Monterey Peninsula. Unlike many areas of today's California, where new housing developments with fancy Spanish names such as Hacienda Royale or Rancho Tranquil are springing up like wildfire, there hasn't been a substantial new subdivision of single-family homes on the Peninsula proper since the 1970s. A few multiunit town-home communities and condominiums have been built in the last two decades, the largest of which is the exclusive Residence at Spanish Bay complex in Pebble Beach. Plus, a few multiacre Pebble Beach estates have been subdivided into smaller parcels, where owners can design and build their custom homes. But new tract-housing subdivisions have been virtually nonexistent on the Peninsula proper for decades. So when we talk neighborhoods in this chapter, we're describing distinct geographic areas within Monterey, Carmel, Pacific Grove, and Pebble Beach where a particular style or age of home is prevalent. Sure, over the years, remodels, rebuilds, and new structures have cropped up that don't fit the overall character of the neighborhoods described here. Still, this chapter should give you a general feel for the locales and might help you focus your search when looking for a home to purchase or rent. (All median prices in this chapter are for the year 2001.)

Monterey

Since the 19th century Monterey has been known for its distinct "Monterey Colonial" and traditional Spanish-adobe style. That architectural influence is still largely felt, even in many of the modern structures. Spanish and similar Mediterranean-style homes circa 1900 as well as circa 2000 can be found throughout the city. The best of this style of architecture generally begins in downtown Monterey and works its way uphill to the west. This area, known colloquially as Spaghetti Hill because of the predominance of Italian families who settled here during the heydays of the sardine industry of Cannery Row, features some fine examples of the Spanish and Mediterranean styles as well as many stately Victorians.

Toward the bottom of the hill, just above Pacific Street, many of the larger homes have since been converted into businesses and multiunit rentals. The higher you progress up the hill, the more residential the area becomes. Head even farther up the hill, above Veterans Memorial Park and below the Community Hospital of the Monterey Peninsula (CHOMP), and you enter the Monterey neighborhood known as Skyline Forest. Here you find newer homes and townhouses set within the eastern edge of Del Monte Forest near Pebble Beach. The many tall pine trees tend to limit the amount of warm sunshine that comes through, and the shallow-rooted

Modest homes out on the Peninsula, like these two Pacific Grove charmers, now begin in the $400,000 to $600,000 range, and up. PHOTO: TOM OWENS

trees can cause occasional property damage when they come crashing down in the high-wind winter storms that can whip in off the Pacific. (This is a problem that occasionally plagues all forested areas of the Peninsula.) But the trees certainly add beauty and an air of tranquillity to the Skyline Forest area. A trip down Skyline Forest Drive from Holman Highway (Highway 68) just north of CHOMP leads you into this neighborhood.

To the northwest of downtown Monterey, out Lighthouse Avenue past the Presidio and toward Pacific Grove, is the neighborhood of New Monterey. Located directly up the hill from Cannery Row, this area of town was populated by the many newcomers who migrated to Monterey during the peak of the fishing industry in the 1940s and early '50s. Strictly a residential area above Lighthouse and Hawthorne Avenues, New Monterey is a hodgepodge of mostly modest single-family homes, peppered with the occasional apartment house, rental duplex, or eye-popping Victorian. Many apartment houses populate the lower streets like Hawthorne Avenue and the main uphill drag of David Avenue, which separates New Monterey from Pacific Grove. Because of the hillside terrain, this area of town affords some of the nicest views overlooking Cannery Row and Monterey Harbor.

East of downtown Monterey toward the city of Seaside is an area of town informally known as "the sunbelt." This part of the Monterey is actually off the Peninsula proper and therefore out of the primary fog belt that extends across the tip of the Peninsula through Pacific Grove and Pebble Beach. The landscape in the sunbelt is a bit flatter and sandier than on the Peninsula, with fewer large Monterey pines and cypress. Homes here are generally less expensive than in other parts of Monterey, and the area has a substantial number of apartments and other rentals due to its proximity to the Naval Postgraduate School.

One neighborhood of note within the sunbelt is Del Monte Beach, a small group of homes and condominiums built on the sand dunes right above the shoreline. The views here are spectacular as you look out across the Bay northwestward toward Cannery Row and Pacific Grove. From Del Monte Boulevard, turn north on Casa Verde Way to enter the Del Monte Beach area.

An amazing aspect of the city of Monterey is that one neighborhood can be situated on a sandy shoreline while another can be nestled in a mountain forest. Jack's Peak, twin summits that rise more than 1,000 feet just a couple miles east of downtown, is home to some of the nicest and most expensive homes in the city. To get a taste of the area, take a drive out Aquajito Road, which forms a loop south of Highway 1 from Fremont Street at Monterey Peninsula College to Holman Highway (Highway 68) at the top of Carmel Hill. There are plenty of large estates on sizable lots here as well as rustic abodes nestled in narrow canyons along each side of the roadway. It's truly mountainous country living less than five minutes from downtown Monterey.

Two more highly populated neighborhoods are also situated in the foothills north of Jack's Peak. Called Fishermans Flats and Deer Flats, these subdivisions were originally built in the 1960s and later. They feature primarily three- and four-bedroom homes. A few have panoramic views overlooking Monterey Bay, while many others face the green hills and canyons of the local terrain. Downhill from both neighborhoods are Josselyn Canyon Road and Sylvan Road, which also have some nice homes in a semisecluded canyon running parallel with the Del Monte Golf Course. On the other side of the golf course lies La Mesa, a housing district for military personnel attending the Naval Postgraduate School.

The median home price in Monterey is $476,000. Entry-level homes near the $300,000 level are primarily in the sunbelt and New Monterey areas, while more expensive homes are generally clustered on the hills of downtown Monterey, Skyline Forest, and Jack's Peak.

Pacific Grove

Think of Pacific Grove, and you immediately think of Victorian architecture with its ornate gingerbread trim. These beautiful stately homes are still common around the downtown area, particularly along the major thoroughfares of Lighthouse, Central, and Pine Avenues. The Pacific Grove Heritage Society has been very active in ensuring the preservation of these homes, and you'll find the society's nameplates on many of the significant residences signifying the date of construction and the name of the original owner. The median price of a Pacific Grove home is $550,000. Because of its splendid location on the northern tip of the Monterey Peninsula, the median price would be higher except that the city was laid out with many small lots that can't handle much more than a small two-bedroom home.

North of Lighthouse Avenue and south of Lovers Point is a portion of town occupied by the original Pacific Grove Retreat. These tiny lots, most created as sites for temporary tent houses, are now packed tightly with some of the most picturesque Victorians in town. Elbowroom is at a premium, but the tight-knit neighborhood has great character, somewhat reminiscent of a small-scale San Francisco.

From Lovers Point, follow Ocean View Boulevard northwest along the coastline to find some of the most spectacular oceanfront property in the state. The famous purple carpet of flowering ice plant provides a breathtaking frame for a bay view that stretches all the way north to Santa Cruz. Prices on large homes here have surpassed the million-dollar range, but smaller beach houses are downright affordable compared to similarly situated properties in Pebble Beach and Carmel.

Just inland from this section of Pacific Grove is the neighborhood known as the Beachtract. Situated on streets named Surf, Shell, and Ripple are mostly 1950s- and 1960s-style tract homes of generally solid construction and prime location. "Bargains" of less than $600,000 can still be found in this area, but they're becoming rare as the Beachtract becomes one of the most desirable areas for newcomers who want to be close to the water but chose to avoid the really high-rent districts.

Keep following the coast out to the Peninsula's northernmost tip at Point Pinos and the shoreline winds south toward Pebble Beach. You're now in the area known as Asilomar, the name taken from the famous Asilomar Conference Grounds that's situated in the area. Stretching inland to Asilomar Avenue and its cross streets, this is a forested beachfront section of town noted for its tall Monterey pines and prolific deer population. (Gardeners here face a triple whammy of chilly fog, salty air, and hungry deer who seem to prefer the most colorful and costly store-bought plants to the natural flora.) The Asilomar section of Pacific Grove can be downright mystical on a fog-shrouded day. If you aren't an ardent sun worshipper and can withstand many cool foggy days, this section of town may be just right for you.

Two other neighborhoods of Pacific Grove deserve mention. One, called Candy Cane Lane, is situated east of Forest Avenue between Morse Drive and Beaumont Avenue. These primarily upper-middle-income family homes become a winter wonderland each December as neighbors vibrantly decorate their houses, yards, and neighborhood parks in holiday decor. In fact, if you decide to purchase a home in this area, you'd better be prepared to join in the fun or be labeled a neighborhood Scrooge! The final Pacific Grove neighborhood of note is Del Monte Park, located at the top of David Avenue west of Congress Road. This district of 1950s and '60s tract homes is one of the more affordable spots in Pacific Grove with ample sized three- and four-bedroom homes. While lacking the Victorian charm of historic downtown, some of the houses here have nice views overlooking the Del Monte Forest of Pebble Beach and the Pacific Ocean beyond.

Commercial and residential buildings in Pacific Grove reflect Victorian architecture.

PHOTO: ROSS ANDRÉSON

Carmel

With a median home price of $850,000, Carmel remains one of the most desirable areas of the Monterey Peninsula among well-to-do retirees who have vacationed here in the past and always dreamed of returning for good. The Carmel most of these visitors are familiar with is the collection of shops, inns, and restaurants on and around Ocean Avenue. Interestingly enough, Ocean Avenue also serves as a dividing line when describing the residential neighborhoods of Carmel. Most of the more prestigious Carmel addresses (that is, if they had addresses) lie in the area known simply as South of Ocean. This is the quaint Carmel of English cottages, English Tudors, Comstocks, and Cape Cod design. The homes range from cozy to palatial, but all share a common village ambiance due to Carmel's abundance of trees, crooked streets, and general lack of street lights and sidewalks.

As a rule, the oceanview factor dictates property values, with homes along shoreline Scenic Road and on Carmel Point demanding the highest premium. Farther south in Carmel, beyond Rio Road and a bit inland, is the neighborhood known as Mission Fields, which gets its name from the neighboring Carmel Mission. Here, outside of the village forest, you find the more traditional 1960s subdivisions of family homes. You can generally buy more

Carmel homes, like this spectacular stone cottage, add great charm to the seaside village. PHOTO: TOM OWENS

home for the dollar in this section of Carmel, but we're certainly not talking low-rent district. One major precaution: During the 1990s, certain areas of Mission Fields were twice hit hard by flooding from the nearby Carmel River. Recent changes in the flood-control levees along the river have improved the situation somewhat. Still, before purchasing or renting a home in this neighborhood, check out its history regarding previous flooding.

Meanwhile, back north of Ocean Avenue is the neighborhood generally known as Carmel Woods. Here, the pine forest shared with neighboring Pebble Beach is denser and the terrain steeper than South of Ocean. Homes are also generally newer here, and the feeling is more rustic Californian than quaint English village. Parts of Carmel Woods lie outside the incorporated city, as does the High Meadow Drive neighborhood of larger homes and townhouses located in the spacious foothills east of Highway 1 at Carpenter Street. Also along Highway 1 is the Carmel neighborhood of Hatton Fields. You'll find a number of California ranch-style homes in this hilly canyon area of gently winding streets. Farther east at the mouth of Carmel Valley is the neighborhood of Carmel Knolls. These fairly prestigious homes of modern design overlook the scenic valley and provide substantially warmer weather than Carmel proper.

Pebble Beach

For some, a Pebble Beach address is the epitome of "making it." Unarguably the most scenic area of the Monterey Peninsula, Pebble Beach is home to the rich and famous from around the world and features some of the most majestic estates on the West Coast. You can get a peek at the cream of the crop by taking the scenic 17-Mile Drive along the coast route from Cypress Point to Pebble Beach Golf Links. But spectacular homes are evident throughout the Del Monte Forest. The median price for a Pebble Beach home is $930,000. An ocean or golf-course view puts you in the $1 million-plus range.

The neighborhoods surrounding Pebble Beach Golf Links, Cypress Point Club,

Spyglass Hill, Poppy Hills, the Monterey Peninsula Country Club, and Spanish Bay Golf Links all feature prestigious homes of various styles and vintages. The more modest homes, at least by Pebble Beach standards, include the inland areas near the Country Club Gate entrance and the neighborhoods below Forest Lake. Another neighborhood of note is atop the western slope of Huckleberry Hill near Holman Highway. Up here among spectacular views you'll find a swath of newer homes, many replacements for those destroyed in a devastating fire that swept through this part of the forest in the early 1990s.

Surrounding Communities

Those considering relocating to the area may find the Monterey Peninsula real estate market a bit too pricey. Fortunately, there are a number of surrounding communities that offer lower housing prices but the same great climate and, in some cases, ocean views. At the same time, some of the other off-Peninsula locales are just as pricey as the Peninsula but offer alternatives in terms of climate and/or terrain. Here are a few neighborhoods to consider.

Big Sur

Author Lillian Bos Ross wrote that "Big Sur is a state of mind." It's also a beautifully rugged stretch of coastline that extends from the southern tip of Monterey County northward to Point Sur. While much of Big Sur is comprised of National Forest and other public lands, there are also privately owned homesites and ranches that provide inspirational solitude and privacy. Real estate prices are all over the map in Big Sur, with a median price of just more than $600,000. Homes range from lean-to cabins located up barely passable dirt roads to hacienda estates in unbelievable settings and with all the comforts of city living. Regardless of which end of the spectrum they fall, Big Sur residents tend to be part of a tight-knit community of friendly semi-seclusionists. Highway 1 is the only route in and out of Big Sur, and its winter closure due to mud and rock slides is practically an annual event. With that in mind, planning to commute from a Big Sur home to a Monterey Peninsula job is an unpredictable proposition at best. But if you have that pioneer spirit, can make a living from your home, or are independently wealthy and not susceptible to cabin fever, there's hardly a more beautiful place on earth.

Carmel Highlands/South Coast

Nestled in the northern reach of the Santa Lucia Range of Big Sur lie the Carmel Highlands. This civilized version of Big Sur sits high above Point Lobos Reserve and Yankee Point, approximately 3 miles south of Carmel. Made up primarily of million-dollar homes, it's becoming an upper-income alcove featuring fine residences with spectacular views. If you have the time after visiting Point Lobos, take a leisurely drive up Highlands Drive, Walden Road, or San Remo Road off Highway 1.

Below Carmel Highlands west of Highway 1 is a beachfront area known as South Coast because of its proximity to the Monterey Peninsula. Here on Yankee Point are some beautifully designed homes situated along breathtaking coastline. Homes are typically in the $1.5 million range and on par with Pebble Beach and Carmel coastal properties. A drive out Spindrift Road or Yankee Point Drive is well worth the time for house-hunters looking in this price range.

Insiders' Tip

Since street numbers and addresses are absent in most of Carmel proper, there isn't any mail delivery in town. Residents retrieve their mail from the post office, which has become a primary social center.

The Residence at Spanish Bay in Pebble Beach was one of the last multi-unit residential communities built on the Peninsula. PHOTO: TOM OWENS

Carmel Valley

Carmel Valley is the Wild West of the Monterey Peninsula area. Stretching inland from Carmel toward the Salinas Valley, it's a vast, largely undeveloped area with pockets of civilization dotting its valley floor and rugged hillsides. With a population of approximately 13,000, Carmel Valley is a mixture of exclusive resort-like properties, sprawling ranches, and cozy mountainside homes. At the mouth of the Valley lie the Carmel Knolls area and the Carmel Rancho district, with its modern homes and townhouses and stylish shopping centers. Continue inland the next few miles along Carmel Valley Road, and you'll discover the golf resort communities surrounding Rancho Canada Golf Course and Carmel Valley Golf and Country Club. Here are exclusive country club neighborhoods such as Quail Meadows and Summit at Carmel Valley Ranch.

Once east of the golf courses you enter the residential Mid Valley area, made up largely of residential family homes and small ranches along the Valley and more secluded neighborhoods up the narrow canyons. Robinson Canyon Road winds south through some beautiful countryside, eventually reaching Rancho San Carlos, a huge private development of more than 20,000 acres.

Approximately 12 miles inland from Carmel is Carmel Valley Village, the heart and soul of this truly Californian community. Here, residential neighborhoods are nestled up scenic canyons and along the broad valley floor north of the Carmel River. South of the river, across Rosie's Bridge on Esquiline Drive, lies another residential neighborhood of both modern houses and rustic cabins situated along hillsides and large open-space meadows. East of Carmel Valley Village, the Valley narrows and the landscape becomes steeper and less populated. A few small communities, such as the gated Sleepy Hollow, are interspersed with sprawling vineyards and ranches. About 25 miles inland is the community of Jamesburg, located 3 miles up Crews Ridge Road. Homes here and farther out toward

Carmel Valley Road to Salinas Valley are mainly rustic cabin-style structures, but larger homes and ranches dot the rural landscape as well.

The median price of a Carmel Valley home is $763,000, but property values vary widely. From the mouth of the Carmel Valley to Jamesburg, you'll find a friendly tight-knit community with a Western flair that prefers the warm inland sunshine to the cooler, foggier coast. If that fits your lifestyle, Carmel Valley is certainly for you. Be aware that wildfires are a concern in the dry seasons, and the Carmel River is subject to flooding in the rainy season. While these events are certainly rare, pick your site carefully out here in the Wild West.

Del Rey Oaks

Incorporated in 1953, Del Rey Oaks is a small city of approximately 1,700 people and 300 acres landlocked between Monterey, Seaside, the Monterey Peninsula Airport, and the former Fort Ord Military Reservation. Canyon Del Rey Boulevard (Highway 218) between Fremont Boulevard and the Monterey-Salinas Highway (Highway 68) is the main thoroughfare through this bedroom community. Quiet neighborhoods of single-family homes and a few condominium projects populate the northern half of the city, while light-industry business parks make up the south end of town. In between, the Frog Pond Natural Area, a 17-acre seasonal freshwater marsh and nature preserve, is the home of the rare Pacific tree frog (see our Parks and Recreation chapter). Homes in Del Rey Oaks are typically in the $350,000 to $450,000 range, with a median price of $435,000. Be aware that on-again-off-again talks of a large hotel project in Del Rey Oaks have been held in these parts. If such a project were to go through, it could change the sleepy nature of this corner of town.

Marina

Located north of the former Fort Ord, approximately 9 miles up the coast from Monterey on Highway 1, is the City of Marina. Marina was originally laid out in 1913 as part of a real estate development among the sand dunes, with five-acre plots selling for $375. It later became a bedroom community for neighboring Fort Ord and today is home to 18,000 residents. Along with Seaside, Marina provides some of the most affordable family homes in the Monterey Peninsula area, with a median price of $343,000. The original section of town east of Highway 1 and south of Reservation Road is primarily of the 1950s and 1960s vintage, while newer tracts are located west of Highway 1 and north of Reservation Road. The Marina terrain is a bit sparse, located among the sandy dunes of this stretch of California coast, but the weather is exceptionally pleasant. Marina State Beach and Locke-Paddon Park provide fine recreation spots for family activities. Plus, Marina makes for an easy commute inland to Salinas and U.S. 101 by way of Reservation Road.

Monterey-Salinas Corridor

Follow Highway 68 out of Monterey east toward Salinas, and you're in the unincorporated Monterey-Salinas Highway corridor. Off this main east-west route to and from the Monterey Peninsula lie numerous canyons, primarily in the southern Sierra de Salinas hills. Up the canyons and along the hillsides, you'll find a variety of fairly recent housing developments of upper-income neighborhoods with names like Bay Ridge, The Villas, The Meadows, and Las Palmas Ranch. You'll find gated communities of single-family homes, townhouses, and condominiums, some with country-club amenities such as golf and tennis. You'll also find older ranch-style and tract homes, a few with considerable acreage. Far back into the canyons of San Benancio and Corral de Tierra are working cattle ranches and large spreads similar to those of Carmel Valley, which lies just on the other side of the Sierra de Salinas range. These hills were the setting for John Steinbeck's *The Pastures of Heaven*. The median home price out in the Monterey-Salinas Corridor is $540,000. Those with a penchant for the sunny country-club style of living and who can benefit from a short commute to Salinas and other cities along

U.S. 101 should definitely check out this area east of the Monterey Peninsula.

Sand City

With barely 200 permanent residents, Sand City is noted as being the second-smallest incorporated city in California. Primarily a commercial district wedged between Monterey, Seaside, and the waters of Monterey Bay, its 350 acres are, aptly enough, mostly sand. In fact, Sand City's sand business was at one time among the largest on the Pacific Coast. Today, however, the sand business has given way to light manufacturing and, more recently, retail businesses. A large center of discount chain stores was established here in the mid-1990s, and it continues to grow, making Sand City one of the busiest shopping districts in the area. Residential real estate in Sand City is made up of a handful of mostly modest homes inland from Highway 1. Some have nice Bay views; others share neighborhoods with commercial properties. Prices are generally in the $300,000-$400,000 range.

Seaside

Directly northeast of Monterey, Seaside is a substantial city of almost 10 square miles and more than 30,000 residents. Long serving as a bedroom community of its neighbor-to-the-north Fort Ord, Seaside, incorporated in 1954, is the most ethnically diverse neighborhood in the Monterey Peninsula area and remains home to a population of retired military. When the army moved out and Fort Ord shut down as part of the nationwide round of military base closings in the early 1990s, dire predictions of economic disaster for Seaside hit the news. But outside of a few closings of businesses directly dependent on the military, the city has survived remarkably well. Light industry, retail stores, hotels and motels, an array of ethnic restaurants, and a major auto center now provide a sound economic base for Seaside. This active commercial district is largely situated on the western side of town, along and between the major north-south thoroughfares of Del Monte and Fremont Boulevards. East of Fremont Boulevard is mostly residential.

Seaside has the lowest-priced homes in and around the Monterey Peninsula. The median price of $317,000 makes Seaside a popular entry point for relocating out-of-towners looking for the most house for the dollar. Favored neighborhoods are generally in the higher elevations along the eastern edge of town. Here, you'll find spacious homes, some with fabulous Bay views looking west toward the Monterey Peninsula. Homes farther west toward the flatter commercial district are generally less expensive but are typically smaller and don't afford the great views. By Monterey Peninsula standards, Seaside has had somewhat of a reputation as a high-crime area. Although problems with gangs and drugs in some of the lowest-income areas of the city cannot be denied, the city has gone through a quiet transformation in recent years. Since the closing of Fort Ord, crime rates have dropped significantly. Active neighborhood groups have reclaimed their streets and parks, and civic pride is on the increase. Economic prosperity has also received a big boost from new construction, such as the lavish Embassy Suites hotel near Laguna Grande Park. Seaside seems poised for a renaissance, and the low home prices now available have nowhere to go but up.

Real Estate Companies

There is no shortage of quality real estate companies staffed with experienced experts on the Monterey Peninsula. Carmel in particular has a number of notable real estate firms, including the oldest on the Peninsula. Most of these major real estate firms cover the entire Monterey Peninsula and surrounding areas. Some of the larger ones have multiple offices in more than one city. Therefore, we list these firms in alphabetical order rather than trying to segment them by locale.

Alain Pinel Realtors
Junipero Street and 5th Avenue, Carmel
(831) 622–1040, (800) 933–1331,
www.apr–carmel.com

Three of the agents used to run local real estate companies of their own. Although specializing in homes in Carmel, Carmel Highlands, and Pebble Beach, the firm covers the entire Monterey Peninsula. Property management, long-term rental, and relocation services are provided. Local owners Robert and Judith Profeta have put together an experienced midsize agency, with branches in the San Francisco Bay Area.

Bratty Real Estate
574 Lighthouse Avenue, Pacific Grove
(831) 375–5173

Bratty Real Estate is synonymous with Pacific Grove. Established in 1957, this one-office, nine-Realtor agency is owned and operated by born-and-bred Pagrovians Bob and Dru Bratty. Although specializing in P.G., Bratty Real Estate covers the entire Monterey Peninsula. Property management and long-term rental services are provided, and the staff is well versed in the tax laws of 1031 "like kind" exchanges.

Burchell House Properties
Ocean Avenue and Dolores Street, Carmel
(831) 626–6461, (888) 441–6914
Lincoln Street and 6th Avenue, Carmel
(831) 626–5045, www.burchellhouse.com

Established in Carmel in 1920, Burchell House Properties is the second-oldest continuously operating real estate business in Carmel. Still headquartered in its original location at Ocean and Dolores, which it used to share with Carmel City Hall, Burchell House is locally owned and operated and serves the entire Peninsula area from two Carmel offices. Its 23 agents are all licensed Realtors, and co-owner Gerry Hopkins says this medium-sized boutique realty prides itself in using sophisticated technology to provide personalized service. Burchell House has a property-management division that specializes in long-term and vacation rentals (see our Vacation Rentals chapter). Uniquely, Burchell House also offers the services of a certified feng shui consultant. Feng shui is the ancient Asian art of balancing energies by aligning space design and furnishings.

Buyer's Real Estate
532 Abrego Street, Monterey
(831) 644–9312, (888) 644–9312,
www.buyersrealestate.com

A real estate company that represents only buyers? Yes, it's Buyer's Real Estate, a five-year old company run by Joel Denning. With only three Realtors on staff, they're small, but they don't take listings or offer property management services. Their sole focus is serving as a buyer's representative, covering the entire Peninsula and all price ranges. As an added value, they rebate 50 percent of their commission to the buyer at the close of escrow.

Calandra Real Estate
708 Forest Avenue, Pacific Grove
(831) 372–3877, (800) 835–7705,
www.calandrarealestate.com

Karen Calandra runs a small, two-Realtor office in Pacific Grove and takes pride in providing personal attention to her clients. She's even been known to help a new homeowner hire a gardener, shop for furnishings, or interview a housekeeper. Founded in 1987, Calandra Real Estate covers the entire Peninsula and also represents properties in the Monterey Dunes Colony, a planned unit development north on Highway 1 near Moss Landing. Limited property-management and relocation services are provided to her clients.

Carmel Cottage Realty
7th Avenue and Lincoln Street, Carmel
(831) 625–1943, (800) 624–4331,
www.carmelcottagerealty.com

With 20 years of experience, owner Terri Gelardi takes pride in operating her small Carmel office in this era of large franchise real estate firms. As a licensed real estate broker, Terri and her four agents emphasize establishing long-term client relationships and then finding that something special within a given price range in Carmel or surrounding Peninsula communities. She invites potential relocators to drop by for a visit and a market overview, even if they're not quite ready to buy. And when it is time to buy, Terri can help you find just the right loan as well.

Insiders' Tip

The Monterey County Association of Realtors has an informative Web site with many real estate facts and figures. Visit www.mcar.com.

Carmel Realty Company
Dolores Street and 7th Avenue, Carmel
(831) 624–6482, www.carmel-realty.com

Founded in 1913, Carmel Realty is the longest continuously operating real estate company on the Monterey Peninsula. As its name implies, the company specializes in Carmel property, yet covers the entire Monterey Peninsula. Partners Bart Whelan, Jim Winterbotham, and Barbara Weymuth Mellon lead a staff of 25 experienced Realtors well versed in the local market. Carmel Realty offers extensive property-management services, including long-term and vacation rentals.

Century 21 Scenic Bay Properties
656 Munras Avenue, Monterey
(831) 648–7271, (800) 723–6887,
www.c21scenicbayproperties.com

Owners Dick Kelly and Erling Andresen lead a team of (appropriately enough) 21 Realtors at Century 21 Scenic Bay Properties. Since 1985 the firm has offered a full range of single-family residences and condominium properties and provided complete investment, property-management, and relocation services to buyers and sellers across the Monterey Peninsula. Agents speak several foreign languages including German, Italian, Spanish, and Norwegian.

Chelew & Campbell Realty
1155 Forest Avenue, Pacific Grove
(831) 649–8888

Chelew & Campbell, a six-Realtor office owned by Rose Marie Coleman, has been selling real estate on the Peninsula since 1958. With 40 years of experience, Chelew & Campbell offers a full range of residential properties. Its property-management department features long-term rentals, including apartment houses. Relocation services are outsourced. Rose Marie invites visitors to drop by her Pacific Grove office with any real estate questions.

Coldwell Banker Del Monte Realty
Junipero Street and 5th Avenue, Carmel
(831) 626–2221
3775 Via Nona Marie, Carmel
(831) 626–2222
Ocean Avenue and Dolores Street, Carmel
(831) 626–2224
Ocean Avenue and Lincoln Street, Carmel
(831) 626–2227
The Shops at the Lodge, Pebble Beach
(831) 626–2223
The Inn at Spanish Bay, Pebble Beach
(831) 626–2225
501 Lighthouse Avenue, Pacific Grove
(831) 626–2226, www.cbdmr.com

With seven offices and approximately 100 Realtors on staff, Coldwell Banker Del Monte Realty offers the combination of nearly 80 years of local experience with the resources of one of the largest real estate networks in the world. Pebble Beach pioneer Samuel F. B. Morse founded the original Del Monte Realty back in 1919, and the company established itself early on as a luxury-home specialist. Real estate giant Coldwell Banker purchased the firm in 1997 and, while continuing its Pebble Beach tradition, lists homes from $300,000 to $20 million across the Monterey Peninsula and surrounding areas. Coldwell Banker Del Monte Realty provides basic property-management assistance and is part of the national Coldwell Banker Relocation System. The extensive Coldwell Banker training program helps ensure that agents are well versed in the latest real estate trends and techniques.

Alan H. Cordan, Realtor
San Carlos Street and 5th Avenue, Carmel
(831) 625–4393, (888) 333–7653,
www.cordan.com

This is the epitome of a mom-and-pop personal-service real estate company. Alan Cordan and his wife, Sandy Stone, have been active in the Monterey Peninsula market for 30 years and have operated their own

Mediterranean is a popular architectural style across the Montery Peninsula. PHOTO: ROSS ANDRÉSON

firm since 1979. You won't find property-management or relocation services here, just the special attention of two dedicated business partners who can help you buy or sell a home. Alan and Sandy specialize in homes at $500,000 or more in the Carmel and Pebble Beach area. Alan is a Certified Residential Specialist (CRS) and a Certified Real Estate Brokerage Manager (CRB).

Fouratt-Simmons Real Estate
Court of the Golden Bough,
Ocean Avenue and Lincoln Street, Carmel
(831) 624–3829, www.fouratt-simmons.com

Since 1946, Fouratt-Simmons Real Estate has been providing personalized service to the Monterey Peninsula. Owner Barbara Simmons and her 11 agents, all licensed Realtors, work to provide one-stop shopping for "castles to cottages" throughout the entire Peninsula and Carmel Valley. Located in the court of Carmel's historic Golden Bough Theater, Fouratt-Simmons has a full service property-management division offering long-term and vacation rentals. The company will even help you with escrow and financing.

Harbor Realty
299 Webster Street, Monterey
(831) 649–6860, (800) 449–6860,
www.harborrealty.net

Harbor Realty has been serving the Monterey Peninsula since 1980. Today owner Richard Fowler and eight licensed Realtors can show you a wide range of residential and income properties, including apartment complexes. Locally owned and operated, Harbor Realty offers property-management and relocation services. It's a member of the Monterey County, California, and National Association of Realtors.

Ben Heinrich Real Estate
26364 Carmel Rancho Lane, Carmel
(831) 625–6225, (800) 585–6225
650 Lighthouse Avenue, Pacific Grove
(831) 649–6225, www.benheinrich.com

Oceanfront homes, like the so-called "Butterfly House" in Carmel, demand premium prices measured in the millions. PHOTO: TOM OWENS

Established in 1981, Ben Heinrich Real Estate is considered one of the local experts in Big Sur and golf course properties. Their offices are staffed with licensed Realtors averaging 20 years of real estate sales experience. A member of Christie's Great Estates, a worldwide affiliation of independent real estate offices listing high-end properties, Ben Heinrich's specializes in prestigious golf resort properties in Pebble Beach and Carmel Valley. Owner Ben Heinrich was the 1998 president of the Monterey County Association of Realtors and is a noted speaker and author.

International Estates
5th Avenue and San Carlos Street, Carmel
(831) 626–5100,
www.internationalestates.com

Specializing in luxury upper-end properties, International Estates has the distinction of being a Five Star-rated real estate agency. Owner Gayle Crusan has been serving the Peninsula since 1989 and has been rated among the top 5 percent in agent sales for the last five years. International Estates has eight Realtors, each representing their own listings throughout the Monterey Peninsula. They are full-service agents who attend all escrow signings. The company offers property-management services including long-term rentals as well as full relocation services.

The Mitchell Group Real Estate
El Paseo Courtyard, Dolores Street at 7th Avenue, Carmel
(831) 624–0136
200 Clock Tower Place, Carmel
(831) 624–1566
312 West Carmel Valley Road, Carmel Valley
(831) 659–2267
1157 Forest Avenue, Pacific Grove
(831) 646–2120, www.mitchellgroup.com

The largest independent real estate firm on the Monterey Peninsula, The Mitchell Group has a staff of 60 licensed Realtors operating out of four busy offices. With a history that dates back to 1926, the Mitchell Group covers the entire Monterey Peninsula area, but partner Kent Nelson says the firm's specialty is waterfront properties from Pebble Beach and Carmel south to the Big Sur coast and large ranch estates out in Carmel Valley. The company provides full property-management services, including long-term and vacation rentals and is an affiliate of Sotheby's relocation services. Mitchell Financial Services offers in-house mortgage lending, making this third-generation Carmel real estate firm a truly full-service operation.

Pan American Real Estate
5th Avenue and Junipero Street, Carmel
(831) 624–3511, (800) 982–2763,
www.panamericanrealestate.com

Pan American, with four licensed Realtors on staff, takes a unique approach to covering the entire Monterey Peninsula. Owner Joe Rousso assigns each agent to a distinct area of the Peninsula, making him or her a neighborhood expert. Pan American also has a licensed and certified appraiser on staff and provides complete estate appraisals and liquidations. You might not only find your dream home, but also that antique bedroom set you've always been looking for. National and international relocation services are provided, as well as property-management services.

Tom Redfern and Associates
26350 Carmel Rancho Lane, Carmel
(831) 625–5200

If you're looking to purchase an apartment building on the Monterey Peninsula, Tom Redfern is your man. Specializing in apartment-house sales and exchanges, Tom Redfern and Associates is a small single-office, two-Realtor agency that focuses exclusively on this niche market. Tom has more than 25 years of experience in the area and a long track record of putting together transactions that provide optimum tax benefits and income opportunities.

RE/MAX-Realtors Monterey Peninsula
26362 Carmel Rancho Lane, Carmel
(831) 625–3535, (800) 347–6835,
www.bertaronson.com

RE/MAX-Realtors is a large international real estate network with more than 2,500 offices worldwide. That network provides local franchise owner Bert Aronson with a wealth of resources from his Carmel office. With 24 licensed brokers on staff, RE/MAX covers the entire Monterey Peninsula offering both residential and commercial properties. Full property-management services are offered, including a separate vacation-rental division called Garden Court Vacation Rentals, (831) 625-1400. The office is part of the worldwide RE/MAX relocation network. Special features include loan-origination services and a training and education center that offers seminars on topics such as real estate investments.

John Saar Properties
212 Crossroads Boulevard, Carmel
(831) 622–7227
26135 Carmel Rancho Boulevard, Carmel
(831) 625–0500, www.johnsaarproperties.com

A former top-10 agent with a Northern California real estate franchise, John Saar left to form his own brokerage in 1997. Today he runs two Carmel offices with more than 10 Realtors. Saar has carved a unique niche in the Carmel and Pebble Beach market, providing out-of-towners with local representation in their search for a Peninsula home or investment property. Saar's marketing skills and hi-tech, multi-media approach serves sellers well too.

Greg Shankle Real Estate
261 Webster Street, Monterey
(831) 646–1401, www.gregshankle.com

Owned and operated in Monterey by the same local family since 1956, Greg Shankle Realty is an accomplished mid-size agency with 16 Realtors serving all of Monterey County. Ten of the agents are brokers and average more than 15 years of experience. The company is a member of RELO, an 1100-member national network offering full relocation services. Owner Greg Shankle, a former member of the Monterey Peninsula Association of Realtors, reports that year after year his firm ranks at or near the top locally in successful transactions per agent.

Retirement

- Activities and Clubs
- Agencies and Services
- Education
- Emergency Services
- Employment and Training
- Health Services
- Housing
- Legal and Governmental Services
- Public Libraries
- Transportation Services

Seniors living in Monterey County, having found such an ideal place to spend their golden years, feel blessed. Recent census data reveals that more than 13 percent of our nearly 375,000 residents are older than 65.

In addition to the moderate clime, the Peninsula offers a realm of beauty not found elsewhere. The magnificent Monterey Bay, a National Marine Sanctuary, offers an ever-changing variety of scenery and seasonal changes.

A myriad of resources serves the growing senior population, providing a wealth of information and assistance and ensuring that Monterey County seniors feel welcome and well taken care of.

Today's seniors are experiencing better health and living longer. Walking along the beach, dining with friends, and enjoying the many social and cultural events are but a few of the activities on the Peninsula most seniors find especially satisfying. It is also a comfort to know that we have excellent medical facilities with many physicians to care for those who have health needs.

Activities and Clubs

Listed below are some of the many agencies that provide services for the special needs of the senior population.

City of Monterey Recreation and Community Services Department
546 Dutra Street, Monterey
(831) 646–3866, www.monterey.org

The Recreation Department plans programs and leisure activities for seniors. Activities include sewing, crafts, exercises, golf lessons, dancing, and other specialized senior citizen classes.

City of Monterey Senior Center
280 Dickman Avenue, Monterey
(831) 646–3878, www.monterey.org

Recreational activities such as card playing, exercise classes, arts, crafts, bingo, tap dancing, line dancing, and international folk dancing are held at this center. Lunch is served weekdays, except Wednesday. For lunch, a $2.00 donation is requested for seniors age 60 and older, $5.00 for others.

Oldemeyer Center
City of Seaside Community Services
986 Hilby Avenue, Seaside
(831) 899–6339, bbs.ci.seaside.ca.us

The Oldemeyer Center offers classes such as dancing, exercise, sewing, piano, and arts and crafts. This is the site for the senior nutrition lunch program. It also provides information referral services.

Sally Griffin Senior Center
700 Jewell Avenue, Pacific Grove
(831) 375–4454, www.93950.com

The senior center in Pacific Grove is also the home of Meals on Wheels, which serves noon meals to seniors. Other activities include guest speakers, classes related to senior life, and holiday, music, and other entertaining programs. Referral services to other senior-related services in the area are also available.

SCORE
Monterey
(831) 372–7761

SCORE (Service Corps of Retired Executives), a nonprofit association, provides free business counseling for small businesses. The counselors are all retired executives who volunteer their services.

Agencies and Services

Adult Day Services/Salvation Army
1491 Contra Costa Avenue, Seaside
(831) 899–4914

This agency provides services for frail or isolated older adults. It offers stimulating and rehabilitative activities for the person in need and a day off for the caregiver. There is also a caregiver's support group.

Adult Protective Services
1281 Broadway Avenue, Seaside
(831) 899–8010, www.co.monterey.ca.us

Run by the Department of Social Services, this agency provides immediate response to emergencies. It provides goal-oriented services as well as information and referral to dependent adults and elderly persons in need of protection. The goal of the program is to prevent or remedy neglect, abuse, or exploitation of dependent adults and elderly persons who are unable to protect their own interests.

Alliance on Aging
2200 Garden Road, Monterey
(800) 510–2020, www.allianceonaging.org

The Alliance on Aging houses administrative offices for community programs such as senior employment services, health insurance counseling, senior homesharing, and tax counseling. It also provides referral information.

The Friendly Visitor Program, operated by the Alliance on Aging, links volunteers with isolated and lonely older people who need the emotional support of a friend in order to continue living alone. Telephone reassurance and limited amounts of escort driving are also provided.

In addition to providing information relevant to senior issues, this service also provides assistance in completing public benefit forms and tax returns. There is a bimonthly newsletter for Alliance members. When appropriate, it provides advocacy for seniors.

Area Agency on Aging
1000 South Main, Suite 211-A, Salinas
(831) 647–7899, www.n4a.org

This regional planning agency administers federal Older Americans Act funds and serves as an advocate for those age 60 and older.

Counseling Center/Community Human Services
590 Pearl Street, Monterey
(831) 373–4775, 24-hour Crisis and Referral Line, (831) 373–4773

This nonprofit organization provides individual, group, and family counseling on a sliding scale fee basis. Counselors are either interns working on a master's degree in Marriage, Family, and Child Counseling or social workers. Counseling sessions are held at the center, and appointments are necessary.

Family Service Agency of the Monterey Peninsula
544 Pearl Street, Monterey
(831) 373–4421

This nonprofit agency offers professional counseling to individuals, couples, and families. Services are designed to promote improved relationships within the family unit. This includes aging and family issues. Fees are based on a sliding scale.

Insiders' Tip

The City of Monterey offers a variety of programs and services that help resident seniors maintain their homes and their independence. Visit the Web site at www.monterey.org or call (831) 646-3995.

Activities abound for active seniors on the Monterey Peninsula. Opportunities to learn new skills and hobbies are available at adult schools and colleges. PHOTO: ROSS ANDRÉSON

In-Home Supportive Services/Department of Social Services
1281 Broadway Avenue, Seaside
(831) 899–8010

The agency provides low-income elderly and blind or disabled persons of any age with nonmedical assistance so that they can safely remain in their homes. This includes domestic services, meal preparation, cleanup, laundry, shopping for food and other essentials, personal care, transportation for medical appointments, and protective supervision.

Injury Prevention Program/Monterey County Health Department
1200 Aguajito Road, Suite 103, Monterey
(831) 647–7949, www.co.monterey.ca.us

This program provides information on how to arrange your home to prevent injuries. It can also provide a home-safety questionnaire.

Meals on Wheels of the Monterey Peninsula Inc.
700 Jewell Avenue, Pacific Grove
(831) 375–4454

This organization provides home-delivered meals to seniors and the disabled. The criteria for delivery are an inability to shop and cook for oneself. Meals on Wheels also provides a congregate lunch program with noon meals to seniors at Griffin Senior Center, 700 Jewell Avenue, Pacific Grove; Monterey Senior Center, 280 Dickman Avenue, Monterey; Oldemeyer Center, 986 Hilby Avenue, Seaside; and the Alzheimer's Day Care Resource Center, 200 Coe Avenue, Seaside. Senior Center activities, services, classes, and information are also provided by the agency.

Education

Adult Literacy Program
550 Harcourt Avenue, Seaside
(831) 899–0417

Trained volunteer tutors provide free, confidential one-on-one literacy tutoring to adults. Tutoring is available for both native and foreign-born speakers. Writing and spelling programs are set up to meet the needs of the individual. The one-on-one sessions are held at the Seaside Library (address indicated above). A volunteer tutor takes part in a two-day workshop where technique, skills, and materials are provided. The tutor must be willing to commit four hours a week, two for preparation and two for the session.

Books-By-Mail Program
26 Central Avenue, Salinas
(877) 848–9100

This program provides free library services to homebound and disabled persons who are unable to get to a library facility. A booklet outlining the choice of books is sent to patrons. Order requests and books are sent and returned by mail.

Monterey County Free Libraries
26 Central Avenue, Salinas
(831) 424–3244

The organization provides free access to information, educational and recreational materials, and lifelong learning experiences. Services include books and other library materials, reference assistance, bookmobiles, Books by Mail program, adult literacy instruction, videos, music cassettes, and magazines.

Older Adult Program/Monterey Peninsula College
980 Fremont Street, Monterey
(831) 646–4058

Continuing personal-enrichment classes structured for seniors are offered at selected community sites and rest homes on the Monterey Peninsula. All classes are free, and registration takes place at anytime by attending the class.

Adult Schools

Adult education is a program of quality academic, vocational, and physical education based on the philosophy that increasing knowledge allows any subject to be enjoyed, pursued, accepted, or defended to greater degrees. The adult education program believes in the right of every adult in the community to gain an education regardless of age, heritage, disability, or background.

Programs for older adults are based on the following categories: scientific and human perspectives, fine and applied arts, cultural studies, mental fitness, and accident prevention. Course offerings include woodworking, where students repair or finish projects; open media art, which allows for creative expression through watercolor, ink, pastel, pencil, and collage; language programs such as French, German, Italian, and Spanish; physical fitness classes; communication improvement, where students use discussion and writing assignments to improve skills; and music appreciation.

Class fees average around $20 per seasonal quarter, depending on class materials. For information about the many classes offered by the area adult schools,

Insiders' Tip

One call to the Volunteer Center of Monterey County and seniors are connected to hundreds of interesting and rewarding volunteer opportunities. The center offers training and placement services for volunteers who want a one-time or an ongoing volunteer position. Call (831) 757-3206 in Salinas or (831) 372-4838 in Monterey, or visit their Web site at www.yesillhelp.org.

call between 8:00 A.M. and 4:00 P.M. on weekdays.

Carmel Adult School
3600 Ocean Avenue, Carmel
(831) 624–1714

Monterey Adult School
200 Coe Avenue, Seaside
(831) 899–1615

Pacific Grove Adult School
1025 Lighthouse Avenue, Pacific Grove
(831) 646–6580

Emergency Services

Dial 911 for any emergency call. Give the operator the location you are calling from and the nature of the emergency. If you are hearing impaired, emergency TDD service is available by dialing 911 then pressing the space bar until someone answers.

Emergency Disaster Services/Salvation Army Monterey
(831) 899–4913

The Salvation Army is ready to respond to community need during emergency/disaster situations. It has a mobile canteen ready to provide communication services, emergency food, counseling, or support services as needed.

Emergency Home Repairs Loan Program/City of Monterey
Corner of Madison and Pacific Streets, Monterey
(831) 646–3995

Low-income Monterey seniors receive top priority in obtaining a loan of up to $5,000 for emergency home repairs. The city staff supervise and pay the repair person(s) and inspect the repairs. The loans are made at 5 percent interest. No payments are made on the loan until the property is sold (deferred).

Employment and Training

Joblink/Older Worker Program
1976 Fremont Boulevard, Suite A, Seaside
(831) 899–8151

This program provides employment and training services at no cost to eligible older workers, age 55 and older, who want to work or re-enter the labor market.

Senior Aides/Senior Employment/Alliance on Aging
2200 Garden Road, Monterey
(831) 655–1334, www.allianceonaging.org

Seniors age 50 and older can find work through this free employment service. It also provides part-time work assignments in nonprofit agencies for low-income seniors.

Health Services

Alzheimer's Association Helpline
182 El Dorado, Monterey
(831) 757–0531

This nonprofit organization offers support groups, peer counseling, information/referral, a lending library, and Wander Protection Program.

Alzheimer's Day Care
Resource Center & Library
200 Coe Avenue, Seaside
(831) 899–7178

The Visiting Nurse Association provides adult day care for dementia-impaired adults, a support group for caregivers, and a lending library regarding Alzheimer's and other diseases common to the aging population.

American Lung Association of the Central Coast
550 Camino El Estero, Suite 100, Monterey
(831) 373–7306, www.alaccoast.org

This organization was set up to help improve the quality of life for those who suffer from respiratory disease. It promotes healthy lungs in a healthy environment. By thorough research it seeks to find answers regarding the prevention, cure, and control of lung disease.

American Red Cross
Dolores Street and 8th Avenue, Carmel
(831) 624–6921, www.arccarmel.org

This disaster-based organization operates a loaner closet of medical equipment. It provides volunteer opportunities and has a knitting club that makes items for veterans and homeless shelters.

Auxiliary/Lifeline Program
Monterey
(831) 625–4516, www.chomp.org

The Auxiliary of Community Hospital of the Monterey Peninsula offers a 24-hour emergency response system for seniors. The program provides a Lifeline unit that is worn around the neck. The unit has a button that, when pressed, alerts the hospital. A hospital volunteer places a call to the person who pushed the button, and if there is no response, help is summoned.

Blind and Visually Impaired Center
225 Laurel Avenue, Pacific Grove
(831) 649–3505

This center provides orientation and mobility instruction, teaches home living skills, gives Braille instruction, and operates a low-vision clinic. It also conducts exercise and ceramic classes. A weekly luncheon is hosted by the center.

Health Insurance Counseling and Advocacy Program
2200 Garden Road, Monterey
(831) 655–1334

This countywide service provides counseling and assistance regarding Medicare benefits, supplemental health insurance, Medicare Risk HMOs, and long-term care.

Hospice of the Central Coast
100 Barnet Segal Lane, Monterey
(831) 649–1772

Hospice, a service of Community Hospital of the Monterey Peninsula, is a team of medical professionals and trained volunteers who provide a wide range of services to patients and families who are facing end of life. The emphasis is on keeping patients at home whether they are pursuing aggressive treatment or are focusing on comfort measures. Services include skilled nursing care, symptom and pain management, medical social services, chaplaincy, home health aids, a pharmacy, support groups, volunteer support, and a free library that is open to the public.

Josephine Kernes Memorial Pool
15 Portola Avenue, Monterey
(831) 372–1240

This is a warm-water pool with individualized exercise swim instruction for mentally and emotionally disabled children and adults. Arthritis exercise classes are also held. A lift is available to assist nonambulatory people with getting in and out of the pool.

Monterey Bay Dental Society
2100 Garden Road
Suite B10, Monterey
(831) 658–0618, www.mbdsdentists.com

This organization provides free referrals to dentists who offer senior discounts. It also assists in patient-dentist conflicts.

Monterey Hearing and Balance Center
1077-D Cass Street, Monterey
(831) 375–5688

This full-service diagnostic center offers audiological testing with complete hearing evaluation, impedance testing, hearing-aid evaluation, balance evaluation, and consultation. Its state-of-the-art,

Insiders' Tip

The Auxiliary of Community Hospital of the Monterey Peninsula sponsors Telecare, a free program designed to give seniors peace of mind and support their independence. Each morning a volunteer places a check-up phone call to older people who live alone and would like the security of daily contact.

advanced technology equipment provides accurate hearing-aid assessment and fittings. Insurance programs are accepted.

Tele-Med/Community Hospital of the Monterey Peninsula
Monterey
(831) 649-1999

This free service provides callers with several hundred prerecorded informational messages on medical/health issues and concerns. Pamphlets are available listing the inventory of topics, or callers can request tape number 429 for details on how Tel-Med works. The service is only accessible with a touch-tone phone.

Visiting Nurses Association (VNA)
40 Ragsdale Road, Monterey
(831) 375-9537, www.ccvna.com

VNA, an affiliate of Salinas Valley Memorial Healthcare System, operates the SHARE Program, which meets the needs of adults who are physically impaired due to a stroke or head injury. Services include speech, physical, and occupational therapy. The Alzheimer's Program prevents or postpones institutionalization of adults who may be frail or have Alzheimer's or other dementia-related conditions. Extended Services Home Care is available 24 hours a day and provides personal care assistance with daily living needs.

Housing

Retirement Communities

Canterbury Woods
651 Sinex Avenue, Pacific Grove
(831) 373-3111, www.ehf.org/cw

Canterbury Woods offers private cottages and apartments on six acres in Pacific Grove. It provides a full range of services including housekeeping, linen service, and three meals a day served in the dining room. There is 24-hour security, and medical facilities are on site. Activities include dancing, tai chi, and exercise classes.

The Park Lane
200 Glenwood Circle, Monterey
(831) 373-6126, www.hyattclassic.com

One of Hyatt's Classic Residences, The Park Lane is on 12 acres overlooking the Monterey Bay and surrounding forest. It offers a wide array of Hyatt-style services and amenities, including spacious balconies; beautiful grounds; choice of lunch or dinner daily; housekeeping; scheduled transportation; cultural, social, and educational programs; a fitness center and spa; a library; and a putting green. Studios, one-, or two-bedroom apartments, or garden chalets with elevators are available.

Forest Hill Manor
551 Gibson Avenue, Pacific Grove
(831) 657-5200, www.cnmh.org

Once a luxurious hotel, this facility offers studio, one-, and two-bedroom suites with various floor plans. The rooms have beautiful views of the Bay and forest. Amenities include weekly housekeeping and linen service, three meals daily, a 24-hour security staff, 24-hour licensed nursing staff, and van service. Forest Hill Manor also has an arts and crafts area, a woodworking shop, expansive gardens, walking trails, and three large libraries. Lectures, seminars, discussion groups, art exhibits, and local entertainment are commonly held on site, and daytrips are offered.

Housing Services

City of Monterey
Corner of Madison and Pacific Streets, Monterey
(831) 646-3995, www.monterey.org

The City of Monterey offers a variety of services to older adults who are homeowners and residents of Monterey.

Mr. Fix-it Program

This program provides grants to a maximum of $600 for minor home repairs. Priority is given to low-income seniors. The city staff inspects, supervises, and pays repair persons.

Social Services Referral and Housing Oversight

Low-income Monterey seniors with housing-related problems can call for information, referral, and staff assistance.

Housing Rehabilitation Program

Giving priority to low-income seniors, this program provides loans for major repairs and renovations of up to $75,000 at 5 percent interest, with no payment until the property is sold or transferred. City staff inspects and supervises the project and pays the contractors.

Senior Homesharing Program/Alliance on Aging
2200 Garden Road, Monterey
(800) 510-2020, www.allianceonaging.org

The agency acts as a clearinghouse service to link people who offer living space in their homes or apartments with people seeking affordable housing.

Legal and Governmental Services

Conflict Resolution and Mediation Center
1900 Garden Road, Monterey
(831) 649-6219

This agency provides mediation and conflict services in the areas of landlord/tenant, neighborhood problems, youth, quality of life, and fair housing. It covers all forms of alternative dispute resolution, including arbitration services.

Eldercare Locator
(800) 677-1116

This Washington, D.C.-based organization provides information on a wide range of state and local services for seniors, including information on agencies that assist with housing issues, financial matters, legal aid, Alzheimer's disease, diabetes, and healthcare matters. Call the number above or write for more information: 1112 16th Street, NW, Suite 100, Washington, DC 20036.

Lawyer Referral Service
Monterey
(831) 375-9889

For a $30 fee, the Lawyer Referral Service arranges a 30-minute consultation with an attorney with a practice in the required area of law.

Legal Services For Seniors
915 Hilby Avenue, Suite 2, Seaside
(831) 899-0492
21 West Laurel Drive, Suite 83, Salinas
(831) 442-7700,
www.legalservicesforseniors.org

Free legal advice and representation is provided to persons age 60 and older through this program. The program has several outreach centers located throughout Monterey County. The priority areas are housing, public benefits (Social Security, SSI), elder abuse, consumer problems, and life-planning issues.

Monterey County Department of Social Services
1281 Broadway Avenue, Seaside
(831) 899-8001

This is the county government agency designated to administer a wide range of community and social service programs that use county, state, and federal funds. The two client-serving divisions within the government are income maintenance (commonly known as welfare) and social services, which encompasses services to adults, families, and children.

Social Security Administration
24 East Alvin Drive, Salinas
(831) 443–9195, www.ssa.gov

This office is administrator for Social Security benefit programs and Supplemental Security Income programs for the elderly, blind, or disabled.

Public Libraries

The following public libraries offer a collection of books and materials in large print, reading aids, closed caption decoder, and TDD. The libraries provide special services to seniors including books on tape, aging and medical information, tax forms, videos, shut-in service, references, and referrals. They also have a special notice and information board for senior citizens.

Harrison Memorial Main Library
Ocean Avenue and Lincoln Street, Carmel,
(831) 624–4629

Harrison Memorial Park Branch
Mission and Sixth Streets, Carmel
(831) 624–1366

Monterey Library, 625 Pacific Street
Monterey
(831) 646–3932, www.monterey.org/library

Pacific Grove Library
550 Central Avenue, Pacific Grove
(831) 648–5760, www.pacificgrove.lib.us

Seaside Library
550 Harcourt Street, Seaside
(831) 899–2055

Transportation Services

Monterey-Salinas Transit (MST)
1 Ryan Ranch Road, Monterey
(831) 899–2555, www.mst.org

MST provides fixed-route bus service between cities on the Monterey Peninsula. Discount fares are available for those age 65 and older and individuals with disabilities. Call for detailed route, schedule, and fare information.

RIDES
Monterey County
(831) 373–1393, www.mst.org

RIDES is a transit service for seniors or special-needs riders. It offers curb-to-curb service anywhere in the county for $1.00 each way. Hours of operation are from 7:00 A.M. to 7:00 P.M. daily. It is best to reserve your ride 24 hours in advance to ensure service.

Senior Taxi Scrip Program
City of Monterey, Monterey Senior Center, 280 Dickman Avenue
(831) 646–3878
Casanova Oak Knoll Park Center, 735 Ramona Avenue
(831) 646–5665
Hilltop Park Center, 871 Jessie Street,
(831) 646–3975
Revenue Office, City Hall, Room 4, Corner of Pacific and Madison Streets
(831) 646–3944, www.monterey.org

Operated by the City of Monterey and the Yellow Cab Company, the Taxi Scrip Program provides seniors age 65 and older who are residents of Monterey with discounted cab fare. Seniors pay $10 for a $20 booklet of taxi scrip (coupons) at any of the locations listed above. The scrip can be used like cash for cab fare to healthcare appointments, the pharmacy, grocery stores, and other locations within the city limits.

Veterans Van Service
445 Reservation Road, Suite E, Marina
(831) 384–0605

This service provides veterans with transportation to and from VA centers for healthcare. It also provides the opportunity for spouses to visit hospitalized veterans.

Healthcare and Wellness

- **Hospitals**
- **Urgent Care Centers**
- **Home Health Programs**
- **Hospice Care**
- **Referral Services**
- **Health Information**
- **Alternative Healthcare**
- **Wellness for Pets**

The Monterey Peninsula offers a kaleidoscope of healthcare options, from traditional to alternative medicine. Scores of physicians have set up private practices here, and medical specialists are in abundance in fields ranging from audiology to urology. Between Monterey County's three hospitals, there are two Comprehensive Cancer Centers, a Heart Center, a Neonatal Intensive Care Unit, and a number of highly-specialized departments and services. One hospital even has a working partnership with NASA. Several options are convenient for the out-of-town visitor in terms of drop in clinics or urgent care needs. Mental health facilities are also available, including those specifically tailored to recovery from substance abuse.

Alternative medicine plays a significant role in the area's healthcare scene, with disciplines represented in the fields of massage, physical therapy, chiropractic, iridology, meditation, herbology, aromatherapy, body contouring, yoga, acupuncture, nutrition, reflexology, and hypnotherapy.

Monterey County residents have access to free information lines that provide data on a number of medical topics; we list them along with general information about how to use the services and the subjects they cover. Finally, those traveling with a pet will appreciate the section we've added on emergency pet care.

Hospitals

Community Hospital of the Monterey Peninsula
23625 W.R. Holman Highway, Monterey
(831) 624–5311, www.chomp.org

With 174 beds, Community Hospital of the Monterey Peninsula is the nearest acute-care hospital and is easily accessible from anywhere on the Peninsula. Accredited by the Joint Commission on the Accreditation of Healthcare Organizations, the hospital provides prevention, diagnostic, treatment, home healthcare, and end of life (hospice) services.

Patient rooms are private and most feature a patio or balcony that looks onto beautiful and fragrant gardens. Through an endowment specifically for art and music, the hospital incorporates fine art and live music into the healing environment. In addition to inpatient, outpatient, and emergency care, a variety of services—education classes, diagnostic imaging, laboratory services, mental health and recovery programs, surgery, and radiation and chemotherapies—are provided here. The hospital also provides selected services at more than 15 satellite offices located throughout Monterey County.

The Family Birth Center, offering single-room maternity care, was built in 1996 and is adorned with many colorful paintings by Hank Ketchum, creator of *Dennis the Menace*. On its campus, the hospital operates a Comprehensive Cancer Center with state-of-the-art diagnostic and treatment capabilities. A Library & Information Center, located in the lower level of the Cancer Center, provides books and tapes, computers with Internet access, and a librarian and volunteers who offer assistance.

Among the many specialized services offered by Community Hospital are a Diabetes Program, a Blood Center, a Sleep Disorders Center, Behavioral Health Services that include inpatient and outpatient mental health and substance abuse programs, hospice services, home healthcare, a Breast Care Center, and rehabilitation services. The hospital provides classes, seminars, and screenings throughout the year in addition to an annual health fair in the fall. A wealth of information and links to other resources can be found on the hospital's Web site.

Natividad Medical Center
1441 Constitution Boulevard, Salinas
(831) 759–6517, (800) 821–2967,
www.natividad.com

Natividad Medical Center (NMC), a county-owned and operated hospital with more than 150 beds, is located in a rapidly growing area of Salinas. Natividad is a full-service acute-care academic center staffed by full-time faculty and community physicians. The hospital, accredited by the Joint Commission on the Accreditation of Healthcare Organizations, is a local leader in managed-care programs with extensive outpatient services.

NMC, affiliated with the University of California at San Francisco School of Medicine, is home to the Family Practice Residency Training Program—postgraduate training for physicians specializing in the board-certified specialty of Family Medicine. It is the only academic medical center on the Central Coast. The hospital also has affiliations with Lucile Packard Children's Hospital, Stanford University, for operation of their adolescent medicine clinic; and with Santa Clara Valley Perinatologists to provide services for women with high-risk pregnancies, genetic testing and counseling, antenatal testing, and ultrasound.

The medical center offers the full complement of inpatient and outpatient diagnostic and treatment services including mental health and substance abuse programs. The Maternal/Child Health Center operated by NMC offers unique services including the Bates-Eldredge Child Sexual Abuse Clinic, a Breast Cancer Early Detection Program, and the county's only Level II Neonatal Intensive Care Unit licensed by California Children's Services. It encompasses the Central Coast HIV/AIDS Pediatric Clinic in partnership with Stanford University and 13 pediatric subspecialty clinics.

Salinas Valley Memorial Healthcare System
450 East Romie Lane, Salinas
(831) 757–4333, www.svmh.com

Salinas Valley Memorial Healthcare System, based in Salinas, is known for its commitment to employing the latest advancements in technology for prevention, diagnosis, and treatment of some of today's most challenging illnesses. In fact, this local hospital works in partnership with NASA on the Virtual Clinic, among other technology developments that have healthcare applications.

Salinas Valley Memorial Hospital is a full-service acute-care facility, accredited by the Joint Commission on the Accreditation of Healthcare Organizations. In addition to a variety of highly specialized clinical departments providing inpatient and outpatient care, the hospital offers 24-hour emergency services, Level II medical and surgical care, a pediatric unit, and single-room maternity care.

Salinas Valley Memorial Healthcare System includes the Harden Regional Heart Center with state-of-the-art open-heart surgery facilities, private patient rooms, a catheterization lab, a special-procedure room, and a radiology suite.

Salinas Valley Memorial also operates a Comprehensive Cancer Center, the highest designation available to a nonuniversity hospital. In May 2000, the hospital affiliated its Cancer Center with Stanford University Medical Center's Clinical Cancer Program, expanding the resources available to local people facing cancer.

The healthcare system also has affiliates that provide home health and hospice services, urgent care at several locations, and an assisted living facility, and is associated with the CSUMB Campus Health Center and Harden Medical Center. Throughout the year, the hospital provides a variety of education classes, seminars, and screenings, and is a Children's Miracle Network (CMN) hospital. CMN funds are used to support newborn and pediatric services at Salinas Valley Memorial, community outreach programs for children's healthcare, and individual children in need.

Urgent Care Centers

Doctors on Duty
501 Lighthouse Avenue, Monterey
(831) 649–0770
2260 North Fremont Street, Monterey
(831) 372–6700
3130 Del Monte Boulevard, Marina
(831) 883–3300
1212 South Main Street, Salinas
(831) 422–7777
1137 North Main Street, Salinas
(831) 757–1110

Doctors on Duty, owned by Salinas Valley Memorial Healthcare System, provides urgent care, family healthcare, occupational medicine, and physical therapy. Physicians treat sports injuries and do physical exams (including immigration physicals), x-rays, and lab work. The clinics are open daily from 8:00 A.M. to 9:00 P.M. No appointment is necessary. The clinics accept more than 100 insurance plans as well as major credit cards.

Monterey Bay Urgent Care Medical Center, Inc.
245 Washington Street, Monterey
(831) 372–2273

Monterey Bay Urgent Care Medical Center, conveniently located near downtown Monterey and Fisherman's Wharf, provides prompt, walk-in urgent care seven days a week. Many of the physicians who work at this facility are also on staff of the Emergency Department at Community Hospital of the Monterey Peninsula. In addition to urgent care, the medical center staff offers family healthcare, occupational medicine, physical therapy, treatment for sports injuries, physical exams (including immigration physicals), x-rays, and lab work. The clinic accepts most health insurance plans and workers' compensation insurance plans, as well as major credit cards. Monterey Bay Urgent Care is open daily from 7:00 A.M. to 10:00 P.M. No appointment is necessary.

Home Health Programs

Home health programs can vary widely in the services they offer. Services range from skilled nursing care, cardiac care, physical and occupational therapy, and mother-baby visits to assistance with daily living activities such as grooming and bathing. A sampling of organizations that offer home health programs is provided here and additional listings can be found in the local Yellow Pages.

Central Coast Visiting Nurse Association and Hospice
An affiliate of Salinas Valley Memorial Healthcare System
40 Ragsdale Drive, Suite 120, Monterey
(831) 375–9882
957-A Blanco Circle, Salinas
(831) 758–8302
191 San Felipe Road, Suite H, Hollister
(831) 637–6724, www.ccvna.com

Community Hospital of the Monterey Peninsula Home Health Services
555 Abrego Street, Suite 100, Monterey
(831) 647–6456
100 East Romie Lane, Salinas
(831) 757–1505, www.chomp.org

Community Care
1900 Garden Road, Suite 280, Monterey
(831) 657–1999
21 West Laurel Drive, Suite 53A, Salinas
(831) 424–1455,
www.communitycaremonterey.com

Country Home Care
995 Cass Street, Monterey, (831) 625–2284
(831) 771–1737 (Salinas),
www.countryhomecare.com

Hospice Care

Hospice services are provided to people with life-ending conditions and their families. For the most part, hospice care takes place in the home and involves a team of medical professionals and trained volunteers who provide a wide range of services including pain and symptom management, respite care, resource referrals, and counseling. Hospice care often enables people to die with dignity in the comfort of their home, surrounded by friends and family.

Insiders' Tip

The Web sites of the area's three hospitals offer quick and easy access to a wealth of information about health and wellness, prevention, medical conditions, pharmaceuticals, treatments, and living with chronic conditions. Visit www.chomp.org, www.svmh.com, or www.natividad.com.

Hospice of the Central Coast
A service of Community Hospital of the Monterey Peninsula
100 Barnet Segal Lane, Monterey
(831) 648–7744, www.chomp.org

Central Coast Visiting Nurse Association and Hospice
An affiliate of Salinas Valley Memorial Healthcare System
40 Ragsdale Drive, Suite 120, Monterey
(831) 375–9882
957-A Blanco Circle, Salinas
(831) 758–8302
191 San Felipe Road, Suite H, Hollister
(831) 637–6724

Referral Services

Physicians

Monterey County Medical Society
(831) 455–1008, www.montereymedicine.org

Chiropractic

Associated Chiropractic Referral Service
(831) 757–2319

Choosing A Chiropractor, USA
(888) 262–4476, www.chiroreferral.com

Dental

American Dental Referral
(888) 657–6453,
www.americandentalreferral.com

Dental Referral Service
(800) 577–7317, www.dentalreferral.com

Monterey Bay Dental Society
(831) 658–0618, www.mbdsdentists.com

Mental Health

Mid-Coast Psychological Association Referral Service
(831) 429–7799, www.calpsychlink.org

Health Information

Facts of Life Line
(800) 711–9848, www.ppmarmonte.org

A community service provided by Planned Parenthood, the Facts of Life Line provides free counseling weekdays from 9:00 A.M. to 5:00 P.M. Free taped messages can be heard 24 hours a day. Callers can hear messages on topics under the following categories: services provided by Planned Parenthood, family planning, pregnancy, prenatal care, childbirth, sexual abuse, sexuality, sexually transmitted diseases, and healthcare. When calling the Facts of Life Line, callers are guided through the system by a series of prompts.

Tele-Med/Community Hospital of the Monterey Peninsula
(831) 624–1999

This free service provides callers with several hundred prerecorded information messages on medical and healthcare issues and concerns. Pamphlets listing the inventory of topics are available, or callers can request tape number 429 for details on how Tele-Med works. The service is available only on touch-tone phones.

Alternative Healthcare

If you prefer alternative healing systems, the range of services available on the Monterey Peninsula will please you. Whatever discipline you're leaning toward, the Yellow Pages of the phone book will be your guide to uncovering the alternative care approach you are seeking.

Alternative Care Clinics

The Preventive Medicine Clinic of Monterey
1084 Cass Street, Monterey
(831) 373–4406, www.wellnessmd.com

Many people prefer to combine the diagnostic capabilities of traditional medicine with gentler, non-invasive approaches to healing. This is the focus of The Preventive Medicine Clinic of Monterey. Run by Abraham Kryger, D.M.D., M.D., the clinic bridges the gap between conventional and alternative medicine, offering the best of both worlds with a multi-disciplinary healthcare approach. Its services include counseling on nutrition, weight loss, natural hormone therapy, massage, and acupuncture.

Monterey Bay Advanced Medical Group
205 Montecito Avenue, Monterey
(831) 372–5602

Operating under a new concept in healthcare, this group clinic combines traditional medicine and chiropractic therapy. Michael Weir, a chiropractor, and Albert Kapstrom, a medical doctor, have teamed up to offer healthcare featuring physiotherapy, radiology, diagnostic testing, medical treatment, and spinal rehabilitation.

Wellness for Pets

Traveling with pets presents a whole set of challenges, but travelers can rest easy knowing that the following pet hospitals and clinics stand by to provide pets with the best possible care. All facilities listed are available for emergency services around the clock, seven days a week.

Emergency Clinic and Critical Care Services
Ryan Ranch, 2 Harris Court, Suite A-1, Monterey
(831) 373–7374

The Animal Hospital
3 The Crossroads, Carmel
(831) 624–0131, www.carmelvet.com

Monterey Animal Hospital
725 Foam Street, Monterey
(831) 373–0711

Education

Education plays a significant role in the community of today's Monterey Peninsula. From a more than 150-year-old religious school to a barely seven-year-old state university campus to world-renowned foreign-language schools, the educational facilities on the Monterey Peninsula provide a wide range of scholastic opportunities for students of all ages. In this chapter we take a look at the public school districts, private schools, community colleges, technical schools, colleges, and universities that contribute so much to the vitality of the area.

Public Schools

Public school students and their parents on the Monterey Peninsula have experienced firsthand some of the same shortcomings that plague school districts up and down the state of California. Tight budgets and aging facilities have led to less than ideal circumstances for at least part of their children's educational experience. The Monterey Peninsula Unified School District, in particular, has faced serious budget deficits that threaten to force closure of some schools and discontinuance of some special programs. That said, the public school systems of the Monterey Peninsula have done a commendable job providing quality educational opportunities for their students from kindergarten through high school.

Active parents volunteering their time to improve the school systems have much to do with the success stories in Monterey, Carmel, Pacific Grove, Pebble Beach, and neighboring communities. In addition to strong efforts by the local PTA programs, groups such as Monterey's Community Partnership for Youth, Pacific Grove's P.G. Pride, and Carmel's Padre Parents have rallied the community to help compensate for budget shortfalls.

Local businesses and community organizations have also contributed greatly to the public school systems, particularly in the area of the arts. The nonprofit Monterey Jazz Festival provides musical instruments, sheet music, and docent training to middle and high schools throughout Monterey County. The AT&T Pebble Beach National Pro-Am raises substantial funds for local schools through its annual golf tournament. The Monterey Bay Aquarium and local museums create special educational programs otherwise unavailable to Peninsula youth.

The Peninsula is not an idyllic sanctuary free of drugs, guns, gangs, and other temptations that face youth nationwide. But it is comprised of a group of highly committed communities that realize the value of education to the present and future well-being of society. What follows is a brief overview of the three public school districts that cover the Monterey Peninsula and surrounding communities. Additional information can be obtained by requesting a School Accountability Report Card from any of the school districts.

Note: All of the school districts in this chapter use the State of California Standardized Testing and Reporting (STAR) Program for assessing academic achievement. STAR utilizes the Stanford 9 (or STAR 9) scoring system, which measures and reports scores for the subjects tested at each grade level: reading, written expression, mathematics, and spelling for grades two through eight; reading, writing, mathematics, science and social science for grades nine through 11. Scores are shown as a national percentile, with 50 percent the norm group average. (The scores

The auditorium at Pacific Grove Middle School has a classic architectural design. PHOTO: ROSS ANDRÉSON

presented here were the most recent as of January 2002.)

Monterey Peninsula Unified School District
700 Pacific Street, Monterey
(831) 649–1562, www.mpusd.k12.ca.us

The Monterey Peninsula Unified School District (MPUSD) covers 67 square miles, including the cities of Monterey, Del Rey Oaks, Seaside, Sand City, and Marina as well as portions of unincorporated areas such as Pebble Beach. Twenty-four campuses comprise the district, including 17 elementary schools (kindergarten through grade five), four middle schools (grades six to eight), two high schools (grades nine to 12) and one alternative high school. According to the School Accountability Report Card, which is required of all California public school districts, MPUSD spends an average of $5,300 per student annually for instruction, supervision, and instructional materials.

Total 2000–2001 enrollment in the 17 elementary schools was approximately 6,500. Current average class size in these schools is 20 students for grades kindergarten through three and 28 students for grades four and five. (The MPUSD Board of Education has adopted a plan to implement a state-funded program that will reduce elementary school class sizes to a maximum of 20 students for all grades.)

Measured by the STAR 9 system, the 17 elementary schools in the district scored in the 21 to 85 percent range for reading, 13 to 90 percent in language, and 18 to 91 percent in math.

The four MPUSD middle schools' enrollment is at 2,500 with an average class size of 26 students. STAR 9 test scores ranged between 27 and 67 percent for reading, 45 and 69 percent for language, and 29 and 69 for math.

The two MPUSD high schools, Monterey and Seaside, are accredited by the Western Association of Schools and Colleges. In 2001–2002 they had a combined enrollment of fewer than 3,000 students with an average class size of 27 students. STAR 9 test scores for grades nine through 11 were in the 24 to 47 percent range for reading, 31 to 59 percent for language, 38 to 55 percent in science, and 31 to 60 percent in social science. Twelfth graders at Monterey High School had SAT scores of 524 for verbal and 526 for math; those at Seaside High School averaged 451 for verbal and 466 for math. Special high school programs include the Academy of Travel and Tourism, the Monterey Academy of Oceanographic Science, the Navy Junior ROTC program, and ArtCareer Academy for Visual or Performing Arts. Unfortunately, these unique programs are in jeopardy due to school district budgetary problems. Central Coast High School, MPUSD's continuation high school, provides an alternative school environment for students who have difficulty in the traditional high school setting.

Pacific Grove Unified School District
555 Sinex Avenue, Pacific Grove
(831) 646–6520, www.pgusd.org

Pacific Grove Unified School District serves the city of Pacific Grove as well as parts of unincorporated Pebble Beach. The district spends approximately $5,600 per student for educational staff, services, and materials. The district schools are comprised of a Kindergarten Center, two elementary schools (grades one to five), one middle school (grades six to eight), one general high school (grades nine through 12), and one community high school.

The two elementary schools in Pacific Grove—Robert Down and Forest Grove schools—have a combined population of more than 1,000 students in grades K-five. Class sizes have averaged 20 to 28 students, on the way down to the state-prescribed 20-student level. The STAR 9 scores for the two schools ranged from 68 to 82 percent for reading, 68 to 74 percent for language, 71 to 78 percent for math, and 57 to 77 percent for spelling.

Pacific Grove Middle School has 570 students with an average class size of 24 to 27 boys and girls. In STAR 9 testing, the sixth- through eighth-grade students scored in the 63rd to 75th percentile in reading, 66th to 75th percentile in math, 59th to 75th percentile in language, and 57th to 61st percentile in spelling. The middle school music program, particularly the Jazz Band, is top-notch, having done especially well in recent state competitions.

Pacific Grove High School has 650 students in grades nine through 12, with class sizes averaging 27 students. In STAR 9 testing the ninth- through 11th-grade students scored 57 to 65 percent in reading, 59 to 79 percent in math, 63 to 71 percent in language, 60 to 66 percent in science, and 63 to 81 percent in social science. The 12th-grade SAT scores averaged 558 on verbal (481 state average) and 544 on math (493 state average).

Community High School provides an alternative for students who have not had success in a traditional school environment. It features a basic curriculum that emphasizes reading, writing, math, science, and art. Graduation requirements are the same as those at Pacific Grove High School. Community High School averages 35 to 40 students who are at various stages of their high school careers. Some may be simultaneously enrolled at Monterey Peninsula College, a two-year school. Class size averages 15 to 20. Students are required to be in school 3.5 hours per day. Independent study is emphasized.

Carmel Unified School District
Carmel Valley Road, Carmel
(831) 624–1546, www.carmelunified.org

Carmel Unified School District (CUSD) serves the cities of Carmel and Carmel Valley as well as unincorporated areas down the Big Sur coast. CUSD is made up of three elementary schools, one middle school, one high school, and a continuation high school, with the district spending an average of $7,900 annually per student for educational staff, services, and materials.

Approximately 1,100 students from kindergarten through the fifth grade attend the three CUSD elementary schools. Class sizes are at or near the 20 student per teacher maximum set by the state except at the fourth and fifth grade levels, which average 25. STAR 9 scores for the three elementary schools were 55 to 89 percent for reading, 53 to 94 percent for math, 50 to 93 percent for language, and 36 to 81 percent for spelling.

Carmel Middle School has a population of 625 students in the sixth through eighth grades, with class sizes averaging 25 to 30 students. On the STAR 9 tests, middle school students scored 71 to 74 percent in reading, 73 to 77 percent in math, 73 to 76 percent in language, and 55 to 66 percent in spelling.

Carmel High School has a current population of approximately 700 students. Class sizes average 20 to 25 students, who now take advantage of computers and wiring for the Internet and cable television in every classroom. On the STAR 9 testing, ninth through 11th graders scored 64 percent on reading, 66 to 79 percent on math, 65 to 72 percent on language, 66 to 70 percent on science, and 68 to 75 percent on social science. On the SAT, Carmel High 12th graders scored an average of 541 in verbal and a 554 in math.

Private Schools

All Saints' Episcopal Day School
8060 Carmel Valley Road, Carmel
(831) 624–9171, www.asds.org

In the sunny side of Carmel, All Saints' Episcopal Day School offers a rigorous academic curriculum within a Christian environment. Although the school has strong ties with All Saints' Episcopal Church, children from various religious backgrounds are admitted. Children as young as four years and nine months can take part in the school's Early Childhood Unit, a five-day morning program. Schooling continues through the eighth grade, with an average class size of 21 to 24 students at the upper levels and 15 students at the kindergarten and younger levels. Founded in 1961, All Saints' School places a strong emphasis on basic grammar, composition, math, and science, and all students study a foreign language (Spanish or French) beginning in the first grade. Latin is required of sixth through eighth graders. A strong fine arts program is also presented, including an annual Shakespeare production. The school hosts a series of "Visitors Days" for parents of prospective students in the fall and winter. Applicants must be in good academic and personal standing with their previous schools. Financial aid is granted on the basis of economic need. All Saints is a member of the National Association of Independent Schools.

Chartwell School
1490 Imperial Avenue, Seaside
(831) 394–3468

The mission of Chartwell School is to educate children ages seven to 14 who have dyslexia and other specific language-learning disabilities so that they can return successfully to mainstream education. Founded in 1983, Chartwell provides a multisensory instructional program that includes language arts, language training, mathematics, fine arts, performing arts, science lab, and physical education. Parent workshops are also provided. Students entering their final semester participate in a formal transition program to prepare them for reentry into a traditional school system. A four-week summer program is also offered to students ages seven to 13. **Note:** At the time of this writing, Chartwell School has plans to build a new 28,000-square-foot facility located on 29 acres of the former Fort Ord army base, land donated by the Monterey Peninsula Unified School District.

Junipero Serra School
2992 Lasuen Drive, Carmel
(831) 624–8322, www.dcsmonterey.org

Junipero Serra School is a kindergarten through eighth-grade Roman Catholic school located on the grounds of Carmel Mission. Founded in 1943, it is fully accredited by the Western Catholic Education Association and the Western Association of Schools and Colleges. Children from all parishes as well as non-Catholic children are admitted. Currently, the school has 230 students, with an average class size of 28. The academic program emphasizes religious education, family life, language arts, science, health, social studies, math, Spanish, computers, music, physical education, art, and drama. A variety of extracurricular activities are provided, including choir, community services, journalism, and speech. Uniforms are required for all grades, and each family is required to contribute a number of hours to school service each year. Extended care is available after school hours for all grades, providing supervised homework, recreation, and arts and crafts.

Lyceum of Monterey County
1073 6th Street, Monterey
(831) 372–6098, www.lyceum.org

Lyceum of Monterey County is a creative program of instruction that offers 400 fun-filled classes to children from preschool age to high school. A private nonprofit organization founded in 1960, the Lyceum offers an incredibly wide variety of instructive programs in the arts, crafts, computers, sports, hobbies, humanities, life skills, science, and nature. Family programs are also offered. Programs can last from one day to one week and range in topic from surfing to baby-sitting safety to international folk dancing to computer-aided design. Kids from outside the county are welcome to join in during their stay on the Monterey Peninsula. Contact the Lyceum of Monterey Peninsula, and see what programs are being offered this year. The Lyceum also sponsors the annual Peninsula Spelling Bee for fourth and fifth graders and Monterey County History Day for middle school and high school students.

Monterey Peninsula Christian Preschool
520 Pine Avenue, Pacific Grove
(831) 373–1922

A ministry of Peninsula Christian Center, Monterey Peninsula Christian School is a preschool and extended-care program for children ages two through five. It offers a flexible schedule, provides a supportive learning environment, and teaches Christian values. The school is open Monday through Friday from 7:00 A.M. to 6:00 P.M., with a preschool program from 9:00 A.M. until noon. Children partake in outdoor play, games, arts and crafts, science and nature observation, music, and story time. Bible stories and verse memorization are included in the daily program.

Mothers' Morning Out
501 El Dorado Street, Monterey
(831) 373–1067

Provided by the First Presbyterian Church of Monterey, Mothers' Morning Out ministers to and provides a school curriculum for children ages two through prekindergarten, with three separate programs developed for different age groups. Children from age two through three years and five months attend the Little Critters school, which is offered on three schedules: Monday, Wednesday, and Friday from 9:00 A.M. until noon, Tuesday and Thursday from 9:00 A.M. until noon, and Tuesday and Thursday from 1:00 to 3:30 P.M. The curriculum includes art, house play, a block area, manipulative materials, cooking experience, story time, science, outdoor play, and math readiness. The Main Room program for children age $3\frac{1}{2}$ to five years old is offered weekdays from 9:00 A.M. until noon. The curriculum is similar to the Little Critters program except that language skills, such as letter recognition, are added. The prekindergarten program for children who will be eligible to enter kindergarten the following fall is offered from 1:00 to 3:30 P.M. Monday through Friday. Curriculum includes math units from UC-Berkeley/Lawrence Hall of Science, "The Gems" (Great Explorations in Math) series, and "AIM" (Activities Integrating Math and Science).

Pacific Oaks Children's School
1004 David Avenue, Building A, Pacific Grove
(831) 373–8853

A licensed, private, nonprofit corporation, Pacific Oaks Children's School provides preschool and kindergarten through second grade classes, as well as after-school programs for children five through 12 years of age. Staffed by a principal and teachers with training and experience in early childhood education, the school maintains a child-to-teacher ratio of eight-to-one. Total enrollment is approximately 100 students. With a philosophy of learning by doing, Pacific Oaks offers preschool and kindergarten classes in language arts, math, social studies, music, art, science, nature, and physical education. The preschool operates year-round, Monday through Friday from 7:30 A.M. to 5:30 P.M. Kindergarten meets during the regular fall to summer school year from 8:30 A.M. to 1:30 P.M., while first and second graders meet from 8:30 A.M. to 2:30 P.M. The after-school program highlights drama, art, music, and science. It meets after the

Insiders' Tip

The Naval Postgraduate School is located on the former grounds of the Hotel Del Monte, Monterey's first world-class resort. It is home to the splendid Arizona Garden of specimen-size cacti and succulents.

regularly scheduled first- through fifth-grade classes of the Pacific Grove Unified School District.

Robert Louis Stevenson School
3152 Forest Lake Road, Pebble Beach
(831) 626–5200, rlstevenson.org

Founded in 1952, Robert Louis Stevenson School, or RLS as locals call it, is a coeducational boarding and day school on a beautiful 60-acre campus within the Del Monte Forest of Pebble Beach. Approximately half of the 500-plus ninth through 12th graders live on campus in six residence halls. Though nonsectarian, Stevenson School encourages its students to attend church as part of its quest to "educate the whole person" and offers vespers and Sunday Christian services at the school's exquisite Erdman Memorial Chapel.

Accredited by the Western Association of Schools and Colleges, RLS has a traditional college-preparatory curriculum. The Secondary School Admission Test (SSAT) is required for enrollment. Among 12th graders the average SAT scores are 592 on the verbal and 618 on math. Advanced-placement courses are offered in art, English, foreign languages, American and European history, economics, mathematics, biology, chemistry, and physics. Average class size is 15 students. Approximately 18 percent of the student body receive financial aid grants, totaling more than $1.25 million in 2001.

Robert Louis Stevenson Lower and Middle School offers a range of academic choices for more than 200 students from kindergarten through eighth grade. Special programs are presented in art, dance, dramatics, music, and physical education.

San Carlos Regional School
450 Church Street, Monterey
(831) 375–1324, www.sancarlosschool.com

Established in 1898, San Carlos Regional School is an interparish Roman Catholic school that covers preschool through eighth grade. Accepting students of all faiths, its focus is providing Christian morals and basic academic skills in language arts, math, science, health, social science, Spanish, computer science, and physical education. Enrichment programs include field trips and interscholastic sports. Current enrollment is approximately 300 boys and girls. Preschool is designed for children ages three to five, with each session limited to 15 children and two teachers. Uniforms are required for grades kindergarten through eight. Parental participation is vital, as each family is required to make a time and talent commitment to the school each year. San Carlos School is fully accredited by the Western Association of Schools and Colleges. All homeroom teachers are fully credentialed. Extended-care services for grades kindergarten through eight run from 7:00 A.M. to 6:00 P.M.

Santa Catalina School
1500 Mark Thomas Drive, Monterey
(831) 655–9315, www.santacatalina.org

Santa Catalina is a Catholic school with a 150-year history in Monterey. Originally founded in 1850 by Mother Mary Goemaere, a Dominican sister, Santa Catalina School operates today as a coeducational lower school and an all-girl upper school. Both are on an expansive 36-acre campus that was once a Spanish hacienda estate. Santa Catalina School is accredited by the Western Association of Schools and Colleges and is a member of the California Association of Independent Schools and the National Association of Independent Schools. Santa Catalina Lower School provides a classic curriculum for students in preschool through eighth grade. The school emphasizes a strong foundation in the basic skills of language arts, social studies, science, and mathematics, along with religious instruction. Catholic students are taught the tenets of Catholicism, while others are instructed in interfaith classes that focus on values and world religions. Students add Spanish in grades four through eight. All classrooms are equipped with one or more computers that have Internet access and CD-ROM capability. Santa Catalina Lower School participates in a local sports league with teams in basketball, flag football, soccer, tennis, and volleyball.

The all-girl upper school combines a rigorous liberal arts curriculum, modern educational technology, and solid Christian principles into a well-rounded high school experience. A student-to-faculty ratio of seven-to-one facilitates individual instruction, while faculty, dorm, and college admission counseling provide on-campus guidance. Performing and visual arts are emphasized, and a full interscholastic sports program offers seasonal competition. The 29,000 volume Sister Mary Kieran Memorial Library and a school-wide Internet and e-mail network promote studying. Residential dorms offer primarily double rooms, with girls changing roommates three times a year to promote new friendships. Student responsibilities and rights vary by class level. School clubs, voluntary service activities, and traditional off-campus events and excursions ensure that all students become an active part of the Peninsula community.

Serendipity Pre-School
1231 7th Street, Monterey
(831) 375–9743

A preschool program for children ages three up to kindergarten, Serendipity Pre-School focuses on developing reading, math, and science readiness skills, reinforced through art and music programs. The morning session runs from 9:00 A.M. until noon, while the afternoon session runs from 12:30 until 3:30 P.M. Before-school care is offered from 8:00 until 9:00 A.M., and after-school care is offered from 3:30 until 5:30 P.M. Extended preschool and day care are available for the full 8:00 A.M. to 5:30 P.M. schedule. Preschool sessions begin with music and group time. The classes are then divided into the Rabbit Group and the Butterfly Group, based on maturity levels and other factors. These groups then rotate through a period of outdoor playtime and learning centers, including the use of the AIMS (An Instructional Manipulative Series) program in prereading, consonants, vowels, comprehension, and math. Story time concludes each preschool session.

York School
9501 York Road, Monterey
(831) 372–7338, www.york.org

York School is an independent, coeducational college-preparatory Episcopal day school in the scenic foothills near the former Laguna Seca Ranch, a few miles inland from downtown Monterey. Serving grades eight through 12, York School enrolls just over 200 students with an average class size of less than 15. A rigorous college preparatory curriculum and an ambitious financial aid program attract a high-quality, culturally diverse student body. On the SATs, York students averaged 665 on the verbal section and 651 in math. More than 48 percent of seniors from the last six graduating classes have been National Merit honorees. Accredited by the Western Association of Independent Schools, the National Association of Episcopal Schools, and the California Association of Independent Schools, York School awards grants and loans—totaling more than $590,000 in 2001—to approximately 35 percent of its students. As an Episcopal school, it emphasizes the development of moral and spiritual values in all aspects of student life.

Colleges and Universities

California State University Monterey Bay
100 Campus Center, Seaside
(831) 582–3330, www.csumb.edu

When President Bill Clinton visited the brand-new California State University Monterey Bay (CSUMB) in 1995, it marked an important day for both the Monterey Peninsula and the United States as a whole. For the nation, CSUMB represents a successful conversion of a former army base, Fort Ord, to a valuable civilian resource. For the Monterey Peninsula, the 21st campus in the California State University system represented yet another high-quality educational facility and hundreds of local jobs. From the humble beginnings of only 650 students that first year, CSUMB now welcomes more than 2,600 full-time students each semester. By the year 2030, that population is expected to grow to 15,000. Many of these students are projected to attend the university off-campus and on-line as part of the California Virtual University system. The campus is already offering some technology courses entirely on-line. CSUMB offers 12 undergraduate majors and three graduate-level programs. The university grants both bachelor's and master's degrees in the arts and sciences as well as teaching credentials. Areas of specialty include human communication; music and performing arts; visual and public art; world languages and cultures; education; CLAD/BCLAD teaching credentials; collaborative human services; global studies; liberal studies; management and international entrepreneurship; earth systems science and policy; telecommunications, multimedia, and applied computing; teledramatic arts and technology; social and behavioral sciences; marine science; and interdisciplinary studies. The majority of students, faculty, and staff live on campus, creating a unique residential atmosphere. More than 44 student clubs have been created, a testament to the close-knit community being established on this once sprawling army base 5 miles north of the city of Monterey.

The CSUMB Otters presently compete in eight intercollegiate sports: men's basketball, soccer, golf, and cross-country and women's volleyball, basketball, golf, and cross-country. The campus prides itself on its full-service childcare facilities for the children of students. This service offers daily or hourly childcare for children ages six weeks to five years, as well as afterschool care for kids in kindergarten through age 18. A baby-sitter referral service is also offered.

Chapman University, Monterey Campus
99 Pacific Street, Monterey
(831) 373–0945, www.chapman.edu

Chapman University, established in 1861, is an independent institution of liberal arts and professional training. With its main campus in Orange, California, it has operated its Monterey Academic Center since 1974, primarily to part-time students who are parents of young children and work full- or part-time. Chapman University offers undergraduate degrees in liberal studies, organizational leadership, and social sciences as well as master's degrees in education, psychology, and human resources. It also offers programs for teaching credentials. To help students balance the demands of job, family, and education, courses are offered in accelerated nine-week terms, one evening per week plus one Saturday class. Chapman University is accredited by the Senior Division of the Western Association of Schools and Colleges, and credits earned may be transferred to other colleges and universities.

Golden Gate University
500 8th Street, Marina
(831) 373–4176, www.ggu.edu

Founded in San Francisco in 1853, Golden Gate University is the fourth-oldest private university in California. The Monterey campus, one of 16 Golden Gate campuses in California and the Pacific Rim, has been offering undergraduate and graduate degrees in business-oriented majors since 1971. Classes in Monterey are held on the former Fort Ord military base. The Golden State University Monterey campus offers bachelor's degrees in business administration, accounting, and computer information systems. Master's degrees are offered in finance, human resource management, information systems, management, business administration, marketing, public administration, taxation, and other areas of business. The university is fully accredited by the Western Association of Schools and Colleges. Average class size is 16 students. Classes meet throughout the year in 15-, 12-, 10-, and eight-week formats. Many courses are available on-line in the Golden Gate Cyber Campus and others in intensive sessions, which meet Friday evenings and all day Saturday on alternate weekends over a six-week period.

Hopkins Marine Station
Ocean View Boulevard, Pacific Grove
(831) 655–6200, www-marine.stanford.edu

Founded in 1892, Hopkins Marine Station is a marine biology research facility of Stanford University's Department of Biological Sciences and was the first marine laboratory established on the American Pacific Coast. Hopkins is ideally situated on Mussel Point, a rocky headland in Pacific Grove surrounded by the rich sea life of the Monterey Bay Marine Sanctuary. The facility is staffed year-round by approximately 20 resident faculty and support staff and is host to visiting researchers and graduate students. Both introductory and advanced marine and general biology courses are offered year-round to qualified students from any college or university. Special areas of study include cellular and developmental biology, immunology, neurobiology, comparative physiology, conservation biology, oceanic biology, marine botany, biomechanics, and marine ecology.

Monterey Institute of International Studies
425 Van Buren Street, Monterey
(831) 647–4100, www.miis.edu

Since 1955, the Monterey Institute of International Studies (MIIS) has served as a vibrant global village on the Monterey Peninsula, offering international courses and degrees to students seeking careers as bilingual, bicultural professionals. More than 700 students, approximately half being foreign students representing 50 nations, gather here to take advantage of four fully accredited graduate schools. MIIS offers master's degrees in international business administration, translation and interpretation, language teaching, commercial diplomacy, international environmental policy, international public administration, international policy studies, teaching English to speakers of other languages, and teaching a foreign language.

Insiders' Tip

The Defense Language Institute serves the entire Department of Defense and is the largest language institute of its kind.

A Bachelor of Arts honors program allows students with two years of undergraduate work to complete both their bachelor's degree in international studies and master's degrees in three years at the institute.

Summer and Winter Intensive Language Programs are provided in Arabic, Chinese (Mandarin), French, German, Japanese, Russian, and Spanish, as well as English as a second language. MIIS's Center for International Trade Strategy trains business executives on the intricacies of international commerce, while the Business and Economic Development Center, the Small Business Institute, and the International Trade Research Center offer international marketing assistance to businesses. The Center for Nonproliferation Studies is the largest private center in the world addressing international weapons proliferation.

The school's library features books and periodicals in more than 30 languages. MIIS is accredited by the Western Association of Schools and Colleges.

Community Colleges and Technical Schools

Monterey College of Law
404 West Franklin Street, Monterey
(831) 373–3301, www.montereylaw.edu

Monterey College of Law (MCL) is a California State Bar-accredited community law school offering a four-year program of instruction leading to a Doctor of Jurisprudence degree. The school was founded in 1972 by local lawyers and judges with the goal of allowing residents to attend law school at night while continuing their daytime careers. Indeed, most of the students at MCL work full-time during the day while attending evening classes from 6:30 to 9:30 P.M. Fall and spring semesters last 16 weeks, while the summer semester is 11 weeks. Courses are taught by practicing attorneys and judges. The age of the student body ranges from the early 20s to the early 60s, with a median age of 36. The average class size is 45 students. In addition to being accredited by the State Bar of California, MCL is approved by the Council for Private Postsecondary and Vocational Education. The school reports that 280 of its 380 graduates have successfully completed the bar exam and are admitted to practice law in California. However, the college has not sought accreditation from the American Bar Association. Therefore, graduates might not meet the necessary requirements to practice law or take the bar examination in other states.

Monterey Institute of Touch
27820 Dorris Drive, Carmel
(831) 624–1006,
www.montereyinstituteoftouch.com

Monterey Institute of Touch offers both a 200-hour Certified Massage Practitioner program and a 500-hour Certified Massage Therapist program from its Carmel location. In addition, the institute offers a series of advanced workshops and seminars in massage techniques such as shiatsu, craniosacral, reflexology, and polarity. The school emphasizes hands-on training and the latest advances in the holistic health-care field.

Monterey Peninsula College
980 Fremont Street, Monterey
(831) 646–4000, www.mpc.edu

Founded in 1947, Monterey Peninsula College (MPC) is part of California's public community college system of 107 campuses throughout the state. Classes are held during two semesters (fall and spring) as well as a summer session, with enrollment reaching 10,000 to 12,000 students per semester. The average student age is 37 years, evidence of the school's significant 40-and-older population. More than 350 international students represent 46 countries at MPC. The 87-acre campus is minutes from downtown Monterey yet enjoys a decidedly rural setting.

MPC confers the Associate of Arts degree in liberal arts and an Associate of Science degree in science, technology, and vocational fields. Its transfer program enables students to complete the first two years in preparation for moving on to a four-year college or university. Occupational education programs provide basic technical and professional curricula. MPC offers a full program of intercollegiate sports, including football, basketball, baseball, softball, and golf. The Maurine Church Coburn School of Nursing offers an Associate of Science degree. It is accredited by the National League for Nursing and approved by the California Board of Registered Nursing. MPC also has special accreditation and certifications from the California State Board of Dental Examiners, California State Fire Marshall, Commission on Dental Assisting of the American Dental Association, Commission on Police Officer Standards and Training, and the National Automotive Technical Education Foundation. MPC is also home to the Marine Advanced Technology Education (MATE) Center, a national consortium of marine technology educational institutes.

Military Schools

Defense Language Institute
Presidio of Monterey, Monterey
(831) 242–5104, www.dli.army.mil

In 1941 the U.S. Army established a secret school on the Presidio of San Francisco. Its mission: to teach the Japanese language to American soldiers of Japanese descent. In 1946 the school was renamed the Army Language School and moved to the Presidio at Monterey, where it expanded to teach more than 30 languages. That was the beginning of today's Defense Language Institute Foreign Language Center, now the world's largest language institute of its kind. The 395-acre campus, known locally as DLI, is comprised of more than 750

The Defense Language Institute (DLI) in Monterey provides language training for the nation's military forces. PHOTO: ROSS ANDRÉSON

classrooms, 21 language labs, and eight computer labs in seven distinct schools. More than 650 civilian faculty, 300 civilian staff, and 250 service members support the school. The primary mission of DLI is to teach the nation's military forces the foreign language skills needed to meet Department of Defense national security needs. In addition, the institute provides language training for other branches of the federal government and, since 1996, to civilians with U.S. citizenship.

DLI is accredited by the Community and Junior Colleges of the Western Association of Schools and Colleges and, in partnership with Monterey Peninsula College, offers associate's degrees in foreign languages. It offers basic through advanced foreign-language studies with emphasis on intensive listening, speaking, reading, and writing development as well as the history, culture, and current affairs of the region where the language is spoken. Courses run 25 to 63 weeks, depending on language difficulty. The wide variety of languages offered will vary depending upon the present needs of the Department of Defense.

Aiso Library, which is open to California State University Monterey Bay students, subscribes to hundreds of foreign-language newspapers, maintains 80,000 volumes of foreign-language books, and provides access to more than 5,000 foreign-language television programs.

Naval Postgraduate School
1 University Circle, Monterey
(831) 656–2441, www.nps.navy.mil

On the former grounds of Hotel Del Monte, Monterey's first world-class resort, Naval Postgraduate School (NPS) offers master's and doctoral degrees to members of all branches of the U.S. military as well as students from more than 25 foreign nations. In Monterey since 1947, NPS now serves 1,500 students on its 627-acre campus. The curricula are designed to meet the defense requirements of the armed forces within the framework of a high-level academic institution. Each curriculum leads to a master's degree, while additional study in certain fields can lead to a doctorate. NPS ranks second of all colleges and universities in its number of alumni who have become NASA astronauts.

While strictly a military school, NPS offers valuable resources to the Peninsula's civilian community. The 100,000-square-foot Dudley Knox Library houses approximately 400,000 bibliographic volumes in hard copy, 500,000 volumes in microfilm, and 1,200 journal subscriptions, making it the largest local research facility. A large staff of librarians and support personnel offers assistance to the general public, though some of the collection is available only to military personnel.

NPS takes an active part in the community by hosting a series of free Concerts on the Lawn, featuring popular classical selections by the Monterey Bay Symphony Orchestra. It also sponsors Discovery Day, a series of interactive science programs created by the academic faculty and targeted toward students between eight and 14 years of age. Finally, the school provides self-guided tour booklets of the former Hotel Del Monte and its fabulous Arizona Garden of specimen-size cacti and succulents. Rebuilt in 1926 after the second of two devastating fires, Hotel Del Monte (now called Herrmann Hall) serves primarily as offices and quarters for naval officers and is home to a small Naval Postgraduate School Museum.

The old Del Monte Hotel is now the site of the Naval Postgraduate School. PHOTO: ROSS ANDRÉSON

Childcare

Childcare is a substantial industry in Monterey County. More than 11,000 Monterey County children spend at least half their day in a child-care facility. Their parents work for the county, at restaurants, for private industry or the military, in hotels, or in the fields. The county has more than 800 licensed childcare establishments: nearly 700 family day care homes and more than 100 centers.

The number of childcare options hasn't kept pace with the rapid growth of the Monterey County work force, and welfare reform is expected to add to the numbers. In an effort to address childcare needs, county and city officials, local businesses, and childcare industry personnel have formed a partnership and are working toward a solution for the ever-increasing need for childcare facilities.

Childcare is usually a family's third largest expenditure, after food and housing. Childcare in Monterey County ranks among California's most expensive. Full-time care costs an average of $100 per week. Family day care providers, usually set up in private homes, are generally less expensive than established centers.

As a result of childcare challenges, some businesses in the Monterey Peninsula area have relaxed their policies on absence and tardiness and set up tax-credit programs to help employees pay for childcare. A few companies provide benefits to help with the expense of childcare. For example, upon discovering through a company study that their employees prefer to place their children in family day care homes, Community Hospital of the Monterey Peninsula set up 14 of them.

Family Daycare Homes

With nearly 700 family daycare homes for children in Monterey County, it is impossible to list them all. In general, as noted above, family daycare facilities are less expensive than childcare centers and have fewer regulations. Family daycare homes for children may offer more flexibility in terms of schedules. For safety reasons, many family daycare facilities are not listed in the phone book. Parents need to work with a referral service such as Children's Services International (see our listing in the "Resources" section).

All family daycare homes must be licensed through the state and are required to provide their license number in all advertisements.

The license for the operation of a family daycare home requires the following:

• The home must be kept clean and orderly with heating and ventilation for safety and comfort.

• It must have telephone service.

• The home must provide safe toys, play equipment, and materials.

• Any food brought from the child's home must be labeled with the child's name and properly stored or refrigerated.

• The home must be free of defects or conditions that might endanger a child.

• All in-ground swimming pools must have at least a 5-foot fence or covering inspected and approved by the licensing agency.

• Outdoor play areas must be fenced, or outdoor play must be supervised.

• An emergency card must be maintained with the child's full name, the phone number and location of a parent or

Insiders' Tip

The Lyceum of Monterey County, 1073 6th Street, Monterey, (831) 372-6098, www.lyceum.org, offers a large variety of family classes and field trips in science and nature, the arts, life skills, humanities, crafts, and hobbies. A program guide, published three times a year, lists more than 375 classes annually.

other responsible adult to be contacted in an emergency, the name and phone number of the child's physician, and the parents' authorization for the licensee to consent to emergency medical care.

• Each family daycare home must have a written disaster plan of action on a form approved by the licensing agency. All children, age and ability permitting, and all others in the household must be instructed in their duties under the disaster plan.

• The licensee must maintain either liability insurance, a bond, or a file of affidavits signed by each parent with a child enrolled in the home. The affidavit states that the family daycare home does not carry liability insurance or a bond according to standards established by the state.

Childcare Centers and Preschools

Nearly 200 childcare centers and academic preschools exist in Monterey County. The social services department inspects them annually to make sure they meet health and safety standards. Childcare center employees are required to take the equivalent of three classes in early childhood development and to be annually certified in CPR and basic emergency procedures.

The requirements for operating a childcare center or preschool match those for a family daycare home but have additional requirements. When seeking a local childcare center or preschool, you may want to consult the Yellow Pages of the phone directory. You can also contact Children's Services International (listed in our "Resources" section) for a referral.

Resources

Children's Services International
344 Salinas Road, Salinas
(800) 273–0274

This organization provides information on childcare, preschool, and family daycare. It also offers a referral service for childcare facilities.

Monterey County Early Start Infant Program
Monterey County Office of Education,
901 Blanco Circle, Salinas
(831) 755–0300

The Early Start education program for special-needs children (birth to age three) serves all eligible infants who reside in Monterey County. The program provides a service model for infant stimulation, development, and parent education. Parent/child classes meet at least two times weekly. Home visits and parent meetings are also provided.

Insiders' Tip

Need information on childcare resources on the Monterey Peninsula? Children's Services International at (800) 273-0274 offers a referral service for childcare, preschool, and family daycare.

Monterey County has an excellent selection of childcare options available for parents and their children.
PHOTO: ROSS ANDRÉSON

Monterey County Child Care Planning Council
1000 South Main Street, # 133, Salinas
(831) 796–3530,
www.co.monterey.ca.us/childcare

The Child Care Planning Council coordinates childcare services for the county. It also provides information and assists other employers in providing childcare services for their employees.

Mexican American Opportunity Foundation
826 North Sanborn Road, Salinas
(831) 757–0753, www.maof.org

This foundation provides food to daycare centers. It also runs a state-funded childcare center. To qualify for the childcare center, parents must be in school or working at least six hours per day. The program is ideal for parents who need to further their education. The childcare center is run by teachers, aides, and other workers. Breakfast, lunch, and an afternoon snack are served. The center has planned activities for the children, including learning activities, games, stories, and craft projects.

Baby-sitting Services and Nannies

When visiting the Peninsula with children, it's still possible for parents to spend some alone time together by using a baby-sitting service. You can find a baby-sitter or nanny from either an agency or through the concierge at your hotel. Sitters or nannies will come to your hotel room or vacation rental. Some services also place full- or part-time nannies who live in or out of the home. We've listed a few local agencies that provide baby-sitting services.

Sitters-by-the-Sea Professional Babysitting
12 Castro Road, Monterey
(831) 656–0107

Sitters-by-the-Sea provides nannies who are CPR-trained and bonded and conducts background checks on all employees. The nannies do on-site childcare at your home, rental unit, or hotel. The company has served the Monterey Peninsula area since 1993.

VIP Child Care Services
(831) 659–2203, www.vipbabysitting.com

VIP provides baby-sitting for infants, children, and teenagers as well as custom children's programs for group events of 10 to 1,500 children. Their staff is insured, CPR certified, fingerprinted (with FBI background check), and registered with Trustline through the State of California. Their staff comes to your location prepared with art materials, games, and activity books for custom events. Reservations may be made 24 hours a day by phone or on-line.

Media

- **Newspapers**
- **Magazines**
- **Television**
- **Radio**

If you're looking for newsworthy items of local, national, or international significance, the media selections in Monterey County can provide you with the appropriate information. For a small market, the Monterey Peninsula has amassed media possibilities in everything from daily newspapers and syndicated news programs to Public, Education, and Government (PEG) Access channels and a Community Media Center.

Newspapers

Dailies

The Monterey County Herald
8 Upper Ragsdale Road, Monterey
(831) 372–3311, www.montereyherald.com

For over 75 years, *The Herald* has provided news to residents of Monterey County. *The Herald,* a Knight-Ridder publication, is now a cousin of the highly respected and well-known *San Jose Mercury News.*

The Herald of today is made up of a main news section. The sports section contains the classifieds, with the ever-popular "New Today" column (a listing of classified ads that are running for the first time) and the help-wanted, rental, real estate, and auto ads. A "Living" section includes the syndicated columns of Ann Landers and Dr. Gott and features on pets. Information on television programming and comics round out this popular section.

Each Thursday, locals and visitors alike check out *The Herald*'s pullout tab *Go!,* a weekly entertainment and dining guide that runs in the paper and is also distributed free as an independent publication. A Saturday *Real Estate* pullout runs with maps, open houses, and residential, commercial, and rental properties and is available free at newsstands.

The Herald, with a circulation of around 40,000, has the largest circulation of local newspapers.

The Californian
123 West Alisal Street, Salinas
(831) 649–6626, www.californianonline.com

The Californian, a Gannett newspaper, has been a respected news source since 1872. Although the paper is based in Salinas, it has a slight presence on the Monterey Peninsula. Published weekdays and Saturday, the newspaper has a circulation of around 20,000. It provides coverage of countywide news with a primary emphasis on the Salinas Valley.

From an editorial standpoint, the paper consists of national and local news, entertainment, features, sports, and classified sections. A pull-out entertainment and dining guide, *411,* is published on Thursdays. *The Californian* is available by subscription and at newsstands.

Weekly, Semiweekly, and Monthly Papers

Coast Weekly
668 Williams Avenue, Seaside
(831) 394–5656, www.coastweekly.com

This paper, with a circulation of more than 42,000, serves Monterey County in the areas of news and entertainment. The free publication comes out each Thursday and can be found at newsstands around the county. Best known for its "Hot Picks" arts and entertainment calendar, *Coast Weekly* is also considered by many to be a good alternative to mainstream media, particularly when it comes to local issues. The paper, founded in 1988, has won more than 25 California Newspaper Publishers Association awards over the past five years. One of the most anticipated issues is "Best of Monterey County," when readers cast their vote for their favorite businesses. It provides insider information on readers' top choices of local restaurants, entertainment venues, and service providers.

Visitors to the area will appreciate the stand-alone product *Best of Monterey Bay,* which recaps the results of "Best of Monterey County" and includes directories for various services, locations for entertainment, maps, and an annual calendar of events. This special edition is distributed at 120 locations, including area hotels, bookstores, and visitor centers.

Community Links
Pacific Grove
(831) 375–2026, www.communitylinks.net

This community calendar, printed monthly, works in unison with radio, television, and the Internet. The concept, created in 1997, is to inform readers about Monterey County's community organizations' events. It is distributed monthly via *The Monterey County Herald,* AMP, KAZU, KBTU, KPIG, KMBY, and KCDU. Around 40,000 are inserted into *The Herald* each month. An additional 25,000 free copies of *Community Links* newspapers can be found at libraries, city halls, banks, bookstores, visitor centers, hospitals, chambers of commerce, and senior centers.

The Connection Magazine
317-A Cedar Street, Santa Cruz
(831) 459–0522, www.ReConnect.com

This free monthly newspaper covers a wide range of topics including health and fitness; arts and events; restaurant, music, and movie reviews; pet health; diet and nutrition; astrology; and relationships. *The Connection Magazine* is circulated throughout Monterey, Santa Cruz, Santa Clara, and San Mateo counties and claims a readership of 100,000. Readers can find it at local hospitals, clinics, coffee shops, restaurants, health-food stores, and fitness centers.

The Monterey County Post
225 Crossroads Boulevard, Suite 408, Carmel
(831) 624–2222

Controversy is the name of the game for this free, weekly, tabloid-sized paper. The editors of the *Post* seek out tough issues and take sides in hotly contested local elections. A group of columnists pontificates on subjects such as jazz, Carmel politics, and furniture. *The Monterey County Post* has the distinction of being the only paper in the county with a weekly column written by a dog.

Peninsula Family Connection
612 Lighthouse Avenue, Suite 101, Pacific Grove
(831) 372–4996

This family-run, quarterly publication, billed as a "Comprehensive Guide to Family Fun on the Monterey Peninsula," has an annual circulation of 40,000. Local writers contribute articles on topics such as art, adoption, holistic living, pets, child development, and various aspects of parenting. A calendar of events provides information on local happenings that are especially suited to families. Listings of family-friendly restaurants and other businesses are also provided. The paper is free and available at libraries, bookstores, restaurants, family-oriented businesses, and social agencies.

The Pine Cone
4th Street between Mission and San Carlos Streets, Carmel
(831) 624–0162, www.carmelpinecone.com

Published since 1915, *The Pine Cone* is a favorite of locals seeking news primarily about Carmel and immediately surrounding communities. This 25,000-circulation weekly is distributed at nearly 300 drop points in Carmel, Carmel Valley, Carmel Highlands, Pebble Beach, Monterey, Pacific Grove, and Big Sur. Highlights include the fascinating (and often amusing) police and sheriff's log, an events calendar, a social column, features on food and wine, a real estate section, and a good-sized service directory.

Magazines

Carmel Magazine
Carmel
(831) 625–9922, www.carmelmagazine.com

The covers of this high-quality, glossy, quarterly lifestyle magazine feature celebrities with local Carmel connections. Recent celebrities so honored include Brad Pitt, Jay Leno, Tiger Woods, and the former mayor of Carmel, Clint Eastwood. Regular features include art gallery showcases, restaurant reviews, topical features, and a regular column that profiles the dogs that Carmel business people bring with them to work. The magazine is free at various businesses around town and is also available by subscription. A companion television show, *Carmel Magazine TV*, airs on local cable stations on the Monterey Peninsula and in Santa Cruz.

Central Coast Adventures
5th Avenue and Dolores Street, Carmel
(831) 626–5143,
www.centralcoastadventures.com

This local lifestyle publication presents beautiful four-color highlights from the menus of local restaurants, features on food and wine, restaurant reviews, and a listing of restaurants throughout the Monterey Peninsula. The free magazine, with a circulation of 60,000, is distributed quarterly in *The Monterey County Herald,* local hotels, and area visitor centers. Also published within the magazine and as freestanding publications (12,000 circulation each) are sections on real estate, galleries, and restaurants.

GuestLife Monterey Bay Magazine
7th Avenue between Lincoln and Monte Verde Streets, Carmel
(831) 624–5740, www.guestlife.com/monterey

This upscale annual tourist publication contains information on accommodations, shopping, culture, and cuisine. Its four-color, slick, and glossy appearance makes it an enjoyable read. More than 10,000 hotel rooms on Monterey Peninsula contain a hardbound edition of *GuestLife*. Local newsstands sell about 5,000 soft-cover editions throughout the year. About 30,000 separately bound soft-cover sections, Culture and Cuisine, show up at the local chamber of commerce, visitor center, galleries, restaurants, and at special events such as the AT&T National Pro-Am Tournament.

Monterey Peninsula Guide
499 Calle Principal, Suite H, Monterey
(831) 648–9242,
www.montereypeninsulaguide.com

Founded 17 years ago, this four-color magazine with an annual distribution of 60,000 is distributed through local hotels and motels, chain supermarkets and drugstores, and various bookstores. It's published twice each year and is replenished at distribution points throughout the year. Visitors receive a copy free in their hotel room, at the concierge desk, or at the airport. On the newsstands, it sells for $4.50. The magazine contains facts about the Monterey Peninsula, maps, a calendar of events, information on things to see and do, and feature articles on the arts, lifestyles, history, and golf. It also contains a lodging guide.

Monterey Peninsula Homes
Lincoln Street and SE 5th Avenue, Carmel
(831) 625–6195, www.homesmagazine.com

Those looking to relocate to the Monterey Peninsula will want to pick up a free copy of this slick, glossy, four-color magazine that acts as an advertising aid for Realtors to promote their listings. The publication, first published in 1996, has a distribution of 30,000 and is published 10 times per year (every five weeks). You'll find the magazine at participating realty offices and on media racks throughout the Peninsula, or it can be ordered on-line.

Monterey Land and Sea
380 Alvarado Street, Monterey
(888) 221–1010, www.montereyinfo.org

The official magazine of the Monterey County Convention and Visitors Bureau, this four-color publication contains a wealth of visitor information, area maps, and brief highlights of the major areas in Monterey County, as well as extensive listings of area attractions, accommodations,

Insiders' Tip

One of the most reliable sources of information about the mercurial weather of the Monterey Peninsula is a Web site maintained by the National Weather Service. Continually updated, the site contains interactive graphics, radar and satellite images, current conditions on land and sea, and forecast discussions revised every few hours. The somewhat cumbersome address is: http://nimbo.wrh.noaa.gov/wrhq/javaLinks/wrhqJava.html.

restaurants, spas, and wineries. A calendar of events gives specifics on the annual recreational and cultural activities available on the Monterey Peninsula. *Monterey Land and Sea* is readily available at the major visitor centers and can be ordered on-line.

Pacific Grove Directory
Pacific Grove
(831) 646–0351,
www.bestofcal.com/pacificgrove/pgweb.html

This free guide for locals and visitors is a directory of accommodations, restaurants, shopping, trades, and personal services in Pacific Grove. There are also maps, interesting collections of historical information, community highlights, and information on Pacific Grove events. The circulation of 20,000 is distributed through the hospitality industry in Pacific Grove and Monterey as well as through the Pacific Grove Chamber of Commerce. The directory is published quarterly.

Television

Peninsula-area viewers can access a variety of programming 24 hours a day through local cable, network, and specialty channels. Residents and businesses in Monterey are also served by Public, Education, and Government Access programming on several cable channels. AT&T Broadband is the current local provider of cable television. Those channel numbers are indicated in parentheses in the listings that follow.

KCBA Fox Channel 35 (3)
Salinas
(831) 422–3500, www.iknowcentralcoast.com

KION CBS Channel 46 (5)
(831) 784–1702, kion.cbsnow.com

KGO ABC Channel 7 (7)
(415) 954–7777, www.abc7.com

KMST MCOE Channel 59 (26)
(831) 373–2955
KQED PBS Channel 9 (9)
(415) 864–2000, www.kqed.org

KSBW NBC Channel 8 (6)
(831) 758–8888, www.theksbwchannel.com

KSMS Univision (Spanish) Channel 67 (4)
(831) 373–6767, www.univision.com

Cable

Access Monterey Peninsula (24, 25, 27)
2200 Garden Road, Monterey
(831) 333–1267, www.ampmedia.org

Access Monterey Peninsula (AMP) is a community media organization created to serve the public, educational agencies, and local governments on the Monterey Peninsula. This local nonprofit organization provides training and access to media technology for residents of Monterey County. AMP also airs programming 24 hours a day on channels 24, 25, and 27. Channel 24 features public access programming that showcases self-expression, from music, dance, poetry, and plays to religious, political, and social views. Channel 25 broadcasts programs about city services and public meetings; federal government programs including Navy/Marine Corps News, Army News, and Air Force Television News; The Research Channel and programs of the University of California. Channel 27 presents community information in the form of an hour-long looping bulletin board. KAZU Public Radio provides the accompanying soundtrack, keeping viewers informed and entertained.

AT&T Broadband
2455 Henderson Way, Monterey
(831) 649–9100

This is the major cable company serving the Monterey Peninsula. The company carries major networks such as ESPN, CNN, USA, and TNT. An optional pay-per-view service can be set up on an automatic system that operates with a converter placed in the home. The monthly fee varies. Please call for more information.

Radio

Radio fans won't be disappointed with the variety of station formats found in the Monterey Peninsula area. The selection includes those you'd expect and perhaps a few that will surprise you.

Adult Contemporary

KBAY 94.5 FM
(408) 287–5775, www.kbay.com

Soft Rock

KTEE 103.9 FM
(831) 655–5833, www.ktee.com

KWAV 97 FM
(831) 649–0969, www.kwav.com

Christian

KLVM (KLOVE) 89.7 and 95.9 FM
(800) 434–8400, www.klove.com

Community/Public

KAZU 90.3 FM
(831) 375–7275, www.kazu.org

Music/information/news 24 hours. Music programming is provided by local volunteer programmers. News content provided by NPR.

KSPB 91.9
(831) 625–8374, www.kspb.org

Students of Robert Louis Stevenson School in Pebble Beach facilitate afternoon and evening programming. Interesting view into the musical tastes of high school students. When not broadcasting live, station airs the BBC World Service.

KUSP 88.9 FM
(831) 476–2800, www.kusp.org

Santa Cruz public radio station. Features classical, jazz, and world music.

Country

KTOM 100.7 and 100.9
(800) 660–5866, www.ktom.com
KPIG 107.5
(831) 722–9000, www.kpig.com

Truly one of a kind, KPIG is an amalgam of musical styles that over time touches just about every nook and cranny of American music, no matter how obscure.

Jazz

KRML 1410 AM
(831) 624–6431, www.krmlradio.com

Straight-ahead jazz featuring local jazz aficionados.

Hispanic

KSOL 98.9 FM
(713) 407–5584,
www.netmio.com/sales/contact.html

The Bear Flag Building was originally an apartment building when constructed in 1929. Today, it houses restaurants, shops, offices, and KNRY radio. PHOTO: ROSS ANDRÉSON

News/Talk

KNRY 1240 AM
(831) 373–1234, www.knry1240.com
Nationally syndicated radio talk shows share airtime with local, community, and issue-oriented hosts.

KSCO 1080 AM/KOMY 1340 AM
(831) 475–1080, www.ksco.com

KGO 810 AM
(415) 954–8629, www.kgo.com
The 50,000-watt signal reaches Canada and Mexico. San Francisco ABC flagship

station features talk show hosts with guests of national renown. News and talk 24 hours.

Rock

KCDU 93 FM
(831) 658–5200, www.cd93.com

KMBY 104.3 FM
(831) 658–5200, www.kmby.com

KSJO 92.7 FM
(408) 453–5400, www.ksjo.com
Part of a network of rock stations covering the entire Bay Area.

Top-40/Oldies

KDON 102.5 FM
(831) 649–5366, www.kdon.com
Contemporary hits.

KIDD 630 AM
(831) 649–0969, www.magic63.com
Music from the '40s through the '60s.

KOCN 105.1 FM
(831) 646–5105
Hits from the '60s and '70s.

Urban

KBTU 101.7 FM
(831) 643–1017, www.1017btu.com

Worship

Religious worship was the foundation of early settlers and today continues to play a major role in the lives of Peninsula residents. The Yellow Pages directory yields nine pages of church listings—a total of 56 denominations, everything from A (Apostolic) to W (Word of Faith). This is after all California, and the tolerant, accepting attitude of Californians for all things unusual extends to the eclectic blend of religious beliefs and choices available here. Of course the traditional religious faiths are well represented.

The religious roots of the Monterey Peninsula began in 1770. Spanish King Charles III chartered missions in California for the purpose of establishing a presence in Alta California by religious conquest. In this way, Spain could take possession of the land before the Russians or the English could lay claim to it.

The Franciscans succeeded in founding 21 missions, with Father Junipero Serra overseeing the founding of the first nine. Serra's ambition, solely missionary, was to win the hearts of the Indians to Christ. With the exception of the San Francisco Mission, all of the California missions were established during the Spanish era. In 53 years, from 1769 to 1822, California was transformed into a Christian province by a handful of Spanish soldiers and a few Franciscan missionaries. The founding of Mission San Carlos de Borromeo de Monterey on June 3, 1770, shaped the little settlement called Monterey.

During Spanish rule the missions were the center of early California life. But after 30 years of being governed by the Spanish, Mexico gained its independence from Spain and things changed in California. Under the rule of the Mexican government, the mission lands were taken from the church and sold at auction.

Until the secularization of the missions in 1842, the Church of Spain dominated the religious scene. Even after the missions were turned over to the Mexican Government, a faction of people remained loyal to their Franciscan faith. The chapel in Monterey became the local parish church, and in 1850 it was designated the Cathedral of the Diocese of Monterey.

Methodists established a presence on the Peninsula in 1875 with the development of a religious camp meeting, the Pacific Grove Retreat. The Methodists didn't build churches in those early years because most of the meetings were held outdoors in the open air during summer months.

Other denominations were also attracted to the area, and Pacific Grove soon became known as the "City of Churches." Among the early faiths established were Episcopal in 1891, Congregational in 1892, Christian Science in 1905, Bethlehem Lutheran in 1925, and Seventh-day Adventist in 1928.

Many of the historical churches in Pacific Grove and other parts of the Peninsula were destroyed as they fell into disrepair. In the early days the churches were constructed quickly and cheaply, and the church leaders were more interested in building newer, more permanent structures than preserving the old ones. A few still remain and are a reminder of our religious heritage; we will briefly mention those who greatly influenced the spiritual development of the Monterey Peninsula.

Founded in 1770 by Father Junipero Serra and completed in 1794, The Royal Presidio Chapel of San Carlos Borromeo de Monterey is the oldest church in continuous use in California. PHOTO: MONTEREY COUNTY CONVENTION & VISITORS BUREAU

Royal Beginnings

The Royal Presidio Chapel, built in 1794, is the oldest building on the Monterey Peninsula and the oldest church in continuous service in California. The first two chapels were constructed of pole, brush, and mud, but the third was an adobe with foundations of stone and lime. It was named the Royal Presidio because it was the place where Spanish governors, representatives of the King of Spain, worshipped.

Today the church, located at 500 Church Street in Monterey, is listed as a California and National Historical Landmark. In 1968 it received the title "cathedral" by the Catholic Church, the smallest church to be so designated. The Royal Presidio Chapel is California's only extant presidio chapel and the last remaining structure of 18th-century Spanish origin.

Mission Moves to Carmel

Mission San Carlos Borromeo del Rio Carmel, founded in 1771 by Father Junipero Serra, was the second of the 21 missions founded in California. It was the first church to be completely built of adobe bricks. Ten years later, a sandstone church was built with stones quarried from the Santa Lucia Mountains in Carmel Valley. At that time the congregation was mainly Indian families.

After the missions were secularized in 1823 and the Franciscans were forced to leave, many missions fell into disrepair as looters stripped the missions of anything of value. The uninhabited Carmel mission was totally destroyed by vandals and lay in ruins for the next 50 years. In 1884, the restoration began with a new roof. Part of the quadrangle was restored and a memorial erected to the four padres buried there. The mission was completely restored in 1931 under the expert direction of Sir Harry Downey. Pope John Paul designated the mission, in 1960, the status of a minor basilica. The Carmel Mission, located at 3080 Rio Road, is considered a Monterey County landmark.

Pacific Grove's First Church

Although the Methodists first established a religious encampment in Pacific Grove, they did not build the first church. St. Mary's by-the-Sea Episcopal Church, 146 12th Street, was the first church building constructed in Pacific Grove. It still holds services today.

St. Mary's was founded on March 25, 1886, by a small group of women who formed St. Mary's Guild. The church was built in 1887 on land donated by the Pacific Improvement Company. The Old English Gothic-style structure was modeled after an ancient church in Bath, England. The building size was doubled in 1911. Architect Lewis P. Hobart, who also conceived Grace Cathedral in San Francisco, devised this plan.

Several stained-glass windows in St. Mary's are of great historical interest. Bruce Porter of San Francisco designed the window over the main altar in 1894. It was created with more than 3,000 pieces of glass. Another, donated by Cyrus H. McCormick, was designed by Louis C. Tiffany and was placed in the church in 1922. Tiffany's window depicts pink foxgloves and white lilies. McCormick, of the millionaire McCormick Farm Implement family, married his wife at St. Mary's in 1889.

The Little White Church

The Christian Church of Pacific Grove, 442 Central Avenue, was established in

Insiders' Tip

John Steinbeck used the Royal Presidio Chapel as his model for the Church of San Carlos in the story of the pirate in *Tortilla Flat.*

St. John's Chapel, Episcopal was consecrated in 1891 and was originally part of the famous Del Monte Hotel. PHOTO: TOM HARDY COLLECTION

1894 by the "Willing Workers," a group of women who organized and laid plans for the church. They struggled for 10 years to raise enough money to build the church, holding fund-raising bazaars where handmade products and baked goods were sold.

In 1896 they purchased a lot from the Pacific Improvement Company for $1.00. The construction of the church, a low-budget plan, was completed that same year. Though simple, the church is quite elegant, a lasting testament to the women who willed the church into existence.

A Church for Hotel Guests

Visitors at the famed Del Monte Hotel found only one thing lacking—a church to serve their spiritual needs. C. P. Huntington and Charles H. Crocker (of the "Big Four"; see our History chapter) and the Crocker sisters, Miss Hattie and Mrs. Rutherford, became involved in the planning and support of the new church. Crocker obtained property adjacent to the hotel and donated it for the site of the new chapel.

Ernest Coxhead, an Englishman living in San Francisco, was the architect for the church. Coxhead was interested in the new "Arts and Crafts" style and felt it would be a good match for St. John's Episcopal Church. However, Huntington disagreed. He felt the church should adopt a typical English Norman style built in granite. The Crockers sided with Coxhead, and the chapel was built with an exterior of redwood shingles.

The new chapel, open to all, was dedicated in 1891. At the service Bishop Nichols said, "This little Chapel-of-Ease is fitted for a unique piece of missionary work. Men and women will worship here who rarely attend divine services in our great city churches."

If you go to St. John's Episcopal Church, notice the elegant rood screen, donated by Mrs. Mary Morrison in 1932 and placed between the nave and the choir seating. Designed by Danish artist Robert Petersen, it has a graceful arch with a rood, or cross, at the top of the curve. Two swinging gates, each with a cross, complete the effect.

Through the years, St. John's has always taken a traditional stance, stressing

St. Mary's by-the-Sea Episcopal Church, founded in 1886, is a landmark in Pacific Grove.
PHOTO: ROSS ANDRÉSON

Biblical faith and worship. After the demise of the Del Monte Hotel, it was moved in 1957 to its present location on Mark Thomas Drive.

First Baptist Church of Pacific Grove

The First Baptist Church, 246 Laurel Street, was the first African-American church on the Monterey Peninsula. Although it was organized in 1909, a church building wasn't erected until 1912. Many of its earliest members were from the Ninth Regiment of the U.S. Cavalry. The Ninth, stationed at the Presidio from 1902 to 1904, was an all African-American regiment of about 300 soldiers. They had been organized toward the end of the Civil War to fight the Indians. During their stay on the Peninsula, they were housed in tents in the area near where the Hopkins Marine Station now stands. This explains, in part, how an all-Black church got an early start among the all-white population in Pacific Grove.

The Church of the Wayfarer in Carmel

The first church in Carmel originally met outside, under the trees on the corner of Dolores Street and Sixth Avenue. The year was 1904. In 1905, J. Devendorf graciously donated two lots he owned on Lincoln Street near Ocean Avenue and shortly thereafter the First Methodist Episcopal Church of Carmel was built and formally dedicated. The name of the church changed to the Carmel Community Church before it received its current name, the Church of the Wayfarer. *The Wayfarer* was a musical pageant written by one of the church members and, in the early 1940s when the name was changed, also reflected the international composition of the congregation.

The church was constructed with pieces of famous estates; the wood panels inside the church came from a house designed by Frank Lloyd Wright and the tile on the floor was originally part of the Hearst estate. Take a minute to stop and look inside the wonderful old church as you visit Carmel, or attend a Sunday service if you prefer—all wayfarers past and present are welcome here.

Today's Religious Scene

Visitors and locals alike refer to the Saturday religion pages in *The Monterey County Herald* for specific information regarding worship services. The religion pages offer information about special activities at individual churches, religious news, and columns by several local religious leaders. The Yellow Pages of the phone book contain listings of all the local churches. Many churches have display ads listing the time of their worship services.

Several churches broadcast services on local public access cable channel 24.

If you are visiting from out of the area, take the opportunity to attend a church service at one of our historical churches, alternative houses of worship, or community churches. From the oldest to the newest, Monterey Peninsula has a form of worship for everyone.

Index

C

K

L

M

S

U

V

W

About the Authors

Tom Owens

A second-generation Californian, Tom Owens was born and raised in the suburbs of Los Angeles and moved up to the Monterey Peninsula in 1980. His first experience with the Monterey area was during his honeymoon in 1978, when he and his bride fell in love with Big Sur and the entire Monterey Bay coastline.

Now a marketing and communications specialist, Tom has an extensive background in magazine journalism and public relations, covering everything from insurance to acid jazz. A communications arts graduate from California State Polytechnic University in Pomona, Tom spent 11 formative years as a writer for and then editor of *Small Business Reports* magazine, a how-to journal on owning and operating small to midsize companies.

When the magazine was purchased by the American Management Association and moved to New York City, Tom bid it farewell and started his own freelance writing service, Good Ink, in Pacific Grove. His writings appeared primarily in business journals, such as *Independent Business* and *Personnel Journal*, but included more leisurely publications like *Golfweek*. His freelance connections led him to the editorship of *Monterey Bay Magazine*, a local lifestyle monthly, and *GuestLife*, a tourist-industry annual that serves as an in-room resource in local hotels. Tom has also served as publication editor and freelance writer for the Monterey Jazz Festival, where he developed his current love for America's greatest contribution to world civilization. Today, he enjoys plying his trade in three-dimensional cyberspace but still relishes putting pencil to paper as well.

Tom lives happily in Pacific Grove with his wife Emily and two Peninsula-born daughters, Kate and Anna. Edie the dog and Gianni the cat round out the Owens household. Tom enjoys hiking, beach combing, softball, badminton, all kinds of music, and most kinds of travel. You'll often find him in the great outdoors soaking in the spectacular scenery of the Monterey Bay.

Melanie Bellon Chatfield

Originally from Michigan, Melanie traveled west in 1994 for a five-day vacation. Starting out in San Francisco, she and a friend drove down Highway 1 to the Monterey Peninsula. One day later, she met Michael, now her husband, and decided to make Monterey her home. Her penchant for discovering new places was ignited when, at age four, she traveled by train to Southern California with her parents and brother. They stayed for two years. Spontaneously moving to California seems to run in her family.

As a young woman with dreams of worldwide travel, Melanie took a job with a bank in her hometown of Lansing. Go figure. With the threshold for boredom of a two-year-old, Melanie worked in just about every department of the bank until she landed in the Marketing Department in 1979. There she found her calling and pursued her degree in marketing in the evenings. She moved to Kalamazoo and served as public relations manager for the banking company until 1990. Seeking to flex her creative muscles, Melanie joined an advertising agency as copywriter and public relations executive.

After moving to the Monterey Peninsula, Melanie started her own writing and communications business. Lured back into the corporate world, she worked as a staff writer for a corporation and then as community relations director for a local hospital. Then, finally, she returned to her first loves: freelance writing and traveling. Melanie and her husband work together in their home office where they provide writing and communications services for local and national businesses. They also write for area lifestyle, healthcare and business publications. On the travel side, she has scoured the countries of Europe during dozens of visits and explored terrain above and below the water (with the aid of SCUBA) on the Monterey Peninsula, and in Bali, Mexico, Honduras, and Italy.